The Biosphere Catalogue

EDITOR-IN-CHIEF

Tango Parrish Snyder

Produced by

THE INSTITUTE OF ECOTECHNICS

Synergetic Press

LONDON . FORT WORTH

First Edition 1985

Copyright ©1985 by the Institute of Ecotechnics

Published by Synergetic Press, Incorporated
    312 Houston Street, Fort Worth, Texas 76102
    24 Old Gloucester Street, London WC1

Editor-in-Chief: Tango Parrish Snyder

Research Editor: John Allen

**Design and
Production Editor:**   Kathleen Dyhr

Cover: Kathleen Dyhr
                          Phil Hawes
                          Marie Allen

Credits   Photo on pg.4 courtesy of NASA.
                 Page 5, copyright 1978, by Charlene Spretnak, reprinted by permission of Beacon Press.
                 Photos on pgs. 102,108,110,112,124,130,142 copyright After Image.
                 Photo on pg. 127 copyright The Image Bank West.
                 Illustrations:
                 Pg. 120, "Human Energy Production as a Process in the Biosphere," by S.Fred Singer, **Scientific American,** Sept. 1970.
                 Pg. 122 top, "The Energy Cycle of the Biosphere," George M. Woodwell, **Scientific American,** Sept. 1970.
                 Pg. 122 bottom, "The Biosphere," G. Evelyn Hutchinson, **Scientific American,** Sept. 1970.

Typeset by Synergetic Press on Studio Software and Laserwriter

Printed by Edward Brothers, Ann Arbor, Michigan, U.S.A.

ISBN 0 907791 12 3

Library of Congress Card Number 85-062154

Contents

Contributing Editors

Lynn Margulis
Professor of Biology at Boston University. As microbiologist and cell biologist, she is interested in the origin of cells with nuclei. Co-authored *The Five Kingdoms: An Illustrated Guide to the Phyla of Life on Earth*, and authored *Symbiosis in Cell Evolution*. Her work has been central in the development of biospherics.

Dorion Sagan
A sleight-of-hand magician and science writer interested in the relationships between science and perception. Co-founder with Dr. Margulis, of *ScienceWriters*, a partnership dedicated to illuminating science writing.

Norman Myers
Environmental consultant for the past two decades to conservation and development agencies of importance from the World Wildlife Fund to the World Bank. Author of several books including *The Sinking Ark*, General Editor of *The Gaia Atlas of Planetary Management*. Awarded Gold Medal by World Wildlife Fund in 1984.

Michael B. McElroy
Professor of Atmospheric Sciences, Harvard University. A committee member on U.S. Congress Space Program Advisory Panel, NASA Space and Earth Science Advisory Committee, National Academy of Sciences Committee on Atmospheric Effects of Nuclear Explosions. He has made significant contributions to the evaluation of Martian atmosphere.

Alwyn Gentry
Associate Curator of Botany, Missouri Botanical Gardens. Outstanding field botanist concentrating on Panama, Columbia, Equador, and Peru. He manages the joint Missouri Botanical Garden/ Field Museum Flora of Peru Project.

Gordon Orians
Director, Institute for Environmental Studies, University of Washington, and member of Scientific Advisory Board of the World Wildlife Fund, U.S.A. Chairman of the Committee on Applications of Ecological Theory to Environmental Problems of National Research Council of the National Academy of Sciences; editorial board member of *Behavioral Ecology and Sociobiology*.

Ghillean Prance
Senior Vice President for Research at the New York Botanical Garden, Director of the Institute of Economic Botany, and Executive Director of the Organization for Flora Neotropica, a UNESCO non-governmental organization charged with studying and publishing a series of monographs on *The Plants of the World*.

Peter Riecks-Marlowe
Culturologist; co-founder and Director from 1971-76 of *Release*, the Berlin drug rehabilitation center for hard-drug addicts; a Director of an open schizophrenic house in Zurich; author of forthcoming book, *Angst to Gotterdammerung and Beyond: A Survey of German Culture;* Director of Caravan of Dreams Theater, Fort Worth, Texas.

Contributing Editors

James D. Hays
Professor of Geology at Columbia University, member of staff at Lamont-Doherty Geological Observatory, and visiting Research Associate of the American Museum of Natural History, New York City. Leading authority on deep-sea sediments and the ocean history they record. Past Executive Director of the CLIMAP Project of the International Decade of Ocean Exploration.

William J. Breed
Expedition Leader, Nature Expeditions International. Former Curator of Geology, Museum of Northern Arizona. Recipient of National Science Foundation's Antarctic Service Medal, 1977. Co-author of several NASA studies comparing Earthian and Martian deserts.

Clair Folsome
Exobiologist, Professor of Microbiology at Univ. of Hawaii. One of the 1969 finalists in NASA competion for Scientist-Astronaut, he remains closely associated in his work with NASA. Founder of Eco-culture, Inc., a research and development corporation which models, designs, and manufactures life-support systems for use in space stations. President of Biofoods, Inc.

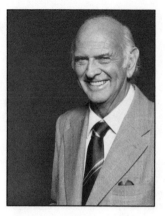

Gordon Hallsworth
Director, International Federation of Institutes for Advanced Studies 'Save Our Soils' Project; FRS of Chemistry. Former Chairman, Land Resources Laboratories, C.S.I.R.O., Australia; and President, International Society of Soil Science; currently Chairman of I.S.S.S. Committee on Rules.

John Allen
Executive Chairman, Space Biospheres Ventures; Consultant, Institute of Ecotechnics; pioneer in metallurgy, ecotechnics, entrepreneurial management and philosophy of systems theory. Poet and playwright.

Rocco Fazzolare
Associate Professor in Energy Engineering, University of Arizona; Director, Solar and Energy Research Program, College of Engineering, University of Arizona; NASA Energy Consultant.

Arthur Reed
Aviation Editor of *The Times,* London; European Correspondent for *Air Transport World,* Associate of Royal Aeronautical Society.

Gavin Trevitt
Writer, top information executive in the international telecommunications industry with special interests in satellite communications.

Contributing Editors

Mark Nelson
Chairman of the Institute of Ecotechnics. Director of Savannah Systems, Pty.,Ltd., a 5000 acre project in Australia for the development of drought-resistant savannah systems and developing halophyte crops; Director/owner of high-desert low-water-use orchard experiment in U.S.A.

Phil Hawes
Architect and Director of Sarbid Ltd. (Synergetic Architecture and Biotechnic Design), A.I.A. Projects built around the planet including such remote places as Ladakh and Savaii, among other places. Studied with Frank Lloyd Wright, and taught graduate architecture at the University of Oklahoma with Bruce Goff.

Roy Walford
Professor of Pathology, University of California, Los Angeles; expert advisor to the World Health Organization in immunology; author of *Maximum Life Span*. Responsible Program Project Director, U.S.P.H.S. Grant -- 'Histocompatibility Systems and Aging' 1984-1989; and avant-garde theater historian.

Donald Paglia
Professor of Pathology, University of California, Los Angeles; member of the Aerospace Medical Association, consultant to Jet Propulsion Laboratory/NASA in radiobiological concerns.

Robert Raffauf
Professor of Pharmacognosy, Medicinal Chemistry, Northeastern University; member of Society for Economic Botany; Research Associate and part-time instructor at Botanical Museum, Harvard University.

Sandra Parker
Conference Coordinator, SunSpace Ranch Conference Center, Tucson, Arizona. Active in travel industry over past decade as operations assistant in travel seminar company, operations manager for an international wholesale tour company, and sales associate at Hotel Tahara'a and Hotel Bora Bora, French Polynesia.

Toshio Murashige
Professor of Plant Physiology, University of California, Riverside. Developed the revolutionary *Murashige and Skoog* Salt Base Medium used in plant propagation, and the basic formulation to derive growth media. Leading consultant in plant tissue culture.

Bill Boyd
World-city traveller, *flaneur;* a sometime film, theater, and art critic.

Contributing Editors

Acknowledgements

We are grateful to the Ansel Adams Trust for making it possible to include his photography in this publication; to the National Optical Astronomy Observatories, Tucson, for photos; to Scientific American for their illustrations; and to Corinna MacNeice for research on symbols.

To V.I. Vernadsky

Preface

Mark Nelson
Chairman, Institute of Ecotechnics

The story of the blind men and the elephant, each complacently studying a different part of the animal, unaware it forms a functioning organism, serves as an apt analogy for the excesses of over-specialized scrutiny. For our planet, the elephant represents our biosphere shaping and directing its evolution within the constraints of solar radiation, moon tides, geological forces, and now the plague effects of man. Unfortunately, scientists, perfecting understanding of the biosphere, also perfected the means to destroy it. However, scientists and managers could reverse this disastrous course and initiate the creative era of "Biospherics" -- a total systems know-how of biosphere operations, launching an endeavor with the potential to integrate the detailed 'elephantine' studies of the varying disciplines. The masters of biospherics rather than the pastmasters of plunder will determine the horizon of man's future in the cosmos.

The Biosphere Catalogue, a guide for students of the biosphere, intends not to present an endless compendium of random facts culled from this truly vast domain, but an investigative approach to those areas of greatest interest and significance by participating in the actual thinking processes of individuals at the frontiers. The *Catalogue* asks: if the individual is potentially part of the brain of the biosphere what does he want, need, wish to know?

The *Catalogue* offers: a fuller access to nature in its varied exuberance, access to wealth -- the ability to forwardly organize our metabolic and metaphysical life, access to decision making to sharpen skills as 'reality-thinkers', access to cultures with their diversity of value systems, and access to cosmological thinking to meditate our place in the universe.

The Institute of Ecotechnics, founded in 1973 with the purpose of beginning and developing a new discipline interrelating man, his culture, and his technics with the evolving biospheric totality of planet Earth, engaged itself in the setting up and ongoing consulting of demonstration cost-effective projects concentrating on areas of ecological risk and opportunity: rainforests, savannahs, deserts, city centers, rivers, and coral reefs. *The Biosphere Catalogue*, produced by the Institute of Ecotechnics, offers opportunities for the interested individual to experience the action of interrelating man, his culture, and his technics with the biosphere.

Humans now have the opportunity and probably the obligation to take their part as creative collaborators with the forces of evolution. We should learn how to act it well.

I am large,
I contain multitudes.
WALT WHITMAN

Biospheric Concepts

The Real Deficit: Our Debt to the Biosphere

Lynn Margulis and Dorion Sagan

Thoughts give birth to a creative force that is neither elemental nor sidereal ...
Thoughts create a new heaven, a new firmament, a new source of energy, from
which new arts flow. PARACELSUS

In an information sense, the world becomes smaller every day. Communications technology improves, the population expands, and relations among peoples and countries become ever more interdependent, intricate, and involved. As human beings evolve with other life during the next twenty to two million years, the earth's potential for change and danger exponentiates. The single greatest challenge becomes getting along with our neighbors, living with each other.

Living with other forms of life is known as symbiosis and has been central to the development of the biosphere. Those organisms that could not tolerate the existence of their neighbors perished; the symbionts survived, flourished and complexified. As human beings exploit the wonderful modeling and representational abilities known as intelligence and technology, they form a break with the past and act as a possible bridge to a future so complex it makes of the earth a sort of single free-living cell, a multicolored gem that has crystalized in the blackness of space.

This book concerns ideas about the biosphere or Gaia, ideas that may influence life, not only in our and our immediate descendants' lifetimes, but millions of years hence, when time has compounded the effects of our present-day decisions. If we are truly in the possession of biological wisdom, these ideas are not simple academic word games but turning points in evolution for the future history of life.

The word "biosphere" was first used by the Russian sage-geologist, crystallographer and cartographer V.I. Vernadsky (1863-1945). Far keener than any biologists of his age, Vernadsky recognized that life "is intimately associated with the structure of the

THE TETONS AND THE SNAKE RIVER, Grand Teton National Park, Wyoming, 1942. Photograph by Ansel Adams. Courtesy the Trustees of the Ansel Adams Publishing Rights Trust. All Rights Reserved.

Earth's crust, it is involved in the mechanism of the latter and in this mechanism it is responsible for most important functions without which the mechanism could not exist." Life, Vernadsky wrote "determines not only the picture of surrounding nature with all its colors, forms, plant and animal communities, labor and arts of civilized mankind, but its impact is much deeper, it effects more magnificent chemical processes within the Earth's crust." We all live inside of "an envelope of life," in other words in an environment of which we form a part. (For these quotes and a description of Vernadsky's life and work, see Balandin, 1982.)

Since the time of Vernadsky there has been a strong undercurrent of scientists recognizing the animation of the environment, among them G. Evelyn Hutchinson who wrote *The Biogeochemistry of Vertebrate Excretion* and *The Earth as a Planet* and Heinz A. Lowenstam whose life-time of scientific papers have been devoted to understanding the mechanism of biomineralization: the production of "inorganic" materials by cells of living organisms. Only these men and a few of their students have regarded the earth and its atmosphere not as a passive container housing life but as a dynamic extension of the organismal life as a whole. This view, of environmental evolution, though very old and almost intuitive, has been broadened in recent years in large part due to NASA's exploration of and search for life on other planets. But an awareness of Gaia still has not been broadcast enough; every student and philosopher really deserves the opportunity to see the earth in this enlightening manner.

The history of our planet is not a series of progressions of plants and animals adapting to static environments. It is a cellular dance of networks in which the most creative and efficient collectives enhance each other and expand. As V.I. Vernadsky said, "The biogeochemical effect of living matter on our planet is the greatest...for unicellular microorganisms. They create the planetary atmosphere, prevail in other geological processes of a global character, change sharply the entire chemistry of the biosphere, and hence the chemistry of the planet.'' Highlights of life include its incredible quality and increasing fidelity of maintaining past environments in the present; they include the development of photosynthesis which caused oxygen to build up on our planet, changing the direction of life forever, the symbiosis of differing bacteria which merged to make the nucleated cells which comprise us, as well as the more recent developments of space flight and flowers. All of these developments had precursors if not precedents. They all speak to us of our present and future. The prevailing view of a static ''environment to which organisms adapt'' is embarrassingly antiquated. Not merely inadequate, it is conceptually vacuous, scientifically sterile and misleading. What the idea of a flat earth was to earlier centuries, so the view of an inert, mechanical environment is to present science.

Jim Lovelock's Gaia hypothesis sprung from this new perception of life as a planetary phenomenon. In looking for a way to detect life through remote sensing, Lovelock became increasingly impressed with the intense chemical disequilibrium of the earth's atmosphere, as compared to those of Venus and Mars. Here, carbon dioxide forms 0.03 percent of the atmosphere. On Mars and Venus the figure looms above the 95th percentile. The reason that earth is shockingly depleted of carbon dioxide is undeniably biological. Photosynthesizers (through the course of natural history at the earliest times bacteria and later bacteria trapped as chloroplasts inside the cells of plants) used atmospheric carbon, as they continue to do today, to make more of themselves. Photosynthesizers, always removing gases from and pumping gases into the atmosphere still are the only ''productive'' forms of life. As Lovelock (1979) has tried to tell us in his little book, our atmosphere is an active part of the biosphere and has been so for over three billion years. The gas-exchanging properties of the biosphere keep the earth habitable for life, different from the rest of the known universe, in a condition of chemical disequilibria that fuels the energetic activities underlying the intricacy and beauty of Gaia.

Gaia is synonymous with the biosphere, a sort of proper noun (derived from the Greek goddess of the earth) we can use to address this provident entity of which our human wisdom is only a small (and perhaps ultimately insignificant) part. The gaia *hypothesis*, on the other hand, is a more strict appellation, referring to the specific possibility that the protracted chemical disequilibria on a planetary scale (of which carbon dioxide is only one aspect) depends on the combined activities of life. This possibility has increasingly seemed to us a probability, the best explanation of the earth's discrepancies relative to other planets. The earth's temperature has never deviated

from beyond the bounds of what is needed to maintain liquid water. We have inexplicably too much oxygen and too little carbon dioxide. We have wildly improbable amounts of methane and dimethyl sulfide. We see these peculiar conditions and rapid elemental cycling of our biosphere as owed in large part to the incessant rapid growth and death of diverse and worldwide communities of bacteria -- microbes. These numerous, ancient exploding populations have metabolical capabilities -- especially involving carbon, nitrogen and sulfur gases -- far exceeding those of conspicuous larger forms of life.

Eighty percent of life's history was microbial. Bacteria seem to have preserved the hydrogen-rich ambience of the early solar system and engineered a program of planetary environmental regulation (homeorrhesis) as early as 3 billion years ago. This modulated environment still supports larger forms of life and, in light of industrial perturbations of the atmosphere, the bacterial players may be busier than ever. The fantastic metabolic activites of groups of so-called lower forms of life reveals the paucity of our former characterization of them as merely ''germs'' to be destroyed (Sonea and Panisset, 1983). As Lewis Thomas succinctly put it microbes ''run the show.'' We ourselves are recombinations of the metabolic processes of oxygen-using and other forms of bacteria that appeared during the Proterozoic accumulation of free oxygen in the atmosphere approximately two billion years ago. Remnants of bacteria, with DNA identified by molecular biologists to be extremely similar to true bacterial DNA, divide as mitochondria in the human cells of the reader as these lines are read.

Thus human beings are not special, apart or alone. A logical extension of the Copernican view that we are not at the center of the universe deprives us also of our place as kings of the beasts. It may be a blow to our ego but we are not masters of life perched atop an evolutionary ladder, the closest living things to God and the angels. Ours is a permutation of the wisdom of the biosphere. We did not invent genetic engineering, we copied it from and harnessed it in germs. We did not invent agriculture or locomotion on horseback, we became involved in the life cycles of plants and animals, whose numbers increased in tandem with ours.

Just so, the much vaunted accomplishments of technology, from the mainframe computers to the microchip, are not *our* property. They came from the biosphere -- from the interconnected environment of *all* life -- and eventually they belong not to us but to Gaia. As with theory and intellect, high technology also is not really ours but planetary in nature. We have been separating ourselves from the rest of life, incubating forms of organization that are ultimately bigger and richer than we. It is time for us to invest in our future by researching our past in the broad sense. We must comprehend the three billion year history of the genes as the thread of life (Lewin, 1983) and see ourselves not as the petty soldiers of obscure kings and citizens of arbitrary nationstates but as bearers of genes allowing us to drink milk as adults. That is, we must master the Timescale (Calder, 1983) and become as fine chronographers as we have become geographers. We must understand the components of the grand biosphere that so recently spawned us, examining its history and patterns. We must trace the connections between the slower tectonic cycles and the more rapid flow of chemical elements essential to growth, death and regrowth. In getting better acquainted with Gaia we need her atlas of planetary management (Myers, 1984). We need to monitor the expansion of the microcosm which produced us (Sagan and Margulis, forthcoming) while establishing the details of the Microcosm's biogeochemistry which sustains us (see the SCOPE books).

In a deep way our economists must be shown that even the most industrious amongst us are never productive: only the photosynthesizers can harvest the sun. Perhaps, with the strategies outlined here by the Institute of Ecotechnics we can go beyond the *domestication* of animals and plants (by "bringing them into the house") and develop *ecopoiesy* -- the making of volumes and even stark planets like Mars habitable (Haynes, 1985). We must bring entire communities of organisms "into the house". No matter the details of our ecopoietic actions, no matter their level of consciousness, we must make up our real deficit and repay our debt to the biosphere by studying it. Otherwise it may foreclose on us.

References Cited

Vladimir Vernadsky (English translation), by R.K. Balandin, MIR Publishers, Moscow, 1982.
Timescale: An Atlas of the Fourth Dimension, by N. Calder, Viking Books, New York, 1983.
Ecopoiesy: Canadian Professor Robert Haynes (York University, Downsview Ontario), a molecular geneticist, coined this phrase (1985) to mean the making of a planet habitable for life. The term encompasses ideas like the "greening of Mars" and the *"terraforming"* of any planets besides the earth. Coming from *eco*, (Gr. house) and *"poiesy"* (Gr. make, maintain), the idea is analogous to *biopoiesy* (origin of life) or *autopoiesy* which refers to the self-maintaining properties of living organisms.
The Earth as a Planet, by G.E. Hutchinson, in *The Planets*, G.P. Kuiper (Editor), University of Chicago Press, Chicago, U.S.A., 1954.
Gaia: A New Look at Life on Earth, by J.E. Lovelock, Oxford University Press, Oxford, England, 1979.
The Expanding Microcosm, by D. Sagan & L. Margulis, Summit Books, New York, in press.
A New Bacteriology, by S. Sonea & M. Panisset, Jones and Bartlett Publishers, Inc., Boston and Portola Valley, 1983.

SCOPE: A series of books by an international group of scientists: Scientific Committee of Problems of the Environment, primarily on the cycling of essential elements through the biosphere. Over seventeen books have been released or are in some stage of planning, for example:
Nitrogen, Phosphorus and Sulphur: Global Cycles (SCOPE 7), B.H. Svenson & R. Soderlund (Editors), John Wiley and Sons, New York, 1975.
The Global Carbon Cycle (SCOPE 13), B. Bolin, E.T. Degens, S. Kempe & P. Ketner (Editors), John Wiley and Sons, New York, 1979.
Some Perspectives of the Major Biogeochemical Cycles (SCOPE 17), G.E. Likens (Editor), John Wiley and Sons, New York, 1981.

Acknowledgements

We are grateful to James E. Lovelock for steady inspiration and to R. Haynes for showing us unpublished correspondence on ecopoiesy. We thank Chris Lyons for her artwork and David Chase for his micrographs. We acknowledge the aid of the life sciences office of NASA. If the question of life on Mars had never been raised and answered we would still be unconscious of Gaia and her microbial activities.

Gaia

Gaia (also called Ge) is the ancient Earth-Mother who brought forth the world and the human race from "the gaping void, Chaos". In the Greek imagination the earth is the abode of the dead, so the earth deity has power over the ghostly world. Because dreams, which often were felt to foreshadow the future, were believed to ascend from the netherworld, Gaia acquired an oracular function. One means of divination was incubation, in which the consultant slept in a holy shrine with her/his ear upon the ground. Another means was the pronouncements of a priestess who spoke of the future while in a trance; she sat on a tripod over vapors arising from a crevice. Gaia's oracular function appears in records of her worship at Delphi, Athens, and Aegae. She was the earliest possessor of the Delphic oracle, before Poseidon, Dionysos, or Apollo.

In the Homeric *Hymn to Ge,* she is praised as "the oldest of divinities"; however, the poem is clearly rooted in the Olympian tradition because it addresses Gaia as "Mother of the gods" and "wife of starry Heaven". Long before she was regarded as mother of the powerful deities, she herself was the powerful deity. In time her son/lover, Ouranos, was added to her mythology.

Although eclipsed during the classical period by the Olympian Gods, Gaia's impressive figure is always in the background. Greek citizens swore their public oaths to her. The priestesses at the oracular shrine of Dodana preserved her name in their chanted litany: "Earth sends up fruits, so we praise Earth the Mother." And at Delphi the priestess began her formal ritual address to the Gods thus: "First in my prayer before all other gods, I call on Earth, primeval prophetess."

Charlene Spretnak

Biomes

Norman Myers

And walk among long dappled grass,
And pluck till time and times are done
The silver apples of the moon,
The golden apples of the sun.
W.B. YEATS

This chapter was originally to be called Ecosystems. As a name for an ecological unit, "ecosystem" is a good name, with its meaning all too plain. Moreover, it is a key concept for anyone who wants to know how the world works. In fact, so important is the notion, that is worth our while to look briefly at what ecosystems are before we go on to consider how they make up biomes.

Ecosystems are basic assemblies of life and habitat. As such, they constitute the building blocks of the biosphere. Wherever we find a distinct community of plants and animals, living together within their own particular patch of environment, there we find an ecosystem. The reader might wonder, how many ecosystems are there on Earth? Well, the biosphere itself is one huge ecosystem. And a grain of soil is an ecosystem, too. This means that the total number of ecosystems becomes a non-issue: too big to grasp, and hardly relevant anyway. So it is more to the point for us to focus instead on large amalgams of ecosystems -- zones where many similar ecosystems exist side by side, making up a super-ecosystem, or biome.

An easily recognizable example of a biome is the tropical forest. From one part of the biome to another, the tropical forest looks pretty much the same, and it works pretty much the same, too. True, the forest of Amazonia contains a basically different set of species from that of Borneo, whether trees or birds or insects; and these species, being different, necessarily interact in somewhat different manner. But these two sectors of tropical forest are more akin to each other than either is to the conifer forests of Canada or Russia.

So the tropical forest deserves to rank as an ecological zone in its own right; and scientists call it a biome. This is not such a striking name as ecosystem, nor is its meaning so obvious. But ecosystem just does not fit. Even if we consider that the Amazonia forest constitutes a single ecosystem, it is cut off from other forests of the tropical belt. An ecosystem must be a continuous entity, and tropical forests are not connected to each other. So there is no such thing as the tropical forest ecosystem. But there is certainly a tropical forest biome.

With biome, then, unprepossessing label as it might be, we must content ourselves if we are to understand the broad classifications of plant-animal communities in our biosphere.

Main Biomes

How many biomes are there? Again, it is almost a case of choose your number. There is much argument among scientists about how many ecological zones merit the title "biome." Of course we soon arrive at an upper limit: we cannot go beyond, say, 30, before we start to abuse the title itself (by marked contrast, of course, with the case for the total number of ecosystems). For purposes of this chapter, we shall settle for a mere nine, which cover all the earth's land surface: tropical forests, of both evergreen and deciduous sorts; tropical woodlands, including bush and thorn areas; tropical savannahs and grasslands; deserts, both hot and cold; Mediterranean-type vegetation, being a short shrubby affair, sometimes known as chaparral; temperate forests; temperate grasslands, including prairie and steppe; boreal forests; and tundra.

These nine categories are enough to give us a good picture of how our biosphere is made up. True, the listing misses out a number of other areas. There is no category for open-ocean zones, even though they feature their own distinctive assemblies of life. But because the main marine realm is not a fraction so rich in plant-and-animal communities as those on land, we shall miss it out here. By the same token, we shall also miss out coral reef and mangrove communities: rich as they are, they cover only very small areas as compared with the nine biomes listed. Nor is there a category for montane zones, since there is no real biome as such -- the montane zones of, for example, the northern Andes are quite distinct from those of the Alps. Nor is there a category for freshwater ecosystems, with their great rivers and lakes; again, they are too differentiated to be considered under a single heading. In any case, if we were to consider all these separate entities in our listing of biomes, we would end up with a chapter at least twice as long as this is intended to be. Enough must be enough.

Clearly it is vegetation that is the deciding factor in the nine biomes we have chosen. Of course each features its complement of animal life as well. In a few moments, we shall look at each biome, one by one. But first let us note the predominance of vegetation as the determining characteristic of biomes. Of all biomass in the biosphere, i.e., plant and animal life combined, 99 percent is plant material. In the end, or rather in the beginning, we are all plants: without the green mantle for our planet supplied by more than one third of a million plant species, animal life (including the human species) simply cannot be sustained -- indeed it would never have evolved. Let us remember, moreover, that many thousands of millions of years ago it was the emergence of plant life that increased the amount of oxygen in the global atmosphere from a trace gas to the one-fifth proportion that slowly led to the proliferation of animal life.

Such, then, is the importance of vegetation. The principal distinguishing feature of the tropical forest is its mass of plant life -- just as the salient characteristic of a desert is its lack of plant life. Indeed the tropical forest contains at least 43 percent of all vegetation in the biosphere, even though it accounts for only 7 percent of Earth's land surface. As for other biomes, tropical woodlands feature 7 percent of all vegetation; tropical savannahs and grasslands, 5 percent; temperate forests, 19 percent; temperate grasslands, 2 percent; chaparral, 1 percent; boreal forests, 16 percent; tundra, 1 percent; and desert, 1 percent (even though tundra and deserts occupy as much as one quarter of Earth's land surface). We see that of all terrestrial plant matter, forests of various sorts account for more than three-quarters, a total of almost 1000 billion tons. To put this figure in perspective, we can consider that all cultivated crops account for only 0.7 billion tons -- even though croplands cover more of the earth's surface than do tropical forests.

Let us look at the situation another way by considering plant growth -- what scientists call primary productivity. This ranges from virtually zero in deserts to huge quantities in tropical forests. A tropical evergreen forest generates 90 tons (metric) of new plant material per hectare per year. This contrasts with an irrigated sugarcane field, 60-120 tons; and a well-watered garden lawn in Britain or New England (virtually all spring and summer growth), 70 tons. A papyrus swamp varies between 50 and 125 tons; and a desert rarely produces more than 3 tons. Forests are so productive that tropical and temperate forests combined account for 37 percent of the biosphere's primary productivity, or 133 billion tons a year; and tropical forests alone account for 23 percent (but because organic matter is speedily decomposed, annual net increment in a virgin tropical forest is usually nil).

Generally speaking, the amount of new plant material generated each year in well-watered parts of the world doubles as we move from the Boreal to the temperate zones, and more than doubles as we move from the temperate zones to the tropics. This is no more than we would expect, when we consider the increasing amounts of warmth as we move from the poles to the equator. Not surprisingly, too, we find that ecological complexity increases as we move along the same gradient: it expands from relatively simple communities with few species in the polar regions, to communities with great abundance and diversity of species at the equator.

Why Are Biomes Where They Are?

Before we go on to look at each biome in turn, let us ask ourselves a key question. How is it that forests are where they are, and deserts, too? What is the rhyme or reason that lies behind the distribution of biomes around the biosphere? What "life strategies" have been devised by evolution in response to environmental pressures, culminating in distinctive communities of plants and animals? What has been needed, in terms of climate and other physical factors, to generate a readily recognizable association such as the "spruce-moose" biome of boreal forests in North America?

Well, we can identify four crucial factors right off: temperature and rainfall, and latitude and altitude. When once we know how warm and wet an environment is, or how cold and dry, and where it is located (high latitude, high elevation?), we can, thanks to the systematized insights of ecology and biogeography, make a good guess at what types of plant life are likely to dominate the scene. For sure, we must often consider further factors, such as topography and soils. But in the main, we can reckon that throughout the equatorial zone we shall encounter year-round warmth and moisture. So we can expect to find evergreen rainforest. As we move away from the equator and toward the tropics, we find that rainfall becomes more seasonal. So we can look for deciduous trees that tolerate periodic drought. In areas where yearly rainfall declines still further, we find woodland, of increasingly open sorts

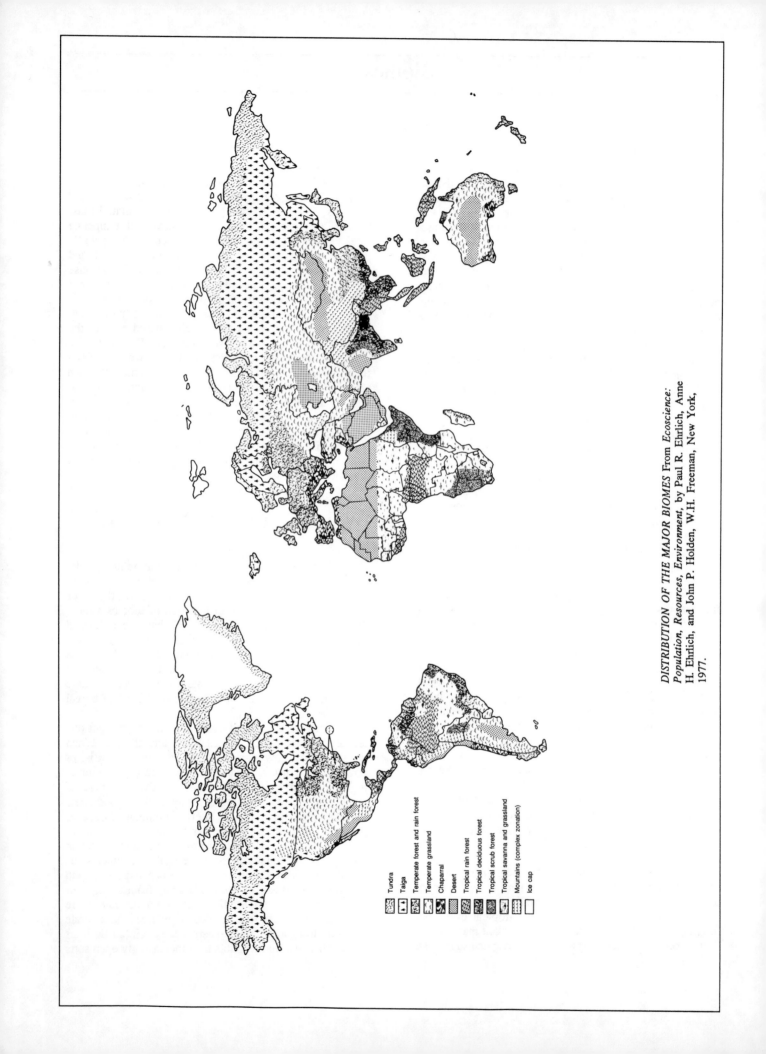

DISTRIBUTION OF THE MAJOR BIOMES From *Ecoscience: Population, Resources, Environment*, by Paul R. Ehrlich, Anne H. Ehrlich, and John P. Holden, W.H. Freeman, New York, 1977.

Tundra
Taiga
Temperate forest and rain forest
Temperate grassland
Chaparral
Desert
Tropical rain forest
Tropical deciduous forest
Tropical scrub forest
Tropical savanna and grassland
Mountains (complex zonation)
Ice cap

before it eventually gives way to bush and scrub. Next along the "hydrocline" are grasslands and semi-arid landscapes, plus thorn-thicket vegetation. Finally we encounter deserts.

Let us note, with respect to tropical deserts, that still further factors can influence the outcome. After all, deserts occur in places other than those predicted by the above analysis -- some of them in rather unlikely localities. Along the coasts of Namibia and Chile, for instance, there are cold offshore currents that cool the moisture-laden air inflowing from the oceans, preventing it from rising high enough to release rain. Results, deserts.

So much for the equatorial/tropical zones. Moving outward again, this time from the tropics into the temperate zones, we find something of the same sequence repeated (albeit with regional variations): forest, woodland, bush, grassland, scrub and desert. But -- and this is a big "but" -- the temperature steadily declines, and soon winter becomes a pre-eminent phenomenon in the annual cycle, bringing a halt to many life processes for months on end. So we encounter communities with much smaller numbers and variety of species. Life is simply less fecund. As a result, life strategies reveal adaptations to the basic factor of seasonal change: birds migrate toward the tropics, caribou among other mammals that assemble in large throngs head toward more promising areas, while bears and squirrels dig themselves into holes where they can close their eyes to the harsh conditions outside.

World Map of Biomes

To give us a better idea of how these life strategies work out in practice, let us look at an illustrative map. The land mass spreads out in the north, the great land masses of North America and Eurasia. It slims down toward the equator, before extending into tear-drop shapes in the southern hemisphere, corresponding to South America and southern Africa. This helps to clarify the disposition of biomes. So if somebody asks us what type of biome we would expect to find at, say, 50 degrees north in a continental heartland, we can come up with a correct answer in terms of the broadscale classification.

Moreover, we can speculate that if, say, Central America were to bulge out along the Tropic of Cancer, instead of almost dwindling away, we would encounter another vast desert corresponding to the Sahara. Similarly if Africa were to extend further along the equator, as does Amazonia, we would find a huge rainforest.

The Nine Major Biomes

Tropical Forests

In tropical areas where temperature and light intensity are always high, and rainfall is greater than 200 cms. a year (and at least 12 cms. in the driest month), there usually are -- or rather, there were -- tropical forests. These are by far the richest sectors of the biosphere, by virtue of the richness of food stocks available, and the relative constancy of environmental conditions throughout the year. Whereas one hectare of a temperate forest may feature no more than 10 dominant tree species, a tropical forest may well feature at least 100 -- and a tropical evergreen forest around 250. Equally to the point, a person walking through a tropical forest may find only a single specimen of each tree species per hectare, again a marked contrast with a temperate-zone forest.

The tallest trees reach 60 meters high, with crowns occasionally covering as much as one quarter of a hectare. The overall impression is of "forest growing upon forest", by virtue of the many epiphytes, lianas, etc., that hang from every branch and cling around every trunk. Well might tropical forests be described as the greatest celebration of nature to appear on the face of the planet since the first flickerings of life almost four billion years ago. While these forests feature perhaps 100,000 plant species out of the biosphere total of a quarter of a million, their animal life is even more abundant, at least 2.5 million species, more likely 5 million, and conceivably, just conceivably, 30 million or more -- the great bulk of them being insects.

The richest tropical forests are the evergreen rainforests, concentrated along the equator. Further away from the equator, as rainfall tends to be more seasonal, we find monsoonal forests and other deciduous formations. The vegetation is not so thick and lofty, and the numbers and diversity of species are not so ultra-great.

A person wishing to view an example of evergreen rainforest could well visit the research station known by its Brazilian acronym INPA at Manaus in the heart of Brazilian Amazonia; or the Finca La Selva research station in Costa Rica; or a patch of forest in Peninsular Malaysia. At each of these sites he will find as many bird species in just a few square kilometers as in the whole of Great Britain or California.

But on his way to these protected-area sites, he will see much forest being destroyed. Through the work of the commercial logger, the fuelwood gatherer, the cattle rancher and the smallscale cultivator, the tropical forest biome is being eliminated at a rate faster than any other ecological zone. Unless present patterns of exploitation and land-use can be radically altered, there may be little tropical forest left within just another 50 years. This gross impoverishment of life's diversity on earth will mean the extinction of millions of species. In terms of the magnitude of destruction, and the compressed time-scale of the process, it will constitute the greatest biological debacle ever to afflict the biosphere.

Tropical Woodlands

This biome includes not only open woodlands, but bush and scrub areas that qualify as part of the woodland biome by virtue of their occasional tall-standing trees. Not nearly so impressive as tropical forests, they are still striking in their appearance, as in their diversity of species as compared with temperate woodlands. A good example occurs in the miombo woodlands of central-southern Africa, which extend for millions of square kilometers, and feature such stately species as the baobab tree.

Whereas tropical forests are super-spectacular forms of nature, tropical woodlands suffer from the unfortunate reputation of being dull -- at least in comparative terms. The miombo in particular is sometimes thought to amount to a mere mammoth expanse of monotonous vegetation. But in spring, the trees break into glorious bright foliage -- at first red, crimson and copper, before gradually turning into bronze, olive and finally glossy bright green. In fact the new growth seems almost as magnificent as the great outburst of color that characterize northern woodlands in autumn.

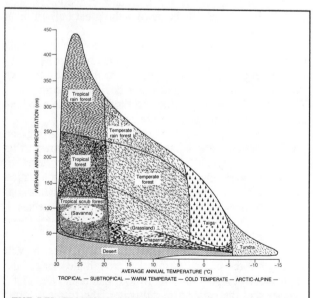

THE RELATIONSHIP OF BIOMES TO PRECIPITATION AND TEMPERATURE From *Ecoscience: Population, Resources, Environment,* by Paul R. Ehrlich, Anne H. Ehrlich, and John P. Holden, W.H. Freeman, New York, 1977.

Tropical Savannahs and Grasslands

Because they occur on very poor soils, and the forest vegetation contains little stocks of nutrients as compared with the vast biomass of tropical forests, this biome does not come under so much pressure from agriculturalists.

Covering a wide belt on either side of the equator between the tropics, this biome is characterized by a warm climate, and only moderate rainfall with a lengthy dry season. The extended drought during the annual cycle means that fire plays an important and constructive part in the annual cycle.

Generally grass grows as high as three and a half meters, with trees dotted around the open plains, notably acacias. Because all plants must be adapted to drought and fire, there is not nearly as much diversity as in tropical woodlands. That is, as concerns plant life. But when we turn to animal life, we encounter an astonishing sight. The most dominant animals are the large grazing mammals, at their most spectacular in the savannah throngs of Africa. The most pre-eminent example is the Serengeti Plains, where a 25,000 sq.km. ecosystem supports two million wildebeest, two million gazelles and zebras, and tens of thousands of buffalo, other antelopes, giraffe, elephant and the like, together with their associated carnivores such as lion, leopard, cheetah and hyenas. This total of four-plus million animals contrasts with only four times as many animals in the nine-million sq.km. United States.

No doubt about it, tropical savannahs feature the most spectacular arrays of mammal life left in the biosphere. Regrettably, the savannahs tend to be increasingly taken by man for his herds of domestic livestock, if not for crop cultivation. The amount of savannah wildlife left in Africa is surely no more than one-tenth of what it was 100 years ago, and it is dwindling fast. If it continues to disappear, this will be a biological tragedy on a par with the demise of the vast herds of bison in the North American grasslands 100 years ago -- and our biosphere will have lost one of its most exceptional phenomena.

Mediterranean-Type Vegetation

Often known as chaparral, this biome occurs where there are mild wet winters and pronounced summer droughts. Overall there is less rain than in grasslands.

The vegetation is mainly sclerophyllous, i.e., hard-leaved. Typical forms include shrubby trees and other low-growing woody plants, together with scrub. Because tall trees, with their greater proportion of wood, burn more readily in the frequent fires, they tend to be few and far between, whereas smaller woody plants are only singed by fire. All of these plants are basically evergreen, with hard leaves, thick and waxy -- features that are adaptations to drought, and to the periodic fires that serve to maintain the dominance of the shrub vegetation. Indeed without fire, many seeds would fail to germinate; and after fire, we see shrubs sprouting vigorously.

We find chaparral-type vegetation around the Mediterranean basin, in northwestern Mexico/California, in South Africa, in southern Australia and in southern Chile. A good place to see chaparral is in the hills backing the Berkeley campus of the University of California, where white-tailed deer are common and mule deer not infrequent. Also among the scrub and bush one can find rabbits, wood rats and chipmunks, also wren-tits and brown towhees.

Temperate Forests

Generally found in areas with warm summers, cold winters and plenty of rainfall, as in most of the eastern United States, much of central Europe and part of eastern Asia, we find communities of broad-leaved trees, such as maples, hickories and many oaks, together with some conifers. Within these forests we find deer, wild boars, woodchucks, and a variety of predators including wolves, foxes and wild cats, plus a few omnivores such as bears. Still richer is the bird life, including woodpeckers, titmice, thrushes, warblers and finches, flycatchers, and wild turkeys.

By contrast with tropical forests, temperate forests often stand on fairly fertile soils. So they have been widely cleared for agriculture. At the time of the first settlers' arrival in what is now the United States, virtually the entire country east of the Mississippi was clothed in original forest. Almost all of it was cleared at one time or another, to make way for farmlands. In certain areas, notably New England, the farms were subsequently abandoned, and forest growth has returned, with more maples than in the original forests. The result is the spectacular colors of the Fall foliage -- a more remarkable phenomenon than was viewed by the Pilgrim Fathers. Here we have, then, a man-influenced vegetation that represents, in some respects, an "improvement" on what was there before modern man intervened.

Temperate Grasslands

A category incorporating prairies and steppes in North America and northern Eurasia, also pampas in South America and veld in southern Africa, temperate grasslands occur where rainfall is somewhere between that of temperate forests and deserts, and where there is a fairly long dry season. Sometimes the grass stands as tall as two meters, sometimes no more than half a meter, and sometimes at in-between height. The roots of certain grassland species penetrate deep into the soil, as much as two meters in some cases, and the weight of their roots can be several times greater than that of the above-ground plants.

The dominant animals of temperate grasslands are large grazing mammals such as bison, pronghorn, saiga, guanaco and kangaroos, plus smaller grazers such as prairie dogs, and omnivores such as raccoons. In addition, the grasslands used to feature sizeable numbers of wild horses and wild asses.

In most areas, the large herds of these animals, many of them persisting until fairly recently, have been largely displaced by man's domestic livestock -- and in the U.S. Mid-West, the prairies have given way to vast grain croplands. Fortunately we can still see remnant throngs, set in their sweeping landscapes, in several parts of the western United States.

Deserts

Many of the large deserts are concentrated roughly around latitudes 30 degrees north and south, where the global weather system tends to produce descending masses of dry air. This means they receive less than 25 cms. of rainfall a year, which is too little even for grasses to survive as dominant vegetation. But hardly any desert receives no rain, the exceptions being the central Sahara and northern Chile.

Deserts can be divided into hot deserts, such as the Sahara, the Kalahari and the Thar region of western India, with daytime temperatures often above 50 degrees C., and with low night-time temperatures that can seem bitterly cold after the daytime heat. One may wonder why the temperature plunges at dusk. Well, it is because of the lack of vegetation that would otherwise moderate the temperature declines. There are also cold deserts, such as the Gobi Desert, with long periods of extreme cold and generally severe winters.

A typical desert features large expanses of barren rock or sand, with very sparse vegetation. Such plants as survive include sagebrush, creosote bush, mesquite, and succulent plants such as cacti and euphorbias. All these plants are adapted to drought in various ways. Some have drought- resistant seeds. Others have small thick leaves that drop off during dry periods. Yet others, as in the New World cacti, store water in their stems.

Animals, too, reveal a range of adaptations. In hot deserts, they are mostly small enough to hide under stones or in burrows to escape the daytime heat. Deep down inside a burrow, the relative humidty remains constantly at 30-50 percent, matching that above the ground during the night, and a great deal higher than that above the ground during the day. A good number of reptiles release next to no urine, as a water-conserving mechanism. The kangaroo rat, the pocketmouse and the jerboa can live indefinitely on dry seeds, and appear to last a lifetime, if need be,

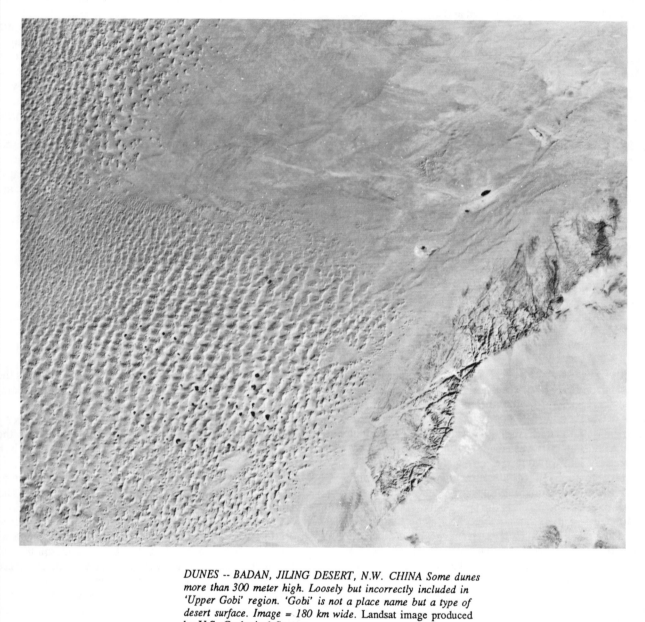

DUNES -- BADAN, JILING DESERT, N.W. CHINA Some dunes more than 300 meter high. Loosely but incorrectly included in 'Upper Gobi' region. 'Gobi' is not a place name but a type of desert surface. Image = 180 km wide. Landsat image produced by U.S. Geological Survey.

without open drinking water -- which means they are much better adapted than is the camel!

Boreal Forests

Also known by the Russian name taiga, the northern coniferous forests form an almost unbroken belt across North America and northern Eurasia, thus forming one of the most extensive biomes. The winters are long and cold, while the summers are short and sometimes very warm.

Boreal-forest trees are mostly evergreen conifers. They are able to photosynthesize year-round, and thanks to their needle-shaped waxy leaves, they can resist droughts which are caused by extreme cold and strong winds. In addition, their tall slim shape enables them to avoid damage by heavy snowfalls. In many areas, a boreal forest features only one or two species of tree, notably spruce, fir and tamarack, plus an occasional deciduous species such as birch, aspen, alder and larch.

The most prominent animals are moose and deer -- there are more species of deer in boreal forests than in any other biome. Also plentiful are rodents. Carnivores include wolves, lynxes, wolverines, martins, weasels, mink and sables. Because of the severe annual cycles between winter and summer, animal numbers tend to oscillate, the snowshoe hare-lynx cycles being a classic example. For similar reasons, coniferous forests are subject to outbreaks of bark beetles and defoliating insects (such as sawflies and budworms), especially in areas where there are just a couple of dominant tree species.

Tundra

A Russian word meaning "north of the timberline", tundra is an expanse of treeless plains, where the average annual temperature is well below freezing point, and many areas remain permanently frozen in a condition known as permafrost. Rainfall is generally less than 25 cms. a year, i.e., equivalent to that of a hot desert. So tundra qualifies as a cold desert.

Because the low temperatures make for a very low rate of microbial decomposition, the tundra is characterized by a thick, spongy mat of vegetation in varying stages of decay. Dominant plants include lichens ("reindeer moss"), mosses, sedges, grasses and dwarf trees such as willows, which rarely reach a height of more than one meter. In fact, the tundra is essentially a wet arctic grassland. Despite the fact that the spring-summer growing season is so short, sunlight persists virtually right around the clock, which means that plants can grow almost non-stop. This means there is a lot more vegetation than we might expect in such unpromising environments. The sudden outburst of plant life helps to stimulate a similar outburst of insect life, especially mosquitoes and black flies.

But because vegetation is sparse on a year-round basis, there are few large animals, the most notable species being caribou, reindeer and musk ox. Smaller creatures include snowshoe hares, lemmings and voles. Carnivores are similarly few and far between, being limited mainly to wolves, the Arctic fox and a few birds of prey. The polar bear eats a good deal of meat, but it counts as an omnivore.

Reading List

There are few books which deal only with biomes as such. The best way to read more about biomes is to consult leading books on ecology, such as *EcoScience*, by P.R. Ehrlich, A.H. Ehrlich and J.P. Holdren, W.H. Freeman, 1977; and *Biogeography*, by C.B. Cox, I.N. Healey and P.D. Moore, Blackwell Scientific Publications, 1976.

Other highly recommended publications include:

Fundamentals of Ecology, by E.P. Odum, (third edition), W.B. Saunders Co., Philadelphia, 1971. The "grandaddy" of ecology in its most modern phase, Odum describes the major biomes in systematic fashion, telling us what we shall find where -- and making it all eminently understandable.
Introduction to Ecology, by P.A. Colinvaux, 1973. Describing ecology as a "pleasant science", Colinvaux regales us with vivid accounts of the broad divisions of the earth, together with chapters on animal geography and plant societies.
Environmental Conservation, by R.F. Dasmann, Macmillan, New York, 1978. Perhaps the most populist account of why plants and animals tend to be where they are.
The Living Planet, by D. Attenborough, Colins, London, 1984. The book of the television series, this is the most easily readable and vivid survey of our biosphere. Sometimes approaches the "can't put it down" category.
Biological Science, by William T. Keeton, (third edition), W.W. Norton, New York, 1976. A trifle technical, and substantive. A fine reference book.
Geographical Ecology, by R.H. MacArthur, Harper and Row, New York, 1972. The standard text on biogeography. Sub-titled "Patterns in the Distribution of Species", which says it all.
Biogeography: Natural and Cultural, by I.D. Simmons, Edward Arnold, London, UK, 1979. Deals elegantly with man's role in changing the face of the earth -- often to the benefit of his fellow species, not invariably destructive.
Of course the reader will want to consult a good map, and the most up-to-date publication is that by M. Udvardy, available through UNESCO and IUCN.

Garden of Earthly Delights

The Biosphere may be looked at as "red in tooth and claw", as a struggle to survive, all-pervasive and relentless, but for the transient forms that populate it moments occur in which the whole process is seen, an identification with the life-force surges through the organism, delight dances our blood. Hieronymus Bosch paints this moment of ecstatic reality.

Atmosphere

Michael B. McElroy

Our experiments...convinced us that the composition of the Earth's atmosphere was so curious and incompatible a mixture that it could not possibly have arisen or persisted by chance. Almost everything about it seemed to violate the rules of equilibrium chemistry, yet amidst apparent disorder relatively constant and favorable conditions for life were somehow maintained. JAMES LOVELOCK

The atmosphere of planet Earth is composed of a bewildering array of gases, many of which reflect either directly or indirectly the presence of life. We can think of the atmosphere as an extension of the biosphere, an essential component of the global life support system. It is alive, ever changing, mirroring in a faithful fashion the variety of subtle changes which characterize the ever-shifting patterns of life on Earth.

Change is the norm, not the exception, for life on Earth. It is easy today to lose sight of the vast significance of the changes which arose in the past, and particularly easy given our current preoccupation with changes wrought by man. It is well, thus, to begin with a brief account of what we believe to be the history of the atmosphere. It is a story which begins with the spinning cloud of dust and gas which composed the original solar nebula. From this relatively commonplace beginning ensued the sequence of events which led to the formation of the sun and planets, the evolution of atmospheres, and, eventually, the appearance of life. With the possible exception of this last event, it is a sequence which must have proceeded in many parts of the universe on many different occasions since the dawn of time.

The early history of the solar system is cloaked in mystery. We believe that the materials which supplied the building blocks for the primitive planets were formed by condensation in the nebula, like ice from water, or liquid from gas. There was an orderly sequence to nebular condensation. Heavier elements such as iron condensed at relatively high temperature; lighter elements such as hydrogen, carbon and nitrogen precipitated at much lower temperatures. This led to a segregation of elements in the nebula. Planets which formed at large distances from the sun, where it was cold, received a preponderance of low temperature material. Planets which formed in the interior of the nebula were composed for the most part of high temperature stuff. They received their quota of low temperature materials during the later stages of planetary formation, as the nebula cooled.

We have a picture thus of the early Earth as a quite heterogeneous body. It evolved rapidly, fueled by energy supplied by decay of radioactive elements trapped in the planetary interior, supplemented by energy added during the accretion process. Heavier elements settled to the bottom forming a primitive core. Lighter elements floated to the top forming the early mantle and crust. The more volatile elements vented to the outside providing an early atmosphere and ocean. Further segregation of crustal and mantle materials led to production of continents and ocean basins, and the process continues, though at a somewhat diminished rate, today.

The initial atmosphere, we think, was composed for the most part of gases formed from hydrogen, carbon, nitrogen, oxygen and sulfur, with trace quantities of helium, neon, argon, krypton and xenon. There is some dispute as to the chemical form of the major elements. Was carbon present in its more reduced (hydrogen-rich) form, as methane, or in its more oxidized (oxygen-rich) configuration, as carbon dioxide? Those who favor the reduced option are usually persuaded by the view that it would be easier for life to evolve in such an environment. I lean toward the more oxidized option, influenced, at least in part, by the fact that atmospheres of our nearest planetary neighbors, Venus and Mars, are dominated by carbon dioxide.

One can estimate fairly readily the total quantities of volatile hydrogen, carbon, and nitrogen evolved by the Earth over geologic time. Most of the hydrogen released over the past 4.5 billion years resides now as water vapor in the ocean. The bulk of the carbon is present as carbonate minerals or as reduced carbon in sedimentary rocks --

residues of once living organisms, relics of the past. Nitrogen is found mainly as nitrogen gas in the atmosphere. We can surmise that the primitive volatiles released by the Earth were dominated by water vapor, with carbon dioxide second in abundance, followed by nitrogen, with trace amounts of hydrogen and carbon monoxide in addition to the chemically inert noble gases. The primitive atmosphere would have been too cold to retain large quantities of water vapor in the vapor phase, much as it is today. Water would have rained from the skies, filling the low areas of the primitive surface. The composition of the early atmosphere would have been dominated by carbon dioxide. The abundance of nitrogen would have accounted for approximately 1% that of carbon dioxide, a situation similar to that which pertains for Venus today.

Carbon dioxide would have slowly infused the primitive ocean forming carbonate minerals. The pressure of the atmosphere would have dropped, approaching the value which holds today. The high concentration of carbon dioxide in the early atmosphere, and the associated greenhouse, would have helped trap heat radiated by the surface, contributing to a relatively benign climate, even though the energy radiated by the early sun was probably less than now. This, I believe, was the environment which nurtured the first living organisms.

It is unclear where or how they first appeared. It is apparent though that life arose early in Earth's history. The oldest surviving rocks, at least those which have been identified, formed more than 3.5 billion years ago, and indicate that the biotic influence was widespread even

COMPOSITION OF THE ATMOSPHERE AT THE SURFACE

Percent by volume

Name	Abundance (%)
Nitrogen	78
Oxygen	21
Argon	0.9
Water Vapor	0.1 – 1.0 (variable)
Carbon Dioxide	0.035
Neon	0.002
Helium	0.0005
Methane	0.0002
Krypton	0.0001
Hydrogen	0.00005
Nitrous Oxide	0.00003
Carbon Monoxide	0.00001 (variable)
Sulfur Dioxide	up to 0.0001 (variable)
Ozone	up to 0.00001 (variable)
Xenon	0.000009
Nitrogen Dioxide	up to 0.0000001 (variable)

then. Free oxygen, was a minor constituent of the atmosphere during the first few billion years of its history. Its subsequent appearance, and rapid rise, was a consequence, we think, of the evolution of plants capable of harnessing sunlight to synthesize organic carbon from carbon dioxide, with a concomitant ability to protect against potentially lethal effects of free oxygen. The composition of the atmosphere has been relatively stable since then. Stable but not static -- hydrogen, carbon, nitrogen, oxygen and sulfur are in constant motion, moving rapidly from atmosphere to biosphere, soils, ocean and sediments, shuffling back and forth between these compartments, spending, with the exception of nitrogen, but a small fraction of their total life in the air.

Consider the case of carbon. Imagine a carbon atom trapped beneath the surface, vented to the atmosphere in the explosive release of a volcano. Consider its fate in the environment today. The atom will appear in the air initially bonded to oxygen atoms, as a molecule of carbon dioxide. It will be carried hither and yon by the wind, and in a matter of a few years will have visited most parts of the Earth. Eventually, within the first ten years of its life, it may be captured by a plant or tree and converted to a more reduced chemical form under the action of photosynthesis. Alternatively, it may make its way into the ocean, where it will be converted to the bicarbonate ion. The atom will wander back and forth between the atmosphere, biosphere, soils and ocean. It will do so for about 100,000 years before finding its way into the ocean sediment. There it may be buried, immobilized for a hundred million years or more.

Life in the sediment is more placid, but even here there is movement. The sediments are transported as passengers on the crustal plates which drive the motion of continents. Sooner or later they are drawn beneath the surface, subjected to intense heat emanating from the planetary interior and returned to the air. The average carbon atom may have made as many as 20 such trips between sediment and air over the 4.5 billion year history of the Earth.

A change in the rate of sea floor spreading or, alternatively, a change in the rate of vulcanism, can lead to a change in the abundance of carbon dioxide in the air. Usually such changes are slow, and their impact on the air is felt slowly on time scales of millions of years or more. A change in the metabolism of the oceanic biosphere, or a change in the rate of ocean mixing can have a more immediate impact on the atmosphere. We have evidence that the abundance of atmospheric carbon dioxide was low during the last ice age, about 200 parts per million (ppm) compared with about 350 ppm today. Most scientists believe that the low abundance of carbon dioxide 20,000 years ago is evidence for a rather different state of the ocean at that time. A more productive ocean would tend to draw carbon from the atmosphere, shifting the balance in favor of the sea. It is possible that the dramatic shifts in climate over the past few million years were caused at least in part by variations in carbon dioxide driven by changes in the metabolism of the sea.

The abundance of free oxygen in the air is linked directly to the fate of carbon. Oxygen is released during photosynthesis. To the extent that photosynthesis is the dominant source of oxygen, we may conclude that for every molecule of oxygen there exists somewhere on the Earth a molecule of reduced carbon. This implies a reservoir of organic carbon equivalent to about 2×10 to the sixteenth power tons C, enough to supply current demands for energy for several million years. Most of this carbon is dispersed, however. Economically recoverable coal and oil represent but a small fraction of the total quantity of reduced carbon in sediments.

The chemistry of the atmosphere is dominated by gases formed directly or indirectly from oxygen under the influence of sunlight. The oxygen molecule can be fractured by sunlight at altitudes above 20 km. One of the oxygen atoms formed in this manner can bond to oxygen forming a triatomic form of oxygen, ozone. Ozone plays an important role in the planetary life support system, shielding the surface from otherwise lethal rays of ultraviolet sunlight. It is a delicate balance. Ozone in high concentration at the surface is toxic, a hazard to plants and animals. It constitutes one of the more noxious compounds of urban smog. Fortunately most of the atmosphere's supply of ozone resides at high altitude, in the stratosphere, where it is produced by sunlight and removed by reactions involving, inter alia, nitric oxide, formed from nitrous oxide. Nitrous oxide is the second most abundant form of nitrogen in the atmosphere, and the eleventh most abundant gas in the air following nitrogen, oxygen, argon, water, carbon dioxide, neon, helium, methane, krypton and hydrogen. A summary of the composition of the atmosphere is given in the accompanying table. It is interesting to note that, with the exception of the noble gases (Ar, Ne, He, Kr, Xe), the abundances of all of the compounds listed here are either directly or indirectly under the influence of the biosphere.

Climate is the long term average condition of the weather. At mid latitudes we expect that it should be warm on average in summer, cold in winter, with the annual temperature range largest in the interior of continents. Within the average though we anticipate considerable variability. Variability is less pronounced in the tropics and subtropics where the annual range in temperature can be as small as a few degrees.

The atmosphere is a vast turbulent fluid, rising in the tropics, sinking at mid latitudes. It is characterized at high latitudes by frequent storms, by alternating high and low pressure systems. The various regimes of the biosphere reflect the prevailing weather and climate. Dense forests are found in the equatorial region where the rising motion of air provides an abundant source of rain. Vegetation is sparse at mid latitudes where the air sinks and is consequently hot and dry. It is here that we find the great deserts of the world. Deserts give way to grasses and deciduous forests at mid latitudes where the climate is more variable over the course of a year and are replaced by coniferous forests and tundras at high latitudes where winters are exceptionally cold and sunlight is essentially absent for much of the year. The biosphere, in its diversity, exists in harmony with climate. Conversely, climate, at least on a local scale, is affected to a considerable extent by the nature of the biosphere. The floor of a tropical forest is relatively cool and moist. Water is conserved there efficiently in contrast to the situation for a desert region where the small amount of water reaching the surface in infrequent rain storms is rapidly evaporated back to the air.

The composition of the atmosphere is changing today at a rate unprecedented in recent Earth history. Carbon dioxide has risen from about 270 ppm a hundred years ago to near 350 ppm today. The increase is due mainly to burning of fossil fuel, with an uncertain additional contribution due to clearance of land for agriculture in the tropics. The abundance of methane is increasing, at between 1 and 2 percent per year, as is carbon monoxide. Again agriculture and energy production are implicated. Similar influences are thought to be responsible for a small but steady rise in nitrous oxide. The concentrations of nitrogen oxides, sulfur oxides and ozone are elevated in industrial regions where large quantities of fossil fuels are consumed in the course of power generation and transportation. The acidity of rain has increased over extensive regions of the northern hemisphere and there are hints that the presence of man may be sensed even in the remote regions of the upper stratosphere where decomposition of chlorinated industrial hydrocarbons and nitrous oxide may contribute to cause a reduction in the concentration of high altitude ozone. The rising levels of carbon dioxide, methane, nitrous oxide and increasing burden of industrial chlorofluorocarbons may be expected to enhance the efficiency of the greenhouse. We may expect subtle changes in the chemical and radiation environment at the surface, generally warmer weather and detectable changes in the distribution of biotic regimes. Even the level of the sea may be expected to rise as warmer temperatures promote melting of land based ice. It is difficult to assess the impact of these various disturbances but it is obviously important that we should do so soon. To this end a number of scientific bodies have combined to propose programs of research to enhance our understanding of the atmosphere, to define the nature of the complex interactions with the biosphere, soils, oceans

HURRICANE. Skylab photograph produced by NASA.

and geosphere. We hope that these programs, under consideration by, among others, the National Aeronautics and Space Administration of the United States, the U.S. National Academy of Sciences, the International Council of Scientific Unions and the Institute for Applied Systems Analysis in Vienna, are successful in stimulating a truly global approach to the study of the Earth and, with it, a deeper appreciation for the unique significance of life.

Catalogue
Regions of the Atmosphere

The region of the atmosphere near the ground is known as the *troposphere*, from the Greek word tropein, meaning to turn or change. This is the zone which contains most of the weather of the planet. The temperature generally decreases with increasing altitude in the troposphere, reaching a minimum value of about -60 degrees centigrade at mid latitudes, somewhat colder, about -75 degrees centigrade in the tropics. The point of minimum temperature is known as the *tropopause*. The temperature increases slowly with increasing altitude above the tropopause in a zone known as the stratosphere. It attains a maximum value near 50 km at a point known as the *stratopause*. The stratosphere is a very stable region, in contrast to the troposphere. Materials added to the stratosphere, debris from volcanoes or nuclear bombs for example, stay there for several years, in contrast to the much shorter residence time, weeks or months, associated with the troposphere. The stratosphere is exceptionally dry, containing most of the atmosphere's supply of ozone. The increase of temperature with altitude is caused by local absorption of ultraviolet solar radiation, a fortunate occurrence since light of this wavelength would otherwise cause serious problems for life below.

The temperature decreases with altitude above the stratopause, in a zone known as the *mesosphere* (middle sphere). It reaches a minimum near 90 km, at the *mesopause*. This is the coldest region of the atmosphere. Temperatures are as low as -90 degrees centigrade. The temperature increases again above the mesopause, in the *thermosphere*. The density of gases is exceedingly low in this zone. Eventually, the density is so low, above about 300 km, that higher speed atoms are able to escape the gravitational field of Earth becoming part of the interplanetary medium. The escape region is known as the *exosphere*. Only the lightest elements, hydrogen and helium, have sufficient speed to escape from the Earth.

The Atmosphere in Motion

The general circulation is the term used to describe the average motion of the atmosphere. It may be simulated on a computer with a numerical model known as a *general circulation model*. We should distinguish between general circulation models and *weather forecast models*. The latter assume an observed initial state for the atmosphere and seek to predict its future evolution. Weather forecast models provide the basis for the predictions which appear daily in the newspaper and on radio and television. Forecasts are reliable only for short periods of time in the future. They should not be trusted on time scales longer than about a week. The difficulty in forecasting the weather is due in part to the problems associated with specification of an initial state, in part due to intrinsic problems which arise in the complex mathematical formulations needed to treat the motion of the air on scales of interest to the user community. The forecaster may be quite successful in describing the weather over a relatively large region, the North East of the United States for example, but, if he predicts heavy rain on average for the North East and if a heavy fall of snow occurs in Boston,

the public response is likely to be less than sympathetic.

An observer from another planet, watching the Earth's weather through the limited eyes of an imperfect camera, would see a relatively ordered structure. He would detect that the air rises in the tropics moving north and south at altitude, returning to the surface at latitudes of about 30 degrees north and 30 degrees south. He would see a return flow along the surface, completing a loop known as the *Hadley Circulation*, named in honor of the eighteenth-century English meteorologist who first proposed the concept of a simple thermally driven circulation. Air in motion in the northern hemisphere is deflected to the right by the rotation of the Earth, an effect of so-called *Coriolis force*, named in honor of the 19th century French scientist Gaspard Coriolis. By the same token air masses in the southern hemisphere are deflected to the left. This gives rise to the characteristic pattern of the *trade winds* which blow steadily from the northeast in tropical regions of the northern hemisphere, from the southeast in tropical regions of the southern hemisphere. The trade winds are a consequence of the surface flows associated with the Hadley cell. At higher latitudes, between 30 degrees and 60 degrees, the circulation of the air proceeds in the opposite sense to the Hadley system. Air rises at about 60 degrees flowing aloft to lower latitudes, with a return flow near surface. The reverse circulation in this case is known as a *Ferrel Cell* named for the American meteorologist William Ferrel. The associated surface winds between 30 degrees and 60 degrees are from the southwest to the northeast in the northern hemisphere, from the northwest to southeast in the south. Winds are more sporadic at high latitudes blowing generally from the east, part of a weak thermal cell driven by intense cooling of surface air near the poles.

Our mythical observer would see a planet covered irregularly by white reflective clouds. With techniques of modern spectroscopy he would conclude that some of these clouds were composed of small droplets of liquid water. Others, particularly those at high elevation, contain ice. With further work he might succeed in classifying cloud types, identifying:

cirrus: thin wispy clouds at high altitudes often aligned in long streamers composed of ice (cirrus = hair);

cirrostratus: thin sheet-like clouds composed of ice covering large parts of the sky, usually at altitudes above 7 km (stratus = spread out);

cirrocumulus: small rounded puffs, frequently aligned in rows, composed of ice and found at altitudes similar to cirrus and cirrostratus (cumulus = heap);

clouds at intermediate altitude, between 2 and 7 km, known as *altostratus* and *altocumulus* (altus = high);

and, at lower elevations, *stratus, stratocumulus, nimbocumulus* (nimbus = rain), *cumulus* and *cumulonimbus*. He would notice that cumulonimbus clouds are often associated with flashes of light and with further study might come to understand the power of a thunderstorm.

Reference

A Field Guide to the Atmosphere, by Vincent J. Schaefer and John A. Day, sponsored by the National Audubon Society and National Wildlife Federation, Houghton Mifflin Co., Boston, 1981. For the atmospheric apprentice, this handbook provides essential information, i.e., how to identify clouds, forecast the weather, distinguish different types of precipitation and air pollution.

Climate Mandate, by Walter Orr Roberts and Henry Lansford, W.H. Freeman, San Francisco, 1979.

Meteorology Today, by C. Donald Ahrens, second edition, West Publishing Company, St. Paul, 1985.

Weather and Climate Modification, by W.N. Hess, ed., Wiley and Sons, New York, 1974.

An Introduction to Dynamic Meteorology, by J.R. Holton, Academic Press, New York, 1972.

Radiative Heat Exchange in the Atmosphere, by K. Ya Kondratyev, Pergamon Press, London, 1965.

Man's Impact on Climate, by W.H. Matthews, W.W. Kellogg, and G.D. Robinson, eds., M.I.T. Press, Cambridge, Massachusetts, 1971.

Climate: Past, Present, and Future, by H.H. Lamb, Methuen, London, 1972.

The Depletion of Stratospheric Ozone, by C.E. Kolb, Technology Review, vol. 78, no. 1, pp39-47.

Stratospheric Ozone Destruction by Man-made Chlorofluoromethanes, by R.J. Cicerone, R.S. Stolarski and S. Waters, Science, vol. 185, pp. 1165-1167 (September 27).

University Corporation for Atmospheric Research

P.O. Box 3000, Boulder, Colorado 80307, U.S.A. 303-494-5151.

Hydrosphere

James D. Hays

Such is the nature of the ocean that the waters which flow into it can never fill it nor those which flow from it exhaust it. I will enjoy myself rambling by it. CHUANG TZU

The hydrosphere -- that fluid envelope that covers more than three-quarters of the earth's surface -- most clearly distinguishes planet Earth from its neighboring planets. Not only is the Earth unique in having so much water in the liquid phase covering its surface, but that water is critical to two other very important features of the planet. Probably the most important is the profusion of life or the biosphere that characterizes the earth, for the hydrosphere is absolutely critical to the biosphere, since life arose from the hydrosphere and most plants and animals are dominantly composed of water. But not only is the hydrosphere chemically important to the origin and evolution of life on our planet, it is also important in maintaining a uniform climate, which has permitted life to sustain itself for more than three billion years. Although there is not a continuous fossil record of life from that time to the present, as more and more fossil evidence is found in the early Precambrian, there is every indication that life in fact has been continuous since that time. Since life requires temperatures to be dominantly between 0 and 100 C, that is, temperatures that allow the hydrosphere to remain dominantly in the liquid phase, the long record of life strongly suggests that the temperature of our planet has been very constant for much of its history.

We are all familiar with the present profusion of life on our planet; on land, in the water, and making use of the air. However, prior to 400 million years ago, life existed only in the hydrosphere. Life in the ocean is different in many aspects from life on land. On land, the basic food-producing processes of photosynthesis take place in green plants of all sizes, some of them many times the size of the animals that browse on them. In the

ocean, on the other hand, the size of an organism and its position in the food chain are related, and the microscopic phytoplankton, which directly and indirectly nourish all other life in the ocean, are the tiniest, although the most abundant marine life. The phytoplankton are restricted to the uppermost layers of the ocean by their need for sunlight. The greatest depth at which they are found vary from perhaps 30 meters in coastal waters to 100 meters in the clearest seas. As a result, the animal life that feeds on the plants is also more abundant in and near the sea surface.

One step removed from the primary food producers are the zooplankton. Many of the zooplankton are microscopic, but this group of drifters also includes crustaceans, larval forms of large marine animals, worms, snails and jellyfish. Smaller zooplankton feed on the tiny planktonic plants; others live by preying on fellow zooplankton.

At the highest levels of the food chain are large, free-swimming predators -- fish, squid, dolphins, seals and whales. These strong swimmers are known as necton, and they too are enmeshed in a hierarchy of predator and prey. Thus plankton-eating fish such as herring are eaten by tarpon and tuna, which in turn fall prey to sharks. In general, the higher the species rank in the food chain, the sparser its population, for the transfer of nourishments from prey to predator is inefficient. It takes roughly ten pounds of phytoplankton to nurture a pound of zooplankton, and ten pounds of zooplankton to produce a pound of herring. And the same rate of conversion continues to the highest levels of the food chain.

Below the sunlit layer lies the cold, dark immensity of the deep ocean. Nourishment enters this realm as a continuous rain of excrement and corpses from the life in the sunlit layers. Although the deep ocean represents the largest habitat on earth, it is also the most sparsely populated.

Even at its surface, most of the ocean does not approach the biological productivity of the land. By one estimate, the average amount of organic matter produced each year beneath a given area of sea surface is less than 1/25 of that yielded by the same area of good farmland. This low fertility reflects the fundamental disadvantage of the ocean as an environment for life. On land the organic compounds contained in excrement and dead plants and animals are released into the soil by the processes of decay, ready for use by the next generation of plants. At sea, by contrast, organic wastes are lost to the depths and life in the surface waters quickly exhausts available nutrients, unless these nutrients are returned to the surface by upwelling deep waters. Consequently, areas where upwelling deep waters do not occur may become biological deserts. The bright blue and aquamarine waters of tropic seas are due to very little life existing in these seas. The grey and dark green waters of northern climates and far southern climes such as the Antarctic and the Arctic indicate abundant life. In fact, the seas around Antarctica, where nutrients lost from the sunlit surface layers are returned to the surface, is one of the most productive open ocean areas in the world. This upwelling nurtures the most spectacular assemblage of marine life. Ceaselessly supplied with nutrients by deep water welling up to replace the chilly, salty surface water sinking to the sea floor, the 12 million square miles of southern or Antarctic ocean host an unparalleled abundance of phytoplankton. These marine pastures in turn nourish zooplankton, primarily two-inch shrimp-like creatures called krill, in concentrations of up to 36 pounds per cubic meter of surface water, a density of living matter that, taking the southern ocean as a whole, amounts to a biomass of perhaps five billion tons. The krill feed 350,000 whales, tens of millions of seals and nearly 200

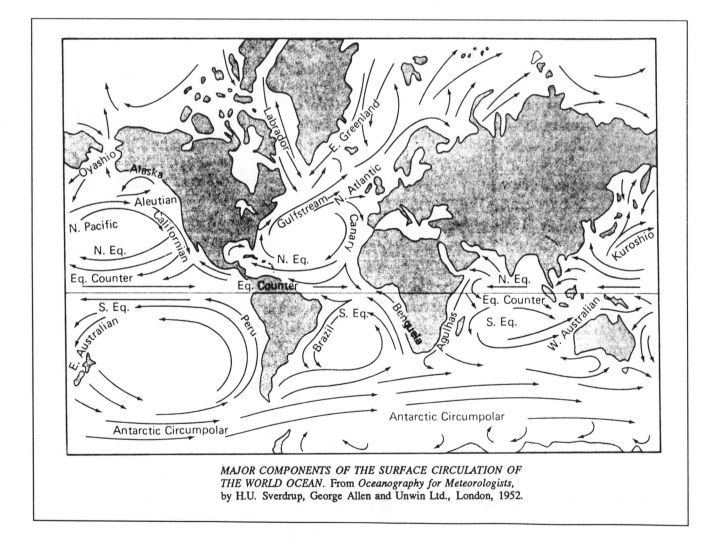

MAJOR COMPONENTS OF THE SURFACE CIRCULATION OF THE WORLD OCEAN. From *Oceanography for Meteorologists,* by H.U. Sverdrup, George Allen and Unwin Ltd., London, 1952.

million sea birds.

Food from the sea is the most important product from the sea for man. In the 100 years after the mid-nineteenth century, the world's total catch of fish, the ocean's most important product by far, increased roughly tenfold. The annual harvest tripled in just two decades from less than 20 million metric tons in 1948 to 64 million metric tons in 1969. In the next decade, the catch continued to increase in volume to 72 million metric tons in 1980. Other profound changes have been taking place all along in kinds of fish caught and the size of regional catches. In the North Sea, for example, for centuries in the area where commercial fishing began, fishermen have pursued only a few of the estimated 20,000 species of fin fish. Sought after species such as herring and cod were once plentiful, but during the early part of the 20th century, North Sea fishermen began to notice that their nets were bringing up smaller catches of smaller fish. It was apparent that the fish had been taken in such large quantity that they could no longer reproduce fast enough to maintain their former populations. Attempts to conserve the supply were ineffectual because the fishermen from different countries could not agree on what limits they should place on their catches. World War I greatly reduced fishing in the North Sea. As a consequence, fish stocks increased. After World War I the stocks gradually decreased again, until World War II resulted in a hiatus in fishing. During that war, fish stocks increased by 400% in the North Sea. But since World War II the harvest has dwindled once again.

The North Sea was not the only place where evidence of over-fishing has been noticed. It has also been noticed in other parts of the North Atlantic where stocks of salmon, sturgeon and shad have become seriously depleted, as have sardines in the North Pacific. As these fish stocks became harder to find, fishermen began pursuing Peruvian anchovy, the Atlantic menhaden and other less desirable fish. These fish, because of their oiliness and pungent flavor, are not widely used for direct human consumption. Most of the secondary catch is processed into meal and fed to livestock and poultry. Before World War II, 10% of the world's catch was converted to meal. In 1980 the share mounted to 30%. In some ways, one could look at this as a food reserve, since the efficiency of converting fish to fish meal and then to beef or poultry is low, compared to direct feeding of fish to human populations. So, if the world were in desperate need of protein, the step from fish meal to beef could be bypassed, greatly increasing the available protein to human populations through direct eating of fish.

Marine biologists do not know how large a catch of primary species of fish can be sustained. This is often referred to as the maximum sustainable yield; in other words, the number of tons of fish that can be caught each year and replaced by the natural reproductive processes of fish. Some think that pushing the catch beyond 100 million metric tons would be dangerous. On the other hand, a lot is unknown about fish populations, and it might be possible to push it further.

But fish are not the only marine resources for food. Instead of eating the fin fish, we could eat the creatures that the fin fish eat. Marine biologists estimate that another 100 million tons of marine creatures other than fish could be taken from the ocean each year without endangering future productivity. To take advantage of this under-utilized marine resource, fishermen and consumers will have to abandon habit and learn to value animals that occupy lower places in the ocean's food chain. The species that has received the most attention as a possible food source for humans is krill; a shrimp-like crustacean that average about 2.5 inches in length. Huge quantities of krill live in the productive waters of the Antarctic. Before baleen whales were hunted almost to extinction, they used to converge by the hundreds of thousands on the fringes of the polar seas, and consume up to three tons of krill per day per whale. According to some calculations, the whales ate more than 250 million tons of krill annually -- enough protein to sustain 200 million people a year. One pound of krill yields more protein than an equal amount of fish, and supplies 460 calories and many essential vitamins.

Indeed, ships from the USSR and Japan have been trawling for krill in the Antarctic since the 1970's. The annual harvest there has reached 80,000 metric tons in 1979 and is used partly for animal feed and partly for human food. Ecologists are concerned, however, about the effects that a greatly increased krill harvest might have on creatures that feed on these crustaceans -- penguins, seals, squid, fish, along with the few remaining baleen whales. The populations of the animals that one had to compete with whales for krill have increased dramatically. But fishermen once again could change the Antarctic ecological balance and perhaps doom the whales once and for all.

The oceans have always been used as the final dumping place for human wastes. Although things are changing slowly, even today most of the large coastal cities of the world dump raw sewage into the ocean. In 1982, twenty-five percent of Americans lived in areas that had no sewage treatment systems at all. And many of the existing plants pump partially treated sewage into rivers that transport it to the sea. Municipalities and states were dredging and accumulating sediments from harbor and river bottoms to maintain channels or open new waterways and dumping the dredged material offshore. The ocean has also been used repeatedly as a means of getting rid of industrial wastes, unused munitions and other war materials, and more recently as a place for nuclear waste, although at this time probably none is being dumped into the oceans. Because the ocean is so vast, people until very recently did not consider its pollution as a serious problem. Nevertheless, with the vast accumulation of refuse from the industrial age, this has become a serious problem. The dumping by ships plying the oceans itself is a problem. Oil spills as well as just the garbage from vessels have been found to concentrate in places like the Sargasso Sea in the middle of the Atlantic, where the great circulating Gulf Stream carries it slowly but inevitably into the middle of that ocean, where it becomes concentrated. Scientists have estimated that bits of styrofoam, bottles, etc., are found on the average of one per square yard in the center of the Atlantic.

However, there is growing awareness of ocean pollution, and an international effort to cope with it is in place. Just as, after years of work, there is nearly unanimous international agreement to cease the hunting of whales, so ocean pollution control is active on the international agenda of concern.

How The Hydrosphere Is Studied

Traditionally the hydrosphere has been studied by marine coastal labs and surface vessels and lake and stream research stations. The goal of much of the early research was to gain a complete census of what lives in the oceans and streams and lakes, and the basic geometry of the ocean, and patterns of deep and shallow circulation.

Since the Second World War, and partly due to technological advances made during that war, the ways the ocean could be studied increased markedly. Today the oceans are still studied from surface ships and coastal stations, but in addition, a wide variety of measurements are made from Earth-orbiting satellites, including sea-surface temperatures and variations of height of the sea surface.

Extensive arrays of buoys have been deployed in many ocean areas to continuously monitor, for years, various aspects of sea surface and sub-surface conditions. The oceans are, today, also studied by extensive over-flights by instrument-laden aircraft, and from submersibles that can sink to the ocean's greatest depths.

The temperature and density structure of the ocean is critical to understanding its deep-circulation, since this is primarily a density-driven circulation, as opposed to the movements of surface waters, that is driven by the stress of near-surface winds. Traditionally, the deep properties of the ocean were probed by lowering strings of metal bottles with attached thermometers. A messenger, sent from the surface ship, would successively trip the bottles on the cast and they would close, capturing a sample of water from a known depth. The thermometers attached to each bottle would record the temperature at the time the bottle reversed. Chemical analyses could then be made on the water sample, either aboard ship or back at the home laboratory.

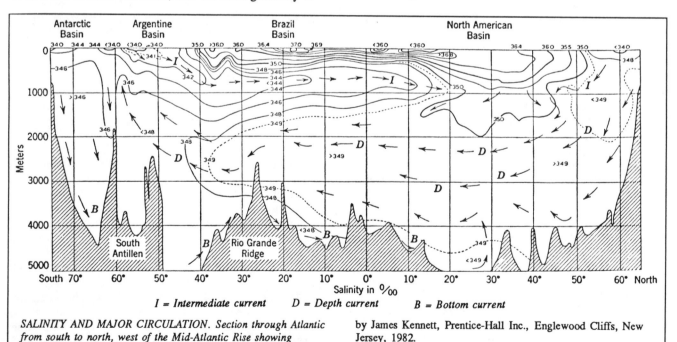

I = Intermediate current   *D = Depth current*   *B = Bottom current*

SALINITY AND MAJOR CIRCULATION. Section through Atlantic from south to north, west of the Mid-Atlantic Rise showing salinity and major circulation currents. From Marine Geology, by James Kennett, Prentice-Hall Inc., Englewood Cliffs, New Jersey, 1982.

Today all these measurements are made continuously by lowering sensors that measure temperature and various chemical properties from the surface to near the ocean floor. These measurements, combined with current meter measurements, provide the basic information needed to chart the direction rate and mechanisms of deep ocean circulation.

Important Past Studies of the Hydrosphere

Important studies of the hydrosphere are often associated with expeditions, institutions or teams of researchers.

Amongst early expeditions, the voyage of *HMS Challenger* in the late 19th Century (1872-1876) stands out as an expedition of outstanding discovery. It circumnavigated the globe and charted many of the major features of the ocean floor; described the dominant types of sediment that blanket the ocean bottom, and sampled life from nearly all depth in the ocean, disproving the theory which helped launch the expedition, i.e., that deeper living creatures are more primitive than those living in shallow depths. The *Challenger* brought back great amounts of information and it took nearly ten years to publish the results. It stands as the expedition that launched modern oceanography.

The expeditions of the German ship *Meteor*, between World War I and II are noteworthy because the *Meteor* established the structure and circulation patterns of the deep water of the Atlantic. Since World War II, major oceanographic efforts have been associated with oceanographic institutions: the study of the deep and surface circulation of the Pacific and its waves and tides by the scientists of the Scripps Institute of Oceanography at La Jolla; intensive studies of Atlantic circulation by scientists at the Woods Hole Oceanographic Institute at Woods Hole, Massachussetts; the mapping of the ocean floor, and the studies of the sediments that blanket it, by scientists of the Lamont-Doherty Geological Observatory, to name several.

Today, as in the past, oceanographic studies are largely team efforts. However, in the past they were centered around data acquisition. Today, with the large amounts of data gathered in the past 20 years, and with the rapidly increasing efficiency of data acquisition, large studies are now possible without going to sea.

Important Aspects of the Hydrosphere

The oceans, covering nearly three quarters of the Earth's surface, form the most important part of the hydrosphere. The oceans fill huge basins with common depths ranging between 2,000 and 4,000 meters. The greatest depths of the ocean (deep-sea trenches) are approximately as far below sea level as Mount Everest rises above sea level (nearly 10,000 meters).

The surface circulation of the ocean is driven by the wind, with tropical waters moving westward driven by the trade winds, and mid-latitude waters moving eastward, driven by the prevailing westerlies. This produces the subtropical gyres which have a characteristically clockwise circulation in the northern hemisphere and a counter-clockwise pattern in the southern hemisphere.

The centers of these subtropical gyres in both hemispheres have generally low productivity, while their edges are more productive. The counter-clockwise gyres that occur in high northern latitudes are more productive than the subtropical gyres, as are the clockwise gyres of the high latitudes of the southern hemisphere.

The deep circulation of the ocean is driven by differences in density. Since both decreasing temperature and increasing salinity make sea water more dense, most of the water that fills the deep ocean originates around Antarctica, or in the far north Atlantic, with smaller contributions from the saline waters of the Mediterranean and the Red Sea. So water sinking around Antarctica, much of it in the Weddell Sea, spreads northward and eastward along the bottom into the Atlantic, Indian and Pacific Oceans. Water sinking in the Norwegian Sea spreads south, joins the Antarctic water near Antarctica, and is carried into the Indian and Pacific Oceans. This deep water collects nutrients from the organic debris sinking from the surface waters. It thus becomes nutrient-rich and fertilizes the surface waters, where it returns to the surface. Although water sinks close to the Antarctic continent, deep water upwells further north, accounting for the high biological productivity of this Ocean.

How the Past Hydrosphere Is Studied

Some of the planktonic organisms (both plants and animals) have shells. When these shell-bearing organisms die, their shells sink to the ocean floor and are incorporated in the slowly accumulating muds there. Since these organisms, when alive, are delicately adapted to the temperature and chemistry of the waters in which they live, certain species can be used as monitors of specific conditions. If the surface water conditions change, then different species will become dominant and a new set of shells will rain to the sea floor. Thus the sediments contain a record of changes in the overlying water. By studying these fossil remains, geologists can reconstruct past patterns of ocean circulation.

By selecting samples of the same age from a global set of deep-sea cores, the sea-surface temperatures can be estimated as well as the surface circulation patterns for that time.

Selected Institutions of Great Importance In Hydrospheric Work

Lamont-Doherty Geological Observatory of Columbia University
Palisades, New York 10964, U.S.A.

Scripps Institute of Oceanography
University of California-San Diego, P.O. Box 109, La Jolla, California 92037, U.S.A.

Woods Hole Oceanographic Institution
Woods Hole, Massachusetts 02543, U.S.A.

Musee Oceanographique
Monaco (Ville), Monaco

National Institute of Oceanography
Wormley, Godalming, Surrey, U.K.

Arctic and Antarctic Research Institute
34, Fontanka, Leningrad D-104, U.S.S.R

Institute of Oceanology
USSR Academy of Sciences, 1, Sadovaya, Ljublino, Moscow J-387, U.S.S.R.

There are over a hundred other fine centers of ocean studies, especially the various national fisheries, and national or state university centers, so non-inclusion in this list is by no means invidious in any degree. The centers listed, however, are all leaders in the study of the total hydrosphere.

Reference

Oceanography for Meterorologists, H.U.Sverdrup, George Allen and Unwin Ltd., London, 1952.
Marine Geology, James Kennett, Prentice-Hall, Inc., Englewood Cliffs, NJ. 1982.

Following is a selection of further references recommended by Dr. Peter Warshall, prominent water systems consultant, for the interested student of the hydrosphere.

General

Sensitive Chaos, Theodor Schwenk, Schocken Books, N.Y. 1965.
Water, Lune Leopold and Kenneth Davis, 196 pp. Life Science Library, Time Life Books, Chicago, 1970.
Water, A Primer, Luna Leopold, W.H. Freeman and Co., San Franciso, 1974.
The Water Encyclopedia, David Todd, Water Information Center, Water Research Bldg., Manhassett Isle, Port Washington, N.Y. 1970.
The Exploration of the Colorado River, edited by John Wesley Powell, Univ. of Chicago Press, 1957. The best book ever written in lay terms about the nature of large river flows.
Biogeochemistry of a Forested Ecosystem, Gene Lekens, et.al., Springer-Verlag, N.Y. 1977. Shows how water is a carrier of chemicals throughout the biosphere.
The Ecology of Running Waters, H.Hynes, Univ. of Toronto Press, 1977.

Water and Humans

Water in Environmental Planning, Thomas Dunne and Luna Leopold, 118 pp., W.H. Freeman and Co., San Francisco, 1978.
Water, Earth, and Man, edited by Richard Chorley, Methuen and Co., London , 1969.

The earth never tires,
The earth is rude, silent, incomprehensible at first,
    Nature is rude and incomprehensible at first,
Be not discouraged, keep on, there are beautiful things well envelop'd,
I swear to you there are divine things more beautiful
        than words can tell.
                                        WALT WHITMAN

Geosphere

William J. Breed

Beneath the Biosphere, the Geosphere shifts
continents, builds mountains, separates the world
ocean into seas, offers up the atoms and
molecules needed to begin and expand life's
moveable feast. THE EDITOR

From space the earth looks serene; a place where nothing much happens. You can see the clouds whirling around and perhaps a difference in color as the seasons change and the snow on the continents advances and retreats. All in all it appears as an unchanging earth -- an earth that is permanent at least as far as the continents and oceans are concerned. This was the concept that the ancients and the early geologists held as well. Even as late as forty years ago geology was taught from a framework that was aware only that mountains were uplifted and that seas sometimes invaded the lands: but in the minds of the German, Alfred Wegner, and a few southern hemisphere geologists did the concept evolve that continents are not always permanent; that they can scurry about like so many pieces of jigsaw puzzle on a table; and that this movement could create mountains and account for the strange distribution of animals throughout the world. They initiated the ideas which eventually would develop into the theory of continental drift which evolved into the theory called plate tectonics -- a concept that would put to rest for eternity the idea that mountains were formed by the contractions of a shrinking earth; and that the strange distribution of animals was evidence for "land bridges" between the continents.

I have often thought that it is too bad that there was not a video camera focused on the earth for the past billion years or so to record the continents careening around the earth and at times crashing into one another. It would also be great to be able to see back into geologic time and watch the various animals and plants moving about the earth and evolving into different forms.

THE GRAND CANYON OF THE COLORADO RIVER, Grand Canyon National Park, Arizona, c. 1942. Photograph by Ansel Adams. Courtesy the Trustees of the Ansel Adams Publishing Rights Trust. All Rights Reserved.

Fortunately at least part of this picture has been recorded in the earth. Exposures of rocks give evidence for a sequence of events of each area. These have been tied with other areas so that eventually the history of the earth has been revealed. Fossils in these rocks give a picture of the animal and plant life during geologic time. So bit by bit with evidence from many different places, we now have at least an outline of the whole story.

Perhaps it is best that we don't know the whole story; for that would leave nothing for future generations to discover. In the words of Seneca, a famous Roman philosopher who lived in the first century, "The world is a poor affair if it does not contain matter for investigation for the whole world in every age. Nature does not reveal all her secrets at once. We imagine we are initiated in her mysteries; we are as yet, but hanging around her outer courts." It is obvious that we do not have the whole picture of the earth throughout time; but we do have at least the outline. This outline has been discovered by many different scientists working in many different parts of the world. In the following pages are listed 24 key areas that are significant in that studies there have revealed different geologic concepts that help us to understand the setting of the Biosphere.

Great Britain: Early Contributions to the Science of Geology

Perhaps modern geology can be traced back to the time in 1795 when James Hutton read his paper on "Theory of the Earth" before the Royal Society of Edinburgh. Early workers in the field of geology in Germany were handicapped by their belief that all the rocks of the earth were precipitated from a universal ocean in a limited amount of time. Hutton, by contrast, accepted the role of volcanism in creating the planet; he would never attempt to precipitate granite or basalt out of an ocean. This step from the "Catastrophism" of the past to the "Uniformitarionism" of Hutton's is expressed in his words, "We find no vestige of a beginning -- no prospect of an end." and summarized in his doctrine "The present is the key to the past." Both of these ideas were taken up by another early English geologist, Charles Lyell who promoted them in his classic book of the time, *Principles of Geology*. Both geologists envisioned a planet in which the processes of weathering and erosion, the wearing down of the land to sea level and the uplifting of that land again above the sea, had been going on since the beginning of time and *at the same rate*.

We now know that even Hutton's concept of the earth has its drawbacks. The main fallacy is that rates of evolution and extinction of species, as well as the movement of the plates and rates of erosion have varied in the past. Nevertheless, Hutton's ideas were more than adequate foundation for the science of geology.

Geologic maps and geologic time also started in Great Britain. William Smith, working as a surveyor on canals in central England, observed that certain strata had the same assemblage of fossils and could be observed throughout much of England with the same distinctive units both above and below. From this he was able to construct a table of these stratigraphic units and eventually a geologic map showing where these different units outcropped. In addition, other geologists working in England were eventually able to give names for the periods of time that these rock units represented, so that a complete scale of geologic time was eventually worked out. It is evident that much of this work was done in England for many of the time periods are named for places or people in Great Britain -- the Cambrian Period was named for the Latin name for Wales; the Devonian Period from the county of Devon; and Ondovician and Silurian from primitive tribes that lived in Great Britain.

Grand Canyon Region: A Textbook of Geologic History

Nowhere else on the face of the earth is geologic history exposed on such a tremendous and complete scale as at the Grand Canyon and neighboring areas to the north and east. Here perhaps half of the history of the earth is revealed in over 20,000 feet of sedimentary and volcanic layers -- layers for the most part undisturbed and exposed over a widespread area so that geologists can study horizontal as well as vertical changes in the various rock layers. In addition, basement rocks of metamorphized sediments and volcanics give evidence for the early history of the area -- 1700 million years ago.

The other unique feature of the Grand Canyon region is that here all of these sediments representing so

much of earth history have been uplifted over two miles without extensive folding or faulting. Thus rocks are essentially undeformed and their integrity is maintained.

The history of this area can be briefly summarized:

ERA ONE (Older Precambrian) -- 1700 million years ago and earlier. Shists, granites and other metamorphic rock represent over 25,000 feet of sediments and volcanics deposited in area. Subsequent uplift produced mountains perhaps 15,000 feet high, which were later reduced by erosion to an almost featureless plain. The core of this mountain range can be seen in the Canyon today in the oldest rocks -- the Zoroaster Granite and the Vishnu Schist. Metamorphism has erased all traces of life from these rocks.

ERA TWO (Younger Precambrian) -- Around 1200 to 600 million years ago. Over 12,000 feet of limestones, shales, siltstones and lava were laid down on the level surface on top of the Vishnu Schist. These rocks were uplifted, tilted and faulted to form another mountainous area. Erosion subsequently leveled these mountains, but resistant rocks stuck up perhaps 600 to 800 feet above the plain. Fossil algae (stromatolites) have been found in these rocks.

ERA THREE (Paleozoic Era) -- On the Precambrian surface, sediments formed in shallow seas, deltas, river channels and deserts were deposited in horizontal layers. These multicolored layers form the bulk of what is known as Grand Canyon today. During this period from 570 to 250 million years ago, an abundance of animals and plants lived in the various environments and their fossils have been found in the different layers.

ERA FOUR (Mesozoic Era) -- This era lasted from 250 to 60 million years ago. During this time, additional layers of multicolored sediments, many representing a desert environment, were deposited. Numerous tracks and bones of dinosaurs and other primitive reptiles and mammals have been found in these beds which are exposed today in Zion and Bryce Canyons to the north; and the Navajo and Hopi Indian Reservations to the east of Grand Canyon.

ERA FIVE (Cenozoic Era) -- 60 million years ago to present. Uplift of the area over 10,000 feet due to a continental plate overriding the East Pacific Rise. Some additional layers added, mainly lake sediments and lavas. Subsequent erosion by the Colorado River and tributaries produced the present landscape. Numerous mammal, bird and fish fossils found in layers of this age.

Thirty years ago the red rocks of the Grand Canyon area were studied by a group from the University of Newcastle in England because the iron in these rocks indicated the polar position while the rocks were being deposited. This resulted in a path of polar wandering from the Precambrian to the present. Similar studies in England and Europe produced a similar path; except the older the rocks, the more divergent the polar paths. This could only be explained by a drift of North America and Europe away from each other. These studies revitalized the theory of continental drift, which eventually became known as the plate tectonics theory.

Dinosaur National Monument, Utah: Dinosaurs by the Ton

Perhaps no aspect of geology has captured the popular imagination as much as dinosaurs. These huge lumbering creatures seem to be everyone's idea of what a fossil animal should be.

No where else in the world have more dinosaur bones been found than at a spot near the Green River now called Dinosaur National Monument. This quarry was developed by Carnegie Museum in Pittsburgh and produced perhaps a greater mass of bones than any in history. There was a complete fauna of gigantic Jurassic swamp-dwelling saurians excavated here including such dinosaur stars as *Brontosaurus* (more properly *Apatosaurus*), *Diplodocus*, *Stegosaurus*, (the dinosaur with the plates on his back), and the carnivorous monster *Allosaurus* who was the ancestor of the most famous meat-eating dinosaur of all time *Tyrannosaurus Rex*. The dinosaurs found in this quarry have often appeared in dioramas, for unlike isolated finds in other areas, this find was a complete assemblage of animals that were living together (or at least died together!). The Morrison Formation is famous as a dinosaur-collecting layer, but this spot was a prime collecting locality.

Most famous localities for collecting fossils are not really very fascinating to visit. It's like going to your friend's house when he is out of town. There is nothing there. However, Dinosaur National Monument is different; here we have dinosaurs on display *in situ*, just as they have been partly excavated from the shales. Here perhaps more than anywhere else on earth you get a feeling for the immensity and variety of these creatures that once roamed the earth.

For 170 million years, dinosaurs were the undisputed rulers of the earth, but now they are gone and speculations over why have been going on almost since their first discovery. We date our time on earth in the thousands of years; the dinosaurs in millions. We consider the dinosaurs failures because they died out; yet I wonder if we will be around 170 million years from now to decide

Using tools as small as ice picks, fossil preparators expose huge leg and shoulder bones of APATOSAURUS (BRONTOSAURUS) in the Dinosaur National Monument Quarry. Photo courtesy of the U.S. Department of the Interior, National Park Service.

whether our sojourn on this planet was a success or a failure.

Italy: An Explanation for the End of the Dinosaurs

Recently, halfway around the world from Utah, a new discovery might give us an explanation for the demise of the dinosaurs. In Gubbio, Italy, along the backbone of the Appenine Mountains, there is a clay layer sandwiched between two marine limestone layers; all deposited on the floor of the Tethys Sea. The lower limestone was deposited while the dinosaurs were still present on the earth; the upper limestone was deposited after they became extinct. The clay layer was formed about 63 million years ago at the close of the Cretaceous Period and represents the approximate time period when the dinosaurs were becoming extinct.

A group of scientists from the University of

California in Berkeley have found in this clay abnormally high concentrations of iridium -- an element that is uncommon on the earth's crust, but often found in meteorites. Their idea is that a giant meteorite struck the earth. The cloud from this meteorite interfered with photosynthesis by blocking out the sun; and this caused the death of great quantities of vegetation. This in turn caused a collapse of the food chain all the way up to the herbivorous and carnivorous dinosaurs at the top. Smaller animals whose food requirements were not so great were able to survive -- particularly mammals who were warm blooded and could stand the temperature change.

Twenty five years ago this explanation would have been ridiculed, but today there seems to be some evidence for it as a high concentration of iridium has been found above the Cretaceous boundary in many parts of the world. This theory may be in error though. Volcanism also produces iridium and a study of the clays at Gubbio has shown them to be of volcanic origin. Also, there is the problem of the location of the crater from this impact. Perhaps the explanation for the extinction of the dinosaurs is still in question.

Alps: An Erratic Mountain Range

Since the Fifteenth Century, scientists working in Switzerland have realized that the beds of the Alps represent deposits from a sea since they contained marine fossils. Later workers recognized the complex folding of the mountain; some of the folds had even thrust older rocks on top of younger rocks. All these features gave the idea of an erratic mountain range -- a range that had been pushed in from elsewhere. With this background, geologists in Switzerland, still did not appreciate the validity of Wegner's theory of continental drift. One notable exception was Angand who accepted these ideas as early as 1915.

When continental drift was accepted as a valid theory in the 1960's, an explanation for the Alps became clear. As Africa moved north, it pushed up the floor of an ocean (called the Tethys Sea by geologists) and these sediments were pushed into folds on top of the European Continent, creating not only the Alps, but many of the other mountain ranges of southern Europe. Mt. Blanc and the Matterhorn were created like all the other large mountains of the world by the processes of continental drift. From this it also seems evident that the Mediterranean will also eventually be pushed into the lap of Europe.

The roots of another theory that now seems all too evident can be traced back to the Alps. Simple peasants in Switzerland had long accepted the idea that huge boulders far out in the valleys had been brought down by glaciers during a time when glaciers were larger and more active.

Learned scientists attributed them to ice rafting during the Great Flood! After it was pointed out that these "erratics" were of a rock type found near the origin of the glaciers at the head of the valley, the concept of wide-spread glaciation began to be recognized. Following the lead of some of his colleagues, Louis Aggasiz became convinced of the validity of an Ice Age when glaciers were much more extensive and in fact covered much of northern Europe. The evidence was there -- erratic rocks, striations on rocks, deposits of unsorted material from the terminus of the glacier, but change in accepted theories comes slowly. With Aggasiz as the spokesperson, however, this theory was eventually established throughout Europe and America.

Iceland: A Portion of the Sea Floor on Land

There was great excitement among the geological community in 1963 when two British geologists, Frederick Vine and Drummond Matthews came up with a new theory called sea floor spreading to account for the positive and reversed magnetism recorded by a geophysical survey on the floor of the Atlantic Ocean. It had been known that the polarity of the earth switched back and forth throughout geologic time. Vine and Matthews assumed that new basalt being formed on the sea floor recorded the earth's magnetism at the time of deposition alternately positive (towards the North Pole) and reversed (towards the South Pole) and that if the sea floor was spreading from a center along the Mid-Atlantic Ridge; the reversals of the earth's poles would be recorded in both directions from the ridge more-or-less like a tape recorder.

A section similar to the sea floor of the North Atlantic is exposed in Iceland; for here, too, the land is being stretched apart and new lava is upwelling in the center. The central portion of Iceland contains the most active volcanism; whereas lavas to the east and west are older and their magnetism is oriented in many places reverse to the present polar direction.

Iceland is on the boundary of the European Plate which is moving towards the east and the American Plate which is moving towards the west. This movement has been measured by geologists at the rate of one-half inch per year. In the thousand years since Iceland was settled by the Vikings -- forty feet has been added to the center of the country. This rapid rate of movement makes Iceland a good place to observe active volcanism. Surtsey, a new volcanic island, was created off the southern coast of Iceland in 1963; on the island of Heimaey, a dormant volcano suddenly became active in 1973 and destroyed part of the town of Vestmannaeyjar -- one of Iceland's main fishing ports.

In addition to active volcanoes, Iceland also contains numerous glaciers and a small icecap; due mainly to its far north location. Interaction between this ice and the volcanism has in the past produced destructive floods and peculiar flat-topped landforms. Similar landforms found on Mars may have been formed by the same process.

Red Sea, East Africa Rift and The Afar Triangle: A Sea is Born and a Continent is Splitting Apart

Looking at a map, or looking down from space, it is difficult not to believe that in some places the continents are moving away from each other. If you could move Arabia towards Africa; the Red Sea and the Gulf of Aden could be completely closed and the land mass that is Arabia and the continent of Africa would fit together like two pieces of a torn-up letter.

One problem, however, in fitting Arabia and Africa together by closing the Red Sea and the Gulf of Aden is the Afar Triangle. This triangular shaped piece of land is bordered on the west and the south by escarpments. If it were not for the presence of this land, the southwest corner of Arabia would fit against these escarpments. This anomaly was investigated by a group of scientists and it was quickly discovered that the Afar Triangle was a piece of the sea floor with faults, lava flows and flat-topped volcanoes -- all of which had evidence that they were formed under the sea. It is also an area of active volcanism with perhaps a hot spot underneath it. All of this would account for the Afar Triangle's presence in a place where there should have been ocean.

Indeed there is evidence from the bottom of the Red Sea that it is an embryonic ocean; that new lavas are being formed on the floor of this sea and the floor is spreading. The Red Sea probably resembles the Atlantic Ocean 150 million years ago when North America was splitting off from Europe. A trench throughout the length of the Red Sea contains pools of hot brine. These pools are mainly salt, but also rich in minerals such as iron, manganese, lead and others. In the Pacific, economic deposits of nickel, colbalt, and copper have been discovered in manganese nodules on the sea floor. These brines and nodules of the sea floor give us a clue as to how minerals eventually get deposited on land. All of the sea floor is eventually subducted under continents; and any mineral on the sea floor will be brought near the surface by superheated mineral-laden waters. In the future this whole of subduction might be bypassed and minerals could be mined directly on the sea floor or on the continental shelf.

Before the Red Sea came into existence it probably resembled the Great Rift Valley of Africa. This valley joins the Afar Triangle at its southern end; then extends 2500 miles to the south almost to Mozambique. Early explorers realized that this valley was not like other valleys. It was not formed by the erosion of a stream; for it contained lakes, no through-flowing drainage and was bordered on both sides by long linear escarpments. Numerous tensional faults indicated that the valley was being pulled apart.

This part of East Africa bordered by the Rift Valley is moving to the northeast in the same direction as the continent of Africa. However, it is moving somewhat faster. A magma layer present under the Rift Valley is spreading these two parts of Africa apart so eventually part of Africa will be an island and the Rift Valley will be an embryonic sea like the Red Sea. Eventually this island will crash into India to form a whole new range of mountains.

Along the flanks of the Rift Valley today can be found the largest mountains in Africa -- Mt. Kilimanjaro and Mt. Kenya -- both volcanoes fed by the magma that underlies the valley. The Great Rift Valley also perhaps nurtured early man; for many of the remains of early man, including footprints, have been found along the length of the Rift Valley.

India and the Himalayas: The Clash of Giants

Only since the theory of plate tectonics has become widely accepted is it possible to explain mountain ranges -- even the Himalayas which contain Mt. Everest, the highest mountain on any continent, which soars over five and one-half miles in elevation (29,028'). Now it has been shown from the evidence from ancient magnetism that India was once connected with Antarctica; but was separated from that continent 100 million years ago and began a slow steady drift northward to eventually collide with the Asian Plate.

When an oceanic plate hits a continental plate; the heavier oceanic plate is forced downwards (subducts); the continental plate overrides the oceanic plate, but becomes crumpled for its forward motion is stopped. A good example of this is the collision of the South American and the Nazca Plates to produce the Andes. However, when two continental plates meet, both are lighter than the underlying mantle. So they both get crumpled much like two cars colliding on a freeway -- and mountains are the result. This collision was initiated about 40 million years ago and continues today with the uplift still proceeding at a faster pace than the erosion. Ultimately, however, this collision will stop; erosion will level the area to a less spectacular elevation; and the roots of the Himalayas will mark where India and Asia became welded together. The region will then look like other areas in the world that mark the collision between two continents -- the Urals and the Appalachians are good examples.

This migration of India is recorded in the fossil magnetism of its lava flows. The magnetism shows that 100 million years ago, India parted company with Antarctica. Fifty million years ago, Indian was astride the equator and then about 40 million years ago it ran into Asia. No other movements of a continent are so clearly marked -- or have such a spectacular climax.

This awesome event in the history of the earth was first recognized by Wegner in his early work. He also recognized that the compression from this collision also formed a series of folded mountains north of the Himalayas.

Chile: A Land of Contrasts

Chile is a land of contrasts. This is in part to be expected in a country that is 2,650 miles in length, but averaging only 110 miles wide. If Chile were in the northern hemisphere hear Europe it would stretch from the western tip of Africa to Scotland. Chile has great contrasts in topography ranging from deserts in the north to rugged mountains in the south; and abrupt changes east to west from sea level to the towering peaks of the Andes. Chile has great contrasts, too, in geology from glaciers and fjords in the south to volcanoes in the central part and sand dunes and other desert landforms to the north.

One of the driest deserts on the face of the earth in northern Chile is produced by the combination of a cold current and upwelling cold water along the coast. Winds moving from a chilly ocean where they can pick up no moisture on to a hot land where they can do nothing but evaporate moisture has created a desert. This desert, called the Atacama, averages 4/100 inches of rain per year, and of course many areas go without rain for years. Because of this extreme dryness, most of the land forms are created by wind rather than water. Hills of soft sediment are shaped into streamlined hills called yardangs, and most of the landscape is made up of dunes, barren hills and desert pavement (rocks left when everything else has been blown away). Although barren, this desert does produce some copper; and evaporates like nitrates.

In addition this extreme dryness along the coast has created another situation which is extremely beneficial to man. The islands off the coast of Peru and Chile contain numerous sea birds feeding off the richness of the sea. The guano that they deposit on these islands accumulates due to the aridity and is rich in nitrates and phosphates -- necessary ingredients of explosives and fertilizer. A pair of cormorants can excrete $2.00 to $3.00 worth of guano per year! Phosphates are also accumulating on the sea floor -- where eventually they can be mined if there is a shortage on land.

This variety of features in Chile was observed by Darwin when he visited the country in 1835, but he saw something else. On a trek of several weeks into the Andes Mountains inland from Valparaiso, Darwin observed fossil sea shells at 12,000 feet and fossil petrified trees at a lower elevation around 7,000 feet. All of this puzzled Darwin, for to explain it, you would have to have a forest that was buried, depressed about a mile so the sea could cover it and then the whole area would have to be uplifted some two miles to form the mountain ranges present in Chile today. His contemporaries would explain this as a result of the great flood, but Darwin thought otherwise. Earlier in 1835, Darwin had been in Concepcion after it had been hit by a terrible earthquake. Much of the town was in shambles, but Darwin also noticed that the land around the harbor had been raised several feet. He did not know the cause of the earthquake, but he did realize that inch by inch, foot by foot, any area could be raised to the level of a towering mountain. All that was needed was sufficient time.

Today we know the cause. Mountain building, earthquakes, volcanoes and even fjords and glaciers as well as the formation of copper all are related to plate tectonics. Chile is at the margin of the South American Plate where it is crashing into the Nazca Plate -- one of the several oceanic plates that underlies the Pacific Ocean. The oceanic plate is forced under the continental plate in a process called subduction. This causes the continental plate to crumple and be uplifted into the Andes. At the same time some of the molten material from the oceanic plate rises in the continental plate in the form of magma and eventually finds its way to the surface forming the numerous volcanoes present here in Chile and elsewhere around the Ring of Fire that surrounds the Pacific. This ascending magma may also contain minerals -- many of the world's copper deposits are associated with present or old subduction zones. Lastly, if it were not for the mountain building associated with the collision of these two plates, the glaciers and fjords of southern Chile would not be present.

When Darwin was in Chile, he realized that much more time was needed to fashion the earth than many of his contemporaries would allow. This gave him the basis eventually to formulate his theory of evolution.

Hawaii: Islands Formed on a Conveyor Belt

North and west of Hawaii a chain of islands, flat-topped submerged islands (called seamounts) and undersea ridges can be traced for 4000 miles. This feature is consistent except that beyond Midway Island it takes an abrupt turn to the northward and becomes known as the

Emperor Seamounts. The American geologist James D. Dana observed as early as 1838 that the Hawaiian Islands get progressively older west from the main island of Hawaii. Dana based this observation on the amount of erosion of the islands. This data has been confirmed by radiometric dating; the northern-most seamount in the Emperor chain is 70 million years old, Midway Island is around 18 million years old.

Tuzo Wilson of Toronto University was the first to give this a logical explanation. He believed that a hot spot exists under Kilauea Crater on the island of Hawaii. This hot spot has produced a chain of islands as the Pacific Plate moved over it in a northwesterly direction (for the past 20 million years) and in a northerly direction (from 20 million to 70 million years ago). This hot spot, thus, has recorded a change in the direction of the Pacific Plate about 20 million years ago.

Hawaii, the main island of the chain, was formed by five coalescing volcanoes. Its classical shield-like form, minimal amount of erosion on the coast, and presence of the world's most active volcano, Kilauea, on its slopes, attest to its youthfulness, and the fact that the hot spot still lies beneath this island. Oahu, about 150 miles to the northwest had active volcanism 3.5 million years ago; its beaches and tremendous eroded cliffs attest to this fact. Midway, formed between 15 and 20 million years ago, is the farthest west of the chain. Since its volcanic core has eroded completely beneath the sea, it is still an island only because of the presence of coral reefs.

Other strings of islands in the South Pacific have a similar trend in direction and age. All of this evidence seems to indicate that the Pacific Plate is moving northwestward at the rate of 5 inches per year. Eventually Hawaii will move away from the hot spot -- and a new island will be formed.

Other possible hot spots throughout the world include Iceland and Yellowstone National Park. The former is of great interest because it lies under a continental rather than an oceanic plate.

Yellowstone: Where the Rocks are Hot

Early explorers referred to the Yellowstone area as the "place where hell bubbles over." The Indians thought that the region was inhabited by spirits. Few who go there are not captivated by the boiling multi-colored springs and pools and the numerous geysers such as Old Faithful which regularly shoots hot water and steam 130 feet into the air for two to five minutes; then is quiescent for over an hour.

Yellowstone is an anomaly for most thermal areas are at the edges of plates. This area, like the Hawaiian Islands, is the result of a hot spot in the mantle of the earth; but in this case the lava erupts onto a moving continental plate. Previous eruptions of this hot spot are present in the Snake River Plain to the south and west where 400 miles of lava erupted over the last 15 million years.

Most of the lava found in the Yellowstone region was erupted slightly over one-half million years ago. The caldera, or collapsed crater, formed during this eruption is known as the Yellowstone Basin and this is the scene for most of the hydrothermal (hot water) activity of today. The high elevation of Yellowstone increases the precipitation in the area, which brings more water into contact with hot rock. Without this large amount of water in the vicinity the display would not be so unique -- and spectacular.

A bulge of about two feet has appeared in the central part of the Yellowstone area that might foretell another eruption. In any event with the slow movement of the North American Plate, the whole thermal area will eventually move into Montana -- if that state exists in the half million or so years that it will take for this to be accomplished.

Mt. Whitney and Death Valley: The Highpoint and the Lowpoint of the American West

Mt. Whitney and Death Valley are neighbors -- only separated by about 100 miles and two mountain ranges. The difference in elevation though is considerable. Mt. Whitney spires some 14,494 feet above sea level, the highest point in the United States outside of Alaska. The lowest point of Death Valley is 292 feet below sea level. This tremendous difference in elevation deserves some geological explanation.

Death Valley is part of a series of north-trending basins and mountain ranges that makes up most of Nevada and surrounding states. This area, known as the Basin and Range Province, was described by the early American geologist Clarence E. Dutton as "an army of caterpillars crawling northward out of Mexico." Mt. Whitney borders on this province; and it, along with the whole Sierra Range, provides the rainshadow effect that makes Death Valley and the rest of the Province a desert.

The peculiar topographic character here has to be due to a large extent to the East Pacific Rise, a sea-floor spreading zone. On a map of the ocean's floor it can be traced paralleling the coasts of South and Central America and Mexico. When the Rise reaches the Gulf of Lower California it disappears under North America, only to reappear abruptly off the coast of Oregon. North America in its relentless movement west must have overridden this rise. After an initial doming and outpouring of lava the West Coast moved west of the Rise; stretched the Basin and Range Province, causing a collapse of the area into a series of north-trending fault block mountains. These mountains rapidly filled their intervening basins with sediment to produce the topography that we know today.

The East Pacific Rise probably still exists under these mountains. Will it eventually start chewing into the Colorado Plateau to the east and disrupt the undisturbed layers there? Other speculation centers on the west coast; will movement on the San Andreas fault eventually separate California from the other states and send it scooting off towards Alaska? The Geospeculator may come up with ideas, but only time will tell if they are right.

Alaska: A Jig Saw Puzzle Put Together

Alaska contains the answer to a few puzzles! How did many of the Ice Age mammals get distributed throughout Europe, Asia and North America? How did man, who probably originated in Africa, get to the New World? The answer is, of course, that during the Ice Ages, much of the water of the earth was tied up in glaciers; sea level was lower and there were land connections between North America and Asia through what is now the Bering Straits; as well an an ice-free migration route to a more equitable climate further south.

The geology of some parts of southern Alaska is also easily explained. The extremities of the Pacific Plate are being pulled under (subducted) at their contact with the North American Plate. This has created the volcanoes of the Aleutian chain -- and southern Alaska. This movement along the margins of two plates is also responsible for earthquakes -- such as the large quake that in 1964 destroyed parts of Anchorage and Valdez and set tsunamis

MT. McKINLEY. Photograph by William Breed.

(tidal waves) throughout the North Pacific. This type of activity -- volcanics and earthquakes -- is common in a belt surrounding the Pacific Ocean, the area known as the "Ring of Fire".

There is, however, another aspect of Alaska that has been a puzzle for geologists. Rocks in numerous areas throughout the state seem to have little relationship to adjacent areas. For instance, you could have pillow lavas formed on a sea floor adjacent to coal deposits formed in a continental tropical swamp environment. Other areas were discovered by paleomagnetic methods to have originated near the equator. Work by Warren Hamilton, a U.S. Geological Survey geologist, had shown that many parts of Idaho and California did not originate there, but were brought in as islands conveyor-like on a spreading sea floor in a small scale fashion, but similar in other respects to India. This provided an explanation for the small diverse areas in Alaska and researchers followed Hamilton's lead. It was soon discovered that most of Alaska was composed of pieces from elsewhere. So Alaska is composed of some 50 different pieces or terranes that were rafted in from elsewhere. In another similar fashion to India, these terranes bumped into one another to form North America's highest mountain -- Mt. McKinley (20,320').

Alaska was originally settled by people seeking gold. This gold originated in crystalline rocks in the mountains, but most of Alaska gold was found in placer deposits. (Heavy minerals such as gold accumulate in stream deposits due to the sorting action of running water.) Obviously much of Alaska's gold was washed out to sea. Eventually as minerals get scarcer these undersea deposits may have to be mined. Similar heavy mineral deposits, such as tin and titanium, are present off the coasts of India and Sri Lanka.

Eastern Canada and Greenland: With or Without Ice

For most of the history of the science of Geology, there have been assumptions about continents; namely that they are the most premanent parts of the earth. Now it is known that continents are nothing more than islands of lighter material floating in the denser rocks of the mantle -- more or less like ice on a lake.

The shield areas are the oldest and were long thought to be the most stable elements of any continent. In addition it was thought that they were formed by differentiation of lighter and heavier materials during the original cooling of the planet from a molten state. Now, however, there is a different view.

With the advent of radiometric dating it is now possible to date the various granitic and metamorphic rocks that make up the hard crystalline shield areas of each continent. It was soon discovered that these shield areas were an agglomeration of different aged parts. In Canada, for instance, the oldest part of the Canadian Shield is 2500 million years old, but it is surrounded by fragments that are as young as 1000 million years old. In adjacent Greenland, an area that split off from Canada about 33 million years ago, are found the oldest rocks on earth -- 3750 million years old. These are very old rocks considering that the whole planet is approximately 4600 million years old.

There are thus two apparent facts about these shield areas: (1) they are composed of an agglomeration of smaller shield areas that vary in age; and (2) these smaller areas collided in the early history of the planet, forming mountain ranges which were then eroded down to an area of low relief. It is thus evident that the shield areas, rather than being the most permanent features on earth, are records of an early stage of plate tectonics.

Canada has another story to tell. During the Ice Ages it was covered with a huge continental glacier -- bigger even than the ice cap that covers Greenland today. This continental icecap covered most of Canada and even spilled over into northern United States. The Great Lakes were eroded by the action of this glacier and were not present before.

These continental glaciers in Canada brought one great benefit to the United States. Tremendous amounts of soil were carried by the outwash from the glacier into the United States. In addition winds blowing off the glacier picked up dried particles of rock and distributed them throughout the Mississippi Basin where vegetation was growing in sufficient quantities to trap this wind-blown rock material. This wind-blown dust called loess was deposited in layers up to 250 feet thick and is the foundation for the rich soils of the U.S. Most of these soils in what is now the most productive agricultural part of the U.S. had their origin in Canada.

This great weight of the continental glacier had one other effect in Canada. We all know that the more passengers we put in a boat the farther the boat sinks in water. In a similar fashion the glacier depressed the crust in Canada so that in some parts, particularly around the center of the glacier at Hudson's Bay, the surface is 2000 feet below its former level. Since the glaciers retreat the surface of the land is rising at a rate of two feet per 100 years. At this rate it will take about 5,000 years for the land to regain its former level. When this happens Hudson Bay will be dry! This property of the crust to rebound after heavy weights have been removed is called isostasy.

Other areas with similar features: Northern Europe.

Antarctica: And Its Exotic Connections

To fly over Antarctica is to experience what the northern parts of North America and Europe looked like during the Ice Ages 10,000 to 2 million years ago. If it were not for Antarctica (and Greenland) glaciers and ice caps of such magnitude would be unimaginable to geologists and the general public as well.

To better visualize the ice cap that covers Antarctica, we need some statistics: Antarctica contains 90% of the ice of the world and 95% of the continent is covered by ice -- in some places to a depth of 2-1/2 miles (ski Antarctica -- 6 inches of powder, 10,000 feet of base!) If all of this ice in Antarctica would melt, sea levels would rise 250 feet, causing the destruction of most of the larger cities of the world.

On the 5% of Antarctica not ice-covered, there have been several important discoveries that have a bearing on continental drift. In 1969, a team of geologists of which I was a member discovered fossil remains of *Lystrosaurus* in 100 million year old (Triassic Age) rock at Coalsack Bluff near the Beairdmore Glacier -- 500 miles from the South Pole. These mammal-like reptiles had previously been discovered in South Africa, India and China. This reptile could not live in a climate where six months out of the year there is no sun. It also could not swim the thousand miles or so of ocean that separates Antarctica from the other land-connected continents where *Lystrosaurus* had previously been discovered. From this the implications for continental drift are obvious.

ANTARCTICA -- Along the Beairdmore Glacer. Photograph by William Breed.

In 1982 fossil remains of a marsupial were found on Seymour Island in the Antarctic Peninsula. This discovery again confirmed the connection of Antarctica with the other southern continents. Indeed, Antarctica was the "land bridge" that enabled marsupials to migrate from Australia to South America, much in the same way they migrated from South America to North America when the connection through Panama was established.

These land connections and the implication that Antarctica once had a more temperate climate were also indicated from discoveries made by Robert F. Scott's expedition to the South Pole. They collected coal samples and fossil plants that were also found in the other southern hemisphere continents and India.

Another important discovery from Antarctica is meteorites. Numerous meteorites land on the 5.5 million square miles of ice that comprise Antarctica. As the ice moves most of these are lost in the ocean. However, in certain areas such as Alan's Nunatak, the termintus of the glacier is ablating; and the meteorites accumulate in one spot. Some of these meteorites found there seem to have originated on the Moon; others on Mars. Perhaps meteorites striking these bodies have thrown off debris that ultimately lands on Antarctica.

Sahara: Sand and Ice

The Sahara is a classic desert, and it is the world's largest. Roughly 3000 by 1000 miles, it is a land of heat, and constant wind. Only 20% of its surface is sand -- the rest is pebbles, rocks and salt flats, but it does contain most of the landforms formed normally in deserts. It is an arid and inhospitable place with fewer than 2,000,000 inhabitants.

It is hard to believe, but the Sahara is caused by the African Tropics. The intense heat along the equator causes a lot of evaporation in the ocean and contributes to a large amount of rainfall in the African tropics. As this heated and moist air rises, it cools and produces rain; but at the same time it draws in air from surrounding zones in the vicinity of the Tropic of Cancer and Capricorn. To replace the rising air in the tropics, the air in these zones descends; and as it sinks its temperature increases and the air becomes drier. It thus sucks up all the moisture in the zones surrounding the tropics.

Strangely enough the Sahara has not always been a desert. During the Ice Ages, climates throughout the world were changed and this acted as a moderating effect on the Sahara. Up to about 2000 years ago, there was rain and grasslands and herds of typical African animals. All of this is portrayed in rock paintings in the Tassili Plateau -- now in the center of the desert.

The Sahara is also a strange place for an ice cap, but 500 million years ago one existed here. A team of

Dune sand diverging around bedrock outcrops in the Sahara Desert near the border of Egypt with Libya and Sudan. Image is 180 km across at bottom. Landsat image produced by U.S. Geological Survey.

geologists, following the lead of some French oil geologists, found striations on the top surface of Ondovician rocks (500 million years old). The only possible explanation for this is for an ice cap of continental proportions to have covered the Sahara at that time. Independent evidence from paleomagnetism has indicated that at that time the South Pole was over the northern part of Africa. At this time all of the southern continents and India were united in one super continent (called Gondwanaland). And, Antarctica was on the equator -- so in 500 million years these two continents have reversed positions.

Egypt: And a Dry Mediterranean

When the Russians were constructing the Aswan Dam on the Nile River in Egypt they drilled numerous bore holes to determine the depth to bedrock. They were surprised to discover that the Nile was actually a huge canyon filled with sediment to depths of at least 1000 feet -- they did not drill deeper. In the bottom of these drill holes fossils of marine organisms were found. No explanation of this was offered, but it was apparent that an arm of the Mediterranean was once present as a salt water estuary in this chasm of the Nile River.

Sometime later the Glomar Challenger -- U.S.

Nile Valley with Aswan Dam and Lake Nasser (lower left corner).
City of Idfu at bend in river (left center). Image is 180 km
across. Landsat image produced by U.S. Geological Survey.

Research Vessel capable of drilling holes and collecting cores from the sea floor -- was taking samples from the floor of the Mediterranean Sea and discovered a thousand feet or so of salt in their cores. This could mean only one thing -- that the Mediterranean was once landlocked and all of the water in the sea had evaporated to leave these deposits. This was an astounding discovery, but these samples plus the information from the bottom of the buried canyon under the Nile River could only be explained by having most of the water in the Sea evaporate. This would lower base level enough to permit the Nile River to cut a Canyon at least a thousand feet below sea level.

Since the Straits of Gilbraltar are the only connection between the Mediterranean and the Atlantic Ocean it is apparent that at one time the movement of Africa towards Europe, or a change in sea level, had created an isthmus where these straits now exist. This happened about 15 million years ago. The sea then dried up until about 5.5 million years ago when this land connection was breached. One can imagine the waterfall and the rush of water pouring into the dry Mediterranean basin when this water connection was established again. It is estimated that about 5% of the world's saltwater thundered through these straits and formed a waterfall that lasted 100 years. When this occurred, sea level around the world dropped 40 feet!

The idea of the Mediterranean drying up had been suggested previously by an oil geologist, Frank Barr, who discovered a buried channel of a river in Libya, but his ideas were considered outrageous and were not accepted by the geologists of the time. It is interesting to note how often the outrageous theories of yesterday become today's dogma. Look how long it took for Wegner's ideas about continental drift to become accepted. And there are arguments about evolution going on even today.

Additional buried channels have recently been discovered in Egypt in the Western Desert. They were discovered this time, not by drilling, but by shuttle image radar. These channels which are buried underneath a sand sheet are not apparent on the ground, or from aerial photographs. The radar apparently is able to look right through a dry sand sheet to reveal the underlying topography -- in this case a complete drainage system. This technique might have applications in the search for underground water in barren desert regions.

Kentucky and Yugoslavia: The Underground World

Caves are a world in themselves. Found in many diverse areas, their total number will forever be unknown and even the known caves have not been completely explored. Caves were once the home of prehistoric man; and even before that the residence of prehistoric animals -- bears, sloths, condors among others.

The origin of caves varies: some are formed in volcanic areas by the draining of conduits through which lava formerly flowed. Others are created in sandstone and related rock types by the sapping action of springs. However, the overwhelming majority of caves are created by the action of water on limestone. Limestone can be slowly dissolved by water -- particularly if it has been made slightly acidic due to plants, or other causes. Water can produce caverns of infinite length through solution in limestone.

The first comprehensive study of caves and the landscape created by water flowing in a limestone region was conducted in the Karst area of Yugoslavia by a geographer, Jovan Cvijic, in 1893. He studied the sinkholes, pits and cracks and disappearing rivers that made up the surface of the land as well as the systems of caves underneath. The type of landscape produced by water in a limestone area is known as Karst topography. These regions are known throughout the world -- in the Alps and Pyrenees, in Kentucky, Tennessee and Missouri in the United States; also in the Kwangsi Province in China to name only a few.

There are many caves in the world, all of them have some similarities, but each is different. Most caves develop at or near the level of the ground water table. The caves at this level are either filled with water or contain actively flowing streams. As the water table sinks through erosion, caves that were once active become stable. Then the slow drip of ground water through the cave deposits an icing of limestone in the form of stalagtites and stalagmites to create the decorated caves that most tourists visit.

One of the longest caves in the world, although not the most beautiful, is Mammoth Cave, Kentucky. In 1982 the total passages explored in that cave along with adjoining systems came to a record 230 miles. (For information: write to the Superintendent, Mammoth Caves National Park, Mammoth Caves, Kentucky, U.S.A., 42259.)

Santorini and Vesuvius: Two Violent Volcanic Eruptions

In the Mediterranean area two violent volcanic eruptions have occurred in historic time. The eruption of Mt. Vesuvius in A.D. 79 destroyed the town of Pompeii; the eruption of Santorini on the island of Thera in about 1450 B.C. wiped out an island and perhaps a whole civilization.

Perhaps no volcano ever has exploded with the force of Santorini. It may have been the most destructive natural event of all time, for 15 cubic miles of debris was thrown into the atmosphere. The center of the volcano collapsed into a large caldera which can be seen today in the island of Thera and a choking cloud of ash covered most of the eastern Mediterranean basin. The noise of the eruption could be heard halfway around the world. Shortly after this eruption, the Minoan civilization centered on Crete south of Thera declined. In addition to the ash Crete must have been hit with a tremendous tidal wave and its most important city, Knossos, is on the northern seacoast of Crete facing Thera. The Legend of Atlantis, the civilization that perished when a continent sank below the waves, may have had its roots in the destruction of Thera. Sailors from Thera traded with the Egyptians, and Plato got the information about Atlantis from Egypt.

The eruption of Vesuvius in A.D. 79 is famous, mainly for the destruction of the nearby town of Pompeii. The people of Pompeii were probably unaware of the destructive nature of the mountain that formed the backdrop for their city, but in A.D. 63 numerous earthquakes rocked the area for some time and destroyed many buildings. These were quickly rebuilt, only to be totally destroyed in A.D. 79, along with the neighboring town of Herculaneum. Most of the 16,000 people who lost their lives that day suffocated from the huge quantities of ash and pumice thrown from the volcano. Herculaneum was drowned in a sea of mud.

The volcanism that caused the eruption of Vesuvius and Santorini came from the same source; all caused by the colliding plates of Africa and Europe. Who knows what influence on the course of Western Civilization these two events had. Survivors from the destruction in Crete and Thera landed in Greece and may have been the impetus that caused the flowering of Greece about that time.

Meteor Crater, Arizona, U.S.A.: The Impact of Space Debris

Twenty five thousand years ago, a meteorite hit Arizona forming an impact crater 4000 feet across and 600 feet deep. At first when this crater was discovered, it was thought to be just another feature similar to the volcanic craters near Flagstaff, 35 miles to the west. Some thought the feature could also be a sinkhole caused by underground solution of the limestone which forms the surface of the surrounding land. However, the upturned sides of the crater negate the latter explanation and the presence of meteoritic iron, shattered sandstone and blocks of limestone on top of the overlying shale give overwhelming evidence that a meteorite once hit the earth here.

Since Meteor Crater was recognized as an impact feature, numerous other craters with a similar origin have been recognized throughout the world -- 110 at last

METEORITE CRATER -- Flagstaff, Arizona. Photograph by Peter Bloomer.

count. However, Meteor Crater is the most prominent and best preserved of the lot; and gives geologists an unparalled opportunity to study the cratering process. In the early history of the earth, space must have been littered with debris -- much of this material struck earth, but most of the evidence has been obliterated by time unlike our neighboring members of the solar system -- the Moon, Mars and Mercury.

It has been estimated by comparing Meteor Crater with similar impacts produced by atomic explosions, that the meteor that formed the crater was approximately 112 feet in diameter, had a mass of 12,000 tons, and was traveling about 21,000 miles per hour. Smaller masses traveling at a greater speed could have also produced the crater.

There is still much debris floating in space. If a similar object struck the earth today in the middle of the Atlantic Ocean, for example, coastal cities such as London and New York would be devastated by giant tidal waves. This is unlikely, but there is always that possibility. Perhaps we will be lucky and if a large meteorite hits the earth again it will be in a remote desert -- or Antarctica.

The Persian Gulf: Oil Needs Time and Great Geological Events

Iran, Iraq, Kuwait and Saudi Arabia are the main countries that border the Persian Gulf. These countries are poor in many respects, mainly fresh water and vegetation; however, they have an abundance of sand, sun and oil!

Why is all this oil found in the areas surrounding the Persian Gulf? As you might expect the answer has something to do with plate tectonics. However, let us look briefly at how oil is formed and where it usually accumulates.

Oil is almost always found in marine sedimentary rocks and is formed from the decomposition of organic matter. Burial of this organic matter is necessary, for only under some heat and pressure can oil be formed. However, once it is formed it tends to migrate towards the surface since it is lighter than water. In some cases the oil moves up to the surface and it is lost. In other instances, though, it enters a reservoir rock, a rock with a high porosity (spaces within the rock through which liquids can flow). If this oil is then trapped in the reservoir rock by some impermeable layer that keeps the oil from flowing to the surface, the oil will be stored until it is drilled -- or lost by some other process.

This Persian Gulf oil and the reservoir rocks were formed under the ancient Tethys Sea. This is being caught up and squeezed in the Arabian Plate as it is moving to the northeast where it is being crinkled by the Eurasian Plate. This crunching of the plate results in a lot of folding and faulting which produces ideal traps to retain oil. It is apparent that a whole series of geological events was necessary in order to produce the oil of the Persian Gulf. Also a lot of time was needed. Oil was first produced in this area commercially in the 1930's, and now the area still has over 50% of the reserves of the world. However, at the present rate of use it is conceivable that within the next century the last oil well will be drilled in the Persian Gulf region.

Great Barrier Reef, Australia: A Masterpiece Made by Corals

In the early 1800's, Darwin solved one of the problems that had been bothering geologists for years. Coral atolls had been discovered that seemed to be composed of nothing but coral -- yet they were growing in the middle of the ocean in water too deep for coral which needs sunlight to grow. Darwin observed volcanic islands that were newly formed; volcanic islands with a fringing reef of coral; coral islands with just a small central mass of volcanics; and coral atolls with no visible volcanic rock present. He, of course, realized from these observations that the coral grew as volcanic islands sunk or were eroded. At the time these ideas were astounding; today the illustrations are in every geologic textbook.

Now we realize that the rise of sea level as the glaciers melted after the Ice Ages contributed to the growth of coral. In addition the concept of Sea-Floor Spreading explains how volcanic islands can move into deeper water and thus slowly sink; for it has been shown that the shallowest part of the ocean is the area adjacent to where new sea floor is being made; as the floor spreads farther and farther from its point of origin; the volcanic rock compacts and the seas get deeper.

Darwin never saw the Great Barrier Reef which is the Coliseum of reef builders. This gigantic animal-made structure stretches for 1260 miles along the northeast coast of Australia and covers 100,000 square miles. This structure, composed mainly of the skeletons of corals cemented by algae, is the largest animal-made structure on our planet. Even our largest cities become the size of ant hills in comparison; and the reef even dwarfs some similar topographic features such as mountain ranges.

On the other side of the Australian continent what may be the world's oldest fossils have been found. In rocks dated at 3500 million years old, fossil algae layers called stromatolites are present in a layer of rock that for its age is essentially undisturbed. Strangely enough, nearby at Shark's Bay are living the present day descendents of these stromatolites. This type of algae is rather rare today as it lives in a relatively restricted type of environment.

New Zealand: Living Fossils

New Zealand is a group of two major and some smaller coastal islands. A unique fauna is always found on islands, and New Zealand is no exception. Before the coming of man there were only two mammals dwelling on land in New Zealand (both bats); The bird population was dominated by huge moas, members of a group of flightless birds called ratites, and smaller flightless birds as well like the Kiwi. The amphibians and reptiles consisted of primitive frogs and a reptile, *Sphenodon,* who is the sole survivor of a diverse reptilian order that with this one exception died out with the dinosaurs. The other components of the fauna and flora of New Zealand have similar ancient lineage.

New Zealand was once attached to the southern supercontinent -- Gondwanaland. We know this because the presence of a fossil plant, *Glossopteris,* ties the island in with the other Gondwanaland continents. Paleomagnetic and sedimentation evidence also shows that New Zealand was attached to the east coast of Australia and West Antarctica. The date for this connection is about 80 million years ago. At this time many of the plants and animals living in New Zealand today must have migrated into the islands. Flightless birds, related to the moas, are found today on most of the southern continents. These are birds that **cannot** fly or swim any great distances so their distribution must be linked to the time 80 million years ago when Gondwanaland existed.

Since New Zealand became isolated, some birds have flown in and become residents; numerous plants, particularly those whose seeds are distributed by wind have also become New Zealand natives. Essentially, though, New Zealand still has a Jurassic aspect to its flora and fauna, and even with the introduction of many new exotics by man, it is still a piece of geologic time floating in the sea.

Like Chile, New Zealand has a great variety of geological features packed in a small area. The South Island has fjords, glaciers and a long mountain chain, the Southern Alps. The North Island has geysers, as well as active and inactive volcanoes. This volcanism is caused by the Pacific Plate subducting under the North Island. The earthquakes from this have been plotted here and in the much more extensive subduction zone to the north, the Tonga-Kermadec Trench. The farther west these earthquakes are recorded the deeper they are up to a total depth of about 435 miles. This zone which is at an angle of about 60 degrees, is characteristic of all subducting zones and is known as the Benioff Zone. The oceanic plate in this area is being devoured at about the rate of 3'' per year.

Panama: The Link That Was Once Missing

In geology classes thirty years ago, before the general acceptance of the theory of continental drift, any strange distribution of animals would be accounted for by postulating a land bridge to connect the continents and thus explain the anomaly. No evidence for these land bridges was ever found when the ocean's floor became better known. The present distribution of animals is more easily explained by the movement of continents according to the plate tectonics theory.

However, there is a bona fide land bridge that connects the continents of South and North America. For a small piece of land, the isthmus of Panama has caused numerous changes in the animal life of the continents it connects and its importance far exceeds its size.

For most of the last 60 million years, the faunas of North and South America have been completely different. South America contained marsupials that had a common ancestry with the marsupials of Australia. Their initial distribution was probably through Antarctica when these three continents were connected and Antarctica was farther north. Primitive mammals also present in South America probably also reached the continent accidently, or by a previous connection with North America 60 million years ago. North America contained advanced mammals which were more in the mainstream of evolution due to its connection at times with Asia and Europe via the Bering Straits. At the same time, tropical parts of the Atlantic and Pacific Oceans were connected and there was a free interchange of marine organisms between these two areas.

Then about 4 million years ago the sea floor spreading away from the East Pacific Rise began to push against Central America. As the floor was subducted, a narrow landmass was pushed up which eventually connected the two continents. This bridge permitted an interchange of animals between the two continents. Some marsupials such as the opossum and primitive mammals such as the porcupine were able to move into North America; but the primary migration was in the other direction with numerous mammals moving into South America and eventually causing the extinction of the less advanced forms found there.

Before the linking of the continents, 29 families of mammals inhabited South America and 27 entirely different families inhabited North America. After the continents were joined they had 22 families in common -- most of which originated in the north. The presence of the isthmus also isolated the marine faunas in the Pacific and the Atlantic and caused them to evolve separately and in different directions.

This connection between North and South America also had another effect. For the past 4 million years the warm water that used to flow into the Pacific now flowed into the Gulf of Mexico. This added strength to the Gulf Stream so more warm, moist water and air has been brought into the North Atlantic to create warmer and moister conditions in Europe.

In a similar fashion, but on a larger scale, the drift of continents worldwide has created high mountains and has placed the North and South Poles in their present land-locked positions. This in turn has created an extreme climatic zonation that would not be present if the continents were much lower and both the poles were in the middle of oceans. The movements of the continents changed the worldwide climates from more equitable to more extreme and set the stage for other smaller fluctuations to create the Ice Ages 2 million years ago.

CONTINENTAL SHIFTS

Early Triassic -- 220 million years ago.

Early Cenezoic (Paleocene).

Mesozonic and Cenozoic.

(From left to right)

Paleocontinental Map, Cambridge University Press, 1977.

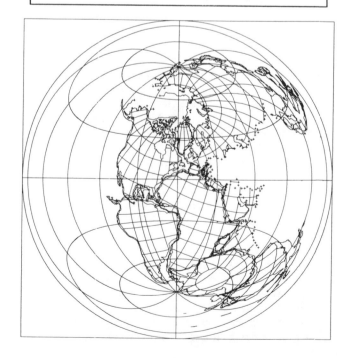

Suggested Reading

The Restless Earth: A Report on the New Geology, by Nigel Calder, Viking Press, New York, 1972 (152 pages). An early popular account of the interpretation of the major features of the earth according to the new geology -- the theory of plate tectonics.

Wandering Lands and Animals, by Edwin H. Colbert, E.P. Dutton, 1973 (323 pages). A book which primarily shows how the distribution of vertebrate animal -- mammals, reptiles and amphibians -- can be correlated in the geologic past with the movement of continents according to the theory of plate tectonics.

Our Wandering Continents: An Hypothesis of Continental Drifting, by Alex L. DuToit, Hafner Publishing Co., 1973 (366 pages). An account by one of the early advocates of continental drift.

Understanding the Earth: A Reader in the Earth Sciences, T.G. Gass, Peter J. Smith and R.C.L. Wilson (Editors), M.I.T. Press, 1971 (355 pages). A compilation of articles by various authors, includes most of the important subjects in geology, particularly those relating to plate tectonics.

The Earth Through Time, by Harold L. Levin, W.B. Sanders Co., 1978 (530 pages). A geological textbook with emphasis on earth history.

Rediscovery of the Earth, Lloyd Motz (Editor), Van Nostrand Reinhold, 1982 (272 pages). This book is a collection of 18 separate articles "regarded as most significant in their documentation of the new view of the planet as it has emerged in the last few years."

Continents Adrift and Continents Aground, Scientific American, W.H. Freeman, 1976 (230 pages). Tuzo Wilson, compiler. A collection of articles on continental drift reprinted from Scientific American.

Continents in Motion; the New Earth Debate, by Walter Sullivan, McGraw-Hill, 1974 (397 pages). A popular well-written account of Plate Tectonics.

New Zealand Adrift, by Graeme Stevens, A.H. and A.W. Reed, 1980 (442 pages). An excellent account of the accumulating evidence that has led to the acceptance of the continental drift theory and its relationship to the geology of New Zealand.

Geology Illustrated, by John S. Shelton, W.H. Freeman & Co., 1966 (434 pages). An easy-to-read and excellently illustrated textbook of geologic principles.

The Origin of Continents and Oceans, by Alfred Wegner, Trans. by John Biram, Dover Publications, 1966. The original written account of Wegner's ideas regarding continental drift.

Conversation with the Earth, by Hans Cloos, Alfred A. Knopf, 1967 (413 pages). An early popular account of geology emphasizing different

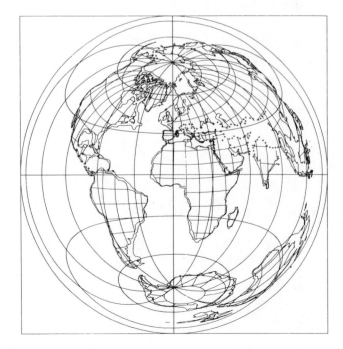

regions. Written before the general acceptance of continental drift.

The Earth We Live On: The Story of Geological Discovery, by Ruth Moore, Alfred A. Knopf, 1956 (413 pages). An excellent popular account of the history of the science of geology before the acceptance of continental drift emphasizing the scientists and their contributions.

Encyclopedia of Geomorphology, Rhodes Fairbridge (Editor), Reinhold Book Corp., 1968 (1296 pages). A convenient book for definitions and explanations of various geologic landforms and processes.

Adventures in Earth History, Preston Cloud (Editor), W.H. Freeman & Co., 1970 (992 pages). This book gives a broad selection of provocative readings from original sources. Everything is included from processes, principles and origins to earth history.

Earth (2nd Edition), by Frank Press and Raymond Siever, W.H. Freeman and Co., 1978 (649 pages). A good general textbook on geology emphasizing processes and plate tectonics.

Putnams' Geology (4th Edition), by Edwin E. Larson and Peter Birkeland, Oxford Univ. Press, 1982 (789 pages). An excellent standard textbook on geology.

Continents in Collision, Russell Miller and the Editors of Time-Life Books, Time-Life Books, 1983 (176 pages). An up-to-date presentation of the plate tectonics theory. Part of the Planet Earth series.

Ice Ages, Solving the Mystery, by John Imbrie and Katherine P. Imbrie, Enslow Publishers, 1979 (224 pages). A synopsis of the various theories that have been used to explain glaciation and the Ice Ages.

Exploring our Living Planet, by Robert D. Ballard, National Geog. Soc., 1983 (366 pages). Some of the most spectacular aspects of plate tectonics are explored in this lavishly illustrated volume.

An Encyclopedia of Geology: Planet Earth, by A. Hallam, Elsevier, Phaidon, 1977 (319 pages). A useful and well-illustrated book.

The Cambridge Encyclopedia of Earth Sciences, by David G. Smith, Crown Publishers Inc/ Cambridge Univ. Press, 1982 (494 pages). A standard comprehensive reference to all aspects of geology.

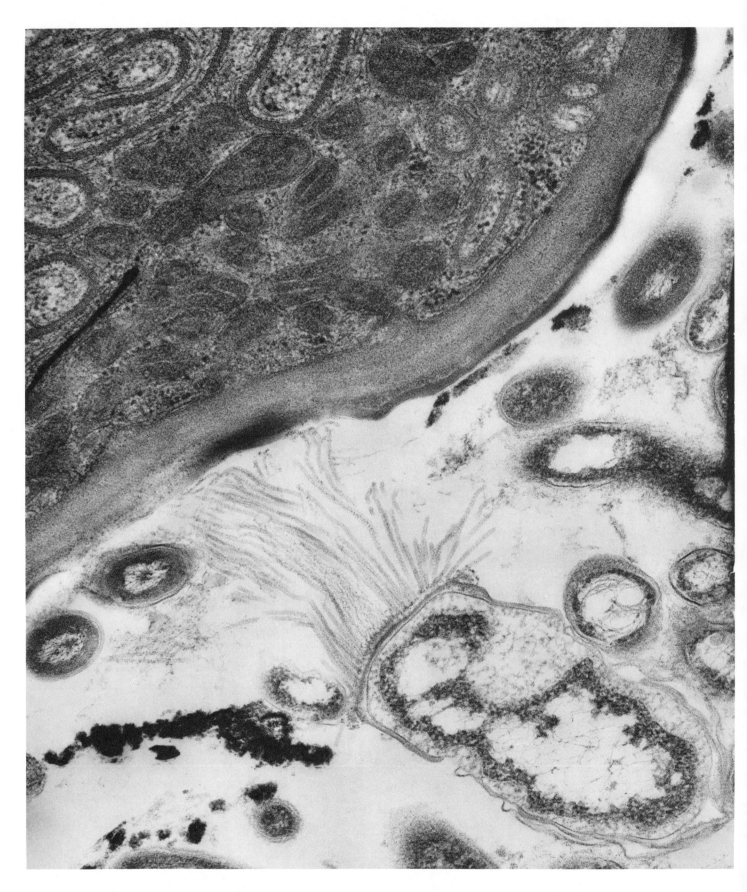

Termite hindgut and its microbial community. Photograph by David Chase.

Microbes

Clair Folsome

The world which was ere I was born,
The world which lasts when I am dead,
Which never was the friend of one,
Nor promised love it could not give,
But lit for all its generous sun,
And lived itself and made us live.
MATTHEW ARNOLD

Anthony van Leeowenhoek discovered microbes in the 1600's and came to the conclusion that these minute life forms were all-pervading. From water-soaked pepper to scrapings from teeth to soil, microorganisms abound. Bacteria have since been found living within rocks in the antarctic, on desert sands, in hot springs, in the air we breathe, and even high in the stratosphere. Microbes have controlled our destinies through plagues upon us, our animals and plants. Foods we enjoy as wine, cheese, yogurt, miso, soy sauce and kefir are a part of our culture's biological heritage. This heritage we will, willingly or not, take with us to space colonies.

The mission of this overview is to show how we will continue to be dependent upon microorganisms when we break the bounds of the earth's biosphere and establish space colonies. We will consider microbial types which can be of benefit to our venture beyond the earth, as well as those kinds which will inadvertently create problems. Then we will extrapolate and suggest potential problems and future benefits our microbial associates might cause. One thing will become clear, and this is that our association with microorganisms will continue into the indefinite future and to the farthest reaches of space.

Microorganisms are so small that fairly sophisticated tools such as microscopes, centrifuges and a well established field of biochemistry were required before we could effectively study them. This is why their existence was not known until the mid-1600's. Less obvious is the way in which early workers, of necessity, had to devise methods to study cells weighing only a millionth of a gram.

The approach to study minute objects with crude tools was to gather great masses of similar cells and to analyze chemically the composition or behavior of the whole mass. Then one inferred the properties of the mass were those of the single cell. In such a manner the concept of a "pure culture" arose. This concept requires that microorganisms be isolated by various techniques until a single cell is obtained from which a line of descent (the pure culture) can be obtained. Once armed with a pure culture, it can be grown in mass, characterized chemically, and classified.

This still is the method microbiologists use to study and classify microbial strains. It works -- for we as yet have few other methods! Yet it does not give the picture of the whole. The ecology of microbial strains as found in their wide-spread environments has only recently become possible to study using more refined tools. This newer work reveals levels of complexity and sophistication which had been undreamed of, and threatens the very nature of the more classical microbial taxonomic methods. It also provides us with a gestalt view of earth's biology.

There are as many different kinds of microorganisms as there are microorganisms. By this, I mean that the metabolic capabilities and the tools we have to measure these attributes can now be extended to set off a single cell from its predecessors. Yet it is possible to defocus this view and to sort microorganisms into a small number of types; all based upon their chemistry. This kind of sorting is based upon a 'divide and conquer' strategy and uses metabolic tests, DNA homologies, size and shape (and whatever else is available) to distinguish major groups of microorganisms. It is by taxonomic convention and convenience that microorganisms are classified in a binomial fashion (i.e., species, genus). Many microorganisms and bacteria mate and exchange genes only in special ways not obligatory to the life cycle. Thus the rigorous concept of "species" (those which can breed with one another) does not apply. The sorting by common characteristics does provide a way of viewing the diversity and molecular virtuosity of these minute life forms.

Of immediate interest to us are the following groups:
protists (algae, fungi and protozoa)
bacteria

First the cellularly complex (eucaryotic) group, as fungi, green algae and protozoa, are separated from the bacterial, structurally less simple (procaryotic) class. These categories separate those which have relatively large and complex cell types from those with relatively little observable structure at the electron microscopic level.

Now, each of the above types can be further separated as:
photosynthetic
heterotrophic

This major division concerns the energy source for biochemical happenings. Photosynthetic organisms use high grade radiant energy (the sun) for energy and effect the conversion of oxidized carbon (carbon dioxide) to organic carbon. These are primary producers; molecular herbivores. Heterotrophic organisms reverse this scheme and obtain energy by dissembling organic carbon molecules. These can be thought of as molecular carnivores. Both are required to maintain the flux of the carbon pool in the world. Indeed, one could argue that the sun-driven cycling of the bioelements from organic to inorganic forms and back again is the major reason why biology exists! But that's another story.

Both types of classificatory chemistries are further distinguished by the way oxygen is used or avoided. Thus

we have those which can and those which cannot use oxygen:
aerobes (using oxygen)
anaerobes (not using oxygen)

Both the photosynthetic and heterotrophic groups are further divided by this characteristic. Hence we have aerobic and anaerobic photosynthetic types, as well as aerobic and anaerobic heterotrophic types.

That's it! The whole of the major taxonomy of microorganisms is contained in these six categories. Of course, when looked at in more detail we uncover layer after layer of complexity of interaction and of degree. Also, we should be aware that we view our microbial world through a window of our own construction: one based upon the availability of our instruments and our notions of biology as related to those sensations we can directly experience with unaided senses. Recall the fable of the blind men who describe an elephant.

To provide some feel for the variety of bacterial groups alone, consider that over 1,576 recognized species of bacteria which are grouped into some 250 genera are currently defined and identified and accepted by bacteriologists. In addition there are hundreds of types which are of "uncertain" identity. Also, over 200 different cyanophytes (blue-green photosynthetic bacteria) are now recognized. In another reality, that of ecology, realize that thousands of ecological niches abound which house microbial types we have yet to imagine, and to catagorize in the laboratory.

Taking the simplistic observations that microorganisms are everywhere, that they can take advantage of life situations of the most diverse kinds, and that they can meet almost any environmental challenge, we can ask -- why? -- how does this impinge on our Biosphere/Space Colony project?

To understand why requires that we reappraise our conventional view of time and the notion that we (Homo sapiens) occupy an unique position in this grand Universe. Civilization has existed on our Earth for only one millionth of the planet's existence. If the entire history of the Earth as a planet were to be compressed into one year, civilization would have existed for only the last half minute.

Let's think again about time in terms of the biological history of humans and microbes. Homo sapiens evolved from recognizable ancestors some 3 million years ago. Biology appeared, as microbes on this planet, over 3000 million years ago. In short, microbes have an enormous evolutionary lead over us, by a factor of at least 1000 fold. When you also consider that the generation time (cell division time) for a microbe might be about 1 to 10 hours, and that our own generation time is 20 years, then we have to acknowledge that the microbes further lead us by an additional factor of 175,000 fold. This gives

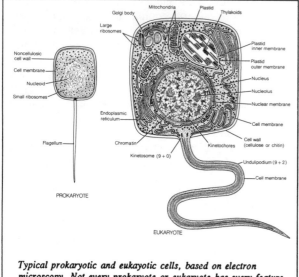

Typical prokaryotic and eukayotic cells, based on electron microscopy. Not every prokaryote or eukaryote has every feature shown here. "9+0" and "9+2" refer to the cross sections of kinetosomes and undulipodia. From Five Kingdoms: An Illustrated Guide to the Phyla of Life on Earth, by Lynn Margulis, W.H. Freeman & Co., 1982.

the microbes a temporal lead over us of some 175,000,000.

This means that microbes have had some 175 million more evolutionary experiments than we to evolve into that wonderous assemblage we now view. Is it any wonder that such creatures, although small, are biochemical and metabolic wizards?

It is due to our cultural heritage that we tend emotionally to view microorganisms as yucky, slimy, smelly, disease-causing, revolting messes. We can do this even while enjoying cheese and wine, bearing our DPT inoculation scars, and using a network of microbe-supported water purification sewage systems for our more basic needs.

More directly to the issue is the role of the microbe in permanently staffed space colonies: Biospheres. Microbes will be a primary requirement for the successful construction of any biosphere. Indeed, it will be impossible to exclude microbes!

To construct a biosphere in orbit or constrained upon the earth imagine a large container which is impenetrable to all matter exchange with the outside world. Now, look at what's to be done to place a complete functioning ecology within that space. (For this thought experiment we shall assume that light energy and heat sinks are available as required.) Certainly we shall want to introduce earth, as shielding and as substrate for plants. Also we will need sources of water, an atmosphere, and an array of plants and animals; not to mention us humans. Such an assemblage of 'hardware' (earth, water and physical substrates) and 'software' (biological entities) will have to be a balanced one. There will be limits imposed upon the quantities and qualities of the software by the hardware. For example, don't expect a model closed jungle of 100 x 100 meters to support even one tiger! The practical aspects of this project dictate that we create initial populations of plants and animals as balanced as present day knowledge permits. So many plants will be needed to support the gaseous and food requirements of so many herbivores which in turn will support so many carnivores, etc., etc.

But this exercise, as presented above assumes we can list those organisms we want, and exclude those we do not want. As the problem is examined in greater depth we will see that we can list with some degree of reality large organisms as animals and plants which we might desire. But each of these biosphere candidates carries along with it its indigenous microbial populations of a complexity as yet undefined, and necessary for its and for our survival. Also, a biosphere, as the earth, is to be a regenerative system. Hence some manner of recycling wastes, dead organisms, etc. will be required. Finally, microorganisms as the blue-green bacteria and green algae will be required to maintain oxygen concentrations and to consume carbon dioxide.

In short, microorganisms will dominate the biosphere, as they do our current one, whether we plan it or not! To get a feeling (unpleasant as it may be) for this reality of biology, suppose that every cell and tissue of which you are composed were suddenly not to exist. What would remain would be a ghostly image, the skin outlined by a shimmer of bacteria, fungi, round worms, pin worms and various other microbial inhabitants. The gut would appear as a densely packed tube of anaerobic and aerobic bacteria, yeasts, and other microorganisms. Could one look in more detail, viruses of hundreds of kinds would be apparent throughout all tissues. We are far from unique. Any animal or plant would prove to be a similar seething zoo of microbes. It is possible, with great effort, to isolate plant seeds or animal embryos under sterile conditions and to rear these aberrations (termed 'gnotobiotic') under continued sterile conditions. Even then such plants or animals will remain infected with viruses descended from their parental germ lines.

By quarantine procedures of the strictest kind it might be possible to eliminate certain disease-causing bacteria and fungi. Even this approach has within it a trade-off. Were we to create a biosphere devoid of human disease causing bacteria, those inhabitants quickly (within months to years to generations) would lose resistance to these diseases. Leaving the biosphere could be an open invitation to death by common diseases of the 'open' earth. Similar arguments apply to plants and animals of the biosphere. Likewise, such a biosphere could become an uniquely sensitive target for any 'open' earth contamination.

These considerations imply that we should welcome our microbial world into the biosphere -- at the risk of failure if we do not.

If we accept this notion, that bugs are here to stay, that they have been about much longer than we, that they have evolved for immeasurably longer times than we, that they are everywhere, then the strategy for the construction of the biosphere becomes more direct (and more Gaian) in philosophy. Indeed, the question becomes: have we neglected any special ecological niches which our microorganisms might require?

In the main, most niches and microorganisms for the niches will abound in any kind of biosphere. Plants harbor thousands of bacterial, fungi, algae, and minute animals within their root balls. Animals carry upon and within themselves not only bacteria and fungi, but whole microbial worlds. Earth soil itself is teaming with an entire gamut of microorganisms, merely 'waiting' for nutritional conditions to arise to coerce them into rapid multiplication. As a trivial example, witness the ease of construction of a cess-pool. All one needs is a dark underground chamber, effluvia from toilets (rich organic matter) and plenty of water. Microbial populations rapidly arise from inocula during construction, from the soil, and from excrement to become dominant populations adept at transforming organic wastes to carbon dioxide, water, and other gases. No doubt cess-pool technology will be one which will see rapid development during early stages of biosphere experiments.

There are special environments on Earth which will not exist in a biosphere, to which are adapted many microbial types. For example, bacteria which can metabolize hydrocarbons, or those which can thrive under extremely acidic conditions, or those which deposit various metals as a result of their specific metabolic processes. These too could be useful in a scheme wherein complete recycling is the goal; yet these might not be included by chance. It would seem reasonable to include inocula from a variety of Earth sources as microbial 'banks' of metabolic potentials.

Since this is to be a catalogue of opportunities providing us with sources of information about specific topics, I list and briefly describe for you some sources below. Please consider these sources as 'leads' into the vast and as yet largely unknown world of the microbe.

Most of these items are crammed with detailed information in density sufficient to overwhelm any but the most persistent! Beware the forest/trees phenomenon and, to get the flavor and essence of the issues presented here, merely read these detailed compendia as you might peruse a novel. Keep in mind that the object is to approach a biological entity (microbes) who are millions of times more ancient (advanced?) than we, and that they offer us Delphic-like answers to our first attempts to create new Gaias.

Sources of Information

Our work at the University of Hawaii shows that the microbial world can be materially enclosed and remain alive indefinitely:

Kearns and Folsome (1981, 1982) have demonstrated persistence of materially closed microbial ecosystems for over 18 years. Measurements of oxygen partial pressures, and of carbon flux rates have been conducted. These data demonstrated that such

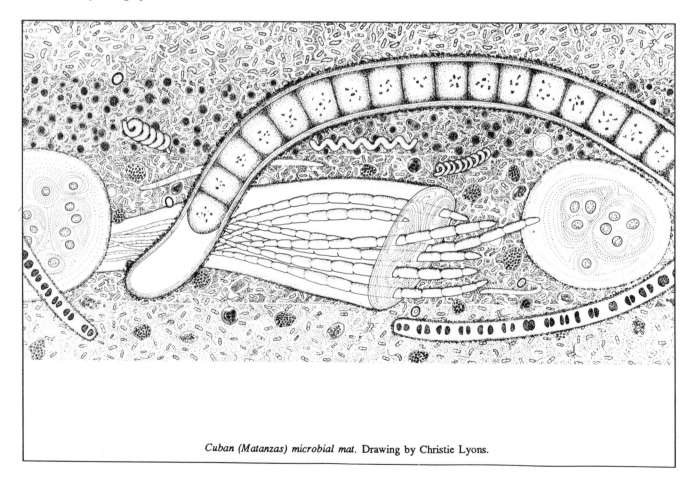

Cuban (Matanzas) microbial mat. Drawing by Christie Lyons.

assemblages persist and maintain biological activity. Also, it is shown that such systems have primary productivity and quantum efficiencies similar to terrestrial estimates: productivity is maintained over at least the 18 year period of closure.

Closely related is the work listed below using shrimp as model biosphere inhabitants. (See Analytics) Note that it is the microbial population which permits the continued existence of the shrimp.

Hanson (1982) has kept large (14mm) crustacea in synthetic brackish water with a variety of algae under absolute material closure for more than five years. His experiments reveal that closure with sustained biological activity is not necessarily restricted to microbial systems but can be extended experimentally to metazoans living with microbes. (See Analytics)

A definition for closed ecosystems has been developed by Folsome, based upon the ideas of Onsager and Morowitz. The reason for constructing such a definition is to provide succinct framework for laboratory experiment, and also to approach ecology in a more Gaian perspective.

An ecosystem can be defined as:

A persistent materially closed energetically open ecosystem is a metastable biological and inorganic assemblage in which the major bioelements (CHNOPS) traverse cycles from oxidized to reduced states. These cycles are balanced, complete, closely coupled and ultimately driven by radiant energy. Following material closure, such systems adjust bioelemental pathways (metabolic networks) to maximize the completeness and energetic efficiency of bioelemental cycling. (Refer to Morowitz, 1968 and Onsager, 1931 for background.)

Technical Papers

There is a vast amount of information on the microbe world. The literature cited below is a collection which focuses on the microbe's role in sustaining closed ecosystems

UNIVERSITY OF HAWAII:
Measurements of Biological Activity in Materially Closed Microbial Ecosystems, by E.A. Kearns and C.E. Folsome, BioSystems, 14: 205-209, 1981. The measurement of the quantum efficiency of closed microbial ecosystems is described and presented here.

Closed Microbial Ecosystems as Gas Exchange Units in CELSS by E.A. Kearns and C.E. Folsome, SAE 12th Intersociety Conf. on Environmental Systems, paper #820857, 1982. A set of calculations which shows how photosynthetic bacteria can provide oxygen for a closed ecosystem.

Energetics of Materially Closed Microbial Ecosystems, by E.A. Kearns, Ph.D. Thesis, University of Hawaii, 1983. A detailed look at the energetic efficiency of closed microbial ecosystems.

ATP as a Biomass Indicator for Materially Closed Microbial Ecosystems, by C. Takano and C.E. Folsome, BioSystems, 16:75, 1983. A technique to measure biomass in closed ecosystems. This provides an indication of the total amount of living matter which a given volume can support.

ATP Measurement of Biomass in Materially Closed Microbial Ecosystems, by C. Takano, M.S. Thesis, University of Hawaii, 1984. A detailed compendium of technologies required to measure biomass in closed microbial ecosystems.

Procaryote/Eucaryote Ratios as an Indicator of Stability in Closed Ecosystems, by D. Obenhuber and C.E. Folsome, BioSystems, 16: 291, 1984. This work shows that by measuring the numbers of major microbial groups, points of populational 'stability' are reached in about 40 days after closure. The rations obtained were compared to a variety of

Microbial marsh world. Photograph courtesy of Lynn Margulis, Department of Biology, Boston University.

natural populations -- polluted streams, open oceans, etc. -- and the closed microbial systems most closely resembled open continental waters in microbial population distribution.

Experimental Approaches to the Measurements of Persistence and Stability in Materially Closed Microbial Ecosystems, by D. Obenhuber and C.E. Folsome, submitted June 1985. A method for measuring oxygen non- intrusively which has been coupled to a data acquisition system. This permits rapid (10 millisecond) determinations of p02 and provides extremely accurate determinations of the state of the closed system.

FURTHER BACKGROUND LITERATURE:
Balanced Aquatic Microcosms -- Their Implications for Space Travel, by R.J. Beyers, Amer. Biol. Teacher, 25: 422, 1963.

The Metabolism of Twelve Aquatic Laboratory Systems, by R.J. Beyers, Ecol. Monogr. 33, 281, 306, 1963. These are open to gas exchange, but still show an approach to the beginnings of study of closed ecologies.

The Microcosm Approach to Ecosystem Biology, by R.J. Beyers, Amer. Biol. Teacher, 26, 491-498, 1964. 'Microcosms' are physically isolated ecologies. But, they are still in contact with the terrestrial atmosphere which can act as an infinite reservoir of O2, CO2, etc.

A New Paradigm for the Examination of Closed Ecosystems, Microcosms in Ecological Research, by D.B. Botkin, J.P. Giesy Jr. (Editor), CONF. 781101, 1978. A ''must read'' paper which depicts the beginnings of the awareness of the necessity of complete material closure, and how such studies might expand our knowledge of ecology.

Can There Be a Theory of Global Ecology? by D.B. Botkin, J. Theor. Biol. 96: 95-98, 1982. Short, provides other good general references -- read it for the answer to its question!

NASA Controlled Ecological Life Support System (CELSS) Program Plan (Draft), by J. Bredt, NASA Life Sciences Division, Washington DC, 1982. The CELSS program stresses largely the matter of 'controlled' ecologies. It seems as though the simpler the biological components of the system become, the more externalized and complete the control must be.

Designing a Microcosm Bioassay to Detect Ecosystem Level Effects, by M.E. Crow and F.B. Taub, *Intern. J. Environmental Studies,* 13: 141-147, 1979. Although not a materially closed system this is a way to determine what's happening to an ecosystem.

Summary Report of the Workshop on Closed Ecosystem Research, by J.A. Hanson, et al, Jet Propulsion Laboratory, 1982. Wherein it is recognized that materially closed ecosystems are to ecology as *E. coli* is to modern genetic technology.

Some Patterns in Post-Closure Ecosystem Dynamics (Failure), in Microcosms in Ecological Research, by B. Maquire Jr., J.P. Giesy Jr. (Editor), CONF. 781101, 1978 (Pages 319-332). These were not failures! The microbial population continues to thrive.

A New Paradigm for the Examination of Closed Ecosystems, by B. Maquire Jr., L.B. Slobodkin, H.J. Morowitz, B. Moore III and D.B. Botkin, (see Giesy, Jr., loc. cit.), 1978. Early awareness that study of closed ecosystems could be of value.

A Synthetic Microcosm, by S.W. Nixon, Limnol. Oceanog. 14, 142- 145, 1969. Not a materially closed system, but still of value.

In Estuarine Perspectives, by L.B. Slobodkin, D.B. Botkin, B. Maquire Jr., B. Moore III and H. Morowitz, V.S. Kennedy (Editor), pages 497- 507. How closed ecology studies can be of use to a general theory of ecology.

Closed Ecological Systems, by F.B. Taub, Ann. Rev. Ecol. Syst. 5: 139, 1974. An excellent review: although somewhat dated it deals with both truly closed systems and with microcosms. A good general source of references to 1974.

A Continuous Gnotobiotic Ecosystem, by F.B. Taub, in *The Structure and Function of Fresh-water Microbial Communities,* J. Cairns Jr. (Editor), Res. Div. Monogr. 3, Virginia Polytech. Inst. and State Univ. Blacksberg, 1969 (301 pages).

Soils

E.G. Hallsworth

Keep it, guard it, care for it, for it keeps men,
guards men, cares for men. Destroy it and man is
destroyed. JOHN STORER

The soil is a living entity, a layer of broken rock and organic matter that lies like a thin skin over most of the surface of the earth. Made up of layers or horizons that differ with depth, the description of its sequence of layers is termed the profile. The sequence of profiles found on moving from the midpoint of a valley up the slope on either side is known as a catena.

The component parts of the land surface of the world, thrust to their various heights and shapes by volcanic action and plate tectonics, are worn down to their present shapes mainly by the effects of climate. Diurnal changes of temperature cause the rocks to be fragmented and broken down to smaller pieces. The rain moistens rock particles and causes chemical breakdown and further comminution of the rock particles. Running water, raindrop splash and wind action transport the weathered particles across the earth. These transported materials, transported in previous geologic periods formed the parent material of the sedimentary rocks of today, the sandstones, clays and shales which occupy much of the present surface of the earth.

Subsequently, green plants, the synthesizer species, capable of synthesizing organic materials from water and from the carbon dioxide of the air, grow on the rock particles and add organic matter. It is on this matrix of mineral and organic matter that plant and animal life and ultimately the life of mankind depends. As a medium for plant growth the soil suffers losses in two ways, firstly by the transport of soil particles from its surface, and secondly by the loss of materials in solution in the water that drains through the soil in those areas or at those times of the year where or when the rainfall exceeds the evaporation.

These factors, the quantity, intensity and distribution of rain throughout the year, the annual march of temperature, and the slope of the land surface, form the physical framework which determines the rate of growth of the soil. Within the constraints imposed by these factors the thickness and organic matter content of the soil are determined by the extent to which the vegetation protects the soil surface from the transporting action of raindrops, running water and wind, and on the amount of organic matter the vegetation can add to the soil. This latter is determined not only by the numbers and types of synthesizer species present, but also on the numbers and types of decomposer species present, which include all species other than the green plants, and whose activities are to an increasing degree controlled by the activities of man.

The synthesizer species require, during their growing period, that the temperature lies between certain limits, during which time the quantity of growth made will depend on the available water supply and on the quantities in the soil of those elements required. These essential nutrients include those needed in larger amounts, phosphorous, potassium, calcium and nitrogen, and those needed in smaller amounts, magnesium and sulphur, or even in trace amounts, iron, copper, zinc, manganese, molybdenum, vanadium and cobalt.

These elements are present in all soils, but the quantities vary from large amounts, as for example, calcium in soils derived from limestone, to very small amounts for the trace nutrients in many soils, particularly sandy or coarse textured soils. The availability of the nutrient elements also varies, depending on which other mineral constituents are present in the soil. In acid soils, particularly those rich in the sesquioxides of iron and aluminum, the phosphate is generally less available to most crop plants, although the availability varies with the type of plant and with the presence or absence of certain strains of mycorrhizae.

The quantity of nitrogen present in the soil in a form

that is, or can become, available for plant growth, is particularly important. The most important single index of a soil's ability to produce good crops is the quantity of nitrogen that can be readily converted to nitrate by the action of bacteria. For all the nutrients, except nitrogen, the plants are dependent on the supply that can be obtained from the soil or rock particles. For nitrogen, however, there are a range of plants that can fix atmospheric nitrogen into a form available for their own use. Those plants in this class used in agricultural practice are mainly from the family Leguminosae. They are not only independent of the soil as a source of nitrogen, but their growth can leave the soil much richer in nitrogen that it was before, and so be able to support growth of other crops.

Fertility, as defined either in the Oxford English Dictionary, or in Webster, is the ability to produce. Soil fertility is, by the same token, the ability of the soil to produce plants. It has three components:

    a. Chemical fertility
    b. Physical fertility
    c. Biological fertility

Chemical fertility is the ability of the soil to supply the plants with the nutrient elements they require, at the times and in the quantities required.

Physical fertility is the ability of the soil to provide a good root-hold for the plants -- particularly important for tree crops -- and to provide air and water to the plants' roots. The ability of the soil to supply water to the plant depends, obviously, on its water holding capacity and on the frequency with which its water holding capacity will be recharged by rain -- or by irrigation. The water holding capacity of the soil varies with its structure, the manner in which the individual particles are organized into aggregates. It also depends most importantly on the thickness of the soil mantle, the depth of the soil that can be explored by the plant roots in their search for water and nutrients.

Biological fertility is the interaction of the different plant and animal species present on the growth of the plant or the crop concerned. The presence of a pathogenic fungus such as a root rot, by limiting the growth of the roots, may prevent the plant from drawing on all the available water, and so lead to an early termination of growth, even when water is present in the soil. Insects and eelworms can have similar effects.

The extent to which soil fertility can be controlled by man is considerable. He can alter the supply, using chemical fertilizers, of those nutrient elements in short supply. He can control, in part, the amount of organic matter returned to the soil by controlling the management of grazing intensity, by the return of crop residues or the use of organic manures. The biological fertility can be altered by changes in the biotic components -- by the use of crop plants resistant to plant or animal pathogens, by the introduction of strains of rhizobia that are more efficient at fixing nitrogen, or by the introduction of plant species or varieties that can make better use of the climatic conditions.

The physical fertility is the more difficult to amend. The greatest cause of deterioration is the simple loss of soil by erosion, and hence a reduction of the depth of soil, with a concomitant reduction in the water storage capacity. Maintaining a higher level of organic matter, which may be achieved by appropriate management of either the chemical or biological fertility, or both, has a marked effect on the rate at which water can enter the soil -- the infiltration capacity -- as well as on the ability of the soil aggregates to resist transport by either water or wind, and so, by resisting erosion, maintain a greater depth of soil.

The type of soil found in different parts of the Earth, consequently, depends on the nature of the parent rock; on the slope of the land surface; on the climate -- temperature range, quantity, distribution and intensity of the rainfall; and the vegetation and animals living on the land.

On land of similar slopes, the poorer the cover of vegetation the greater will be the erosion and hence the less soil that remains in place. As a consequence, steeply sloping lands in the cold alpine or arctic conditions, or in hot arid conditions, will show the same features of thin

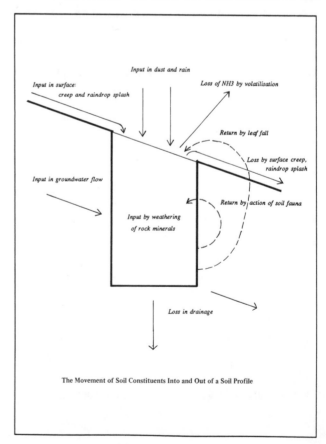

The Movement of Soil Constituents Into and Out of a Soil Profile

*Erosion in northern Andes, Venezuela. This land was
cleared of trees by the Spanish Conquerors, c. 1650, and used
for growing wheat.* Photograph by G. Hallsworth.

soils and exposed rock surfaces. Similar slopes, under gentle rains well distributed through the year, with temperatures favorable to plant growth, will normally have a much greater thickness of soil, unless the activities of man, either through excessive cultivation or overgrazing by his domestic animals, have so reduced the protective cover of vegetation or the amount of organic matter returned to the soil, that erosion is occurring, and soil is being lost more rapidly than it is being formed by weathering.

The depth of weathering and the nature of the profile are also functions both of the character of the parent rock and the climate. In general, fine textured rocks such as basalts and shales give rise to fine textured soils, whilst coarse textured rocks such as granites and sandstones give rise to coarse textured soils. Since the rocks are fractured

initially by the changes in temperature, the depth of the profile varies with the mean annual temperature and the frequency of temperature changes sufficient to cause rock fracture. The soils of the tropics in medium to high rainfalls are usually deep and sometimes 150 to 200 ft. of weathered material overlies the unbroken rock. In cold climates, the soils are invariably shallow, and on flat areas may consist largely of organic material that has accumulated because either the temperature is too low or the ground too waterlogged to allow the organic matter to decompose as fast as it is produced. Under climates in between these extremes, the profile varies according to the particular combination of slope, parent material, climate and land use that is found. Since the surface horizons of the profile are subject to more frequent temperature changes, the quantity of stones and boulders present in the profile increases with

Sand dunes advancing in wheat country in the Mallee of South Australia. Photograph by G. Hallsworth.

Terracing in China near Wugong, Shanti. These were cut by men and women with shovels and handwork. Note the column of soil left to support the telegraph poles. At the deepest cut 2 meters of soil were removed. Photograph by G. Hallsworth.

depth until the unfractured rock is reached.

In sloping country the lower parts of the catena receive water which flows down the slope. When the flow is over the surface it may carry particles of rock or soil material with it. Both surface flow and water which drains through the soil will carry substances that have been dissolved from the land higher up the slope. Depending on the balance between rainfall and evaporation, the compounds dissolved by the water from the higher parts of the catena may either be washed right out of the catena where or when rainfall exceeds evaporation, or they may be deposited in the lower parts of the catena, or in the lower horizons of the profiles of the lower parts, when the evaporation exceeds rainfall.

These different soils, formed under different conditions in different parts of the earth, are the soils that support us, and provide mankind with the food, fiber and timber for his daily life. In the temperate climates of the great land masses of the northern hemisphere the soils generally accord with the climatic conditions of the present day, for most of them are post-glacial in age. In the tropics and sub-tropics the position is different for there the land surfaces are much older than those of northern and central Europe, Asia and North America. They have formed under several different climates, under different epochs of erosion, and the pattern is complex. To farm them for optimum production, as will be needed to feed the expanding population of the earth, it will be necessary to appreciate the extent to which the soils as we find them now are the product of human activities. To what extent have we produced deserts where grass and trees grew before? To what extent have we made saline swamps where once were fertile valleys? The basic problem has been that over much of the earth mankind has taken from the soil all that it had to give, and has left areas largely denuded of the elements essential for the growth of plants.

But things are changing. There is a widespread appreciation that one cannot take out of the land more nutrients than are in it. Moreover, the progress in science over the last 150 years has been immense. Mankind now has in its power the ability to put back the nutrients lost, to put them in to areas that have been infertile for lack of them for centuries; to control the acidity of high rainfall lands of potentially great fertility; to prevent salinization of irrigation areas, and to control it when it happens; and above all to prevent the erosion of the topsoil which has made thousands of square miles less productive than they used to be.

Socio-Economic Effects

How effectively can mankind control the fertility of

the world's soils? Do the people cultivating the soil in different parts of the world know what they are doing to it? What must be done to stop the continuing degradation? These were the questions asked at a conference organized by the International Federation of Institutes of Advanced Study and the United Nations Environment Programme and hosted by the Council of Ministers of the U.S.S.R. at Samarkand in 1976. To supply the answers a widespread enquiry was made of the small farmers of the tropics and sub-tropics to find what they thought about the situation. More than 10,000 people were questioned, the size of the farms ranging from less than 1/2 hectare to 25 or more hectares.

The answers showed clearly that most of the farmers knew that their land was declining in fertility, but few of them connected this with erosion. Erosion they related to the big gullies, and rarely realized that the gullies were formed when water washed down too quickly from the higher land above the gullies. Their understanding of the decline in fertility, however, was quite unrelated to the size of the farms, the size of the farm families or their level of education. Most people knew about chemical fertilizers, but relatively few used them. Chemical fertilizers were often expensive and sometimes were not available at all. With regard to soil conservation the situation was different, and in many parts of the world traditional systems of conservation were in use that had persisted since ancient times. In some parts these ancient systems were still in use, but in other parts they had been forgotten. In parts of the Andes old systems were still practiced but most of the people using them did not know that they concerned the soil. These systems included the massive stone terrace of Baguio in the Philippines and in Peru, the almost universal soil or clay banks and the twig and plant debris banks of east and west Africa. The problem today is that all these systems are labor intensive, and are not susceptible to the use of machinery. They can be used in consequence in subsistence farming, when a man and his family grow just about enough food to keep them alive throughout the year, but it is often difficult to extend the system to allow a better standard of living. As population grows the pressure on the land increases.

In literally all parts of the tropics, where there is sufficient land, a system of "shifting agriculture" is used. This is where the farmer cuts down the trees to make his 'garden', burns the branches, etc., and grows his crops on the land for two or three years until the yields begin to drop. Then he abandons the plot and cuts another out of the forest and lets trees grow again on the plot he has left. In every area, the farmers said this was the best way to restore fertility.

For a period the general opinion was that this "slash and burn" shifting cultivation was the main cause of soil erosion in the tropics. Recent work, however, has shown that this is not necessarily so. Careful studies in Venezuela have shown that three years after cutting down the forest there is still enough nitrogen in the topsoil to grow another crop of trees. The tree roots go deep into the soil and draw up nutrients from drainage waters and from decomposing rock, which they return to the soil in leaf fall. The leafy litter protects the surface soil from the action of raindrops, and if standing trees are left they not only supply seed for the next crop, but protection for the soil surface. Clearing and cultivation have been found to drastically reduce the earthworm population, with a concomitant reduction in the rate at which water enters the soil. Minimum cultivation and the use of a litter mulch is an old practice in some parts of the tropics, but totally unknown in others.

The socio-economic restraint to the more widespread use of fertilizers, mulching, cultivating on the contour and the use of terraces usually arise from bad communication and lack of a good extension service. Very few countries have extension service officers with any training in soil management. There are, in most countries, too few extension officers and they are often without adequate transport. Very few plots are laid out to demonstrate the value of the proposed techniques on farm fields. In those areas in the world where the wise use of fertilizers is spreading, or where conservation practices are extending, it is found that the farmers have seen demonstrations of the technique in a manner that they can see will bring them more money in this year. Where they can see this, the good techniques and good management will spread, but unless there is profit in the new techniques the first year they are used, the small farmer cannot adopt them.

The control of soil fertility now lies squarely in the hands of man himself. The question is whether it can be effectively implemented by a human population made up increasingly of city dwellers, remote from what is happening to the land.

Books on Soil

Soil has been studied in greater detail during this century than ever before and the detail in which it is presented makes it difficult for a newcomer to the field to get a picture of the whole -- soil types, water relations, effects of animals and so on. No recent books give a satisfactory overview of all aspects.

Some of the older books, which are listed below as classics, do this better than their modern counterparts. For the newcomer to the field I would suggest starting on Robinson's letters to a colleague, published as *Mother Earth*. It doesn't have all the latest information, but nothing written there is wrong. After that the 6th Edition of Sir John Russell's *Soil Conditions and Plant Growth* is the best

The start of an irrigated forest, Abu Dhabi. The young trees have to be protected by plastic shields from the blasting effect of the driven sand. Photograph by G. Hallsworth.

attempt by one man to encompass the whole field. Of the modern books, *The Soil Resource*, by Hans Jenny is the most outstanding.

The Classics

Mother Earth, by G.W. Robinson, Murby, London, 1937.

Soil Conditions and Plant Growth (6th Edition), by Sir. E. John Russell, Longmans Green & Co., London & New York, 1932.

The Physics of Blown Sand and Desert Dunes, by R.A. Bagnald, William Morrow, London & New York, 1940.

Factors of Soil Formation, by H. Jenny, McGraw-Hill, New York & London, 1941.

A Source Book of Agricultural Chemistry, by C.A. Browne, Chronica Botanica, Waltham, Massachusetts, 1944.

The Great Soil Groups of the World and Their Development, by K.D. Glinku (translated from the Russian text by C.F. Marbut), Edwards Bros., Ann Arbor, Michigan, 1927.

Le Profil Cultural; Principles du Physique du Soil, by S. Henin et al, Soc. d'Editeurs des Ingenieures Agricoles, Paris, 1960.

Micropedology 1938, by W.L. Kubiena, Collegiate Press, Ames, Iowa.

Soil Zoology, D.K. Kevan Mc E (Editor), Butterworths, London, 1955.

The Russian Chernozem (in Russian), by V.V. Dokuchaev, 1883.

Soil Science (in Russian), by N.M. Sibirtzev, 1901.

Soil Science (in Russian), by K.D. Glinka, 1908.

Soil Chemical Analysis (in Russian), by K.K. Gedroiz, 1923.

Soil Organic Matter, by M.M. Kononova, Moscow, 1963; Pergamon Press, New York, 1961.

Genesis and Regime of Saline Soils, by V.A. Kovda, Moscow-Leningrad, Pt. 1 -- 1946, Pt. 2 -- 1947.

The Cycles of Weathering by B.B. Polynov, Thomas Murby, London, 1937.

Soil Science (in Russian), by A.A. Rode, 1955.

Water Regime and its Regulation (in Russian), by A.A. Rode, 1963.

Serozems of Middle Asia, by A.N. Rozanov, Moscow, 1951.

Russian School of Soil Cartography, by D.G. Vilenski, Moscow, 1945.

Modern Selections: English

World Soils, by E.M. Bridges, Cambridge Univ. Press, Cambridge, England, 1970.

Minerals in Soil Environments, J.B. Dixon & S.B. Weed (Editors), Soil Science Soc. of America, 1977.

Man, a Geomorphologic Agent, by Dov-Nir, D. Reidel Publishing Co., Dordrecht, Holland, 1983.

Improved Production Systems as an Alternative to Shifting Cultivation, F.A.O. Soils Bulletin 53, 1984.

Soils of the World (2 Volumes -- Russian Translation Series), by M.A. Glasovskaya, A.B. Balkema, Rotterdam, Holland.

Experimental Pedology, by E.G. Hallsworth & D.V. Crawford, Butterworth, London, 1965.

Negev. Land, Water and Life in a Desert Environment, by D. Hillel, Praeger Publishers, C.B.S. Inc., New York.

Soil Conservation, by N. Hudson, Batsford Press, London, 1981.

The Soil Resource, by H. Jenny, Springer-Verlag, New York -- Heidelberg & Berlin, 1980.

Termites and the Soil, by K.H. Lee & T.G. Wood, Academic Press, London & New York, 1974.

Earthworms; Their Ecology and Relationship with Soils and Land Use, by K.H. Lee, Academic Press, 1985.

Trace Elements in Soils and Crops, Ministry of Agriculture & Fisheries U.K., Technical Bulletin 21, 1971.

Quantitative & Numerical Methods in Soil Survey (The Oxford Monographs on Soil Survey), by R. Webster.

Soil Classification for Soil Survey (The Oxford Monographs on Soil Survey), by B. Butler

Agricultural Physics, by C.W. Rose, Pergamon Press, 1966.

Soil Conditions and Plant Growth (8th Edition), by E. Walter Russell, Longmans Green & Co., London.

The World of Soil, by E. John Russell, Readers Union -- Collins, London, 1959.

Soil Factors in Crop Production in a Semi-Arid Environment, by J.S. Russell & E.L. Creacen, University of Queensland Press, 1977.

Salt Affected Soils in Europe, by I. Szabolks, Nijholt, The Hague, Netherlands, 1974.

Ecology of Soils, by V.R. Volubaev, Academy of Sciences of the Azerbaijan S.S.R. Baku (Available in English from Israel Program of Scientific Translations, Jerusalem, Israel).

Pedogenesis and Soil Taxonomy (I. Concepts and Interactions; II. The Soil), by L.P. Wilding, N.E. Smeck & G.F. Hall.

German

Entstehung, Eigenschaften und Systematik der Boden der Bundesrepublik Deutschland, by E. Muchenhausen, F. Kohl, H.P. Blume, F. Heinrich & S. Muller, DLG-Verlag, Frankfurt, 1977.

Lehrbuch der Bodenkunde, by P. Schachtshabel, H.H.P. Blume, K.H. Hartge & U. Schwertman, I. Szabolks, Ferdinand Enke Verlag, Stuttgart, 1982.

Bodenkundliches Praktikum, by E. Schlichting and H.H.P. Blume, Parey -- Berlin u. Hamburg, 1966.

French

Pedologie (Soil Science), Volume I: Pedogenese et Classification (2nd Edition), by Ph. Duchaufour, Masson Edit., Paris, 1983.

Pedologie (Soil Science), Volume II: Constituants et Proprietes (1st Edition), by B. Souchier & M. Bonneau, Masson Edit., Paris, 1979.

Livre Jubilaire de l'Association Francaise por l'Etude du Sol (Volume I), G. Pedro (Editor), AFES, 4, rue Redon -- 78370 Plaisir, France, 1984 (349 pages).

Russian

Fundamentals of Soil Science and Soil Geography (Available in English), by I.P. Gerasimov and Glasovskaya.

Soil Map of the World (Scale 1:10 mln), V.A. Kovda & E.V. Lobova (Editors in Chief), 1975.

Basics of the Study on Soils (Volumes 1-2), by V.A Kovda, Moscow, 1973.

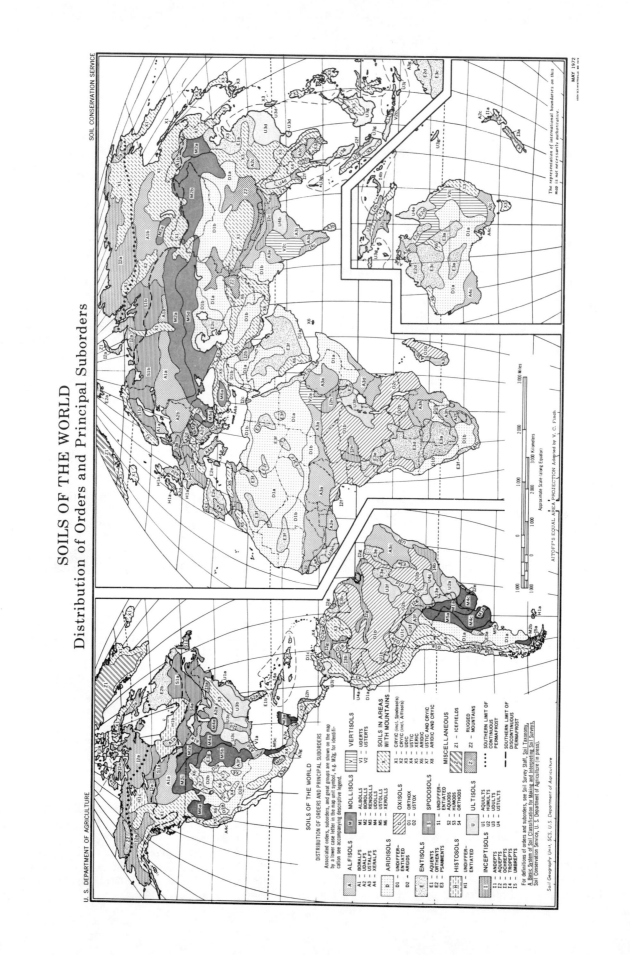

SOILS OF THE WORLD
Distribution of Orders and Principal Suborders

U. S. DEPARTMENT OF AGRICULTURE

SOIL CONSERVATION SERVICE

MAY 1972

The representation of international boundaries on this map is not necessarily authoritative.

AITOFF'S EQUAL AREA PROJECTION Adapted by V. C. Finch

Approximate Scale (along Equator)

SOILS OF THE WORLD

DISTRIBUTION OF ORDERS AND PRINCIPAL SUBORDERS

Associated orders, suborders, and great groups are shown on the map by a lower case letter in the map unit symbol, e.g. M2g, for identification see accompanying descriptive legend.

ALFISOLS
A1 – BORALFS
A2 – UDALFS
A3 – USTALFS
A4 – XERALFS

ARIDISOLS
D1 – UNDIFFERENTIATED
D2 – ARGIDS

ENTISOLS
E1 – AQUENTS
E2 – ORTHENTS
E3 – PSAMMENTS

HISTOSOLS
H1 – UNDIFFERENTIATED

INCEPTISOLS
I1 – ANDEPTS
I2 – AQUEPTS
I3 – OCHREPTS
I4 – TROPEPTS
I5 – UMBREPTS

MOLLISOLS
M1 – ALBOLLS
M2 – BOROLLS
M3 – RENDOLLS
M4 – UDOLLS
M5 – USTOLLS
M6 – XEROLLS

OXISOLS
O1 – ORTHOX
O2 – USTOX

SPODOSOLS
S1 – UNDIFFERENTIATED
S2 – AQUODS
S3 – HUMODS
S4 – ORTHODS

ULTISOLS
U1 – AQUULTS
U2 – HUMULTS
U3 – UDULTS
U4 – USTULTS

VERTISOLS
V1 – UDERTS
V2 – USTERTS

SOILS IN AREAS WITH MOUNTAINS
X1 – CRYIC (incl. Spodosols)
X2 – CRYIC (incl. Alfisols)
X3 – UDIC
X4 – USTIC
X5 – XERIC
X6 – ARIDIC
X7 – USTIC AND CRYIC
X8 – ARIDIC AND CRYIC

MISCELLANEOUS
Z1 – ICEFIELDS
Z2 – RUGGED MOUNTAINS

•••••• SOUTHERN LIMIT OF CONTINUOUS PERMAFROST

— — — SOUTHERN LIMIT OF DISCONTINUOUS PERMAFROST

For definitions of orders and suborders, see Soil Survey Staff, Soil Taxonomy, A Basic System of Soil Classification for Making and Interpreting Soil Surveys, Soil Conservation Service, U. S. Department of Agriculture (in press).

Soil Geography Unit, SCS, U. S. Department of Agriculture

Soil Research Centers

International Centers

International Rice Research Institute, Los Banos, Laguan, Philippines (For studies on waterlogged soils).

International Crop Research Institute for the Semi-arid Tropics, Hyderabad, India.

International Institute for Tropical Agriculture, Ibadan, Nigeria (Studies in fertility of tropical soils, in selection of land for clearing, and erosion).

Australia

Waite Agricultural Research Institute, University of Adelaide, Glen Osmond, South Australia 5064.

C.S.I.R.O. Division of Soils, Glen Osmond, South Australia.

Centre for Australian Environmental Studies (for Soil Physics), Griffith University, Nathan, Brisbane, Queensland.

C.S.I.R.O. Division of Environmental Mechanics, Canberra A.C.T.

Belgium

Rijkslandbouwhogeschool, Royal University of Gent, Coupure Links. 533, 9000 Gent (Soil structure, soil erosion).

University of Louvain, Place Crois du Sud 1, 1348, Louvain la Neuve (Soil physical chemistry, soil mineralogy).

Canada

Department of Soil Science, University of British Columbia, Vancouver, B.C. V6T IWS.

Department of Soil Science, University of Saskatchewan, Saskatoon, Saskatchewan.

Soil Research Institute, Agriculture, Canada, Ottawa, Ontario K1A 0C6

Department of Soil Science, University of Alberta, Edmonton, Alberta TCG 2E3.

China

Academica Simica, Institute of Soil Research, P.O. Box 821, Nanjing (Director: Prof. Zhao Qi-gao).

Institute of Forestry and Pedology, Academica Sinica, Shenjang, Liaoning (Director: Dr. Tao Yan).

Institute for Research in Soil and Water Conservation, Academica Sinica, Wugong, Xansi (Director: Dr. Zhu).

Federal German Republic

Institut fur Okologie, F.G. Bodenkunde, Salzufer 11-12, D-1000 Berlin 10.

Institut fur Bodenkunde, Nussalle 13, D-5300 Bonn.

Institut fur Bodenkunde und Waldernahrungslehre, Bertoldstr, 17, D-7800 Freiburg.

Institut fur Bodenkunde, Herrenhauserstr. 2, D-3000 Hannover 21.

Institut fur Bodenkunde und Standortslehre, Emil-Wolff-Str. 27, D-7000 Stuttgart 70. (Hohenheim).

Institut fur Pflanzenernahrung und Bodenkunde, Olshausenstr. 40-60, D-2300 Kiel.

Institut fur Bodenkunde, D-8050 Freising-Wehenstephan. (Munchen).

France

Centre National de Recherche des Sols, Route de Mende, Montpelier (Especially soil zoology).

Centre de Pedologie Biologique, 17 Rue N.D. des Pavvres, 54506 Vandoevre les Nancy.

Laboratoire des Sols, C.N.R.A., Roote de St. Cyr, 78 Versailles.

Institut National de la Recherche Agronomique (I.N.R.A.).

Institut Francais de Recherche Scientifique pour le development en cooperation (O.R.S.T.O.M.).

Centre National de la Recherche Scientifique (C.N.R.S.).

Centre International de Recherche Agronomique pour le developpement (C.I.R.A.D.), Cet organisme s'appellait GERDAT jusqu'en janvier 1985. Il incorpore notamment l'Institut de Recherches Agronomiques tropicales (I.R.A.T.).

Holland

The Agricultural University, Wageningen, Holland.

The International Centre for Aerial Survey and Earth Sciences, Enschede, The Netherlands.

Hungary

The Research Institute for Soil Science and Agricultural Chemistry of the Hungarian Academy of Sciences, Herman O.U. 15, Budapest 11.

India

Central Soil Salinity Research Institute, Karnal, Haryana.

Division of Soil Science, Indian Agricultural Research Institute, New Delhi 110012.

Central Arid Zone Research Institute, Jodhpur.

Sweden

Department of Physical Geography, University of Lund, Lund (Physics of erosion in Africa).

The Agricultural University, Upsalla (Forest soils, N-cycling).

New Zealand

D.S.I.R. Soils Bureau, Lower Hutt, North Island, New Zealand.

Union of Soviet Socialist Republics

Faculty of Pedology of Moscow State University (6 departments).

Dokuchaev's Soil Institute of Lenin Agricultural Academy, Moscow.

Institute of Soil Science and Photosynthesis of USSR Academy of Sciences, Moscow region, Puschino.

Institute of Soil Science and Photosynthesis of USSR Academy of Sciences, Novocibirsk.

Institute of Soil Science of Academy of Sciences of Kazakhstan, Alma-Ata.

Institute of Soil Science and Agrochemistry of Academy of Sciences of Azerbaidjan, Baku.

Institute of Soil Science and Agrochemistry, Tashkent.

Sokolovsky's Institute of Soil Science and Agrochemistry, Kharkov.

All-Union Institute of Fertilizers and Agropedology of the All-Union Academy of Agricultural Sciences, Moscow.

United Kingdom

Rothampstead Research Station, Harpenden.

Macauley Soil Research Institute, Aberdeen, Scotland.

National Institute for Agricultural Engineering, Silsoe, Bedfordshire.

Department of Soil Science, University of Reading.

Department of Soil Science, University of Aberdeen.

National College of Agricultural Engineering, Silsoe, Bedfordshire (For soil conservation).

United States of America

Department of Soil Science, University of California, Berkeley, CA.

Department of Soil Science, North Carolina State University, Raleigh, NC 27607.

Cornell University, Ithaca, NY 14850.

Purdue University, Lafayette, IN 47907.

USDA-ARS & University of Minnesota, St. Paul, MN 55101.

Iowa State University, Ames, IA 50010.

University of Maryland, Amherst, MD 01003.

U.S.D.A. Salinity Laboratory, Riverside, CA

West Indies

Department of Soil Science, University of the West Indies, St. Augustine, Trinidad.

Venezuela

C.I.D.I.A.T., Apartado 219, Merida.

Consider the lilies of the field,
They sow not, neither do they reap,
Yet Solomon in all his glory
    is not clothed such as these.
ISA IBN MARYAM

Plants

Alwyn Gentry

Green plants are the earth's only means of converting sunlight into a form of energy utilizable by life. This process, called photosynthesis, is one of the most astounding of nature's miracles. Because of this unique photosynthetic ability, plants can use the energy of the sun to bind together the hydrogen, oxygen and carbon atoms of carbon dioxide and water into a simple sugar called glucose; excess oxygen is converted to molecular form and liberated into the air as a by-product. Glucose and the various more complex sugars and other organic compounds derived from it are the basis for life on earth. Over the eons since some lowly protozoan evolved the ability to photosynthesize and became the first plant, the oxygen released by this process has accumulated in the atmosphere, where it is now available to us to breathe. We call plants "primary producers" because they alone can produce from inorganic matter the energy rich carbon-carbon bond on which all other life depends. In addition to the carbohydrates formed from photosynthesis, plants take up other nutrients from the soil, using some of their energy to convert them into the complex organic molecules that make up the tissue of the plant. This nutrient uptake is accomplished largely through the process of transpiration, with evaporation of water from a plant's leaves providing the force necessary to pull ground water with its dissolved nutrients into and through the plant.

Most of the energy fixed by photosynthesis builds the more complicated organic molecules that make up wood, bark, leaves, and other parts of the plants themselves. Some supplies the chemical energy needed by the plant for its own life processes. Some passes to animals that eat various plant parts. Thus everything we

eat, be it plant or animal, and in a very real sense, we ourselves, are ultimately made from plants. As their energy fuels life processes, both in animals and in the plants themselves, some complex sugar and carbohydrate molecules are oxidized, breaking down once again into carbon dioxide and water. When a plant dies, most of its organic matter is decomposed by fungi and other soil microorganisms thus fueling their microbial life processes. The simpler organic molecules produced by this decomposition are once again in water soluble and membrane-permeable form ready to be taken up and re-utilized by another plant.

While many fungi gain their livelihoods primarily by decomposing dead plants, others form complicated, mutualistic and symbiotic associations with living plants. Thus the great majority of green plants have special fungi called mycorrhizae associated with their roots. These mycorrhizal fungi aid the plant in nutrient uptake, at least in part because their extensively branched network of hyphae is able to reach more of the soil's nutrient molecules than are the plant's own root hairs; in return the plant supplies some of the carbohydrates fixed by its photosynthesis to its mycorrhizal symbionts.

In certain situations, for example the anaerobic conditions typical of stagnant swamps, plants that die are not decomposed by soil microbes, which cannot function in such oxygen-depleted environments. In such situations fossils may be formed as the preserved plant parts are slowly replaced by minerals dissolved in the ground water. More important to modern civilization, the organic matter of the undecomposed dead plants may, over time, be converted through heat and pressure inside the earth into coal or petroleum. We are accustomed to think of coal and petroleum as falling into the sphere of geology, but their origin is entirely botanical, as is the photosynthetic energy trapped within them. It is really plants, albeit plants dead and buried for millions of years, that now fuel our cars and heat our homes. From this perspective the "new" idea of producing such gasoline substitutes as gasahol directly from plants is hardly novel. We are utilizing exactly the same solar energy, photosynthesis-fixed by green plants, that we always have: the only difference is in not letting it sit underground for 300 million years before we use it!

The fuels that run our cars and factories and the raw materials for our petrochemical industry are not the only ways in which our modern civilization depends on plants. The history of the beginning of human civilization is largely the story of the domestication of plants. The cooperative behavior needed for complicated agricultural systems has been the *sine qua non* in development of all of the world's civilizations. Each of earth's great centers of civilization has grown up based on a different indigenous plant -- Egypt and Mesopotamia on wheat, China and southeast Asia on rice, the Mayas and Aztecs on corn, the Incas on corn and potatoes, Ethiopia on millets. It is not coincidental that North America, whose only contribution to world food supply was the sunflower, produced no great civilization. Amazingly, only about 20 plant species account for 90% of the world's food today. Worse, the extant cultivars of many of these species originated from a very limited genetic base. It seems clear that new food crops and other natural products must be developed, especially in the tropics, if the world is to prosper in the future.

Plants are important to mankind not only because they feed us and supply much of the energy and raw materials needed by our industrial society. They also play extremely important and often little appreciated environmental roles. Plants clothe the soil surface of much of the planet, protecting it from erosion and temperature extremes. The infamous "dust bowl" years of the midwestern U.S. during the Great Depression resulted directly from plowing up the protective cover of prairie grass for farming. The unprotected topsoil was carried away in gigantic clouds to be redeposited as thick layers of suffocating dust over the whole Great Plains area. Similarly we now know that cutting down the forests of a river's watershed produces devastating hydrological and erosional effects. In the intact forest, rain water is held by the root mat and leaf litter long enough to percolate into the ground. On bare ground, after the forest is felled, instead of soaking into the ground, the rain runs off carrying much of the topsoil with it. Today these processes are especially prevalent in the tropics. On largely deforested Madagascar, the rivers run red from the dissolved lateritic soil, their mouths forming gaping red wounds jutting miles into the blue sea. Floods engendered by runoff from the deforested Himalayas now devastate much of India and Pakistan and cause billions of dollars of damage a year. On the other hand, deforestation of the

Venezuelan coastal cordillera has lead to the annual drying up of formerly permanent rivers crossing the Llanos. In monetary terms, the value of the earth's forests and other plant formations is almost incalculable. We remove the living green skin from the earth's surface at great risk to the delicate balance of the planetary ecosystem.

Erosion control is not the only ecological service to the planet performed by its plant cover. Each year small amounts of carbon dioxide gas are released into the earth's atmosphere through geochemical reactions inside the earth. Through millions of years most of this carbon dioxide has been accumulated in the earth's plant biomass. This delicate balance is now being upset by the burning of tropical forests and ever-increasing amounts of fossil fuel. Oxidation of these long immobilized hydrocarbons result in adding ever more carbon dioxide to the atmosphere, in turn causing the "greenhouse effect", with less reradiation of the sun's energy back into space leading to a warming of the earth's surface. Ultimately melting of the polar ice caps, raising of sea level, and flooding of our coastal cities will result. (Luckily (?) we are also adding enough particulate pollution to the northern hemisphere atmosphere to balance out most of the heating that would otherwise come from the excess carbon dioxide; only in the southern hemisphere -- into which carbon dioxide gas diffuses more freely than does particulate matter -- is increased atmospheric warmth and melting of the polar ice cap being observed.)

At a more local level, also, its plant cover is vital to proper functioning of the earth's ecosystem, in sometimes unexpected ways. For example, about half of the Amazonian rainfall is water continually recycled through plant transpiration; cutting its forest thus automatically halves an area's rainfall, in many places converting rich forest to near desert. On the other hand, some widely reputed effects of plants on the biosphere are minuscule or non-existent. The tropical rain forest, far from being the "lungs of the earth" whose demise would lead to loss of the oxygen we breathe is an equilibrium climax system wherein oxygen release (from photosynthesis) is exactly balanced by oxygen consumption (from the respiration of plants and animals).

Because they are stationary, most people think of plants as inanimate organisms whose "behavior" is limited to photosynthesis and nutrient uptake. Actually, most plants have a complex repertoire of behaviors varying from simple movements of leaves or growth tips, to maximize (or minimize) exposure to the sun, to intricate highly co-evolved reproductive strategies. The tremendous success of the flowering plants, or angiosperms, is due largely to their more precise ability to move gametes (pollen) and propagules (seeds). A beautiful flower or tasty fruit may give us pleasure, but it was not for our benefit that they evolved. Flowers and fruits are a plant's way of getting around, substituting a pollen-carrying insect or fruit-eating bird for adult mobility. Both floral and fruiting behavior can be very complex.

The more consistently a pollen vector visits it, the better off the plant, since a higher proportion of its pollen will end up deposited on the stigmas of conspecific plants rather than wasted by deposition on other flowers the pollinator may also visit. Thus different kinds of plants evolved different kinds of flowers, each adapted to a different pollinator. In some plant families, floral diversification reflects differential use of a single kind of pollinator. For example, all *Aristolochia* flowers look and smell like rotting meat and trap flies that function as their pollinators. In other families evolution led to different taxa having flowers adapted to attract and exploit different pollinators. For example, in *Bignoniaceae* there are genera adapted to pollination by bats, hummingbirds, perching birds, hawkmoths, butterflies and small bees, and large to medium-sized bees (figure 1). Even within some genera different species have evolved to make use of different pollen vectors. In such highly evolved systems there are often elaborate flowers with complicated patterns of morphology and movement of floral parts.

The extreme case is the orchid family. Not only have orchids differentiated to make use of many different pollen vectors, but they have also developed such precise mechanisms for channelizing the behavior of their visitors that all the pollen of the orchid flower can effectively be transferred in a single mass called a pollinium. Some orchids have fragrant white flowers with long nectar-containing spurs and are pollinated by long-tongued hawkmoths. Other species with nectar spurs have red flowers and are hummingbird pollinated. The flowers of some species function as fly traps; others are pollinated by mosquitos, midges, or butterflies. Most species are pollinated by bees. In many of the showy-flowered neotropical orchids, pollination may be exclusively by male bees, each bee species uniquely attracted by the specific fragrance of a certain kind of orchid. These bees collect the orchid chemicals and become inebriated. Consequently the orchids are able to put their drunken visitors through all manner of indignities to ensure that they precisely contact pollinia and stigma in the prescribed manner; some fall down chutes, slide down slippery slides, are catapulted into space, or are dunked in a bucket of water. Orchid flowers also specialize in deceit. Some look like spiders and are pollinated by wasps looking for prey to provision their nests; some look like bees and are pollinated by aggressive territorial male bees trying to defend their territories. Perhaps the ultimate in deception are orchid flowers that look so much like female bees, complete with wings, head, and hairy abdomen, that male bees mistake them for females of their own species and try

to copulate with them, effecting pollination in the process! No matter whether pandering to a pollinator's vices or providing it with a legitimate nectar reward, all orchids have in common a wonderfully specific pollination system -- no wonder there are more species of orchids, about 20,000 of them, than of any other plant family.

Plant "behavior" relating to seed dispersal can be almost as complex as that pertaining to pollination. Of course, the fruits we eat evolved their attractive flavor not to entice us but to attract some other mammal with tastes similar to our own, which might sloppily discard some seeds after carrying away the fruit to munch on. Other plants evolved fruits attractive to birds, gaining the advantage of winged dispersers. Some plants take to the air themselves with wind-dispersed propagules sometimes sailing with wings or plumes, sometimes minute and dustlike. Some of these disseminules have remarkable aerodynamic properties and can swoop and glide over long distances even with little or no wind. Other plants have disseminules specialized for floating and water dispersal. A few plants have no obvious seed dispersal specializations and may be merely gravity dispersed. Some plants, especially weeds, have evolved "stick-tight" fruits with sticky or prickly coverings that adhere to the fur of passing animals (and nowadays to our stockings as well). Many plants are self-propelled or autochorous, often having elastically dehiscing capsules that project the seeds some distance from a parent plant. A few plants even have propagules with hydroscopically triggered twisting appendages that can actively crawl across the ground and on occasion burrow themselves into the soil as well. Many plants rely on ants for dispersal, especially to place their seeds in an appropriate site for germination.

It is in the tropics that the incredible potential diversity of seed dispersal strategies begins to be realized. The fruits of plants specializing in monkey dispersal are rather large, have fruity odors, and are often pubescent or softly spiny to create a texture easily visible against the green forest canopy. In the Neotropics, where the native primates are apparently red-green color blind, monkey fruits are commonly yellow, brown, tan, or greenish at maturity. Fruits adapted for bird dispersal usually have smaller dispersal units and are a bright shiny red or black or open to expose seeds with bright red or contrasting white arils. Bat dispersed fruits usually remain green at maturity, since bright colors are not very useful at night, and are held away from the main leaf mass where they are more easily accessible. They often have single seeds that the bat drops after gnawing off the pulp, but some kinds, like figs, have tiny seeds that pass through the bat and are eliminated with its excreta. Other tropical trees have very large thick-shelled fruits or seeds that can only be chiseled open by the sharp teeth of squirrels and other rodents; some of these animals, such as the agouti, scatter-hoard

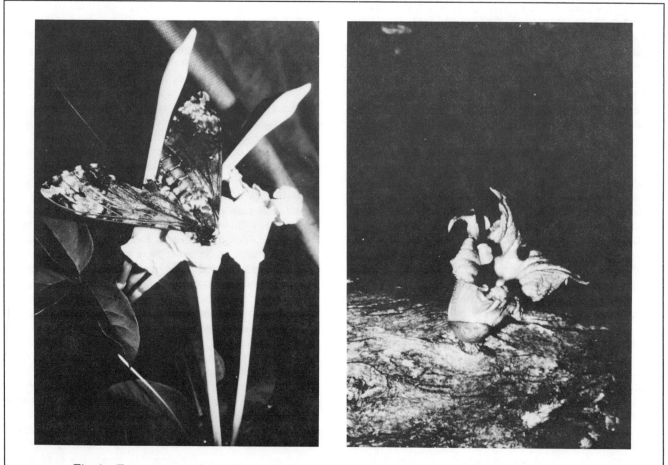

Fig. 1. *Tanaecium, with very long-tubed night flowering sweet-smelling flowers is pollinated by long-tongued hawkmoths (left). Crescentia, with tannish unpleasant-smelling night-blooming flowers, is bat-pollinated (right).*

uneaten seeds for later consumption, effective dispersal of the uneaten remainder. In Africa, many trees have elephant-dispersed fruits, typically with an exceedingly large thick-walled endocarp adapted to survive the no doubt arduous passage through an elephant's gut, in other cases with small flat smooth slippery seeds adapted to slide readily through the same elephant. Of course, many other tropical forest species, especially in dry forests, have winged, wind-dispersed seeds. Different plant species have different strategies for presenting their fruits to their dispersers and for protecting their unripe fruits from premature consumption. Moreover, the plant community as a whole must feed its dispersal agents through the whole year. Often different species fruit in succession, sometimes with wonderful synchrony. At certain times of year a single critical species may stand between the whole frugivore community and starvation. The intricate co-adaptations of plants and animals in such systems is truly marvelous.

There are also wonderful interactions between plants and the herbivores that eat them. Most plant families have some kind of biologically active chemical to protect them. Many plant families specialize in toxins such as alkaloids; others have digestibility-reducing compounds like tannins and lignins that combine with and inactivate digestive enzymes. With sufficient quantities of the latter, an insect can eat itself full and still starve to death. In contrast to these generalized compounds, plant families with toxins often have specific types of protective compounds, e.g., sesquiterpene lactones in compositae, cardiac glycosides in *Asclepiadaceae* and *Apocynaceae*. Certain herbivores, especially insects, may evolve special adaptations for dealing with some of the novel chemical structures by which plants protect themselves. A frequent result is a kind of co-evolutionary race, with a genus of insect specializing on eating a certain family of plants, with speciation in the plant often related to evolution of new biochemicals to which a new species of the insect taxon subsequently may accommodate itself. Whole series of species specific interactions may result, e.g., between passion flowers and heliconiine butterflies, pipevines and pipevine swallowtails. One outcome of the biological warfare is that many unusual and biologically active molecules are evolved, especially in the tropics where such interactions are most intense. Modern, as well as primitive, man has learned to turn this to his own advantage. Today almost half of all prescriptions filled in U.S. pharmacies contain natural products and about a quarter contain compounds from tropical plants -- e.g., tranquilizers from *Rauwolfia,* birth control pills from *Dioscorea,* the muscle relaxant curare from *Menispermaceae,* the leukemia drugs vincristine and vinblastine from *Vinca.* Other elements of modern society turn plant protective compounds to different uses, e.g., as psychoactive and hallucinogenic drugs.

The astonishing diversity of earth's plant life is concentrated in tropical forests where the majority of the earth's plant and animal species live in a minuscule one-sixteenth of the planet's land surface. Most of the world's plant species are angiosperms, highly successful because of their evolution of the specialized reproductive structures we call flowers and fruits. There are perhaps 240,000 angiosperm species in the world with at least 155,000 of these in the tropics. There are many more kinds of plants in tropical America (ca. 90,000) than in tropical Africa (ca. 30,000) or tropical Australasia (ca. 35,000). The other most diversified group of plants are fungi, sometimes considered not to be plants at all but to constitute their own kingdom, with at least 120,000 species and perhaps many more, again with the large majority in the tropics, especially the Neotropics. Ferns, sharing with flowering plants the evolutionary advance of having a vascular system but reproducing by spores rather than having flowers and seeds, constitute a mere 12,000 species, perhaps 11,000 of these in the tropics. Less evolutionarily advanced non-vascular plants -- mosses, liverworts, algae and lichens -- also have relatively few species, each of these groups with between 11,000 and 17,000 species. Such figures are mere guesses, since the basic inventory of the world's plant (and animal) life is very far from complete, but they do serve to emphasize how many of the world's life forms occur in the tropics. How much, or rather how little do we know about the organisms with which we share the planet? We estimate that there may be 10,000 species of yet-to-be-discovered plant species in the Neotropics alone. Many of these undiscovered plant species may have potential uses as may the even more numerous described but otherwise unstudied plants.

Perhaps the greatest tragedy facing the world today is a botanical one. We are on the verge of a mass extinction of life forms on our planet, greater than the one that wiped out the dinosaurs at the end of the Cretaceous 65,000,000 years ago. The very plant resources which might make it possible to feed and make healthy the earth's burgeoning population are being destroyed at an unprecedented rate, even as we begin to think of how the world might take better advantage of this rich evolutionary heritage. Unless we come to better appreciate how dependent we all are on the earth's wonderfully complex and intricately interacting plant life, and do something to preserve the tropical forests where that botanical largesse is greatest, our children will find the world an infinitely poorer place in which to live.

Some Botanical Facts

Largest Flower
Rafflesia arnoldii, parasitic on the roots of Southeast Asian Vitaceae, with flowers to 1 m across and weighing 15 pounds. The aroid *Amorphophallus titanum* of Sumatra has an inflorescence almost as tall as a man but the actual flowers are small.

Oldest Living Tree
Bristlecone pines of the Sierra Nevada mountains of California can reach 5000 years; one tree cut down in the 1960's was 4900 years old. *Cryptomeria japonica,* Japanese cedar, can be as old as 5200 years according to the Guinness Book of Records.

Largest Tree
The giant redwood, *Sequoiadendron giganteum,* is probably the world's largest, though not tallest, tree. The "General Sherman Tree" in Sequoia National Park, California is 280 feet tall, measures 80 ft. around, and is estimated to weigh well over 2000 tons.

Tallest Tree
Several coast redwoods, *Sequoia sempervirens,* have been recorded to exceed 360 ft., the tallest was 367.8 ft. tall in 1963 but has been dying back slowly. According to the Guinness Book of Records, a *Eucalyptus regnans* tree in Victoria, Australia was measured as 375 ft. tall but the tallest living tree of that species, in Tasmania, is only 325 ft. tall.

Heaviest Wood
The black ironwood (*Olea laurifolia*) of South Africa has a specific gravity up to almost 1.5. Several trees of subtropical dry areas like lignum vitae (*Guaiacum*) and

quebracho (*Schinopsis*) have specific gravities around 1.3.

Largest Seed

The double coconut (*Lodoicea seychellarum*) has a single-seeded fruit that may weigh 40 pounds. The largest dicot seed may be that of *Mora megistosperma,* a species of coastal swamps of the Neotropics.

Most Species Rich Forests

The upper Amazonian lowlands of Peru are richer in tree (and animal) species than any others yet known in the world. The record for trees in a hectare is 300 species out of the 600 individual plants ≧ 10 cm. dbh. at Yanamono, near Iquitos, Peru.

Best Botanical Gardens

The Missouri Botanical Garden, in St. Louis, Missouri, oldest in the U.S., is often acclaimed as the world's greatest. Its greatness stems largely from its extremely active tropical research program, with a staff of 25 Ph.D. botanists searching for plants throughout the world's tropics, a library estimated to have almost 90% of everything ever printed (since invention of the printing press) that relates to plant classification, and the world's most active herbarium, to which 100,000 plant specimens a year are currently being added.

Historically, the most important botanical garden in the world has been the famous Royal Botanical Gardens at Kew, near London. The third member of the "top 3" is the New York Botanical Garden in the Bronx, long active in neotropical plant exploration, especially in Brazil and the Guayana area, which is currently developing a more economic and anthropoligical focus aimed at developing new uses for tropical plants.

Some Outstanding University Programs in Botany

The two best botany departments in the States, as judged by the American Association of University Professors, are the University of Texas and the University of California, Davis. Some other outstanding botany programs include those at Berkeley (University of California); Michigan (with a separate but complementary Wildlife Biology and Natural Resources program); Duke University (the home office of the Organization for Tropical Studies); Washington University, St. Louis (tops in Population Biology and very strong in physiology and systematics). The largest, and among the best, in Latin America are at the Universidad Nacional Autonomo de Mexico and the Universidad Nacional de La Plata (Argentina). Some other outstanding botany programs in Latin America are at the Universidad Central de Venezuela; Universidad Catolica in Santiago, Chile; Instituto de Botanico in Sao Paulo, Brazil; Universidade Estadual de Campinas, also in Sao Paulo. The best botany program in Africa is at the University of Witwatersrand, Johannesberg, South Africa. Among top botany programs in Europe might be mentioned Oxford and Cambridge in England; Montpelier in France; Goteborg and Uppsala in Sweden; Aarhus in Denmark; Utrecht in Holland; and Munich and Gottingen in West Germany.

Some Useful General Reference Books about Plants

Best Botany Text

Biology of Plants (3rd Edition, 1981), by P.H. Raven, R.F. Evert and H. Curtis, Worth Publishers, New York , 1971 (686 pages). The leading as well as best college botany text, both well-written and well-illustrated.

Some Important Works Related to Economic Botany

Plants and Civilization, by H.G. Baker, Wadsworth Publ. Co., Belmont, California, 1965 (183 pages). A generalized account of the importance of plants to human beings, the best non-technical introduction to economic botany.

Plant Science: An Introduction to World Crops (3rd Edition), by J. Janik, R. Schery, F. Woods and V. Ruttan, Freeman & Company, San Francisco, 1981. A more or less complete botanical text focused almost entirely on crop plants and how plants relate to man.

Plants, Man, and Life, by E. Anderson, Little, Brown, and Co., Boston, 1952. A wonderfully written and non-technical essay on how plants relate to man, with delightful insight into how botanists relate to plants as well.

Dictionary of Economic Plants, by J.C. Uphof, Verlag-Cramer, Wurzburg, 1968. The most complete compilation of useful plants and their uses.

Green Medicine: The Search for Plants That Heal, by M.B. Kreig, Rand McNally, Chicago, 1964 (462 pages). A fascinating account of some of the recent discoveries of new medicines from plants.

Some Important Works Related to Plant Classification

An Integrated System of Classification of Flowering

Plants, by A. Cronquist, Columbia Univ. Press, New York, 1981. A rather technical and expensive summary of mainstream ideas on plant family classification.

Taxonomy of Vascular Plants, by G.H. Lawrence, MacMillan, New York, 1951 (and many reprints) (823 pages). A rather old fashioned, very concise summary of the major plant families with an excellent glossary of taxonomic terms.

Flowering Plants of the World, by V.H. Heywood (Editor), Mayflower Books, New York, 1978 (335 pages). A nicely illustrated, surprisingly inexpensive compendium of the families of flowering plants (but the distribution maps are very poor).

Some Miscellaneous and Tropical References

Island Life, by S. Carlquist, Natural History Press, Garden City NY, 1965. A nicely written non-technical natural history of selected unusual and distinctive features of island plants and animals.

The Tropical Rain Forest by P.W. Richards, Cambridge Univ. Press, 1952 (and reprints)(450 pages). The classic reference on this botanically most important part of the world.

Tropical Nature, by A. Forsyth and K. Miyata, Charles Scribner's, New York, 1984 (248 pages). Catches the essence of what the tropics are all about in a very readable style.

Costa Rican Natural History, by D.H. Janzen (Editor), University of Chicago Press, 1983 (816 pages). A wonderful potpourri of tidbits of tropical natural history.

Animals

Gordon H. Orians

For the animal shall not be measured by man. In a world older and more complete than ours they move finished and complete, gifted with extensions of the senses we have lost or never attained, living by voices we shall never hear. They are not brethren; they are not underlings; they are other nations, caught with ourselves in the net of life and time, fellow prisoners of the splendour and travail of the earth. HENRY BESTON

Animals exist in an astonishing variety of forms, the full richness of which is yet to be appreciated. About four-fifths of the approximately 1.5 million kinds of living organisms that have been described and named are animals, but the number actually living on earth is much larger than that. Only about 500,000 of the organisms so far named live in the tropics. In the relatively well-known groups, such as birds, mammals and reptiles, the number of species living in the tropics is two to three times the number living in temperate regions. If these ratios are typical, we have probably named less than one-fifth of the organisms living in tropical regions. The proportion could actually be much less than that.

Even though many species of animals are yet to be described, enough is known for us to be able to discern the major patterns in their distributions. The most familiar pattern is that the number of species in most groups decreases with increasing latitude. A tropical forest supports several times the number of species of birds, mammals and reptiles found in a temperate forest of similar overall structure. The number of species of molluscs found on sandy and muddy beaches along the Atlantic Coast of North America decreases steadily from Florida to Newfoundland. There are, however, exceptions in some groups of animals. There are more species of bees in warm temperature deserts than anywhere else. Sandpipers are both most abundant and richest in species in high latitude bogs and tundra. Salamanders are most varied in moist temperate forests. Nevertheless, there are many more species of animals in tropical regions than in higher latitudes.

The numbers of species of animals are also correlated with habitat types. Breeding birds respond primarily to the strutural complexity of the vegetation, probably because complex habitats afford more types of food and provide more different ways of seeking foods.

In a grassland there are only a few ways that a bird can seek food and a small number of different prey types. A forest offers a dark understory, tree trunks, branches of many sizes and shapes, and the complex canopies of trees, none of which are found in a grassland. Interestingly, these substrates exist even if the forest has only a few species of trees in it. Consequently, for birds, the number of breeding species is determined mostly by structural complexity of the vegetation and is little influenced by the number of plant species.

Mammals do not respond to vegetation structure in the same way that birds do, primarily because, except for bats, mammals cannot fly. Most mammals in a forest get their food from the ground and are little affected by the structural complexity of the trees above them. Indeed, except for bats which do exploit the canopy in a variety of ways to obtain insects and fruits, mammals are often as rich in species in grassland areas as they are in forests.

The situation is quite different for insects. Most herbivorous insects are specialists that eat only one species of plant or, at most, a few closely related ones. Therefore, the number of insect species found in an area is positively correlated with the number of plant species. There are, however, also strong correlations with plant structure. Larger, more structurally complex plants support more species of insects than do smaller, simpler ones. In addition, common plants have more insects on them than do rare ones and widespread species also have more associated insects than do plants with more restricted ranges. Food specialization by insects is favored by the complex differences among plants in the chemistry of their tissues. This makes it difficult for any one insect to use the tissues of many species of plants. Also insects are very vulnerable to predators while they are feeding externally on plants. More complex plants afford a wider variety of places in which to hide and more backgrounds that can be mimicked.

The Animal Way of Life

Because all animals require food in the form of energy-rich organic compounds produced directly or indirectly by green plants, much of the diversity of animals relates to what the different species eat, how they find it, and how their foraging activities influence the distribution, abundance, and evolution of their prey and the other species that utilize the same prey. Because the density of energy-rich molecules is generally not extremely high, most animals are mobile and seek out their food. The main exceptions are aquatic areas where a regular supply of food is delivered by flowing water (streams and rivers) or by wave action (ocean shores). In these environments many animals are sessile and compete for space such as plants do. These are also the only environments in which animals exert community-wide effects via their structure. Elsewhere, animals exert their primary effects through the consumption of their prey.

Searching for prey in the highly structured environments provided by terrestrial plants has led to the evolution of adaptations among predators that help them find prey in different types of locations. Smaller predators and parasites are, like small herbivores, often specialists that attack one or a few prey types.

Predator-Prey Interactions

As energy is transferred from one trophic level, such as herbivores, to another, such as carnivores, most of the energy present in one level is "lost" before it reaches the next level. Several reasons contribute to this progressive loss of energy. First, all living organisms expend large amounts of energy simply running the machinery of their bodies. None of this is available to their predators. In addition, many organisms are killed by agents other than predators. When they die they are eaten by detritivores which reduce them to simpler compounds. As a rough approximation, only about ten percent of the energy entering one trophic level in an ecological community is captured by the next level. In the case of woody plants, the percentage is much lower because of the low digestibility of wood. For grasses and marine algae which have no difficult-to-digest tissues, the percentage is usually much

Giraffes, zebras, wildebeest and buffalo, Masai-Mara Game Reserve, Kenya. Photograph by Elizabeth Orians.

higher, but whatever the exact value, much less energy flows through higher trophic levels than through lower ones. This is why big, fierce animals are always rare and why there are no predators on wolves -- they are simply too rare to make it worthwhile!

As predators, animals often exert important influences on the structures of the ecological communities in which they live. The savannah vegetation of much of Africa is kept open and the trees pruned by a combination of the grazing and browsing activities of large mammals, especially elephants and giraffes, and fire. In the North American grasslands, prairie dogs, by clipping and heavily grazing plants in the vicinities of their towns, alter the plant community from one dominated by long-lived perennial plants to one in which short-lived, fast growing annual plants dominate. In the Aleutian Islands, sea otters, by preying upon sea urchins, convert subtidal communities from ones in which algae are kept low and widely spaced by the intensive grazing activities of the urchins, to communities dominated by lush beds of large algae.

When animals have major effects on the composition of communities in which they live, they are referred to as "keystone predators". Many keystone predators have been identified, most of which eat prey that are sessile and compete for space, whether they are animals or plants. Keystone effects are most likely to occur when the predator prefers to eat species that are competitively dominant in the absence of predation and would, therefore, crowd out many other species if they were not held back by predation.

Predators and prey mutually influence one another's evolution as well as determining distribution and abundance patterns. In general, prey evolve to be more difficult to capture and utilize by their predators while predators evolve to become more effective in capturing and using the tissues of their prey. Many of the obvious features of animals are defenses against their predators. Among these are noxious chemicals, toxic hairs and bristles, hard outer coverings, large false eyes that make the animal appear to be much larger than it really is, and mimicry of inedible objects such as leaves, branches, flowers and thorns. Animals also evolve to mimic one another. Many insects are mimics of bees and wasps and some spiders mimic ants. The palatable viceroy butterfly mimics the unpalatable monarch. Other cases of mimicry involve the convergence in appearance of two or more species, all of which are more or less toxic, to create a mimicry complex. These systems function because as naive predators

Three immature Galapagos Hawks on the rim of Volcan Alcedo, Galapagos. Photograph by Elizabeth Orians.

learn that one member of the complex is unpalatable, they generalize and avoid other similar-looking members of the complex. There is probably a great deal of chemical mimicry in nature, but we find it difficult to detect such mimicry because we are such strongly visual animals.

Competition

Animals also exert important influences on community structure by competing with one another. Some types of animals, such as insects that eat plants, seldom compete with one another, but competition is widespread among such animals as mammals, birds, reptiles, amphibians and fishes. Usually, competitive interactions depress one species more than another.

This is revealed by removing one of the competitors and observing the effects on the others. Typically the removal of the larger of the two competitors has a larger effect on the smaller than does the reverse. The ability of the larger species to physically exclude the smaller one from access to resources is the most important reason for this asymmetry. Nevertheless, larger animals need more food per day than do smaller ones and, therefore, smaller species can often exist on lower levels of resources than can the larger ones. Therefore, the larger, more dominant species are often more vulnerable to disturbances that reduce food availability than are smaller ones. Conservation efforts often must be directed toward the large, conspicuous species that are the most successful competitors in communities not being heavily influenced by human activity because they are more susceptible to disturbance than are smaller species.

Mutualistic Interactions

Animals are also involved in mutualistic interactions with one another and with organisms belonging to all other groups of living organisms. Even though mutualistic relationships yield benefits for both species, the "evolutionary interests" of the interacting mutualists are never identical. A plant benefits by having its ova fertilized by a pollinator but it must pay for those services by providing rewards in the form of pollen and nectar. A plant could produce more seeds if it could attract visitors with lower rewards. The pollinator, on the other hand, visits flowers to find food and selects plants to visit on the basis of the quality and quantity of rewards offered. The actual amount of reward offered evolves as a compromise between the level that is best from the pollinator's perspective and what is best from the plant's perspective.

Interactions between plants and pollinators and plants and frugivores are among the most important and conspicuous of mutualistic interactions. Animal pollination has the advantage that pollen can be directed to appropriate sites because there is a "payment upon delivery" system in which the visitor is rewarded when it arrives at another flower of the same species it has just recently visited. Wind, which also disperses pollen and does so at no cost to the plant, nonetheless scatters pollen more or less randomly over the environment. Most of it drops on unsuitable substrates fairly close to the plant producing it. The major dispersers of pollen are mammals, primarily bats, birds, and insects. The number of plant species in an area is always much greater than the number of species of pollinators so that, on average, each species of pollinator visits many species of plants. There are places, however, such as the hot deserts of North America, where many species of bees visit just one or a few species of plants and have their life cycles precisely timed to the period when their particular plant species bloom. Most plants, however, can be pollinated by a wide variety of pollinators, which is why a single species of bee, the honey bee (*Apis mellifera*) can be used so successfully as a pollinator of crops over much of the world.

Fruits and frugivores are also not involved in close co-evolutionary relationships. Nearly all frugivores eat many different kinds of fruits and most plants are visited by many kinds of frugivores. Nonetheless, it is not unusual to find plants that depend primarily upon a single species of frugivore for dispersal of their seeds. An extreme case occurred on Mauritius Island in the Indian Ocean where the now extinct Dodo *(Raphus cucullatus)*, a large, flightless ground pigeon, was the only disperser of the fruits of the tree *Calvaria major*. *Calvaria* seeds failed to germinate for several hundred years following the extinction of the dodo, and the plant survived only because of the great longevity of the adults. Other means of inducing germination of the seeds have now been discovered.

Different groups of animals are most important dispersers of fruits in different geographical areas. In the American tropics, birds are the prime dispersers of fruits. South America is sometimes referred to as the "Bird Continent" because of the richness of its bird species, many of which are frugivores. In Africa, by contrast, mammals are much more important dispersers of fruit. Many species of African plants have very large fruits that drop to the ground where they are picked up by mammals up to the size of elephants. Many plants in Africa also bear their fruits on large branches where they are readily accessible to monkeys. Primates are also important dispersers of seeds in South America and Asia but their role is greater in Africa than elsewhere.

Many of the most spectacular and colorful birds of the world, such as quetzals, bellbirds, umbrella birds, cocks-of-the-rocks, toucans, hornbills, touracos, and birds of paradise, are primarily fruit eaters. These species have not only high esthetical value, they are also the most important dispersers of seeds of many trees that have large-seeded fruits that cannot be eaten by most of the smaller fruit-eating birds. Thus, their loss might well strongly affect the population dynamics of many species of trees in the tropical forests of the world.

The associations of animals with microorganisms are very important but less familiar because they are not obvious. Insects that eat plant tissues are involved in a rich variety of mutualistic relationships with microorganisms that help the insects digest the complex and often heavily defended tissues of plants. Herbivorous mammals have microorganisms in their guts that help them break down the large cellulose molecules of plant cell walls, molecules that are extremely resistant to chemical degradation. Indeed, nearly all multicellular animals are unable to digest cellulose by themselves and

Adult male Marine Iguana. Galapagos. Photograph by Elizabeth Orians.

must rely on mutualists in their guts.

Animals are involved with mutualistic associations with one another. Many birds feed around grazing mammals, catching insects flushed by the mammals. Some species of brightly colored small fishes and shrimp function as cleaners of the gills and teeth of larger fish. The cleaners have particular "stations" where they live and the fish to be cleaned visit these stations and adopt a special cleaning invitation posture.

Aesthetic Value of Animals

Animals play very important roles in the lives of people simply by being there to enjoy. We all feel a deep sense of affinity with the other organisms that have evolved on earth with us by the same processes that produced our own species. People spend vast sums of money to observe animals, study their behavior, or simply accumulate lists of what they have seen. This "biophilia" has been underestimated in the past as a contributor to the quality of human life, but today its importance is being more widely recognized, due in part to the increasing needs felt by people in urban settings for contacts with animals, both domestic and wild.

The utilitarian values of animals in the production of food and fiber, as beasts of burden, as sources of chemicals for industry and medicine, and as biological control agents are enormous and are destined to increase rather than decrease. Often the species with great utilitarian value are small and inconspicuous and do not, therefore, attract much attention. This is why large, spectacular species with high esthetic value are so important as symbols of our interdependence with other animals. As we attempt to preserve them, we set aside parks, reserves, and zoos and, in the process, we achieve

the preservation of many other species that enrich our lives in less obvious but no less important ways.

Catalogue of Investigations for Promising Students at Biosphere University

The enterprising student of animals studies *both* nature *and* books so that accumulated knowledge of humanity can be integrated with the motivating force of interacting with living animals. The best way to do this is to visit areas where natural communities of living organisms can still be found. Even though such areas are scattered and often under pressure for alternative uses, opportunities to study animals in these areas are good today because of the relative ease of travel and the existence of suitable accommodations in most areas. The larger vertebrates are the group that has been most reduced in both species and areas in which they occur as a result of human intervention, mostly shooting and habitat destruction. In the drier portions of the world, large grazing and browsing mammals formerly exerted major influences on patterns of vegetation in those areas. Therefore, visiting areas in which large mammals are still common is an important part of the education of biologists in today's world.

Lake Manyara National Park, Tanzania

This small park, which covers only 123 square miles, is nonetheless very diverse. Included in the park are the northern and western parts of the lake and adjacent slopes to the top of the Rift Valley. The Lake Manyara Hotel, situated on the rim of the valley wall, is an excellent place from which to explore the wet forests, acacia woodlands and grasslands. Large mammals found in the park include lions, leopards, elephants, black rhinoceros, Burchell's zebra, hippopotamus, giraffe, Coke's hartebeest, common waterbuck, Boho reedbuck, impala, and African buffalo. Bird life is especially rich. Thousands of flamingoes are often present on the lake and over 30 species of birds of prey have been found there. Lake Manyara National Park is 26 miles southwest of Arusha just beyond the village of Meo-wa-bu. In addition to accommodations at the hotel, there are some officially designated campgrounds near the park boundary.

Ngorongoro Crater Conservation Area, Tanzania

This important area of 22,500 square miles was established in 1959 to conserve the region's wildlife and to serve the interests of the Masai people who continue their long-term tradition of pastoralism in the area. The crater itself, one of the world's largest, is over nine miles in diameter, over 2,000 feet deep, and covers 102 square miles. The descent into the crater is negotiable only by four-wheel drive vehicles. The floor of the caldera is mostly grassland interspersed with fresh and brackish water lakes, swamps and two acacia woodlands. Large mammals are abundant inside the crater, including spotted hyena, cheetah, lion, leopard, African elephant, black rhinoceros, Burchell's zebra, hippopotamus, giant forest hog, warthog, giraffe, Coke's hartebeest, wildebeest, common waterbuck, impala, Thompson's and Grant's gazelles, bushbuck, eland and African buffalo. Birds are abundant and rich in species because of the varied habitat types found within the park. Accommodations are available at the Ngorongoro Crater Lodge on the rim of the crater and in designated campgrounds.

Serengeti National Park, Tanzania

This, the largest and best known of Tanzania's National Parks, covers over 5,600 square miles in the northern part of the country and is contiguous with the Masai-Mara Game Reserve in adjacent Kenya. The largest and most spectacular concentrations of large mammals found anywhere on earth live in the Serengeti, undergoing extensive annual migrations in which they follow the rains and the green grass they produce. These migrations take the herds into Kenya from June to September. May and early June are the best times to observe the animals on their northward migrations. The most abundant migratory mammals are wildebeest, Burchell's zebra and Thompson's gazelle. As might be expected, predators are also common. Serengeti is famous for its lions, leopards and hunting dogs. Accommodations are available at Seronera Lodge at an

African Buffalo. Photograph by Elizabeth Orians.

elevation of 5,000 feet, and at nine officially designated campsites in the park. There is an airstrip at Seronera. The drive from Arusha, where there is an international airport, is 198 miles.

Amboseli National Park, Kenya

This relatively small park, situated at the northern base of Kilimanjaro, which dominates the skyline, is one of the best places for observing large mammals and their seasonal movements. At the heart of the park are the lakes and swamps at the foot of Kilimanjaro which provide water during the dry season. At this time of year, which can be highly variable but is usually February-May and July-October, large herds of wildebeest, zebras, gazelles and elephants congregate in the lush marshlands of the park. When the rains fall, the animals fan out in all directions into the surrounding savannahs where they find ample pasturage and water for the duration of the rains. Amboseli is the best known of African parks ecologically because of a long series of studies by scientists from many countries. The park is reached easily by road from Nairobi, 150 miles away. Accommodations are available at one of several hotels at Ol Tukai village. There are also designated campgrounds. Much of the valley floor is open grassland but there are savannahs of acacias in several areas and some dense palm swamps.

Lake Nakuru National Park, Kenya

Lake Nakuru, a shallow alkaline lake about 24 square miles in area, is famous for its flamingoes and other water birds. The lake is flanked by marshes, acacia woodlands and hillsides covered with cactus-like Euphorbias. The park was established in 1960 as a bird sanctuary but there are large numbers of common waterbucks, Bohor reedbucks and many leopards. The cliffs surrounding the lake are excellent for viewing rock hyraxes and the powerful Verreaux's eagles which prey upon them. The park is easily reached by a trip just under 100 miles on paved roads from Nairobi. A road circles the lake, providing viewing of birds at a number of locations. The fever tree woodlands are excellent for observing the rich birdlife of the Rift Valley of Kenya. The water level of Lake Nakuru fluctuates in accordance with rainfall and during periods of unusually high water most of the flamingoes leave the lake. Even during those times, however, the park is well worth visiting because of the abundance of water birds that are always present.

Galapagos National Park, Ecuador

No place on earth has played a more prominent role in the development of the theory of natural selection than the Galapagos Islands. Located 600 miles off the coast of Ecuador, these relatively young oceanic islands are a marvel of both volcanic activity and evolution. Because of their isolation the islands have been colonized by a small number of species of animals and plants but many of those have undergone adaptive radiation on the islands to produce clusters of species. The most spectacular radiation has occurred among the finches of the subfamily Geospizinae which now number 13 species ranging from seed-crushing ground species with very large bills to slender-billed insect-eating species. The woodpecker finch, which uses thorns and spines to probe for insects in crevices in bark, is one of the few avian species to use a tool. Radiations have also occurred among the mockingbirds, lizards, snakes and tortoises. The marine vertebrates of the Galapagos are less unique but their abundance and tameness make for spectacular opportunities to observe and study their behavior and ecology. The most unusual among the sea birds is the endemic Swallow-tailed Gull, the only gull in the world that feeds nocturnally.

The Galapagos Islands can be visited by means of tours organized by a number of companies and on vessels ranging from small ones that accommodate less than 10 people to large luxury liners. All tour groups are accompanied by government-approved guides who are knowledgeable about the geology and natural history of the islands. Because of the vulnerability of these island ecosystems to invasions by foreign species, there are strict controls over importation of organisms from elsewhere and visitors are not allowed to spend the night on most places in the islands. At Puerto Ayora on Santa Cruz Island the Charles Darwin Research Station carries out research on the unique plants and animals of the islands and is engaged in attempts to remove foreign mammals that threaten the existence of some of the vulnerable native species of vertebrates.

Yellowstone National Park, Wyoming, USA

This, the first national park to be established in the United States, preserves a large ecosystem with all of its native predators except the grey wolf. In addition, the park provides opportunities to study many unusual geological features such as geysers, mudpots, hot rivers, and rugged canyons. Most of the birds typical of the mountains of western North America are found in the park and its lakes have breeding colonies of the rare Trumpeter swan and white pelican. The size of the ecosystem in which the park is situated is made much greater because of adjacent parks and national forests into which many of the large mammals travel at some times of the year. There

Copulating pair of tortoises on the rim of Volcan Alcedo.
Photograph by Elizabeth Orians.

are many hotels and campgrounds in the park.

National Bison Range, Moiese, Montana, USA

This range, operated by the United States Fish and Wildlife Service since 1908, is located along Highway 93, 37 miles north of Missoula. Its rolling hills are dominated by grassland, but there are deciduous trees along the streams and open forests of pine and Douglas fir on the higher hills. A self-guided nature tour 19 miles in length is available to visitors June 1 through September 30. The range features bison, white- tailed and mule deer, elk, bighorn sheep and pronghorns, as well as many small mammals and birds of the region. It is an excellent place to observe large mammals in their natural settings. A visit in September when bison are in the rut is especially exciting.

Everglades National Park, Florida, USA

Extensive marshlands, punctuated with small patches of subtropical woody vegetation, and extensive mangrove islands make this large park a superb one for viewing and studying the wildlife of tropical wetlands. Waterbirds such as herons, egrets, ibises, and spoonbills, are the major attraction of the park but reptiles, particularly alligators, are also conspicuous. The movements and feeding behavior of many of the animals are related to seasonal changes in rainfall and water levels in the marshes of the park. A number of species of birds breed in late winter when the falling water levels of the dry season trap fishes in shrinking ponds where they are readily captured. Such fluctuating water levels are typical of marshlands of most of the hotter parts of the earth and

the Everglades are an excellent place in which to study these important processes. A number of trails lead to excellent viewing places where the birds and their varied foraging tactics can be observed.

Parque Nacional Braulio Carillo, Costa Rica

This magnificent rain forest park extends from the summit of Volcan Barba, one of the high volcanoes of the backbone of Costa Rica, down to the adjacent Atlantic lowlands. A new extension, the Zonal Protectora, will join the park with the field station of the Organization for Tropical Studies at La Selva, one of the most important research and teaching stations in the tropics. A newly built road takes the observer directly from San Jose, the capital of Costa Rica, to the park. Rainfall is very high and only during the brief and unpredictable dry season in February and March are sunny days at all common. The park, together with its extension to La Selva, preserves a block of rain forest in which seasonal altitudinal movements of birds and butterflies, a phenomenon increasingly being recognized as important in tropical regions occurs. Courses taught by the Organization for Tropical Studies have introduced hundreds of students to the tropics.

Heron Island, Great Barrier Reef, Australia

An impressive mixture of drowned hills and coastlines and over 2,500 coral reefs extends for 1,200 miles along the coast of Queensland. A number of resorts on the Great Barrier Reef can accommodate visitors. Heron Island, one of those, is easily reached from Gladstone by helicopter or, for the more adventurous, by boat. Heron Island, as is typical of coral islands, rises only a few feet above sea level and is covered with dense vegetation. The University of Queensland operates a marine biological station on the island. Coral reefs are among the richest of biological communities and are unusual in that the organisms that form the complex structure of the community are animals rather than plants. The growth forms of corals are extremely diverse and the adaptive significance of those forms is just now becoming understood. In addition to the corals, the reef abounds with clams, sea cucumbers, starfish, sea urchins, limpets, chitons, nudibranchs (sea slugs), and about 850 species of fish. There is no more exciting environment on earth nor one in which there remains so much yet to be learned.

Punta Tombo, Chubut, Argentina

A small projection on the bleak coast of Patagonia, Punta Tombo is famous as a mainland breeding site of over 500,000 Magellanic Penguins. Also present and breeding are skuas, gulls, cormorants and terns. Sheathbills and Giant Petrels patrol the shores for carrion, and the offshore waters harbor sea lions, seals, and whales. The accessibility of Punta Tombo by road from Trelew, a city with good air service from Buenos Aires, and its mainland location, make the area excellent for observing sea bird behavior. The adjacent dry deserts are home of guanacos and foxes. Scientists are carrying out detailed studies on the biology of the penguins at Punta Tombo under the auspices of the New York Zoological Society.

Parque Nacional Aguaro-Guariquito, Venezuela

The extensive llanos of Venezuela, flooded during the rainy season and baked dry under the tropical sun in the dry season, are one of the world's most remarkable environments. A representative mosaic of llanos communities, from open grasslands, to permanent lakes, forests, and riparian communities, is preserved in this important park. Established in 1974, it covers 569,000 hectares. An excellent representation of the unusually rich fauna of the basins of the Amazon and Orinoco Rivers is found in this park, including species of electric eels. Also characteristic of the aquatic environments of the park are large numbers of capybaras, the largest living rodent. Among other interesting mammals, are several species of monkeys, giant anteaters, giant armadillos, pumas and jaguars. Bird life is extremely rich. Among the more striking species are spoonbills, scarlet ibises, and hoatzins, the remarkable cuckoos whose nestlings have claws on their wings and are able to crawl through the branches of shrubs at a very young age. As might be expected in such a region, reptiles, especially caimans and crocodiles, and amphibians abound. The park is not yet well developed, due to its newness and large size, but it is easily reached on its east side by a paved road Las Mercedes-Cabruta. Accommodations are available in the towns of Calabozo, El Calvario and Cazorla. Research stations and visitor accommodations are being planned.

Zoos

Observing and studying animals in their natural habitats usually provides the most satisfying experiences. Nonetheless, zoos have changed dramatically in recent decades from their former role of simply showing as many animals as possible, to one in which animals are exhibited in natural settings. They provide excellent opportunities for the study of the behavior of animals that are very difficult to observe in the wild. Indeed, most modern zoos actively encourage the study of the behavior of captive animals and are involved in breeding programs to aid in the conservation of rare and endangered species.

The tradition of showing a great variety of animals continues in many of the larger zoos of today, even though animals are housed very differently than they were formerly. Some of the newer zoos, particularly those associated with smaller metropolitan areas, do not attempt to exhibit a wide variety of animals. Rather, they specialize on particular kinds of animals or they exhibit primarily species found in the local region, sometimes using the natural habitats of the region as the background for their exhibits. I first discuss some mainline zoos and then mention some of the more interesting specialized collections that are worthy of visits. Of necessity, this list represents a selection from a much larger list of zoos, many of which should be visited by anyone travelling to the cities in which they are located.

MAINLINE ZOOS

Brookfield Zoo, Brookfield, Illinois, U.S.A.

This large, modern zoo, first opened in 1934, is easily reached from Chicago by car, train and bus. It exhibits animals primarily in natural settings. Especially interesting are the tropical forest exhibits and the Seven Seas marine mammal exhibits.

San Diego Zoo, San Diego, California, U.S.A.

One of the world's largest zoos, its location permits tropical species to be displayed out of doors all year. The zoo features over 1,300 species of animals and 1,800 species of plants. There are two large walk through aviaries with rich collections of birds. The active captive breeding program is a very successful one.

St. Louis Zoological Park, St. Louis, Missouri, U.S.A.

Opened in 1915, this is one of the most popular zoos in the world. It features nearly 100 species of mammals, nearly 300 species of birds, 140 species of reptiles, 40 species of amphibians, and over 100 species of fishes.

New York Zoological Park (Bronx Zoo), New York City, U.S.A.

New York Zoological Park (Bronx Zoo), New York City, U.S.A.

This large zoo, which opened in 1899, has one of the largest collections of mammals, birds and reptiles in the world. The spacious locality has allowed much modernization of the enclosures. Special exhibits feature African Plains, Wild Asia and a valley filled with exhibits of birds.

Regents Park Zoo, London, England

A classical mainline zoo featuring over 1,400 species of animals. Facilities have been extensively modernized during recent decades.

Whipsnade Park, Dunstable Downs, England

Opened in 1931 in rolling country 30 miles from London, this modern zoo features animals in semi-natural habitats.

Berlin Zoo, West Berlin, West Germany

Almost totally destroyed in 1944-1945, this great zoo has been rebuilt to again become the largest one in Europe. On exhibit are 250 species of mammals, 750 species of birds, almost 300 species of reptiles, 70 species of amphibians and nearly 800 species of fishes. Because of the recency of its construction, all facilities are modern.

Tiergarten Schonbrunn, Vienna, Austria

The unusual buildings of this zoo were a gift of the Emperor Franz Josef to Empress Maria Theresa in 1752. About 750 species of animals are exhibited and there is a very good aquarium.

Zoologischer Garten, Frankfurt-am-Main, West Germany

This important zoo was first opened in 1858 but most of the current buildings, which house an excellent collection of about 900 species of animals, are of recent construction. Excellent viewing conditions.

Zoologischer Garten, Basel, Switzerland

A zoo dating from 1874 but mostly with new buildings, it is one of the world's best zoos for breeding of unusual animals in captivity. It houses about 450 species.

Parque Zoologico de Barcelona, Barcelona, Spain

This, one of the most popular zoos in the world, houses about 350 species of animals in modern buildings in an excellent location.

Melbourne Zoo, Melbourne, Australia

This zoo was started in 1857 to encourage importation of foreign species into Australia. Fortunately, attitudes have changed and Australia now has very strict laws prohibiting the importation of non-native species. Consequently, most of the extensive bird collection features Australian species. There are extensive plantings of native trees and shrubs among which the animals are exhibited. The great flight aviary simulated three different Australian environments (wetlands, scrublands and rain forest).

Taronga Zoo, Sydney, Australia

This zoo, begun in 1881, houses the best collection of Australian birds in the world. It also has an excellent aquarium into which water is pumped from Sydney harbor. Excellent views of Sydney harbor and the city are afforded from the zoo grounds.

SPECIALIZED ZOOS

Arizona-Sonora Desert Museum, Tucson, Arizona, U.S.A.

This small zoo exhibits over 200 species of animals and 300 species of plants, nearly all native to the southern Arizona region. Extensive use is made of native vegetation for displaying animals in their natural habitats. The zoo, located 14 miles west of Tucson, also features an Earth Sciences Center which helps visitors understand the geology of the region.

Jersey Wildlife Preservation Trust, Channel Islands, Britain

This is the first zoo established specifically to build up breeding groups of endangered species for the purpose of aiding re-establishment programs in the wild. The collections feature 30 species of mammals, mainly primates, about 40 species of birds, especially parrots and pheasants, and about 20 species of endangered reptiles. Success in breeding rare species in captivity has been excellent.

Oceanographical Museum, Monaco

Founded in 1910, this museum deals with all aspects of undersea exploration, but also features an excellent marine aquarim.

Wassenaar Zoo, The Hague, The Netherlands

This small zoo specializes in birds, especially song birds. Large walk-through aviaries house these excellent collections under ideal conditions for observation.

Askaniya-Nova Zoopark, Ukraine, U.S.S.R.

This zoo, which is spread out over 4,053 acres, making it the largest zoo in the world, specializes in native ungulates, and is also involved with acclimitization of antelopes.

Wildfowl Trust's Waterfowl Gardens, New Grounds, Slimbridge, Gloucestershire, England

This is the most comprehensive collection of aquatic birds in the world and is also a sanctuary where thousands of ducks and geese spend the winter.

Western Plains Zoo, Dubbo, New South Wales, Australia

This modern zoo, completely without bars, was opened in 1977. It displays animals from six continents in 460 acres of landscaped, open-range, moated areas. Excellent viewing.

Books

The literature on animals is extensive and growing rapidly. The following books are those that give general accounts of species in the major taxonomic groups. Local and regional books exist for most geographical areas and there are many books dealing with special topics such as behavior, ecology, morphology and taxonomy.

General

On the Origin of Species, by C. Darwin, 1859. The book that caused people to think about evolution is still worth reading.

The Growth of Biological Thought, by E. Mayr, Belknap Press, Cambridge, 19892.

A Wealth of Wild Species, by N. Myers, Westview Press, Boulder, Colorado, 1983.

The Primary Source. Tropical Forests and Our Future, by N. Myers, W.W. Norton & Co., New York, 1984.

Vertebrates

Morphology and Biology of Reptiles, by A. Bellairs and C.B. Cox, Academic Press, New York, 1976.

The Life of Sharks, by P. Budker, Columbia University Press, New York, 1971.

Reptiles of the World, by C. Gans, Bantam Books, New York, 1975.

The Life of Fishes, by N.B. Marshall, World Publ. Co., Cleveland, 1966.

Fishes of the World, by J.S. Nelson, John Wiley & Sons, New York, 1976.

The Encyclopedia of Birds, C.M. Perrins and A.L.A. Middleton (Editors), Facts on File Publications, New York, 1985.

Living Mammals of the World, by I.T. Sanderson, John Wiley & Son, New York, 1967.

Mammals of the World (Third Edition), by E.P. Walker, John Hopkins Univ. Press, Baltimore, 1976. (Two volumes)

Vertebrate Natural History, by M.F. Willson, Saunders College Publishing, Philadelphia, 1984 (621 Pages).

Vertebrates: Their Structure and Life, by W.B. Yapp, Oxford University Press, Oxford, 1965.

Invertebrates

Invertebrate Zoology (Third Edition), by R.D. Barnes, Saunders, Philadelphia, 1974.

Introduction to Insect Biology and Diversity, by H.V. Daly, J.T. Doyen and P.R. Ehrlich, McGraw-Hill, New York, 1978.

Insects on Plants. Community Patterns and Mechanisms, by D.R. Strong, J.H. Lawton and T.R.E. Southwood, Harvard University Press, Cambridge, 1984.

Evolution

Ghillean T. Prance

A struggle for existence inevitably follows from the high rate at which all organic beings tend to increase...Hence, as more individuals are produced than can possibly survive, there must in every case be a struggle for existence, either one individual with another of the same species, or with the individuals of distinct species, or with the physical conditions of life. CHARLES DARWIN

Just one hundred and twenty five years have passed since Charles Darwin scandalized Victorian England by announcing the theory of evolution in 1858. Yet evolution is the basis for the diversity of life in the biosphere in which we live. Although the wife of the then Bishop of Worcester reflected the thoughts of many people when she said "Descended from the apes! My dear, let us hope that it is not true, but if it is, let us pray that it will not become generally known," evolution could not be hidden because it is the mechanism by which primordial life has developed into the wonderful array of plants and animals which we know today.

Darwin was by no means the first person to suggest that species were changeable and not immutable, but he and his contemporary, British biologist Alfred Russel Wallace were the first people to discover the mechanism of evolution which they termed natural selection. In 1808, fifty years before, French naturalist Jean Baptiste Lamarck asserted that all life forms arose by a continuous process of gradual modification from generation to generation, i.e., transformism of species not immutability. Lamarck, however, believed that this came about by acquired characteristics. That is, that new traits develop in an organism because of a need in the environment and are then transmitted to its offspring. For example, there was a need for the giraffe to reach higher to browse in the trees and therefore its neck stretched and this was then passed on to subsequent generations.

Darwin, as a result of his voyage around the world as naturalist on *HMS Beagle* in 1831, and Wallace, as a result of his travels in Amazonia and the East Indies Archipelago, came up with a different theory: that changes or mutations occur in any organism and that any that cause it to be better adapted to the environment survive. This concept of the survival of the fittest is the basis of evolution. The two pioneers of evolution were both fine observers of nature, and through their understanding of life and of the interactions between organisms they both independently came to the same conclusions.

They realized that organisms produce a far greater number of reproductive cells than mature individuals as can be seen by the quantity of seeds produced by an oak tree. The world would be overrun if all acorns developed into mature trees! They also observed that the number of individuals of each species remain more or less constant over a long period, which means a high mortality rate for reproductive cells or of young individuals. Since all individuals of any species are not identical, they concluded that some variations succeed better than others. There must be a great competition for survival between the excess of juveniles, and those individuals that are better adapted to the environmental conditions will survive. Thus an organism will gradually change in response to environment.

As Darwin travelled he was able to observe such things as the finches on the Galapagos Islands that differ slightly from island to island yet are more similar to each other than to other finches. They are also closely related to the finches of the adjacent mainland of South America. He observed the ways in which the finches had adapted to the different food resources and niches available to them and began to think about the reasons for this.

Darwin understood that variations which arose were transmitted to offspring, but he did not work out the mechanism by which they were transferred. That is explained by the science of genetics which began with pioneer work with garden peas of the Austrian Augustine monk Gregor Mendel, but not really developed until the early twentieth century when Dutch botanist Hugo de Vries explained mutation or the sudden occurrence of well-defined and inheritable variation. Today we know

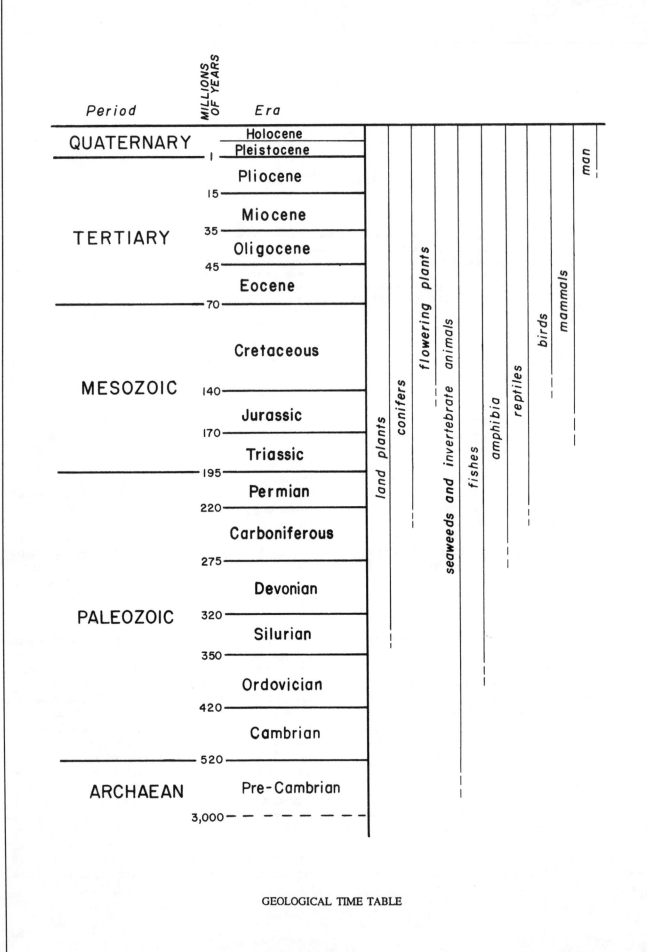

GEOLOGICAL TIME TABLE

much more about genetics, the genes which carry the message of inheritance and the structure of DNA of which the gene bearing chromosomes are made. Through its unique helical structure, DNA can divide into two through the process of mitosis or meiosis and thus pass on the characteristics from parent to offspring.

The story of Darwin and Wallace and later evolutionary scientists and controversies which surround them is recent history and has filled many books. The excitement is that evolution began when life was created over three thousand million years ago in the Pre-Cambrian era either in the sea or, as most recently proposed, in clay on land. Since that time the original primordial protoplasmic mass has evolved through many long extinct forms into the plants and animals which we know today. The competition for survival has been great and so organisms have managed to adapt and fill every niche in the biosphere where it is possible for life to exist. Thus, today we have living creatures adapted to inhospitable environments such as fish that inhabit the depth of the seas, algae that live in the rocks of Antarctica, plants which occur in the most arid desert regions, sightless fish that pass their entire lives in constantly dark underground caves, or even the recently discovered Rhodophyta crustose coralline algae that have been found living at 268 meter depth off the coast of San Salvadore Island in the Bahamas.

The rather incomplete fossil record shows us that the process of evolution has been dynamic and continuous throughout the geological eras. Cataclysmic events may have caused leaps and bounds in evolution and extinctions, but where there is life there is the potential for mutation, change and development. We have fossils of transitional forms between fishes and amphibia such as *Ichthyostegia,* amphibia and reptiles *(Seymouria)* and the famous *Archaeopterix* between reptiles and birds. The latter with its feathers and a reptile-like tail shows that birds were derived from the reptiles.

The species known as man *(Homo sapiens)* is a recent arrival on the scene. Life arose over 3,500 million years ago and the origin of man is less than 3 million years ago. Thus if we encapsulate life into a 24 hour clock, there was no sign of man or his ape-like ancestors after 23 hours. At that time, 145 million years ago, the world had primitive land plants, fishes, amphibia and reptiles and the mammals had just arrived on the scene. Man arose within the last 3 minutes of our clock showing that the organism which now dominates the biosphere is indeed a new-comer.

Man's origin can be traced back to the small insect-eating mammals from which the primates were derived. The tree-shrews are the most closely related living survivors of these animals and the lemurs also belong to the Prosimians. From these the monkeys and apes arose

and man evolved from the apes with whom he still shares the same blood group.

Today scientists are learning much more about both genetics and evolution and we are learning how life of the biosphere is made up both through detailed laboratory studies of genes and the potential of genetic engineering and from field observations of organisms living together. It is such field studies that show us how different organisms strive to outcompete each other and also use each other for their mutual advantage. The whole biosphere is intimately linked together through this network of interactions, through who eats who, through pollination of flowers and dispersal of seeds and through an array of chemical defenses to avoid predation. One of the most exciting evidences of evolution is that of the number of different organisms that have evolved in close dependence on one another. This phenomenon of co-evolution includes many of the features that Darwin and Wallace observed such as the pollination of orchids. But recent work has shown a myriad of closely co-evolved relationships especially in the species-diverse tropical rain forest. Darwin found a Madagascan orchid *(Angraecum sesquipedale)* with a spur on the flower which was 11-1/2 inches long. Although no such moths were known at the time, Darwin predicted that one would be found with a tongue of the same length as the spur of the flower so that it could reach the nectar at the bottom of the spur. The long-tongued moth pollinator *(Zanthopan morgani* forma *praedicta)* was discovered decades after Darwin's prediction and the form was named for that.

Many other marvellous relationships of plants with closely co-evolved pollinators could be given such as the scarab beetle that pollinates the Royal water lily of the Amazon and gets trapped inside the flower for 18 hours.

Another fine demonstration of evolution is mimicry where one noxious species has a harmless look-alike. This is common in butterflies and moths where some foul-tasting ones are exactly copied by other often unrelated species. The predators learn to avoid a certain pattern of butterfly and the harmless good tasting species is safe also because it cannot be distinguished from the poisonous one by the bird predators. It is easy to see how natural selection would favor the harmless butterfly that most resembled the noxious one. That is why there is a true coral snake that is deadly poisonous and the false coral that is harmless. This phenomenon was first described in 1862 by another great Amazonian explorer naturalist, H.W. Bates, and is consequently called Batesian mimicry. He proposed the theory of mimicry shortly after he had read Darwin's *Origin of the Species.* Evolutionary theory enabled Bates to interpret the results of his field observations in the Amazon. About twenty years later, German naturalist Fritz Muller pointed out that frequently two distasteful species also can converge in appearance for protection and this is now known as Mullerian mimicry. In this case the cooperative education of predators by two species would require fewer deaths of each species.

Camouflage is another example of evolution. There are so many insects that look like leaves, the bark of the tree upon which they rest or like a twig.

The Industrial Revolution of nineteenth-century Britain affords us an example of how camouflage can occur. The peppered moth was a light-gray color with a pattern of darker spots and stripes.. It blended well with the bark of birch trees and was little preyed upon. In the 1850's the new industries of Midland England changed the color of the tree barks with their smoke pollution. The light-colored moths began to stand out well against the background of the dark trees and became an easy target for predatory birds. Fortunately for the peppered moth, there was a tendency for occasional individuals to be a darker color. This phenomenon of melanism, as it is called, produced moths that were well hidden against the new background of soot-polluted trees. In time the whole population of the peppered moth changed its color to a darker variety because now the darker ones survived while the light ones were eaten by the birds. For a while it was possible to find only dark moths. Today, with recent cleanup of pollution, the tide is turning and it is again common to see light peppered moths well disguised against unpolluted tree trunks. This changeover has been in effect a laboratory to demonstrate the evolution of camouflage in insects and the powerful effect of predator selection.

These few examples should help to show that evolution is a response to pressure. It makes use of the fact that each individual is slightly different and favors those which can survive best. This dynamic process is continually occurring wherever there is competition or environmental change. For example, a natural change to a drier climate will favor individuals that are better adapted to drought, perhaps those with the deepest roots or thickest or hairiest leaves that will reduce water loss. The biosphere in which we live and the organisms in it are not static. The change in species is still taking place from generation to generation in response to any environmental changes to which it is subjected.

Places to Learn About Evolution

The American Museum of Natural History
Central Park West
New York, NY, USA

The British Museum -- Natural History
Cromwell Road
London, UK

The Desert Dome
312 Houston Street
Fort Worth, Texas, USA

Field Museum of Natural History
Lake Shore Drive
Chicago, Illinois, USA

Museum National d'Histoire Naturelle
Rue de Buffon
Paris, France

The Smithsonian Institution
Washington D.C., USA

Travel to See the Products of Evolution

Amazon River: The locality of Bates and Wallace.

Australia: The isolated marsupial fauna.

Galapagos Islands: The finches and turtles observed by Darwin.

Society Expeditions remain the best way to travel to all these places. See Tours, Travels and Adventures for details.

Bibliography of Further Reading on Evolution

Just Before the Origin: Alfred Russel Wallace's Theory of Evolution, by John Langdon Brooks, Columbia Univ. Press, New York, 1984. The best modern summary of Wallace's contribution to the theory of evolution. A very fair assessment of the importance of the life and work of Wallace.

Animal Species and Their Evolution (Revised Edition), by A.J. Cain, Hillary House, New York, 1966.

The Evolution and Classification of Flowering Plants, by Arthur Cronquist, Houghton Mifflin, Boston, 1968. A good review of the evolutionary classification of flowering plants giving the reasons behind the Cronquist system of classification.

On the Tendency of Species to Form Varieties; and On the Perpetuation of Varieties and of Species by Natural Means of Selection (1858) (Reprinted in: Darwin, C. *Evolution by Natural Selection*), by Charles Darwin and Alfred Russel Wallace,

Cambridge, 1958. This is the paper that started it all. It was read before the Linnean Society of London in 1858. It is interesting that evolution was first presented jointly in the names of Darwin and Wallace, but that Darwin gained most of the credit.

On the Origin of the Species by Means of Natural Selection, by Charles Darwin, 1859. First edition by J. Murray, London. Many subsequent reprints, for example Avenel 1979 edition, Crown Publishers, Inc., New York. Once Darwin and Wallace's paper was read to the Linnean Society, Darwin rushed to produce this full-length book to present the reasoning behind his theory of evolution. Today this book still makes fascinating reading and is full of biological facts about plants and animals that showed what an acute observer of nature Darwin was.

Evolution. Essays on Aspects of Evolutionary Biology, by G.R. De Beer, Clarendon Press, Oxford, 1938.

Embryos and Ancestors (Reprint 1971), by Gavin De Beer, Clarendon Press, Oxford, 1958.

Atlas of Evolution, by Gavin De Beer, Nelson, London, 1964.

Genetics and the Origin of Species (Reprint 1982), by T. Dobzhansky, Columbia Univ. Press, New York, 1937. This book by the father of modern genetics was the first synthesis of evolutionary systematics and experimental genetics. This book finally linked convincingly the theory of evolution and genetic mechanisms by which it functions.

Evolution, by T. Dobzhansky, F.J. Ayala, L. Stebbins and J.W. Valentine, W.H. Freeman, San Francisco, 1977.

The Process of Evolution, by Paul R. Ehrlich and R.W. Holm, McGraw-Hill, New York, 1974.

The Genetical Theory of Natural Selection, by R.A. Fisher, Clarendon Press, Oxford, 1930.

Mendelism and Evolution (8th Edition), by E.B. Ford, Methuen, London, 1965.

Ecological Genetics (3rd Edition), by E.B. Ford, Chapman & Hall, London, 1971. This book helped develop the relationship between genetics and ecology, the basis for modern population biology. This is a fascinating well-written account of ecological genetics.

Coevolution, D.J. Futuyma and M. Slatkin (Editors), Sinauer Associates, Sunderland, Massachusetts, 1983.

Coevolution of Animals and Plants, by L.E. Gilbert and P.H. Raven, Univ. Texas Press, Austin, Texas, 1975. This book brought together the recently emphasized subject of the co-evolution of plants and animals. It explains how the pollinators and the plants which they pollinated have evolved together and many other examples from modern field biology such as mimicry and dispersal biology.

The Causes of Evolution, by J.B.S. Haldane, Longmans Greene & Co., London, 1932.

Evolution in Action, by Julian S. Huxley, London, 1953.

Evolution As A Process, by J.S. Huxley, A.C. Hardy and E.B. Ford, Allen & Unwin, London, 1954. An excellent explanation of the process of evolution by three of Britain's leading experts of evolution and ecological genetics.

Darwin's Finches, by D. Lack, Cambridge Univ. Press, Cambridge, 1947.

Philosophie Zoologique, by J.D. de Lamarck, Paris, 1808. In this treatise Lamarck expounded on the mutability of species and his theory of evolution through the transmission of acquired characteristics from one generation to the next.

Evolution of the Brain and Intelligence, by H.J. Jenison, Academic Press, New York and London, 1973.

The Species Problem, by Ernst Mayr, Amer. Assoc. Adv. Sci., Washington, 1957.

Systematics and the Origin of Species (Reprint 1982), by Ernst Mayr, Columbia Univ. Press, New York, 1942. Although systematics began to accept and apply evolutionary theory directly after Darwin's '*Origin*', this book was a landmark publication that showed how systematic data about species are consistent with the principles of genetics. The nature of a species began to become known and the science of population genetics was born.

Evolution and the Diversity of Life. Selected Essays, by Ernst Mayr, Belknap Press, Cambridge, Massachusetts, 1976.

A Synthesis of Evolutionary Theory, by H.H. Ross, Prentice-Hall, Englewood Cliffs, New Jersey, 1962.

Understanding Evolution, by H.H. Ross, Prentice-Hall, Englewood Cliffs, New Jersey, 1966.

Tempo and Mode: In Evolution, by G.G. Simpson, Columbia Univ. Press, new York, 1944. This book along with those of Dobzhansky (1937) and Mayr (1942) was one of the early syntheses of evolutionary theory that showed the relevance of modern genetics.

The Major Features of Evolution, by G.G. Simpson, Simon & Schuster, New York, 1953.

Splendid Isolation, by G.G. Simpson, Yale Univ. Press, New Haven, 1980. This is a most readable account about the isolation of South America as a large island continent for many millions of years. The result was the evolution of many animals that are different from the rest of the world. This is one of the most fascinating accounts of the role and value of paleontology, the study of fossils, of many extinct animals.

Variation and Evolution in Plants, by G.L. Stebbins, Columbia Univ. Press, New York, 1950.

Contributions to the Theory of Natural Selection, by Alfred Russel Wallace, London, 1870.

The Geographical Distribution of Animals: With a Study of the Relations of Living and Extinct Faunas as Elucidating the Past Changes of the Earth's Surface, by Alfred Russel Wallace, Harper Brothers, New York, 1876.

A Narrative of Travels on the Amazon and Rio Negro, by Alfred Russel Wallace, Ward, Lock & Bowden, London, 1895. This is one of the classic nineteenth century natural history books on the Amazon. Since Wallace's observations there led him towards the formulation of evolutionary theory this is a particularly significant book in the history of evolution.

Modes of Speciation, by M.J.D. White, Freeman, San Francisco, 1978.

Cultures

Memes, Themes, Scenes and Dreams...

Peter Riecks-Marlowe

A culture represents as much organically-grown inherited
information, acquired by selection, as a species of
animal. KONRAD LORENZ

"Culture is the sea in which the human fish swims." This phrase pithily describes the essence of the phenomenon culture, a key to the approach under which we could possibly understand it, and the challenges and paradoxes awaiting the budding apprentice in culturology. Apprentices we might term all of us, for the attempt to understand culture from the point of view of biosphere can only be undertaken now that we are beginning to understand our planet as a total system. The study of culture throws light upon the mind itself, for as Konrad Lorenz so aptly put it, "The human mind is a supra-individual phenomenon" or, in the words of Edward T. Hall, "... human mind is internalized culture." It is, in the meantime, well-established that the evolution of human cultures is a process structurally identical, though on a different level, and therefore analogous, to that of biological evolution. Eric Erickson coined the term, "pseudo-speciation" for a Darwinian approach to the evolution of culture. Thinkers as diverse as Lorenz, Skinner, Dawkins, and Erickson have acknowledged the power of this concept to bring science to the cultural field, as it had before to the biological.

The process of "cultural-speciation", which we shall use instead of "pseudo-speciation", explains the first basic difficulty presenting itself to an observer of culture. While it might be relatively simple though dangerous to break through and explore the taboos of culture, totems may be much more significant in preventing us from seeing the real motivations and basic assumptions of the repertoire of *creencias* composing a culture. Ortega Y. Gasset used creencias to signify those firm beliefs each man as part of a culture possesses about parts of reality. Ortega puts it precisely: these creencias are not ideas that we have but ideas that we are. The creencias of any given culture at any point in time and space may be so unconscious to the conditioned individual that they may never even be formulated, expressed or acknowledged.

The secondary difficulty deriving from this is that each methodology devised for the study of culture (even given that the methodologist has striven with all his/her might to cancel cultural bias), is ultimately part of and derived from culture, possessing its own set of creencias (e.g., objective physical science, and its creencia experimental approach), or idealistic/materialistic philosophies and their creencia of coherent systems. The very nature of culture may defeat devising an objective methodology for again, as Ortega Y. Gasset puts it, creencias are a repertoire of a given culture at a given time/space intersection and this repertoire may not now or ever possess a logical structure; its parts may not fit one another, they can contradict one another. Each cultural-species like a biological species, must be seen as a unique history striving to adapt to and gain energetic advantages from an ever-changing environment. How long a given culture will last, and if it disappears, leaves a descendant(s) behind, remains as problematic as the fate of chimpanzee, redwood and syphilis.

In the following section I will describe basic approaches to culturology and their strong points and evident short-comings. I urge the reader to consider the quoted books and authors as basic tools for conceptualization; each one is a legitimate method in its own right and can be applied to all cultures that the biosphere contains. That they each have limitations should not deter their use any more than the biologist inhibits himself from using in turn chemistry, physics, genetics, or anatomy to study his species.

As the key to this new approach to culturology, those of us engaged in the task use the idea of *meme*, first adumbrated by Richard Dawkins in his book *The Selfish Gene*, as the culture-species' equivalent of gene.

Cultures

Memes, materially manifested building blocks of culture: postures, tones, phonemes, gestures, movements, colors, weaves, substances, rhythms, objects, spaces, foods, habits, move through time (history of a culture), space (meme transferral from one cultural-species to another, memetics developed long before genetics), energy (pointing the index finger varies greatly in the power that it holds in different culture-species), and, of course, some memes disappear and others are mutated into being.

Carrying forward the study of the meme, we found blocks of related, attracted, or opposing memes to organize, or cluster, into larger units, *themes*. Each culture-species studied then proceeds to provide *scenes* to enact the recurrent drama of the clash of great themes.

Finally scenes are organized into the highest unit of dramas, *dreams,* or rituals determining or at least pervading the world-view (the Weltanschaung), the entelechy, of a culture-species.

These dramas, dreams, or rituals may be tangibly expressed in an architectural *Now* as in the landscaping of the entire Chinese culture, or the ancient Egyptian, or it may take centuries of time to act out the scenes that no one without initiation or vision can witness: from such a culture-species viewpoint, a World War may appear as but one scene in the pursuit of its innermost dream.

The works of authors so diverse as Frazer, Mircea Eliade, Elias Canetti and Claude Levi-Strauss and, to a lesser extent, Edward T. Hall, typify what may be called the comparative-structural approach to culture-species. They trace great memes, themes, scenes and dreams through ages and across space. Such an approach advantageously provides us with the big picture, the overview, lets us see that the same cultural building blocks are or can be almost universally deployed, and makes us actively doubt our own cultural species' universality. As to its limits, this approach pretends too easily to contain *the* answer (and has been quite virulently attacked for doing so), seductively luring us into glowing pictures of a grand scheme of relationship or an underlying causal connection where in reality they be related by only chance, mutation, necessity and adaption. Still, the short-comings of this method spur us toward an exact tracing of cultural migration and relation and toward the goal of eventually realizing a transformational cultural grammar.

Ruth Benedict's *Patterns of Culture* stands well for what I would term the classic Anglo-Saxon school of anthropology. The method of observation and description of habits, ritual and belief lets the observed culture stand out alive like a clearly-lighted street fair, risky generalization seems to be avoided; but this method implicitly imposes a tribal scale culture to be the only workable object of such studies; a larger phenomenon, like "Western culture", can only be touched by inference and gradual circumspection. The general short-coming of this method lies in its "a-historicity". Not only is the object of this school of thought more often than not a small culture which, in itself, has little historic dynamism, but its very method tends to avoid history. The described cultures therefore sharply stand out, like glaring totem poles, cruelly lit up to the finest detail, yet strangely wooden and inaccessible, a museum of rare cultural-species, a stuffed wombat next to an encased monarch butterfly, taken into the great theme of North American culture, *things* and their acquisition. Furthermore, seeming contradictions between cultural patterns and ecological adaption seem never sufficiently open to question or reconciliation. Epistemologically, the split individual-society (culture) cannot be satisfactorily explained; this approach does not consider normative processes as important as averaging ones. However, this method teaches one photographic precision on memes and themes. In about roughly 50 pages of *Beyond Freedom and Dignity*, B.F. Skinner, exponent of the school of behaviorist psychology, studies culture as the way to do memes. Describing meme transmission as a positive-negative reinforcement conditioning-process and banning words like "idea", "value", "spirit", "group-mind" from any "scientific" investigation of culture he very soberly reminds us of the fact that there is no study of higher systems which must not ultimately face the acid-test of being checked by a method of thinking based on the assumption that truths can only be expressed/stated via quantity and fact. This successful reduction of culturation processes to the level of learning by maze-running rats obviously does not take into account the synergistic properties of systems. It makes clear, however, how important the process of ensuring meme distribution throughout each cell of the culture-species is in the struggle for survival of each culture-species variation.

At the opposite level of complexity of Skinner on the thinkers' scale, we find the cultural historians & philosophers describing culture in terms of value and idea systems moving through time and space, that is dreams, drama and ritual. An excellent compilation of some of the outstanding exponents of this method (from Herodotus to Voltaire to Gasset) is Karl G. Weintraub's *Visions of Culture*. The methods described therein place high emphasis on the automony of values, ideas, and the individual's work to come to terms with the "historicity" of culture. Needless to say the fact that nearly all the memes and indeed most of the themes and scenes of homo sapiens sapiens stems from the need to survive, eat, fight, mate and die could easily be overlooked in such a scheme of things.

The most viable foundation for future biospheric investigation of culture has been delivered by Konrad Lorenz in his *Behind The Mirror*. Taking as subject of evolution integrated systems developing from simple to complex, and establishing that the more complex system will have properties not deducible from the properties of the simple system it is composed of, he attempts a history of evolution of systems from simple cell to complex culture. "Society is the most complex of all living systems on earth...the direct comparison of animal species with human cultures tends to arouse the opposition of those with a highly developed sense of the difference between higher and lower living systems. The undeniable fact that cultures are highly complex, intellectual systems, resting on a basis of symbols expressive of cultural values, causes us to forget, given, as we are, to thinking in terms of opposites, that they are natural structures which have evolved along natural lines." And, "A reflecting self-investigation of a culture has never yet come to being on this planet just as objectivating science did not exist before the time of Galileo." *Behind The Mirror* is an indispensable tool and a foundation for a biospheric culturology. It becomes by now clear that just as the specific shape of a fin of a fish in the sea is product of interplay between genes and environment that cultures are part of the biosphere and the "human fish" must try to understand himself and the "sea" as integrated system.

Over 3000 known and perhaps a greater number unknown culture-species, each with its distinctive world-view or entelechy giving rise to a relatively non-outside "breeding" program, compete for econiches in the biosphere. The sheer number of these culture-species and their difference in areal domination make it difficult to perceive the patterns. So we shall follow the ecologist's principle of looking for "the top of the pyramid", only in this case a dominant culture contains also the most biomass, unlike, say, tigers who make up a small percentage of the natural ecosystem's biomass.

Twelve major culture-species can be mapped occupying most (often along side other smaller ones to be sure) of the biosphere together with other naturally arising species. These major culture-species can be provisionally named North American, Latin American, West European, East European, Far Eastern, South Asian, Malaysian, Afrasian Aridzone, Australasian, Sub-Saharan African, Pacifican, and Globaltech.

The culture-species range shows up on the map with cross-lines for frontiers to indicate that the boundaries are not like political-economic frontiers, but are more fluid. Also the interior of these regions are not the monocultural habitat of a single culture-species. Kalmuck and Uzbek live in the area marked Eastern European, Israeli and Sabaean continue in the Afrasian Aridzone culture-species, Northern Cheyenne and Orthodox Judaism survive in the North American, and so on. However, an individual or group from the major culture-species in the area demonstrates a comparative mastery of traveling, breeding, eating, and ability to act out freely his memes, themes, scenes, and dreams.

Globaltech, the newest of the major culture-species to form, does not find either the nation-state dominated by cities (West European), the imperium dominated by a great bureaucracy (East European), the religion dominated by its mullahs (Afrasian Aridzone), or any other land-space contiguous area, the best way to manifest its memes, themes, scenes, and dreams. Rather, Globaltech uses the market dominated by those time-space networked kshatriya-led economic voting forums called planetary corporations linked together in multi-national and regulatory professional associations.

Globaltech's eating, breeding, and dying take place in enclaves of metal, concrete, electronics, and relatively free interchange of information: Singapore, Frankfurt airport, Hong Kong, World Trade Centers, Free Ports of all kinds, the associated hotels, restaurants, and shops, on-board a vehicle regulated by an international association, airplane or ship and soon satellite, they read their own newspapers, the *International Herald-Tribune* and the *Far Eastern Economic Review,* have their own movie seats, their own telephone connections, even their own ever-growing production zones. Some individuals of some other culture-species launch occasional territory-defending terrorist forays against Globaltech meme carriers, but to date the territory of dominance keeps expanding and it definitely seems not to have reached its eco-equilibrium.

The following is a purely preliminary survey of selected access to dreams for three of the twelve great cultures prevailing on the planet at this time.

Impressions of Dreams of Three Culture-Species

West European

West European culture is built upon the past -- figuratively and literally speaking. W. Europe's present culture is historic heir to seven civilizations and several Empires spreading over the soil it inhabits. The basis of its nature, however, is its fascination with the *city.* The memes of its culture are imbedded in the city. It did not invent the city -- it is heir to it. The original waves of barbarians had nothing in mind but destroy, sack, plunder. The survival of the city is due to the fascination that the artificial stone beehive must have exerted upon their progenitors. Cities existed long before European culture. Yet one look at the geography, ecology and history of W. Europe makes clear the advantage and fascination the city exerted upon its successive native and invading tribes -- historically, geographically, and ecologically so diverse

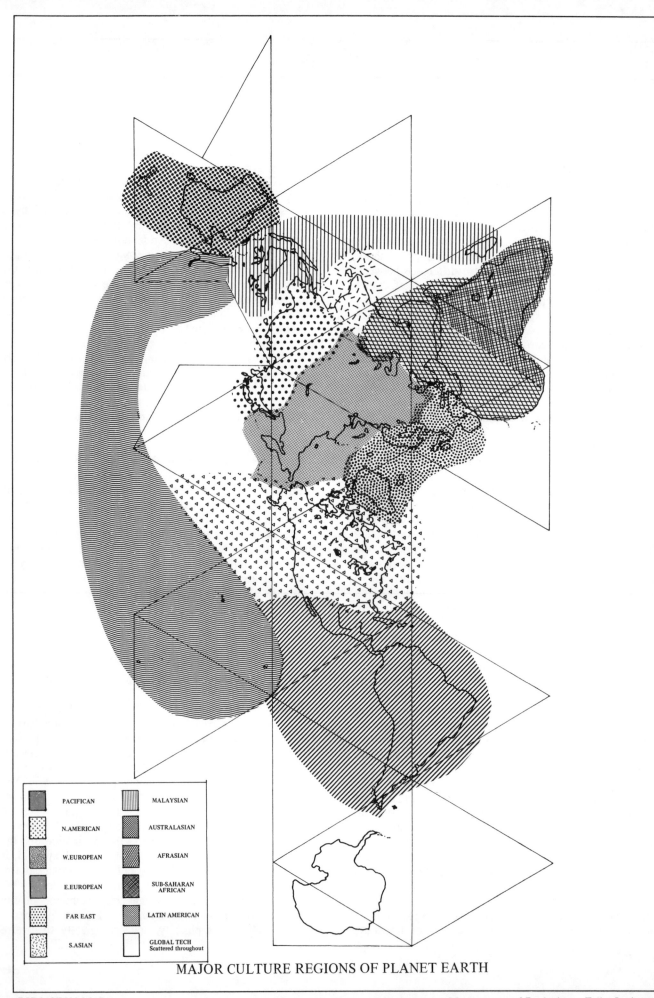

MAJOR CULTURE REGIONS OF PLANET EARTH

PACIFICAN

N.AMERICAN

W.EUROPEAN

E.EUROPEAN

FAR EAST

S.ASIAN

MALAYSIAN

AUSTRALASIAN

AFRASIAN

SUB-SAHARAN
AFRICAN

LATIN AMERICAN

GLOBAL TECH
Scattered throughout

DYMAXION MAP

Map courtesy of Buckminster Fuller Institute.

that cities could grow up short distances from each other.

The city became the basic social organism. The great European cultural themes centered around social cooperation/conflict which solidified into a strong, simple (compared to South Asia) class-structure. This structure had great explosive potential in comparison with other cultures and their class structures, due to the closeness of its cities and villages. No land to escape to, emigrate to, until the American discovery, and then so far away as to suffer a cultural mutation into a new species, the scene in Europe has always been divided into the *forum* where the themes of equality and fraternity took place and *privacy* with the themes of romance and sacrifice. And this drama between forum and hearth, honor and love, shapes and is shaped by the city.

North American

Americans are to be recognized as such by three traits: a) fascination by things; b) importance of prowess and display; c) happiness in tribal number, quantity, gregarious gathering at any price. North American culture is perhaps the greatest *thing-* culture that ever existed. Things are the theme of life, dominate life. "Life is a great thing." This is hardly surprising. Most white settlers arrived in America (coming from a thing-rich culture, Europe) with few things. Things proved to be essential for survival. They were met by tribal Indian cultures which also placed great value on things.

The theme of and handling of things integrated into a scene: know-how. Prowess and display were of know-how. The know-how, of course, is the magic key to acquire/produce more things. As a magic secret it has to be guarded. You may display your skill, but you guard your know-how. West European culture bearers are sometimes baffled at the reluctance that a true, well-bred American shows at displaying his know-how. But every Indian guarded his personal *medicine* with the same degree of jealousy.

The know-how cannot resist the urge to display itself, and so the dream of North American culture is revealed in *play*. A random element is introduced or a situation is created which is not serious, which is not really survival-related. Play creates happiness and the survival situation can be forgotten. Play, gregarious by its essence, provides opportunity to neglect quality in favor of quantity. The American astronaut who upon setting foot on the moon then proceeded to play the first golf-game on this heavenly body was indeed a true child of his culture. Play is by its very nature timeless, for the duration of the game. The mythological expression thereof is both the God of Eternal Youth and the Trickster, the two central figures being worshipped in American popular culture.

Play is deceptive. Revealing the nature of the Universe as random it searches for a meaning beyond. It must be remembered that the tribal Indians already shared a belief system postulating a *Great Spirit*. *Spirit* became a key word for naming an ultimate reality. *Dream* became another. From the Spirit of the class of '45, to the Spirit of St. Louis, to the Great American Dream -- there's hardly anything in America that doesn't have a spirit. Many Americans began to think this is all hype. Indeed, so it is. *Hype* became the other side of the *Great Spirit*. No escape from the trickster mentality. *Hype* in present day is both worshipped and despised. The nature of a supernatural being, mysterious as it is, has always had the light and the dark side.

The two nation-states whose borders roughly coincide with the borders of North American culture on the whole are, or were, the foundation of probably the most powerful Empire ever. No accident. The true nature and potential of the culture-species that hides its scenes, its know-hows, is as yet unknown, even to itself. "Out of sight", as the Americans say, and they also add, "out of mind". Neither North Americans nor, I believe, their fellow culture-species are yet capable of comprehending this formulation of ultimate frontier.

South Asian

The basic fact of life confronting the West European traveller in South Asia is that there is a crowd or if not that, a crowd can quickly form out of *nowhere*. The South Asian crowd is a phenomenon; indeed, really there is no crowd, that is West European perception: an examination of the metaphysics as well as the praxis of this area reveals that its culture is built upon and centers around the individual human body. The metaphysical expression of this statement would be that it is the Karma of this particular "I"-dentity to be imprisoned in such and such a body under such and such circumstances. It is therefore essential to master the body. The crowd is not a crowd -- it's not going to do anything. It's a test. One of the basic rituals of South Asian culture, the juggernaut, is centered upon the technique to assemble an ecstatic crowd under the very bad survival conditions. The aim of such ritual makes sense: only the mastery of body assures survival. Here all Karma comes to a test. The great themes of this culture must therefore center around a quite obvious predicament, for example, what, why, and how to do anything.

So, tasks are not opportunities, they are recurrences, programs, which one makes one's body perform daily. The culture's name for this operation is *dharma*. Supposing one's observations about the body function were right, the routine and observance of routine are most economical. All these themes of dharma, however, provide the material for the scenes India finds in *Kama*, pleasure, and in *Artha,* wealth.

But pleasure and wealth are also bound to the body, and must become wearisome. Who hasn't tried to fulfill all the prescriptions of the Kamasutra and the Artharastra. The drama of this culture must be Moksha, liberation, the I's triumph and rulership over matter, the body, and its reflecting mirror, the ever-changing mind.

Some Fundamental Books on Culture

The Golden Bough, by James G. Frazer, St. Martin (abridged version pub. by MacMillan), 1980 reprint of 1890 edition (13 volumes).

The Decline of the West, by Oswald Spengler, Knopf, 1945 (2 volumes).

A Study of History, by Arnold Toynbee, Oxford University Press, 1961 (12 volumes).

Imperial Germany and the Industrial Revolution, Thorstein Veblen, University of Michigan Press, Ann Arbor, 1966.

The Theory of the Leisure Class, Thorstein Veblen, Houghton Mifflin, Boston, 1973.

Democracy in America, by Alexis De Toqueville, Random House, 1981.

Notes on the State of Virginia, by Thomas Jefferson, Norton, 1972.

Agricola & The Germania, by Tacitus, Penguin, 1971.

History of the Persian Wars, by Herodotus, Harvard University Press (4 volumes).

Elementary Structures of Kinship, by Claude Levi-Strauss, Beacon Press, 1969.

Structural Anthropology, by Claude Levi-Strauss, Allen Lane, London, 1968.

Crowds & Power, by Elias Canetti, Continuum, 1982.

Behind the Mirror, by Konrad Lorenz, Methuen, 1977.

Image Music Text, by Roland Barthes, Hill and Wang, New York, 1977.

Primitive Mentalities, by Lucien Levy-Bruhl, Ams. Pr., 1976.

Patterns of Culture, by Ruth Benedict, Houghton-Mifflin, 1961.

Ancient Society, or Researches in the Lines of Human Progress from Savagery Through Barbarism to Civilization, by Lewis H. Morgan, MacMillan and Co., London, 1877. Latest edition may be: Charles H. Kerr, Chicago.

Man & Culture, by Clark Wissler, Johnson reprint in 1923.

Beyond Culture, by Edward T. Hall, Doubleday, 1977.

The Origin of the Family, Private Property and the State, by Friedrich Engels, Path Press, New York, 1972.

Argonauts of the Western Pacific, by Bronislaw Malinowsky, Waveland Press, 1984.

Facing Mount Kenya, by Jomo Kenyatta, Random House, 1962.

The Track of Man, Adventures of an Anthropologist, by Henry Field, Greenwood, 1969.

The Wheel of Life

This Tibetan Yantra shows an artistic rendition of the Biospheric System which symbolizes how the Biosphere assumes different shapes from Paradisial Bliss to Hellish Terror depending upon the state of consciousness of the participating observer. *(Painting by Renchen Norbu.)*

Doom! Doom!
You have destroyed
A beautiful world
With relentless hand,
Hurled it in ruins,
A demigod in despair!
We carry its scattered fragments
Into the void
Mourning
Beauty smashed beyond repair.
Magician,
Mightiest of men,
Raise your world
More splendid than before,
From your heart's blood
Build it up again!
Create a new cycle
For the splendors of sense to adorn;
You'll hear life
Chant a new and fresher song.

Goethe's *Faust*
translated by Caravan of Dreams Theater

Commodity Production

John Allen

The Commodity Production, Cities, Energy, Transport and Communications sections can be read separately, but taken together they deal with what has been called the Technosphere. The Noosphere as an active force consists in the harmonious synthesis of the Biosphere and the Technosphere by intelligence. One of the major purposes of *The Biosphere Catalogue* is to assist this process. THE EDITOR

The economic-political-social world of eighteenth century England possessed an expanding planetary empire in which to circulate masses of commodities. The vast unleashing of man-altered and in increasing numbers man-invented gases, liquids, and solids with known, unknown, and doubtless unknowable effects -- many of which have been disastrous not only on a species but even on whole ecosystems -- now begin to threaten biospheric integrity itself (atomic weapons).

A commodity X sold on the market for money which can then buy commodity Y acts as part of an intricately linked system, the *World Market*, in which no one knows where any given product will end, while the rate of production of commodities, including labor, follows exponential growth curves. The system of external controls on man's activities, already severely weakened by the introduction of agriculture after a million and a half years of hunting and gathering existence, collapsed. The factory, the refinery, the voting booth, the city, the studio, the vehicle, in short, the productive unit can overwhelm the surrounding region's ability to neutralize the noxious by-products of the process and send off on planetary cycles its exhausts, its fluids, its suspended solids. Finally the World Market grows big and complex enough to overwhelm a civilization's ethics, and the commodities in many cases such as DDT, dieldrin, and autos become directly polluting devices themselves.

The scale and rate of increase of this vast tonnage moving throughout the biosphere can be contemplated from studying the accompanying figures (table 1).

By the post-World War II era, the world market had outgrown national and even imperial state negotiations, outgrown giant corporate advertising and promotion efforts, outgrown multi-sided international tariff agreements. Beginning with three World Trade Centers in 1968, Houston, New Orleans, and Tokyo, one hundred and fourteen are now operating or being built. Significantly the two New York World Trade Towers, the world headquarters for World Trade Centers, are each higher than the world's previous tallest building, to give an indication of the scale. In these World Trade Centers anyone with a commodity may meet buyers from the Capitalist states, the Communist states or the mixed Third World states.

In addition, the number of great world fairs and festivals grows apace. At Frankfurt, book commodities are shipped in by the ton for the annual fair. At Cannes, movies, at Edinburgh, even theater companies. In all, over 800 international trade fairs are listed in British Business Trade Commodities Guide of January 1985.

In vain the Communist states strive to resist the force of commodities. Their plans everywhere crumble and erode in the face of cheap commodities that batter down not only the Chinese Walls mentioned by Marx but Iron Curtains. Third World attempts at autarchic growth wither.

American and West European protectionist

Table 1
PRODUCTION IN MILLIONS OF TONS

	Oil	Cars (Units)	Raw Steel	Wheat	Fertilizer
1900	.025	–	70.0	69.0	–
1920	5.6	–	80.00	105.0	–
1940	20.00	5.0	95.0	140.0	31.0
1960	125.0	16.4	336.0	250.0	62.0
1980	260.0	30.0	716.0	445.0	210.0

fail to protect their industries' outmoded commodities produced by outmoded methods.

The vast, and every twenty-five years doubling, amounts of raw material and the finished commodities made from them have become forces that geologists and ecologists dare not fail to include in their planetary and biospheric calculation. We must also see that the technical requirements of the commodity production system have produced surveying (landsat, etc.) and measuring devices and scientific disciplines that allow an opportunity for humanity to attain a conscious and creative econiche as a partner in evolution.

However, all attempts to deal with the biospheric problematique are fated to remain utopian and impractical without coming to grips with the producers-consumers-market commodity system. The closed material-energetic-information loops necessary for biospheric equilibrium cannot be achieved with such a rapid exponential growth factor forcing its way to the very center of biogenic material transfers occurring on the planet. And this exponential growth factor carries at least two other exponential growth factors along with it: human population and pollution. And when a fourth, weapons of planetary and even space war, are also tied to the commodity system, the ultimate entropy stares us directly now in the face.

Commodity Exchange

To see commodity trade in action visit the Chicago Commodity Exchange. There, coffee, cocoa, sugar and other primary products are bought and sold. Such trade determines the fates of nations, populations and ecosystems. Deserts are created, millions may starve as land use shifts from subsistence farming to production of commodities for international trade.

World Trade Centers

"An organization that stands outside of politics across national boundaries, in service to those who develop and facilitate international trade." World Trade Centers offer services that government agencies and other organizations do not provide. These often include consultation on import- export regulations, investment and exchange rules, and market research. Some also offer training programs in practical matters such as preparation and documentation of international shipments. Members of the World Trade Centers Association host trade shows and conferences. The Association's literature states "Our meetings are not segmented by political or economic blocs, and there are no confrontations on grounds of race or ideology. Our assemblies are devoted to one essential topic to which all participants are committed: the practical development and facilitation of trade." A look at the membership of the Information and Communications Committee of the World Trade Centers Association shows the range of the World Trade Centers:

Thomas J. Kearney
World Trade Center New York
Director, World Trade Institute
The Port Authority of New York and New Jersey
Herman H. Schurink
World Trade Center Rotterdam
Chief Adebayo Adeleke
World Trade Center Nigeria, Ltd.
David Collins
World Trade Center of Orange County
Roberto Fendt, Jr.
World Trade Center do Rio de Janeiro
H.W.N. de Jong
World Trade Center Amsterdam
Nona Haimer
World Trade Center New York
Robert Hobart
World Trade Center Melbourne
Sensuke Igarashi
World Trade Center of Japan, Inc.
Michael Merton
World Trade Center Geneva
John Raven
World Trade Center London
Gary Reid
World Trade Center Toronto
Vjatscheslav I. Teleguin
World Trade Center Moscow

World Fairs

The following selection of great World fairs will give anyone who wishes to invest a certain portion of his time a thorough understanding of the situation. No one interested in the biosphere should fail to attend at least two or three of these extraordinary events and make calculations as to the total tonnages and kinds of materials involved in order to have a "feel" for this dynamic and two-centuries exponentially expanding process.

Frankfurt: International Book Fair
October 8-13, 1985
Dubai: Arab Municipal Services Exhibition
October 26-30, 1986

Florence: Uomo Italia (Men's Fashion Show)
January 1986

Paris: Salon Internationale De La Lingerie
February 1986

Basle: European Cable and Satellite Exhibition and Conference
March 4-6, 1986

Cannes: International Television Program market MIP-TV.
April 1986

Chicago: Association for Information and Image Management
April 1986

Gothenburg: Scanautomatica '86. Noventer Hydraulics, Pneumatics and Automata Trade Fair
October 1986

Houston: ISA International Instrumentation Automation Conference and Exposition
October 1986

Zurich: International Trade Fair for High Precision Techniques, Dimensional Measurement and Control Dusseldorf: Wire
April 1986

Cologne: International Sweets and Biscuits Fair
January 1986

San Francisco: International Gourmet Products Show
May 1986

Chicago: Contract Carpeting Promotion/Chicago Merchandise Mart
February 1986

Houston: 18th Offshore Technology Conference
May 1986

Bleiswijk: Horticultural Industry Exhibition
February 1986

Poznan: International Trade Fair of

Medical Equipment (SALMED)
April 1986

Munich: International Trade Fair for Watches, Clocks, Jewellery
February 1986

Montreal: Montreal Salon de L'Auto (International Auto Salon)
January 1986

Frankfurt: International Exhibition of Automobile Workshop and Garage Equipment (Automechanica)
September 1986

Cannes: International Record and Music Publishing Market
January 1986

Riyadh: Saudi Computer '86 (Computer and Computer Graphics Show)
March 1986

Geneva: International Exhibition of Technologies and Services for Banking and Finance (Technobank)
June 1986

Dusseldorf: International Printing and Paper Fair (DRUPA)
May 1986

Beijing: Multi-National Instrumentation Conference and Exhibition
April 1986

Pireaus: International Shipping Exhibition (Posidonia)
June 1986

Tokyo: World Sport
March 1986

New York: Knitting Yarn Fair
September 1986

Sydney: International Toy, Hobby and Leisure Fair
February/March 1986

Moscow: Anti-Pollution
July 1986

Libreville (Gabon): International Water Supply Exhibition
June 1986

Madrid: International Security Safety and Fire Exhibition
March 1986

Amsterdam: International Traffic Engineering Exhibition
April 1986

Cannes: International Film Market
May 1986

Essen: International Postage Stamp Fair
May 1986

Amsterdam: International Trade Fair for Safety, Health and Welfare at Work
May 1986

New Orleans: International Association of Amusement Parks and Attractions
November 1986

Kuala Lumpur: Asian Defense Exhibition
February 1986

Information

The Statistics and Market Intelligence Library offers an important service to exporters, and may save you time, money and research abroad.

The library holds a large collection of foreign trade directories, including telephone directories and specialized directories on particular sectors of industry.

If you think SMIL has some information of interest to you, why not phone them on 01-215 544/5 or call into the library between 09:30-17.30 hours, Monday to Friday? Last admissions at 17.00 hours.

The library is situated at 1 Victoria Street, London SW1H OET.

Futures and Options

METALS

COMMODITY RESEARCH BUREAU INDEX

Today	Previous Day	Year Ago
227.8	227.4	268.7

GRAINS & OILS

PLATINUM (NYM)
50 troy oz.; $ per troy oz.

FINANCIAL

WHEAT (CBT) 5,000 bu.; $ per bu.

SILVER (CBT)
1,000 troy oz.; ¢ per troy oz.

U.S. TREASURY BONDS (CBT)
8%-$100,000 prin.; pts. and 32d's of 100%

WHEAT (KCBT) 5,000 bu.; $ per bu.

CORN (CBT) 5,000 bu.; $ per bu.

SILVER (COMEX)
5,000 troy oz.; ¢ per troy oz.

GNMA CERTIFICATES (CBT)
8%-$100,000 prin.; pts. and 32d's of 100%

OATS (CBT) 5,000 bu.; $ per bu.

COPPER (COMEX) 25,000 lb.; ¢ per lb.

U.S. TREASURY BILLS (IMM)
$1 million; pts. of 100%

SOYBEANS (CBT) 5,000 bu.; $ per bu.

10-YEAR U.S. TREASURY NOTES (CBT)
$100,000, pts and 32d's of 100%

GOLD (COMEX) 100 troy oz.; $ per troy oz.

CERTIFICATES OF DEPOSIT (IMM)
$1 million; pts. 100% add on

SOYBEAN OIL (CBT) 60,000 lb.; ¢ per lb.

3-MONTH EURODOLLAR DEPOSITS (IMM)
$1 million; pts of 100%; add on

SOYBEAN MEAL (CBT) — 100 tons; $ a ton

STOCK INDEXES

PALLADIUM (NYM)
100 troy oz.; $ per troy oz.

BRITISH POUND (IMM)
25,000 pounds; $ per pound

VALUE LINE STOCK INDEX (KCBT)
$500 x index number

CANADIAN DOLLAR (IMM)
100,000 dollars; $ per Canadian dollar

S. & P. 500 STOCK INDEX (CME)
$500 x index number

LIVESTOCK

WEST GERMAN MARK (IMM)
125,000 marks; $ per mark

N.Y.S.E. COMPOSITE INDEX (NYFE)
$500 x index number

CATTLE, Live beef (CME)
40,000 lb.; ¢ per lb.

JAPANESE YEN (IMM)
12.5 million yen; $ per yen

MAJOR MARKET INDEX (CBT)
$100 x index number

CATTLE, Feeder (CME)
44,000 lb.; ¢ per lb.

SWISS FRANC (IMM)
125,000 francs; $ per franc

INDUSTRIALS

PORK BELLIES (CME)
38,000 lb.; ¢ per lb.

FUTURES OPTIONS

LUMBER (CME)
130,000 bd. ft.; $ per 1,000 bd.ft.

U.S. TREASURY BONDS (CBT)
$100,000 prin.; pts. and 64ths of 100%

HOGS, Live (CME) 30,000 lb. ¢ per lb.

COTTON (NYCTN) 50,000 lb.; ¢ per lb.

HEATING OIL No. 2 (NYM)
42,000 gallons; cents per gallon

GOLD (COMEX)
100 troy oz.; $ per troy oz.

NY GASOLINE, LEADED REG. (NYM)
42,000 gallons; cents per gallon

FOODS

COFFEE (NYCSCE) 37,500 lb. ¢ per lb.

FINANCIAL OPTIONS

U.S. TREASURY BONDS (CBOE)

CRUDE OIL (NYM)
42,000 gal.; $ per bbl.

SUGAR, World (NYCSCE)
112,000 lb.; ¢ per lb.

Cities

Bill Boyd

"Let us not flatter ourselves overmuch on account of our human conquest of nature. For each such conquest nature takes its revenge on us. Each of them...has in the first place consequences on which we counted, but in the second and third places it has quite different unforeseen effects which only too often cancel out the first...It is still more difficult in regard to the remote social consequences of these actions." FRIEDRICH ENGELS

The vast movements of matter detailed in the Commodities section focuses on the cities, each of which is the center of a network and then in its turn becomes part of the network of a world-city, and these world-cities -- Moscow, New York, Paris, London, Delhi, Beijing, Tokyo -- are where the biospheric action's concentrated as far as homo sapiens sapiens is concerned.

Bill Boyd and a few other lovers of cities have taken the challenge of the Biosphere Catalogue to muse on certain cities which have concentrated the quintessence of one or another quality of that most protean species yet evolved by the biosphere ...

The City!

Glamour, gods, gold, gossamer, and go, cities, these so far supreme inventions for storing knowledge (because knowledge is power) and ensuring the exchange of knowledge, by means of streets, plazas, cafes, theater, dance, music, parks, museums, fashion, monuments, media, demonstrations, parades, riots, revolutions, processions, anonymity, fame, facade, architecture, clubs, societies, banks, offices, laboratories, directories, ports, airports, parties, sexuality, games, bombings, threats, slander, sports, temples, warehouses, bazaars, exchanges, hospitals, cemeteries, utilities, and libraries, control the life of humanity in the biosphere, setting its tone, its values, its governments.

Not always was this so. The United States in its Jeffersonian foundations relied on the farmer, old England on the yeomen, pre-Solonian Athens on the tribes, the Latin oligarchies on the latifundia. Today we go for business, pleasure, enlightenment, escape to the city and those who retire to the country to write their books or stay there to manage their farms address both their ideas and their fruit to the city which dominates their consciousness.

Following is a catalogue of cities to visit, each of which illustrates a different aspect of the being of *The City*.

Paris: The Feminine City

Cafe au lait, omelette and orange juice at the Boul'Mich cafe across from the Seine bookstalls for leisurely breakfast, stroll through Saint Chapelle, the flower market, and Notre Dame, then to lunch at the Apollinaire on the Boulevard St. Germain, wander a couple of hours on the back streets of the Rive Gauche, stop in for infusion, cafe, or drink at the Deux Magots, charm away the late afternoon in the garden of the Luxembourg or the Tuilleries, dress according to mood for dinner at La Coupole to see and be seen, cross the Seine, idle up the promenade of the Champs Elysees, to arrive at the Cafe de la Paix for the late glass of wine, meander back to your hotel so that when you are asked the next morning "did you sleep well?" you say yes.

What has one accomplished? Nothing, only lived for twenty-four hours, created a touchstone of well-being, allowed one's subconscious to proceed a little ways towards integrating one's being.

The most feminine city, Paris surrenders its inner beauty only to disinterested contemplation, and invites you, whatever might be the path of your twenty-four hours, to the Remembrance of Things Past including Lost Illusions in the Moveable Feast of Being and Nothingness.

New York: Information and Image City

Bagdad-on-the-Hudson O. Henry called it, meaning that he who roamed its streets could live a life as magical as Haroun-al-Rashid's encounters in the stories of Scheherezade. Walt Whitman wrote it a poem, *Mannahatta*, and Mayakovsky turned on. From Washington Irving to William Burroughs nearly every American writer has lived there as have its musicians, its artists, its theater companies, its dancers. They found and find there a refuge from the Babbitry of Main Street, Eliza's southern boarding houses, and What Makes Sammy Run.

Built along an old Indian trail that forked in two at Cold Spring in front of what is now the Flatiron Building to become two trails (now Fifth Avenue and Upper Broadway), Manhattan found itself on metamorphosed rock whose strength could easily support the tallest skyscrapers.

The Erie Canal bypassed Boston which also refused to invest in trains, as did Virginia's Chesapeake Bay, and New York soared into the financial preeminence by which it predominates in world markets today.

Art and wealth join hands with fashion and world politics (the United Nations and multinationals), media and mafia and a hundred ethnic groups to produce perhaps the keenest-witted population in the world. Unlike its great compeers, London, Paris, Mosow, Beijing, Tokyo, and Delhi, New York's not saddled with the withering hand of national bureaucracy, war, and secret police. Its mayor the second strongest political leader of the country, its government can and must respond quickly or be thrown out. Washington is insignificant on every count except nation-stating activities and the so far invincible cultural mediocrity of the rest of the vast country leaves it without other competition in the U.S.; New York thus becomes free to enjoy and improve its role as premier world city -- the place where it's more likely you find the information, the right people, the financing, the management, the image, than anywhere else.

Don't miss the Natural History Museum, the Frick Museum, Washington Square, the Stock Exchange, the Staten Island Ferry, China Town, Little Italy, Off-Broadway, the Gotham Bookmart, the Public Library, the $1.00 breakfast, walking Fifth Avenue and 57th Street, and just "following your nose" to see what story Scheherezade will tell you. If you're loaded, Hotel Pierre will show you *luxury*.

Beijing: An Eternal City

If you have a taste for scale, you will have a feast in Beijing. Truly a world city strategically situated on the edge of the fertile great North China Plain 70 miles from the Great Wall, Beijing has been a center of power and trade for as long as 3000 years. The original city, already powerful, was chosen by Kublai Khan in 1267 as the seat of his great empire. Small thoughts are swept aside in this city whose main boulevards were designed for armies. Up to 300 feet wide the great roadways march across the city for swift exit and entrance to and from any part of China.

Beijing's *inner cities* -- the Forbidden City, the Imperial City, the Tartar City and the Chinese City -- were expanded again by Ming and Manchu Dynasties. Flanking the inner city's immense and beautiful "Gates of Heavenly Peace" are modern government buildings and monuments. The boulevards now extend to east and northeast to the new technical centers and universities

while the Tienanmen Square in front of the great gate provides an arena for modern rallies.

In the early dawn the ineffable eternal pace is evidenced in the graceful movements of the streetside Tai Chi, the wave of bicycles in the wake of armies, billows of steam from streetside rice makers, the rustle of willow trees, the glisten of ancient palaces, the buzz of business, the promise of a long future. Immense, eternal and truly beautiful is this great city of China. *Marie Allen*

London: A Finance City

Start your journey through Greater London with the Standard of Time in Greenwich at Wren's Royal Observatory which determines the GMT and has set the world's clocks since the seventeenth century including London's biggest time keeper, Big Ben. Up the great Serpentine River, the Thames, dividing London, past the Isle of Dogs, and the main harbors one of which is where the fish market of Billingsgate relocated. Empty warehouses and docks haunt the shores, monuments of former times when hundreds of ships created traffic jams between London Bridge and the Tower. Those were the days of the Moscovy Company (1555), the Turkey (later Levant) Company (1581) and the East India Company (1600) which established London as a center for world trade and where the World Trade Center is still located.

Commuters invade London from its five main railway stations, buses, underground railway, and with briefcase and umbrella cross London Bridge and enter *The City*, one of the world's great financial centers. Called Londinium by the Romans, it was a mart as early as 604. By the end of the twelfth century Danish, Gascons, Flemish, and Italian merchants flourished. Here at 10:30 each morning the world price of bullion is set in the Gold Room of N.M. Rothschild and Sons. Here is the international money market of banks, the Stock Exchange, insurance headquarters, and the Guildhall, seat of the Corporation of London built in the 1400's when Guilds bought freedom from intrusion in their affairs from needy monarchs. And you can read all about it on Fleet Street.

Nearby another trade begins before sunrise as hundreds of carcasses of beef, lamb, hare, and fowl are carried to hang in Smithsfields market.

Cut down the Strand towards Covent Garden, now transformed into boutiques and restaurants. Here is the heart of the Theater, World Dance, and Opera. Flashing neon lights titilate the flesh in SoHo, ancient home of the French Huguenots and headquarters of General de Gaulle during World War II. On to Bloomsbury, haven for writers and scholars researching in the British Museum where the bounty of ancient civilizations from around the world can be found.

A shopper's paradise. Fashion is hip and dictates to youth what the next *look* is. The auction houses of Sothebys and Christies determine the value of painting, objects d'art, and antiques for the world. For *color* -- the October Gallery and Portabello Road; for sound -- Ronnie Scotts.

Nelson's triumphal monument at Trafalgar Square, St. James Square, Big Ben, Parliament, Buckingham Palace symbolize order and continuity. Calibrator of theater, literature, art, science, law, and free speech, it's to London one must go for planetary accreditation. *Chili Hawes*

Tokyo: A City of Tempo

Like London, a World-City on an Island, with royalty in the center, Tokyo also maintains the traditions. But the traditions are different, psychological rather than theological or ideological, and the new is welcomed rather than being allocated to Cambridge.

For tradition first see a Noh play, then go to the Kabuki-za, the House of Kabuki theater. Some say that Kathakali in Cochin, or the court drama of Jogjakarta, or the all-night dramas of Bali are the greatest theater in the world, but they alone can be mentioned in the same breath as Tokyo's two theaters. If you're a tourist don't go, they do not exist for entertainment but for beauty...the first, the beauty of contemplation; the second, the beauty of action. Kabuki can be five hours, and you purchase lunch at your level of choice.

Eat at a sushi traditional style amidst the hustle and bustle of Japanese business meetings, watch the Kendo battles, soak in the hot bath.

For the new, take the great subway, contemplate the feel of a world city protected only by a small defensive army, try to negotiate a business deal, hang out at the United Nations University.

Gradually, it becomes clear: Tokyo runs on tempo. Not on time, like New York, but tempo, the inner experience of passing time, snowflakes, cherry blossoms, speeches, bows, significant glances, meetings, meals, no inner shuffling about, each appears and disappears, on tempo. A vast inner music suffuses the city.

Moscow: A Dramatic City

Intensive, dramatic and closed, Moscow sits like a gem on seven hills surrounded by forest, with Asia's glamour and Europe's dynamism. Prince Uri Dolgoruki founded the city in 1147: his father was prince of Kiev, and his mother an Englishwoman. Moscow and Britain share the same patron, St. George slaughtering the dragon.

Moscow: formal as the Bolshoi Ballet, vital as its circus' dancing bears, frivolous as the restaurants that serve only champagne and ice cream, stern as the Marxist-Leninist Institute, sophisticated as Sputnik, grandly luxurious as the Metros, many-faceted as the Kremlin's facade, majestically melancholy as the Eisenstinian clouds that sit enthroned in the Moscow skies. The light, though bone-chilling, has at the same time a reddish glow, as if the city were illumined by embers. Golden onion-skinned cupolas symbolize the many-layered skins of a country of at least Byzantine complexity.

The city revolves around the Kremlin and Red Square. The Russian root word for red also means beautiful. Red Square, beautiful square, hosts visitors and students from around the planet. The square contains the elbow-rubbing feeling of cosmopolitan fraternity of this world city.

The constitution recognizes the new forces unleashed by the scientific-technical revolution, and the intelligentsia as well as workers and peasants are now considered as an official class.

One cannot help but willy-nilly encounter the Russian babushka. She is as key in Russian culture as the concierge to the French, but she is more grandmotherly than her French counterpart, who behaves more like a mother-in-law. Omnipresent in hotels, trains, shops, she scolds, nurses, cheers and annoys. The key to her heart is to allow her to serve you tea from a steaming samovar. She commands respect from youth, and youth, in Moscow, is everyone under 50 years.

A dramatic city -- of Stanislavsky, Vaktangov, Meyerhold, Eisenstein...a literary city, home to Dostoevski, Mayakovski, Gorki, Chekhov, Gogol, Tolstoy, and the honored Pushkin, the most revered of all poets. The inscription on his grave represents the aspiration of the Soviet people: "I shall be loved and long the people will remember/ the kindly thoughts I stirred -- my muse's brightest crown./ How in this cruel age I celebrated freedom,/ and begged for truth toward those cast down." *Kathelin Hoffman*

Delhi: An Imperial City

Capital of the second-largest empire on the planet Earth, Delhi's magnificent distances quite outdo Washington and Moscow, but then the present capitol complex is the seventh along the banks of the Jumna.

However, start with Shah Jehan's capitol at Red Fort and make your way up Chandni Chowk to Fateh Puri and then to Jamni Masjid (great mosque). Stay open to experience, and what you will encounter is truly as they say in Asia dependent only upon your level of understanding.

From Connaught Circle you can start out in any direction for other New Delhi sights, but it itself is a bustling world. Breakfast or salad bar at Nerula's.

Delhi basically exists as the poetry of emperors, crowned and uncrowned, and, for perhaps the best way to enter into its world, stroll the Lodi Gardens with a volume of Urdu poets, and engage in conversation with some interesting looking habitue of the grounds. Climb the Qutub Minar with a *Veda* or *Upanishad* or *Naropa's Teachings* or the *Way of the Sufi,* and see from where the poetry came that inspired the architects.

The two months before Monsoon, which is inspiring, are very hot. Winter is splendid. Whatever befalls you, consider as your karma, the effects of the causes within your mind, but in Delhi men say we have more than one mind, so beware.

Mexico: City of Volcanoes and Flowers

Mexico City settled by 600 B.C. later became the Toltec City of the Gods. There nomadic warriors also found a legend-sought home: a cactus growing from a rock, an eagle devouring a snake. On islands surrounded by snow peaked volcanoes, it had canals, floating gardens and three access routes to the mainland. The canals became streets, the gardens courtyards, but the three Calzadas still form the main autoroutes. Montezuma greeted the Spanish with hospitality. Two years later the new rulers rebuilt the city with their architecture and religion. The political process repeats itself: leaders rise, then fall like hats blown off by rushing winds. Expected population 2000 A.D.: 25 million. The vacuum cleaner sucks silver and leather; fruits and seafoods from both coasts; campesinos looking for work; provincials preparing their careers; anthropologists; ethnocollages; exiled philosophers. They meet: eye contact at the pyramids; coffee talk at the Zona Rosa; singing with mariachis at Garibaldi; backing into each other at the murals or the Museum of Anthropology. Dinner at an amigo's house after a stroll in Parque Chapultepec. No other megalopolis' altitude makes even the Olympic champions lose efficiency. The City offers not exports, but a site: a culture that hardly gels before the next one is stirred in; contradictions coexisting like a Monumento a la Revolucion by Porfirio Diaz. The city lives off the uncompounded interest of the Royal Aztec Jewels. Some say it offers the opportunity to watch the first megalopolis die a natural death. *Norberto Alvarez-Romo*

Florence: An Historic Living City

A thriving prosperous artisanal life with excellent cuisine continues at this biospheric center where Roman, Cluniac, and Synthetic civilizations flourished, both the Etruscan and Renaissance civilizations climaxed, and the Renaissance was conceived on the banks of the Arno. Galileo created the scientific method (with the support of the Academy of Lynxes in Roma and a few years free sojourn in Venezia). Don't miss his workshop where the quantitative approach to the universe was developed with its vast achievements that open up space and vast misuses that threaten life. Machiavelli contemplated the iniquity of man, the preferability of the Republic, and the near-inevitability of the tyrant and gave advice to both. DaVinci created himself to be a new exemplar to humanity, the universal man. Michelangelo surveyed the poetry and tragedy of the effort. Mantegna gazed on being itself. Giotto stared at Eternity. Brunelleschi crafted space. Savanorola nearly destroyed it all. Lorenzo managed it with sublime subtlety. Dante, exiled, immortalized his enemies and his mistress, contemplated its Divine Comedy.

Much remains. Richard Burton, the sufic explorer, and D.H. Lawrence added to it. Maybe you will, too.

Amsterdam: A Far-Out City

Canals with slowly drifting October yellow leaves, canals along which the rich ruthless burghers flourished who, for a brief period between the decline of the Austro-Spanish Hapsburg world-ocean empire and the rise of the British world-ocean empire, dominated the commerce and plunder of Planet Water. Here Rembrandt explored the inner lives of the men and women who broke the advance of the Counter-Reformation and set the stage for science to supersede dogma. His house still stands. A population from the East Indies has settled here emanating a nostalgic exotica.

But Amsterdam today is perhaps the freest major city in choice of life-styles. The police and city government do not act as if the structure of society totters if the conventions of Babbitry or Tartuffery do not uniformly prevail upon the streets, in the plazas, even inside public buildings.

For the taste of personal freedom with Mrs. Grundy safely out of power in a city secure enough to grant it in the mellowness of centuries of conquest, wealth, art, and architecture, poodle aimlessly in October in Amsterdam's water-dappled charm, see where you're really at.

Rome: The Church City

Its founder, Romulus, killed his brother Remus for laughingly jumping over his newly set-up boundary of rocks; from the moment of foundation Roma stood for a strict interpretation of right and wrong. Numa, the first king, says Plutarch, cleverly used religiously endorsed superstition to control the people. Titus' arch commemorates the destruction of Jerusalem and the dispersal of the Jews for refusing to worship the emperor. Constantine's arch recalls the imposition of state Christianity. The Colisseum behind recalls the previous martyrdom of these same Christians along with that of animals and slaves. In the Vatican, books found in every major library remain on the Forbidden Index for the Faithful. Mussolinian pseudo-grandeur reminds of castor oil and prison for democrats.

One can hear the present Pontifex Maximus pontificate his condemnations of birth control, promising hell to all who disobey.

A fantastic study of organized dogma. The Pantheon to the Caesars, the temple of the Vestal Virgins, and the capital of the Inquisition remain inviolate amidst the ruins.

Cairo: A Monument to Memory

Six crumbling stories above the heart of the city the desert can be seen beyond the haze. Midway, a clearing: the river writhes through the vortex of Cairo. The Bab el Louk train whistles and hundreds of shuffling feet funnel out to the street. They merge with the metal tangle moving slow round and light. Boys jump busses, braying hulks, red and green lights playing on their flanks. Beneath a coincidence of overpasses, Egyptian boys play ball. They are handsome and agile, born of shadow and silence, familiar treachery. The shadows of headlights passing through the gratings above become the boundaries of their field. Two stones and a feared arbiter are the net. "I have created you in joy and in sorrows: out of so many things," -- the field. "You have become all feeling for me" -- the net. Elsewhere, the *toorab* (arabic for both cemetery and dust) forms a vast crescent around the city. The dead do not hoard their dwellings. Their survivors live there: a prototype of the modern suburb. They sell vegetables, make matresses, repair radios in the tombs. The children are coming home from school in the tombs. They are nurtured on sound and light. The wealth of the people is a space they invent for themselves and can be found behind their eyes. Accessible, limitless, you are welcome there to participate in the last confessions and gracious death of a relic. *Maria Golia Czerkinskaya,* (quotations from C.P. Cavafy, *In the Same Space*)

Ife: A Jungle City

Thrown upon the West route by a wave of the furious Atlantic, passing by Lagos and Ibadan, to the end of the taxi ride -- Ile-Ife, the cradle of the Yoruba culture.

North desert winds pick up in December. By March the greatest heat has passed. Rain comes. Light. Tenacious and violent. It's August. The dirt roads in the heart of the city, chilis and tomato sauce to spice the yam, cries, laughter, anger -- the color red dominates.

Time is elastic and passes in all imaginable directions.

Ifa, divinity of science, throws the shells and consults the traditional proverbs for answers to questions concerning business, children, old age, youth, rights, and wisdom. But one must stay humble.

The moment for palm wine in the Haoussa area arrives.

Eccentric University of Ife, with its buildings designed for the power of progress, hosts a play of "giants" by Wole Soyinka. A little farther stands a statue in the memory of the students killed by the army.

Ile (the city)-Ife (love), vital and mysterious. Where "talking drums" pick up the ancestral phrases, and the energy is given freely. Allez-y! *Gisele Pierra*

Hardwar: Pilgrimage City

Hardwar is a pilgrimage city which can support a population fluctuation of millions. One of the seven holy cities of India, it is also one of the four sacred places where the Kumbh Mela or 12 year meetings of holy men are held. The Kumbh Mela takes its name from the Hindu legend which tells how four drops of holy nectar fell to the earth from a *kumbh* or water pot during a struggle for possession between angels and demons. The next full Kumbh Mela will be held at Hardwar in February of 1986. For the Vaishnavites it is Hari-dwara, the Gate of Hari or Vishnu. For the Shivites it is Har-dwara, the Gate of Shiva. For most it is the Gate of Heaven or God's City. No static city, but a *door* through which multitudes can flow. There is no better place than Hardwar to experience the simple clarity of the Ganges and the religious purity it engenders. A vegetarian city of saffron swamis where everyone knows that life is a game of karma where no animal is killed and even the eating of eggs is forbidden. See the steamrollers prepare for a new invasion as millions arrive to take the sacred bath. Across the river is a thick jungle which extends all the way to the border of Nepal and sometimes you can hear the elephants roaring in the night. You look at the Ganga flowing at great speed like cold coffee swirling with milk and hear the Baba say, "Money is like water. When it is flowing it is good. When it stays in one place it gets dirty." Dwarf lady with marigolds around her neck nods agreement as she passes by in a ricksha. Endless movie music blares out of loudspeakers while in the not too distant shadows sit the deformed and untouchable beggars like a wall before the river. Somewhere an unexpected telegram is put into your hands. It reads -- SKY INVADERS CLAIM ASYLUM/ IF YOU WANT TO ESCAPE THE CYCLE OF DEATH AND REBIRTH/ COME TO HARDWAR RIGHT AWAY/ *The door opens two ways. Ira Cohen*

Kathmandu: A Shangri-La City

The cool winds and sacred lakes of Gosunkund murmur and beckon "leave the plains below -- in an Emerald Valley find the Mirror City." The land of sun and mountain, wind and rain, temple and flute, where processions pass by and people celebrate in ecstasy and song the cosmic range of creation. At the end of life's road death waits, the sky band declares our journey shall be full of feast and dream.

Today the buffaloes die in honor of Durga of the Night, the people feast on meat and wine. The bats wake, the herons nest, the full moon rises. Candlelit spaceships spin to the sounds of horn and cymbal, while ruby and saffron-robed monks turn the wheel of the law.

Magicians dance their skeleton dance along the river by the burning ghats, while a young bride passes in her carriage. Tonight she will meet her life's love. Her golden bangles and red sari tinkle and whisper her fate.

The gods and goddesses gather on the hill dancing around the holy fires while Nagas attend with pipe and drum, calling the wanderer "without possessions, without cares -- go to the holy shrines, the dwelling places of the gods, where no man need bear his burden. Go empty and without fear -- wanderer go!" *Mary Evans*

Peshawar: A Tribal City

In Peshawar, a foothills city not far from Khyber Pass, one can meet a member of any of the hill tribes of the Northwest Frontier as the Raj called it, and today even more tribals visit the city as Afghanis of various cultural backgrounds arrive from beyond the pass.

A beggar here may be a shaven-headed Qalandar going through his sufic training period, a loafer on the street turns out to be an expert thief or a guide to whatever you may wish to see, or both.

Alexander, Babar, and Burton rode through here; the Aryans swept through with the Laws of Manu, the Greeks erected agora and temples, Buddhists turned the wheel of dharma, the Moguls made their synthesis of gardens, terror, and poetry, the British brought justice, irrigation, and hypocrisy, the Pakistanis (Land of the Pure) speak with two voices, the nation-state and the Mullah; the tribal areas remain independent and in Peshawar come to see the big world, and having seen it, most return, perhaps with a better rifle and more ammunition the better to defend themselves.

Leningrad: A Heroic City

Built by the heroism of the people of Peter the Great, making a gateway to Western Europe in swamp and tide and cold, constructed on into harmonious magnificence by Catherine the Great, swept by Revolution that today rules one of the two global superpowers, name then changed from Petrograd to Leningrad, this city gained its title not from these resounding events, but from its resistence to Nazi armies who surrounded it for two and a half years while it fought on under casualties unequaled by any city in World War II. Here the Russian avant-garde, the Futurists, dreamed their poetry, plays, and art of the fusion of intelligentsia and people destroying the restrictions of bureaucracy, war, priesthood, and monopolist to create a society based on productivity and creativity. "The streets shall be our brushes, the squares our palettes," wrote Mayakovsky.

Berlin: The Divided City that Reflects the Divided World

1985: Berlin -- the capital of two would-be empires -- the most short-lived ones in world history; occupied by five armies; divided in two by a wall and machine guns. Why?

The true reality of all great cities is their myth. The weary traveller from the west, driving to Berlin through 4 border checks will see nothing mythical at first glance. The weather can be grey and nasty or depressingly hot, except for a few redeeming moments at glorious spring or fall. Dreary provincialism camouflages the hidden magic of Nekropolis.

A walk along prosperous Ku-Damm, through Ku-Damm's fashionable side-streets, through punk-ridden Kreuzberg ("no future" say the black graffitis), a stroll along the wall, an outing by sailboat on one of the numerous lakes, a traditional morning coffee in a sidewalk cafe, the obligatory beer-pub ("Kneipe') in the evening -- our traveller shakes his head -- pleasant enough but -- a former world city?

Berlin's real world is the world of history. She forsook life, beauty, things, energies, for its great passionate love- affair between madness, empire and intelligence.

The one "must" in Berlin: visit the Reichstag -- a curious structure, symbol of German unity, centering the powers of the empire in a petrified conglomerate of stylistic elements from Egypt to Greece to Rome to Byzantium to Firenze. Hybris of proud hopes: the first world empire-to-be founded on the principle of Hegelian dialectics and synthesis. This former powerhouse is situated in a desert created by Allied bombers and Russian artillery in '45...but on Sundays the desert is populated: thousands of tribals gather to celebrate the weekly flea market, situated in this man-made desert, a city that has run through the life cycle -- polis, metropolis, megalopolis, now Nekropolis, the city of the historically dead, inhabited by Fellaheen.

Ironically, the second "must" in East Berlin are the Ishtar Walls of Babylon, the greatest Nekropolis of Antiquity.

Berlin: the city where even Voltaire became a courtier, the city Kant reported to, where Hegel taught to thousands, city of two revolutions, of expressionism, Weimar Republic, Bertolt Brecht, Max Planck, Otto Hahn, Hitler and John F. Kennedy. Here people believe in one God and one only: the court of world history. Leaders? They've seen them come, they've seen them go. The wall -- just a material manifestation of antithesis calling down a new synthesis.

Berlin is unsurpassed at certain unusual moods -- a stomping ground of the seven deadly sins -- yet all in style and with some dignity. Brecht found alienation incarnate here.

The battle between New York and Berlin as the focal point for history in the twentieth century has not yet been decided for, after all, Moscow bases itself on Marx, who stated that, finding Hegel standing on his head, he had set Hegel on his feet.

While New York still pauses at the phase of megalopolis, Berlin stands austere, the living city of the dead, a sister to Egyptian Thebes. Curious the emotion a simple statement can evoke: "I am a Berliner" (consider J.F.K. saying "I am a New Yorker"). It is yet undecided if Thornrose-at-the-Spree will again awaken. Undoubtedly the uncertainty as to what that resurrection might imply explains why it is the only city ever to exist under the semi-permanent occupation of five armies.
Peter Riecks-Marlowe

Uruk: A Dead City

Desert. Mounds, mountainlike, dominating the landscape. A sheik with his family the sole guardian, guide, companion of the place now that the Germans have left with the treasures of their mining operations, leaving only the ruins of their railway hauling systems.

A vast ruin of the old city wall around the mounds. The garden district of Ishtar ever-shrinking through centuries of increase of power of the palace. Home of Gilgamesh, epic hero who sought, found, and lost the secret of immortality. First source of the legend of the Flood. Monument to destruction of an ecology wrought by man, and the accompanying inevitable death of its own life and glory. Reminding factor that disastrous consequences do indeed follow destructive behaviour persisted in against the warnings of prophets.

There it is, the city of Uruk. Urshunabi, climb up on that wall, the outer all shining with the brilliance of burnished copper, the seven wise men laid the foundations. One-third of the city is buildings, cunningly executed, one-third of the city is garden with rose and bird, one-third of the city is field with the temple of Ishtar within, Goddess of love and struggle.

Gilgamesh, translated by Caravan of Dreams Theater.

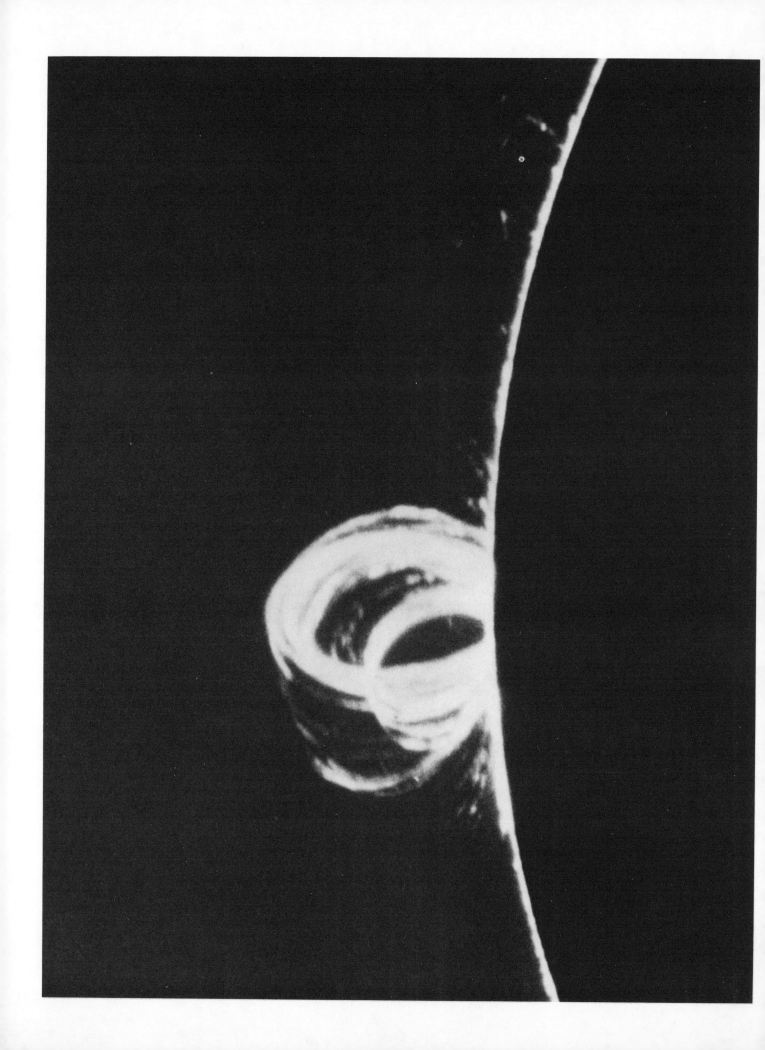

Energy

Rocco Fazzolare

Energy is Eternal Delight. WILLIAM BLAKE

$E=mc^2$. ALBERT EINSTEIN

Energy is Information. DISCOVERY OF THE
SCIENTIFIC-TECHNICAL REVOLUTION

Energy can be defined technically as the capacity to do work or to transfer heat. There are many common manifestations and forms of energy around us that we all recognize, such as the sun, a TV picture, the lights in the street, a moving car, air conditioning, a warm fire, to mention a few. There are also latent or potential forms of stored energy that can be liberated under certain conditions, i.e. the water behind a dam, a lump of coal, a bottle of alcohol, an apple or a car battery. For the most part, the energy used on earth originated at the sun, and also some minor contributions from nuclear and geothermal sources. Most importantly, solar energy sustains all life and powers the biosphere, its ecosystems and climatic variations.

Natural Ecosystems

Less than one percent of the energy from the sun gets fixed or stored by the plants through photosynthesis; the rest is briefly held by the biosphere and then released by reradiation to space. The plants in turn convert carbon dioxide to form breathable oxygen and supply the animal with food energy. An increasing fraction of fixed solar energy in the form of plant food and fuels as coal, oil and gas is being diverted to support man and his needs.

Green plants are the primary "convertors" of solar energy fixing it in organic compounds to maintain themselves and indirectly other living organisms which consume the plants and further convert the energy to flesh and work. The plants trap the sun's energy to build molecular structures such as sugars, starches, proteins, fats and vitamins. On land these are grasses, leaves, berries and nuts; in water the vegetation is plankton and

A loop prominence of the sun -- a result of strong magnetic fields. Sacramento Peak Observatory, 1979. Photograph courtesy of National Optical Astronomy Observatories, Tucson, Arizona.

sea weed. The consumers are animals, birds, insects, people and fish. Some consumers are herbivores such as cows and grasshoppers, others are carnivores that consume only animal matter such as cats and sharks, and some species called omnivores such as humans, get their energy both ways eating plants and animal flesh.

The chemical energy available for life processing decreases through the food chain. The plant itself uses roughly half the energy that it fixes from the sun for its own respiration. An animal eating the plant dissipates ninety per cent of the energy to maintain its own metabolism and muscular activity leaving ten per cent for conversion to weight if it is growing. A carnivore eating the animal would likewise be inefficient in converting the food to body weight. The plant and animal matter that does not get consumed as food ultimately dies and is attacked by decay organisms which extract the remaining energy and return the basic minerals and gases back to the biosphere at essentially zero energy state. The components are eventually recycled however, in new plants and animals by the infusion of solar energy thereby perpetuating the cycle.

The natural ecosystems in the biosphere depend on the incident solar radiation which varies on the earth's surface because of the geometric planetary relationships and most importantly because of the local weather conditions which are in turn influenced by solar heating. Clouds, rain and humidity are due to water evaporation from the oceans, lakes and rivers. The 24 hour average of sunshine on the earth surface varies from 100 watts per square meter in the arctic regions to 250 watts per square meter in the tropics. Very little of the incident radiation gets diverted into the life-support processes of the biosphere, with only about a kilogram per square meter of dry organic matter being produced per year. The forests, which cover about a tenth of the earth surface, fix about half the energy; other land vegetation and the oceans convert most of the remaining energy. Lands cultivated by the human population fix about five per cent of the solar radiation, using an equivalent addition of energy from the fossil fuel reserves in the form of fertilizers and pesticides. The yield of agricultural lands can be increased many fold by the addition of external energy sources. Six to ten kilograms of plant growth per square meter is possible in the most productive agriculture with proper infusion of oil and gas for fertilizers, pesticides, irrigation and machinery.

Technological Man

Agriculture is but one area where modern man has intervened in the natural energy flow of the earth's ecosystems in order to maximize real time benefits in

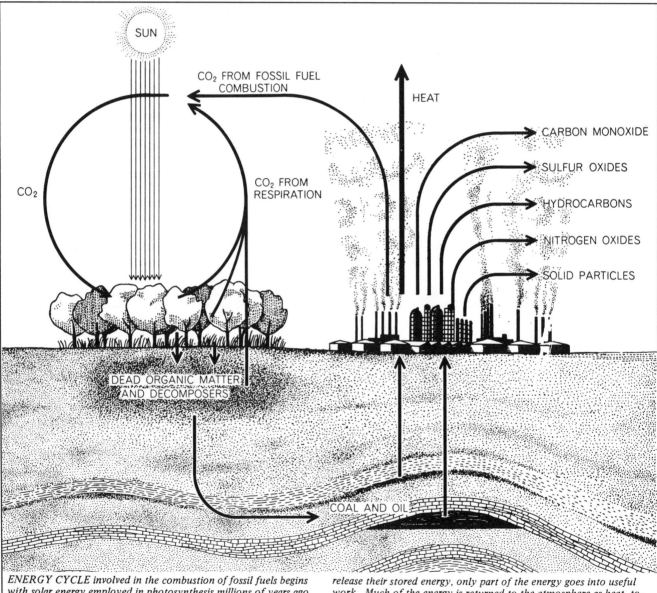

ENERGY CYCLE involved in the combustion of fossil fuels begins with solar energy employed in photosynthesis millions of years ago. A small fraction of the plants is buried under conditions that prevent complete oxidation. The material undergoes chemical changes that transform it into coal, oil and other fuels. When they are burned to release their stored energy, only part of the energy goes into useful work. Much of the energy is returned to the atmosphere as heat, together with such by-products of combustion as carbon dioxide and water vapor. Other emissions in fossil fuel combustion are listed at right in the relative order of their volume.

terms of human well being and material goods. The human intelligence has learned that man is not constrained by the limits of his own body to convert energy to achieve his ends. Other converters of a biological nature such as animals and plants as well as mechanical devices of his own fashion can be used to accelerate and concentrate energy flow to produce food, clothing and shelter. Technological man's needs far exceed the basic biological requirements for subsistance. Human nature however, has not yet allowed for an equitable distribution of these material benefits which accounts for existing starvation and suffering in the world.

The amount of solar energy falling on the earth is immense and far exceeds man's ability to convert it; the amount of heat that falls on one-and-a-half square miles is equivalent to the 20 kiloton atom bomb dropped on Hiroshima. Man's ability to convert radiant energy however is very limited and requires a high initial investment. For the most part man depends on and has depended on plants and other natural earth systems such as hydro and wind to harness the power from the sun. Industrialized society today is very dependent on fossil fuels which originated by photosynthesis millions of years ago. This stored and compacted form of solar energy conveniently packaged for distribution around the globe is relatively cheap since there is no cost of conversion from the incident radiation, just drilling and pumping costs. However, the fact that it is exhaustible and not equitably distributed on the earth surface is responsible for much of the political unrest in the human world today. In addition, its concentrated form permits exaggerated and localized liberation of combustion products and heat which tax the biosphere's ability to absorb the products in the environment.

The massive conversion of energy by man has taken place in a relatively insignificant time period -- 100 years -- compared with the millions of years of life in the biosphere. It is inevitable to question if this accelerated release of energy might not, in fact, affect the life cycles themselves. At one time all human beings depended on organic energy produced by green plants for survival and well being. The primitive societies of the past and very few today live by means of food gathering and hunting which is completely in a harmonious, yet very vulnerable, coexistence with the natural cycles of the biosphere. Slightly more advanced energetically are the food cultivators which through agriculture grow their food and related by-products. Much of the world's population now is in this stage of early development with a very limited control over their own destinies. These low energy societies are to some extent self perpetuating inasmuch as a critical balance between the in and out flow of energy exists. The institutions and energy use patterns tend to be stagnant because a surplus of energy is required for change

to occur. Modern technology for improved conversion cannot be easily introduced because the investments generated by the surplus are not available.

Energy Impact

The organization of the human species into economic and political units has been historically influenced by man's knowledge and capabilities to harness the energy available in the biosphere. In the last 100 years oil, gas and coal and the inventions of steam and combustion engines have greatly magnified human capabilities to construct buildings, transport man and materials and in general alter the environment. Modern man requires and utilizes orders of magnitude more energy for his external environment than he needs to keep alive. The accumulation of energy wealth and associated technology is the source of political and economic power which often results in serious world conflicts and divisions.

Before the era of fossil and nuclear fueled technology, the human race depended almost entirely on renewable solar energy. The lower level of energy availabilities, however, did not relieve the quest for individual accumulation or ameliorate the distribution of benefits. Animals and human slaves were used as energy convertors from Roman times until recently. Water power and wind were used to transport ships and grind grain. The sea powers of Europe dominated the world economically and politically. The new knowledge in using fossil and nuclear fuels has unleashed the industrial revolution and changed the economic institutions and organizations of man. The human condition has in general benefited and the limits and constraints of the biosphere have been expanded. Managed agriculture has increased the yield of crop production feeding a greater population; controlled and designed environments have provided for comfort and leisure regardless of the natural climatic conditions. Outer space beyond this biosphere is now accessible. The effects of this concentrated and localized release of energy and by-product pollution on the natural ecosystems are not clearly understood and remain a consideration for future generations to resolve. However, it is inevitable that the feedback systems of the biosphere will ultimately control our destiny.

Human Needs

The basic necessities of human life go far beyond the energy to supply food, and they include shelter, clothing, health care, transportation, communications, education, recreation, and security. Although only about 40% of the population on earth today enjoys all of these benefits, in 1900 only 1% of the society was so privileged. The availability of fossil fuels and related technology for

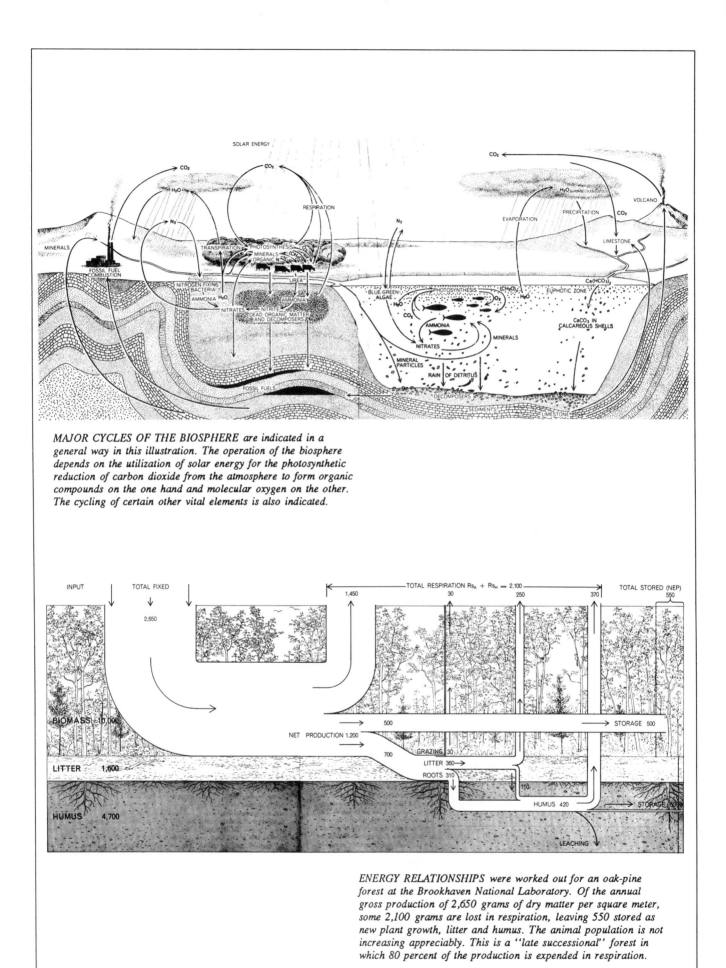

MAJOR CYCLES OF THE BIOSPHERE are indicated in a general way in this illustration. The operation of the biosphere depends on the utilization of solar energy for the photosynthetic reduction of carbon dioxide from the atmosphere to form organic compounds on the one hand and molecular oxygen on the other. The cycling of certain other vital elements is also indicated.

ENERGY RELATIONSHIPS were worked out for an oak-pine forest at the Brookhaven National Laboratory. Of the annual gross production of 2,650 grams of dry matter per square meter, some 2,100 grams are lost in respiration, leaving 550 stored as new plant growth, litter and humus. The animal population is not increasing appreciably. This is a "late successional" forest in which 80 percent of the production is expended in respiration.

conversion to useful products and services is primarily responsible for this growth in the standards of living. Energy consumption has grown from 11 to 83 trillion kilowatt hours since 1900. A major problem facing the world today is how to get enough energy to satisfy the 100% of the population with an equitable distribution of benefits yet minimize the disturbance of the natural biological systems of the biosphere.

The magnitude of the problem is made more acute when one considers how the population and its growth rate have grown in recent times. 250 million people were alive during the time of Christ. By 1650, the population increased to 500 million and doubled again in 200 years, so that it was 1 billion by 1850. In 1930 the population doubled to 2 billion and then reached 4 billion by 1975. The doubling rate is now 35 years and programmed to double again early in the next century.

The complexity of the energy resource expansion problem is further aggravated by societies' dependence on non-renewable and finite reserves of oil, gas, coal and uranium. All estimates show that at current usage patterns these free stored energy sources will be depleted within the next century. To what extent these predictions are to become reality depends on the modifications that society can adopt in both the supply of energy and demand for its use.

The energy crisis and shortages of the seventies were just a prelude to a new era of necessary adjustment. The scarcity of supply has increased prices and motivated a significant improvement in efficiency of use through conservation. Consider that the overall energy consumption in the United States has not changed in the ten year period from 1973 to 1983. Although the available fossil fuel reserve has not changed radically, the perception of an energy crisis no longer exists; oil and gas energy supplies are now apparently more stable because of increased production and present political considerations. The motivations for improved efficiency in energy use have consequently diminished. The underlying issues of continued population growth, limited resources and environmental pollution have not changed for the long term, however, and must ultimately be dealt with.

The biosphere is an automated system which will function with or without the human intelligence. However, some sound and critical human thinking, vision and planning can make for a more harmonious integration of societies' needs within the natural systems of the biosphere yet provide adequate energy for man's needs both in the present and the future.

References

The Energy Cycle of the Biosphere, by Georges M. Woodwell, The Biosphere, W.H. Freeman and Co., 1970.

Ecoscience, by Paul R. Ehrlich, Ann H. Ehrlich and John P. Holdren, W.H. Freeman and Co., 1977.

Energy and Society, by Fred Cottrell, Greenwood Press, 1955.

Ecosystems, Energy, Population, by Turk, J.T. Wittes, R. Wittes and T. Amos, W.B. Saunders Co., 1975.

Energy, Earth and Everyone, by Medard Gabel, Anchor Books, 1980.

The Biosphere, Scientific American Book, W.M. Freeman and Co.

Earth's Energy and Mineral Resources, Brian Skinner (Editor), William Kaufman Inc., 1980.

Energy Basis for Man and Nature, by Howard T. Odum and Elisabeth C. Odum, McGraw Hill, 1976.

Darest thou now O soul
    Walk out with me toward the unknown region
    Where neither ground is for feet
    Nor any path to follow?
                    WALT WHITMAN

Transportation

Arthur Reed

A man can walk four miles in an hour. The supersonic Concorde airliner covers 1,350 miles during the same period. These two parameters sum up graphically the advances that there have been in world transportation within the space of one lifetime, for it was as recently as 1903 (at 10:35 a.m. on December 17, to be precise) that the Wright brothers made the first man-powered flight, covering a distance about the same wingspan as one of today's jumbo jets.

The year 1903 was, therefore, a watershed, marking as it did a transition from a transportation "dark age" to a regime whose future possibilities have no real bounds. The 19th century had seen, it is true, the beginning of the railroads, with Stephenson's *Rocket* running in Britain in 1829, the first crossing of the Atlantic by steamship three years earlier, and the first motor car in 1885, while canals for the moving of coal and other heavy goods had been dug in Britain as early as 1761.

But before Orville and Wilbur Wright demonstrated the practicalities of using the sky as a transportation medium, rather than the surface of the earth, the populations of the world remained largely static. During the 19th century, and in the opening years of the 20th, residents in towns 40 miles distant from a capital city would most likely never visit that city during their lifetimes whereas, today, millions of commuters the world over, from Tokyo, to London, to Washington DC, think nothing of covering such a distance twice each day of their working lives.

There is no doubt that the First World War, breaking out only 11 years after the Wrights' first flight, provided the most significant transportation catalyst that the world has known. Within the four years which that conflict lasted, manpower, and research and development funding were poured in to an extent which would have been unthinkable in peacetime, so that by the time of the armistice in 1918, the technology of road, rail, sea, and particularly air had accelerated wildly.

Aircraft which had entered the war as uncertain contraptions of spruce, fabric, and wire, powered by converted motor-cycle engines, emerged with the beginnings of all-metal construction and custom-designed power plants able to make the bombing of Berlin from London a feasibility. Out of these types came the first airliners, the forerunners of today's fleets which, each year, carry some 700m people, and which draw the continents together as they race seven miles above the surface of the earth with up to 450 passengers on board.

The introduction of the jet engine into air transport on the British Comet airliner in July, 1949, was a transportation revolution as important as the Wrights' first flight, for the low cost of operating jets brought aviation within the financial reach of the ordinary people of the world, so that today the "man in the street" is able to take himself and his family on an annual vacation thousands of miles distant from his home.

So efficient did the jets become that by the 1960's they had sounded the death knell for the passenger-carrying ocean liner. Only those on vacation cruises now choose to cross the North Atlantic by ship in five days, as opposed to the seven hours taken by a subsonic airliner, and the three hours and 50 minutes by Concorde.

But while 700m do make air journeys each year, the bulk of the world's populations still have not flown, and it is the internal combustion engine, rather than the jet, which continues to make the most significant impact on daily lives. The man who can walk four miles in an hour has become the man who can drive, or be driven, ten miles an hour over the worst terrain, or 100 miles an hour on a motorway. The motor car has opened up the world to leisure pursuits, but more importantly, to business.

Transportation

Interlinked with the other three great forms of transportation, sea, rail, and the air, it has facilitated the great traditional trading patterns, so that the products of the soil, which are largely produced by the poorer nations whose countries lie below the equator, may be more easily exchanged for the technological products of the countries in the northern hemisphere.

Thus it is that today a housewife in London will buy in her local market exotic fruits which, 48 hours earlier, were growing on a plantation in East Africa, while the businessman in Rio de Janeiro will draw up his accounts on the latest computer from the robotized factories of Japan. The fruit will have been delivered to the distant airport by road; the computer will have arrived in South America on a container ship, having been sent from the factory to the great Japanese port of Yokohama by rail.

With certain exceptions, the world's railroads have become concentrated on commuter systems serving large conurbations, or on freight. In the United States, for instance, a country whose vast potential was opened up by railroad building in the last century, long-distance passenger services have been virtually ousted by air transport, but freight services by rail are of increasing importance to the economy. The exceptions are in countries like France and Japan, where high-speed trains running on dedicated tracks have been developed to such an extent that they provide real competition with commercial aviation over distances up to 200 miles.

Transportation is thus the muscle which flexes the biosphere, which brings the nations of the world closer geographically together, which influences patterns of trade and vacations. Forecasting how it will develop in the future is notoriously difficult; nobody in 1903 could have foreseen the strides that would have been accomplished before that new century was out. Technologically, the limits are almost infinite. Man landed on the moon as long ago as July 20, 1969, and the ability already exists to fly an airliner with passengers on board safely over long distances with computers, rather than human beings, controlling take-off, cruise, and landing.

But there are other types of limits with which one must temper the wilder prognostications. Infrastructures must put a brake on the future flowering of transportation systems, the seaports, airports, and rail termini through which the passengers and the goods must pass before they board the actual vehicles, the roads on which cars and trucks must drive. Such facilities must be finite, otherwise the smaller countries will become ruined environmentally as they strive to keep up. The strident world-wide environmental movement which sprang up in the 1960's, and which has already had a deep impact on the siting of airports, and the muting of aircraft noise, will resist the unlimited enlargement of transportation infrastructures. A further limiting factor is the amount of GNP which any country is prepared to spend in these directions.

Such inhibitions are bound to hit vacation and leisure travel hardest, for no country will curb its export and import flows for lack of freight sheds. Under pressure, airports will tend to price vacation traffic out in favor of business traffic and the movement of goods. At the same time, the objects of interest which tourists travel to see -- the castles, the palaces, the churches, the works of art -- are likely to become overwhelmed by the numbers of their visitors -- so providing a further limiting factor.

A further finite commodity is the fuel which drives transport on land, sea, or in the air. Petroleum-type fuels from the oilfields beneath the surface of the earth are the most common power source for each transportation type, but during the two fuel crises of the 1970's, various efforts were pursued to find alternatives, particularly in aviation.

Hydrogen was examined closely, as was synjet -- kerosene produced from coal -- nuclear power, even power from the sun, but they were all set aside as being too difficult, too expensive, or too dangerous to develop at this stage. With the ending of the fuel shortage, and a lowering of world prices for kerosene, the incentive to discover an alternative evaporated, but there is no doubt that this research will start up again in any fresh crisis. The most likely substitute seems to be hydrogen, always providing that its proneness to flammability can be curbed.

In the meantime, the various transportation industries are pursuing research into new aerodynamic shapes and lighter structures which will result in their vehicles moving through their various elements with less resistance, thus using less fuel to drive them. In the case of the aerospace industry, the use of lightweight and strong new materials such as carbon fibers to replace the traditional metals is being allied to the increasing employment of on-board computerization to fly the planes more precisely -- once again reducing the amount of fuel used, while also lowering operating costs because fewer cockpit crew need be employed.

The number of people moving about the world in the future may also be checked by the increasing sophistication of international communications, so that executives who now fly thousands of miles to go into conference with colleagues may choose, in future, to talk with those same colleagues on large-scale video screens, and so not have to leave their offices.

Similarly, much of the data which is at present flown or shipped will be transmitted over satellite systems. This is, however, a somewhat academic debate, for there is the important, but indefinable, ''meeting and greeting'' factor to be taken into account. Human beings like traveling to meet other human beings, and it could be that important orders will continue to go to those who fly to shake hands with the client, rather than talk with him over communications links, however advanced those links are.

For all these reasons, transportation progress has reached something of a plateau, and research in the foreseeable future will concentrate on improving the methods which have been developed so far this century, rather than chasing after totally new modes. In the 1970's, it was fashionable to talk about the 1,500-seat airplane, and the 5,000mph supersonic, but for the reasons adduced earlier, and the horrendous costs of such programs, such developments are almost certainly ruled out in current lifetimes.

There is one exception, however -- the exploration of space. This is the area where real transportation progress will occur as the world moves into the 21st century. Nations such as the United States, the Soviet Union, and the European allies, appear prepared, at present, to bear the high financial price of such research, and it is by no means beyond the bounds of imagination that many of us will live to see shuttle services to and from colonies living and working in outer space, and airline flights using the sub-stratosphere to link Britain with Australia in less than one hour. Inconceivable? But so was the Concorde when the Wrights made man's first faltering hop in 1903.

Transportation Appendix

Museums

National Air and Space Museum, The Mall, Washington DC, USA.
The Franklin Institute, Philadelphia, Pennsylvania, USA.
Musee de l'Air, Le Bourget, Paris, France.
The Science Museum, South Kensington, London, England.
The National Railway Museum, New Delhi, India.
The National Maritime Museum, Greenwich, London, England.
The Montagu Motor Museum, Beaulieu, near Southampton, England.

Books

Empires of the Sky, by Anthony Sampson, Hodder and Stoughton.
Three Centuries to Concorde, by Charles Burnet, Mechanical Engineering Publications.
The Sporty Game, by John Newhouse, Knopf.

Films

The Great Waldo Pepper
The Blue Max
No Highway
The Right Stuff

Communication

The Nervous System of the Biosphere

Gavin Trevitt

What happens to the best laid plans of mice and men in
any organization when the instant speed of information
movement begins? MARSHALL McLUHAN

We have all read the statistics, so often repeated
they have almost become a cliche, which show that the
sum total of knowledge in the biosphere is doubling now
every couple of years and that the rate of accumulation
is accelerating.

But, regardless of the sheer volume available,
knowledge left on its own, in a book or a computer file,
does not really exist in a usable way. Knowledge does not
become worthwhile until it is transferred to someone --
or in the not too far distant future something -- who/that
can use it. To state the obvious, it is that process of
transferring knowledge that is communications.

The often-drawn parallel between the world's
communications system and the human brain now
becomes evident, although not quite perfect; the
communications system does not comprise the ''brain''
of the biosphere, rather it is the nervous system which
enables the ''brain (substitute mankind)'' to process
knowledge and use it.

Two Heads Better Than One

Without communications our ability to accumulate
and apply knowledge would be very limited -- limited to
what we could deduce for ourselves and how much of
that we could remember. Our Neanderthal ancestors
didn't have it easy. The emergence of oral
communications improved things no end. Two heads that
could talk to each other probably almost doubled the
amount of usable information, or knowledge, available.

Oral languages also introduced the possibility of
communicating over time. Information garnered,
analyzed and applied by one generation could be passed
on to the next, and the next ... unless, of course,
someone forgot or was prematurely wiped out. Then it
was back to square one.

Necessity being the mother of invention, along came
symbol or written communication to assist mankind. This
solved the posterity problem but ... a cave wall filled with
the most wonderful, meaningful hieroglyphics was of
absolutely no use to you, if you happened to be in the next
cave. Or, leaping ahead a few eons to the middle ages,
while a great deal of usable information could be crammed
into a hand-written book or scroll, this information could
not be transferred from one place to another any faster than
a man could travel.

The first attempts to solve the speed problem,
sacrificed a great deal in the quality of communications
achieved. Smoke signals or a fire beacon on a distant hill
certainly meant that something was afoot. But whether
that something was an enemy army approaching or a
signal for a victory celebration was open for interpretation.
Devices such as semaphores or heliographs were more
precise, but still very limited in the quantity and quality of
the communications conveyed. And they were absolutely
useless beyond the horizon, unless you set up a relay
chain, which slowed down the speed and lessened the
precision of the communications.

With the development of steam power and the
railways in the 19th century, the embarrassing situation
arose where man could physically travel faster than he
could communicate by other means -- a situation which led
to some rather disastrous misadventures on the permanent
way. The solution proved to be the electric telegraph, the
first electronic means of communications.

Innovations followed with comparative rapidity --
distances between telegraph stations, where signals still
had to be physically received and retransmitted,
lengthened and new codes or methods of sending
information were evolved to suit the new medium. Cables
tied cities, then countries, and soon they were tentatively
reaching across the world's oceans. The biosphere's first,

albeit limited, nervous system was being formed. The limitation of the "wonder-working wire" was that it could transmit only small quantities of information and then only to a small number of places. But no longer did information have to be physically transported to the man -- or the man physically transported to the information -- before it became usable knowledge.

The telephone, of course, increased the speed and quantity of information that could be transferred and for the first time made the information stream a two-way transfer. Except for a few exceptional cases, the telephone also allowed the first human-to-human real-time communications.

Broadcast Information

The development of radio, as well as freeing communicators from confining their activities to tenuous threads of copper wire, brought with it two other great advantages. It could be used to transfer information to things that were moving, and it could, through broadcast, be used to transfer information to many people at once. The frustration of it was that, with the exception of some very interference-prone frequencies that were deflected back to earth by the ionosphere, most radio transmissions traveled in straight lines and were therefore only usable for short distances. If you wanted to transfer your information a long way, or overseas, your only options continued to be cable, which could still only carry telegraph signals, or the static, fading and other peculiarities of short-wave, or high frequency, radio. It was generations later that coaxial cables with electronic signal amplifiers, or repeaters, spaced along them on the ocean floor, finally provided a reliable telephone service across the oceans.

The next major development -- satellite communications -- brings us up to the present time and will carry us some way into the future. Satellites, generally located in the Clarke orbit (named after Arthur C. Clarke, who first hypothesized that not only would a satellite 22,300 miles or 36,000 kilometers above the equator stay stationary in the sky above the earth, but that it would also make a wonderful radio repeater station) do well what the ionosphere does in a mediocre fashion. From their geostationary perch they can receive signals directed up to them and retransmit them downwards to be received anywhere over the third of the earth's surface visible from the satellite. Suddenly, distance was not only conquered, it was irrelevant. And the sheer power of this new medium meant that there was no longer any restrictions on the type and quality of communications. A high-definition television relay would take only a small fraction of the capacity of a modern satellite, and thousands of telephone calls ebb and flow via the satellite path as a matter of routine.

As Santiago Astrain, the first Director General of INTELSAT, the world satellite communications cooperative, put it: "With satellites, things which were local events can be world events. Everyone in the whole world can share in the same experience at the same time."

Anyone, Anywhere, Any Time

In other words, the biosphere's nervous system is now virtually complete. Almost everyone on earth can share and use the same information simultaneously. Or almost anyone can transmit instantly almost any information to almost anyone else anywhere. Knowledge is no longer subject to time or distance. Knowledge can be universal.

So let's take stock of the nervous system of the biosphere, as it exists in the latter part of this century.

For convenience sake, a clear distinction should be made between the media -- or the types of systems used to transmit information -- and the services -- or form of information transmitted.

Media can be divided into the three broad categories of cable and landline, radio and satellite. Services need to be subdivided into broadcast and public (those services provided by the public networks for point-to-point private communications). Under broadcast put radio and television and under public put telephone, telegraph, telex, facsimile, data transmission (at any speed), closed circuit television and teleconferencing.

As far as media are concerned, satellites are dominating current developments. Satellites are currently carrying about two-thirds of the world's international communications and about 30 countries are now operating satellite systems to provide domestic communications services. However, over the next few years the emphasis will shift back to land, or at least surface, based links with the application of fibre-optic technology. Because of the tremedous band-width available in the light frequencies, one hair-like strand of optical fibre can carry the equivalent of many thousands of telephone calls. In the developed world, fibre-optic inter-city and local networks are already being installed and there are now no less than four separate proposals for fibre-optic submarine cable across the northern Atlantic Ocean.

Cables and satellites are also changing the broadcast industries, particularly in Europe and North America. Satellites have become a major distribution medium for television programing, both internationally and domestically. A scan across the transponders of many of the communications satellites in geostationary orbit would reveal an enormous variety of TV programs. While conventional broadcast systems are still flourishing, in many instances these programs are received by relatively small and economical dish antennas and fed into cable distribution networks. Cable networks, both conventional and fibre-optic based, can be as small as one hotel or apartment block or as large as a city. They can carry dozens of TV channels and so can cater to minority as well as majority tastes. And they can be interactive, allowing the viewer to participate in the programing or to use the television set as a two-way, rather than one-way communications tool. For the television industry, today's problem is not so much how to get the program to the viewer as it is how to find sufficient program material to satisfy the enormous number of distribution channels available.

With the great strides now being made in the technical development of transmission media, there are associated advances being achieved in transmission methods. The gradual conversion from analogue to digital transmission techniques will enable vastly larger quantities of information to be moved on existing systems and will provide a much more flexible world communications network, capable of handling all types of communications through the same transmission and switching facilities.

The Next Development

The next major development in the world telecommunications system may well be the final one. Nothing sinister is meant by this. It is this final step which will put knowledge -- or usable information -- at the disposal of all human beings who need it, regardless of where they are and what they are doing. It is the mobilization of communications.

With a few notable exceptions, the systems and networks which provide global ''public'' communications are fixed. They provide communications between fixed points. From the telephone in one office or home to another. From one village call box to another. From a telex machine in an agency in Stockholm to a telegraph office in New Delhi. From a news bureau in London to a television network in New York. The messages or communications go from one place to another. As anyone who has experienced the frustration of an unanswered telephone or, worse still, the ominous clicks and white noise that signal the presence of an answering machine can attest, humans still have to be in the right place at the right time to receive the information.

Two technologies -- computers and satellites -- are coming together to enable us to jump this last hurdle in connecting the network with the real recipient.

Computers provide the capability to carry out the extremely complex real time network management and interconnection functions which enable cellular radio land mobile communications systems to function. Cellular radio comprises a series of overlapping small radio transmitting and receiving systems, or cells. A mobile telephone unit requires then only a comparatively low powered transmitter, with the management of its signal being handled by computer as it moves from cell to cell. Because it can carry high volumes of traffic flexibly and comparatively economically, cellular radio is ideal for developed and urbanized areas. Its impact is already being felt in many countries and cities. Cellular radio terminals are already available that can fit unobtrusively in a car, briefcase, pocket or handbag. Wristwatch size units can't be far away.

Satellite Mobile

There are large areas of the world -- the oceans and comparatively undeveloped land areas -- where cellular radio may never be a viable proposition. For these areas, satellites will provide the final human connection.

Remember, satellites from their lofty orbital perches,

can see almost a third of the earth's surface. And, as their transmission and reception medium is radio, they can be used to communicate with anything, anywhere in their coverage area, whether it is stationary or moving. There is already in existence a satellite system which provides instant, on demand, dial-up communications services to shipping world-wide. Plans are well advanced to extend this to aeronautical and, possibly, land mobile applications. Other systems are being discussed or proposed in the U.S. and elsewhere which will provide almost instant position location and rudimentary "paging" type communications services. (Want to know if Dad is still in the pub? Ask a satellite, then summon him home!)

The continuing development of satellite spot-beam techniques and on- board dynamic switching facilities, along with communications links between satellites themselves, hold promise of extensive "satellite cellular" systems in the future, operating to tiny personal terminals and providing an extensive range of high-quality communications services.

It is an odd thought that, just as we get the biosphere's nervous system to this final completed stage, our communications needs may change. It does not require much effort to imagine that the pocket or wrist communicator we will all be carrying will also contain a high-powered ultra- micro computer holding in its micro-mammoth memory all of mankind's accumulated knowledge, updated to, say a couple of seconds ago, via the network. Our only need of communications will then be for the periodic updates from, and for relaying our own contributions to, the knowledge bank.

Focal Points

U.S. Federal Communications Commission

1919 M Street NW, Washington D.C. 20554, U.S.A.

In most countries, telecommunications are still conducted and administered by Government departments or authorities, which do not generally give priority to the provision of information to the public. However, the highly competitive telecommunications environment in the United States is overseen and regulated by the Federal Communications Commission. As a government instrumentality, the F.C.C. is compelled by freedom of information legislation to make information on its proceedings, and the information considered in those proceedings, available to the public. Because of the dynamic nature of the U.S. scene, you can almost be sure that any new telecommunications idea, technology, service or application will make its first public appearance somewhere in the voluminous documentation generated by the F.C.C.

International Telecommunication Union

Place des Nations, CH 1211 Geneva, Switzerland
An instrumentality of the United Nations, the I.T.U. is considered by many as a model of international co-operation for the overall good of mankind. As well as providing a forum for information exchange and discussion, the I.T.U. -- through its committees, principally the C.C.I.T.T. and the C.C.I.R. -- formulates and administers international regulation of common telecommunications standards and practices and radio frequency usage. It also administers the regulation of international satellites in the geostationary (Clarke) orbit.

International Institute of Communications

Tavistock House South, Tavistock Square, London WC1H 9LF, England
World-wide non-governmental membership organization concerned with communications research and policy. Has over 1,000 members in 75 countries, including many in developing countries and more than 80 institutional and corporate members. I.I.C. organizes major conferences, publishes numerous reports and participates in communications orientated projects. An excellent source of information on telecommunications subjects and on communications in a more generic sense. Publishers of *InterMedia* (see Magazines).

Database

Tele/Scope

EIC/Intelligence Inc., 48 West 38th Street, New York, New York 10018, U.S.A.
A comprehensive telecommunications news and information database, with a menu covering business intelligence, product developments, legal actions and issues, industry personnel, emerging technologies, and meetings and conferences. Updated daily.

Programs

School of Management & Strategic Studies

Western Behavioral Sciences Institute, 1150 Silverado Street, P.O. Box 2029, La Jolla, California 92038, U.S.A. 619-459-3811

A two-year program in management education designed for individuals working at or likely to occupy key future roles in the upper ranks of business, governments or non-profit institutions. The program involves mastering the new medium of teleconferencing, as well as the art of intelligent communication of concepts and ideas on contemporary issues. Participants pursue the program "on-line" from their homes or place of work, meeting only four times for one-week sessions over two years. The objective of this program is to prepare the individual to meet radically changed requirements for leadership in the coming decades. Pioneering in computer teleconferencing as a communication tool for the development of intelligent networks -- getting the right information to the right person at the right time, increasing rapid decision-making possibilities and creating immediate feed-back loops -- this intensive program is for the qualified and motivated individual.

American University, School of Communications

4400 Massachusetts Avenue NW, Washington D.C. 20016, U.S.A. 202-885-1394

Offers professional communication skills in journalism, film, video, broadcasting and public affairs. The program structure interfaces with the scene in Washington -- communication center of the world.

George Washington University

2121 First Street, Washington D.C. 202-676-7062

The University provides one of the outstanding telecommunication studies curriculum in the United States. The three major programs offered are Telecommunication Management, Telecommunication Policy and Telecommunication Technology.

The Annenberg School of Communications

3620 Walnut Street, Philadelphia, Pennsylvania 19104, U.S.A. 215-898-7041

Magazines, Periodicals

Telecommunications Reports

1293 National Press Building, Washington D.C. 20045, U.S.A.

Known in the trade as the "Yellow Peril" because of the color of the paper on which it is printed, this weekly newsletter is recognized as the document of record as far as the U.S. telecommunications scene is concerned. Although its layout and reporting style are stiflingly dull, you can be reasonably sure that if it happened and it had something to do with telecommunications, it will find its way into *Telecommunications Reports.*

Communications Daily

Satellite Week, 1836 Jefferson Place NW, Washington D.C. 20036, U.S.A.

One of a stable of newsletters printed by the Washington-based Television Digest group. Good for detailed, day-to-day coverage of the industry. Sister publication to *Satellite Week,* which covers the whole satellite industry including a great deal of communications reporting. Known in the industry to enjoy a controversy and to conduct regular editorial crusades.

Connections

25 St. James's Street, London, SW1A 1HG, England

A collaboration between *Satellite Week* and the English weekly, *The Economist,* this publication inherits its forebearer's controversy-seeking, crusading style but concentrates its coverage more on the European scene.

Telecommunications Journal

International Telecommunication Union, Place des Nations, CH 1211 Geneva, Switzerland

Another publication of record, this time produced by the International Telecommunication Union. The Journal covers the activities of the Union and its various committees, as well as carries articles on actions, operations and technologies from its many member countries and contributing administrations. You could call it the publication of the telecommunications establishment. Don't look to the Journal for up-to-date hot news -- because of publishing lead times, everything you read there will be at least three months old.

Communications International

Elm House, 10 -- 16 Elm Street, London WC1X 0BP, England

In-depth quality coverage of world telecommunications policy and activities, as seen through the eyes of a London-based publication.

Intermedia

International Institute of Communications, Tavistock House South, Tavistock Square, London WC1H 9LF, England

The multi-disciplinary view of the world communications scene. In depth coverage of policy issues, technology impact and future scenarios. Also a discussion forum for topics relating to the social and cultural impact of communications and telecommunications.

Books

From Semaphore to Satellite, International Telecommunication Union. Produced to mark the centenary of the I.T.U., this well-written and nicely-illustrated book traces the history of telecommunications in an interesting and comprehensive way. It is also a good read.

Global Talk, by Dr. Joseph Pelton. A perceptive view of the world telecommunications situation as it stands and the present and future impact of the combination of communications and computers on world cultures and social development. Dr. Pelton is an articulate, recognized expert in the field.

The World's Telephones, A.T.& T. Communications. A periodical publication containing all the statistics and detailed information you would ever want about the world's telephone systems...and more!

Broadcasting and Telecommunications -- An Introduction, by John R. Bittner, Prentice-Hall Inc., Englewood Cliffs, New Jersey, 1985. The development of electronic communications from the telegraph through to the personal computer.

Introducing Satellite Communications, by G.B. Bleazard, NCC Publications, Manchester, 1985. A broad and comprehensive treatment of the subject of satellite communications, expressed in non-technical language.

The International Telecommunication Union in a Changing World, by George A. Codding and Anthony M. Rutkowski, Artech House Inc., Dedham, Massachusetts, 1982. The history of the I.T.U. and a description of its decision-making machinery, structure, problems and prospects.

Competition for Markets in International Telecommunications, by Ronald S. Eward, Artech House, Dedham, Massachusetts, 1984. Considers telecommunications policies and structures of 17 countries.

Forum '83 -- Proceedings of the Fourth World Telecommunications Forum (in three parts), International Telecommunication Union, Geneva, Switzerland, 1983.

International Telecommunications and Information Policy, Christopher H. Sterling (Editor), Communication Press Inc., Washington D.C., 1984. Papers from a Symposium held at George Washington University in May 1983 and a report of the U.S. N.T.I.A. "Long Range Goals in International Telecommunications and Information".

The Missing Link (The Maitland Report), Report of the Independent Commission for World Wide Telecommunications Development, International Telecommunication Union, Geneva, Switzerland, 1984.

Multi-National Study of Telecommunications Structures, by Robert R. Bruce, International Institute of Communications, London, 1985. Comprehensive analysis of the legal and regulatory framework surrounding national information services and telecommunications policies in eight countries.

Telecommunications -- An Interdisciplinary Text, Leonard Lewin (Editor), Artech House Inc., Dedham, Massachusetts, 1984. A comprehensive survey of the subject by various experts, 687-pages strong.

Space Biospheres

John Allen and Mark Nelson

The water we live in is Time. That alien medium we
glimpse beyond Time is Space. And that is where we are
going...WILLIAM BURROUGHS

Equipped with the grand concepts, insights, data
and modelling from Vernadsky, Lovelock, Margulis, and
Folsome we poise ready now not only to cooperate
consciously and creatively with the evolutionary
potential of our present biosphere but also to assist in its
mitosis into other biospheres freeing our earth-life to
participate in the full destiny of the cosmos itself, both by
giving the possibility to voyage and live throughout space
and also to improve ''Biosphere I'' here on planet Earth.

Space Biospheres Ventures bought in July 1984, a
2,300-acre ranch north of the Santa Catalina Mountains
near Tucson, Arizona, and engaged the Institute of
Ecotechnics to manage the scientific-technical aspects of
its project to build Biosphere II, an energetically and
informationally open but materially closed structure
containing seven ecosystems including a human habitat
and an intensive agricultural system. Other ecosystems
are: freshwater, saltwater, desert, savannah, and
rainforest. The size of the structure will be more than
three million cubic feet.

Sarbid, Ltd, a London-based architectural project
firm headed by Margret Augustine, is in charge of the
project design and construction. The Environmental
Research Laboratory of the University of Arizona,
renowned for its innovative agri-systems work, headed
by Carl Hodges, is the chief engineering contractor.

The scheduled engineering, construction and
operation is as follows:

Engineering mid 1986
Construction of Human Habitat and Agriculture
    Systems 1986-88
Fully Materially Enclosed Operation 1989
Debugging 1990
Marketing, Production Program 1991

Milky Way. Cerro Tololo Inter-American Observatory, c. 1978.
Photograph courtesy of Association of Universities for Research
in Astronomy.

The aims of the project are fivefold:

Informational

For the first time a communication between two
biospheres will be established. At present all our
information comes from within Biosphere I or from a
non-biospheric material-energetic universe inside or
outside Biosphere I. Hence, there must exist permanent
hidden constraints on observations. One constraint that is
obvious is a definite length of time for cycles to close their
loop. In Biosphere II, cyclic time will be different.
Another constraint is that in Biosphere I a non-biospheric
core forces Biosphere I into a sphere-surface form with a
non-biospheric interior, whereas in Biosphere II all non-
Biosphere II activity will be exterior. A third is that human
population is unplanned and uncontrolled as indeed are
essentially all the populations in Biosphere I. A fourth is
that Biosphere I is the everchanging resultant of a
continuous, albeit with catastrophic intervals, evolution
and no or little selection has occurred in a non-Darwinian
mode, including that of technics and culture. Therefore, in
Biosphere I there may be teleonomy as Konrad Lorenz has
pointed out, but no teleology. In Biosphere II it is at least
possible that the artistic mode of selection could
predominate over the Darwinian.

The result of these and other differences will be the
exchange of two sets of information ranging from
atmospheric cycles to human physiology to different
technics to different rates of molecular transfer throughout
the Biosphere. We will attain at a bound, the ability to
compare -- the basis of objective thought.

Modeling

Biosphere II will serve as a model for the scientific
manager and managing scientist to upgrade their handling
of energetically open, informationally open, and only

semi-materially enclosed ecological regions due to the strength of the paradigm. They will use it to develop a graded series of analogies, for example: islands, mining regions, forests, deserts, continents, etc.

Space Travel

Biosphere II, by showing the practibility of small-scale stable, complex, evolving life-systems, will open up space to biospheric mitoses and hence to man who can travel only as a part of a greater whole, that is, a biosphere. So, at the minimum point of view, our meaning rises to being co-equal with the cosmos rather than as an insignificant episode in the midst of vast material-energetic exchanges.

Refugia

Biosphere II will serve as a prototype for production of Refugia, which will serve as insurance to protect higher forms of life against the nuclear winter that could well result from a quite possible nuclear interchange between super-powers or an alliance of great powers. A hundred Refugia protected by their own energy resources in mountain caverns could again (in the worst possible case) release full-scale life into Biosphere I after the skies begin to clear. Perhaps even the existence of the Refugia could bring home to peoples and states the gigantic risks they run and thus alter the behavior itself.

Art and Architecture

Biospheres could begin to be the great work of art for cities and peoples to aspire to attain and biospheres will be built in the centers of cities, on the historic plazas of nations, and revolving in splendor around the planet Earth.

A new understanding of the potency of harmony will attract the virile and intelligent of all nations to work on such projects and those, the vast majority, who remain in Biosphere I will be challenged to put forth their best efforts to make it as equal in beauty and interest as it will perhaps remain for a billion years superior in size to its descendants.

Project Information

Those interested in Space Biospheres Project information may contact:
Space Biosphere Ventures
SunSpace Ranch Conference Center
Post Office Box 689
Oracle, Arizona 85623 U.S.A.

Reference

Disturbing the Universe, by Freeman Dyson, Harper & Row, 1979. Dyson reveals the thinking processes of some of the leading physicists and scientists at the forefront of space. ''Pilgrims, Saints & Spacemen'' (Chapter 11) opens one's eyes to the real value/costs of space exploration and colonization today by comparison to the earlier colonial expeditions such as the Mayflower and the Mormons.

(Biospheric book reviews are to be found in the Information section.)

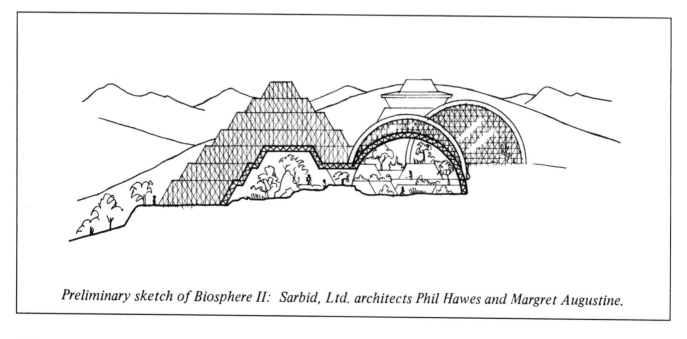

Preliminary sketch of Biosphere II: Sarbid, Ltd. architects Phil Hawes and Margret Augustine.

Two Biospheric Architects

Phil Hawes

The two modern guiding lights in the art of realizing the necessary and critical relationship between man's architecture and the biosphere are Frank Lloyd Wright and Bruce Goff.

Both from the Midwest of the United States, both shared the same birthday, although Goff was thirty-seven years Wright's junior, and both were totally dedicated to their individuality, visions, and understanding of *organic architecture*. Wright's child-mind playing with smooth wooden geometric shapes, running in the Wisconsin woods and fields, "awakened to the rythmic structure in nature", learning to "see constructive pattern evolving in everything he saw". He bridled at the adult utilitarianism and he realized that "a flower was a worthwhile fruit too", and that impressions were vital food.

He studied botanical field drawings as well as plants in nature and translated these into stone and cast iron details for his master, Louis Sullivan, architect-teacher. To Wright "folk buildings that fit their environment are better worth study than all the self-conscious academic attempts to create the beautiful".

"Organic architecture will be a native growth and cannot be put on from the outside." Wright mused, "What is style? Every flower, animal and every individual worthy of the name has it." *"Organic architecture,* the architecture of Nature for Nature, proceeds from the ground; and somehow the terrain, the native industrial conditions, the nature of materials, and the purpose of the building must inevitably determine the form and character of any good building. There is a kinship of the building to the ground." Wright's approach was that good

architecture was indigenous architecture in that it should be inborn, innate, inherent in the symbiotic relationship between the site, the client, the architect, the available technics.

"The law of organic change is the only thing that mankind can know as beneficent or as actual." Based on his childhood love of triangles, squares, and circles, Wright sought organic diversity and harmony through the use of these shapes as modules to develop his plans and elevations for the majority of his work.

Scale to Wright meant human scale which he expressed by making the elements in the building visually manageable. The parts and repetitions of his modules are not so massive as to be visually intimidating to the viewer. This characteristic gives his drawings and photos of his work a deceptively large appearance which becomes intimate relationship when viewed in the actual environment.

If you will slide your eyes over a Wright floor plan or section as if you were wielding the pencil yourself, while keeping in mind where your mental feet are taking you and looking with your mind's eye at the three dimensional forms that evolve, you can become aware of the interlocking relationships between his forms, their functions, and the environment. Particularly exciting are those buildings in which the environment penetrates the building with massive stone outcroppings or when the forms of native living rock are reflected in the shape of the building.

Bruce Goff, a lifelong spiritual heir to Frank Lloyd, discarded the simple geometric modules of his mentor as unnecessarily restrictive. He mentioned that, "mystery is necessary to sustain our interest and mystery defies analysis".

"We shall take the first and most urgent idea and develop it into the final forms. In this way we are more apt to come up with a truly organic performance. In nature the forms are the result of a growth and development; they are arrived at rather than started with." "The building is of the site, not on it." Goff was another who spent his childhood often in the fields and woods and some of his favorite teaching comments were "Look into a building as you look into a tree", and, "We can have harmony in diversity with nature as the supreme example".

A great visionary often accused of *going too far* in his designs, Goff stated: "An artist cannot go too far out; any idea that can be conceived in our time can also be executed in our time".

As with any great architecture, there is no substitute for directly experiencing the buildings of these two great fashioners of *organic architecture*. Experiencing many of the buildings will create in your own organism emotions, understanding, and sensations which constitute a permanent objective impact much akin to experiencing and understanding a phenomenon of the biosphere.

References

Frank Lloyd Wright: An Autobiography, Duell, Sloan, and Pearce, N.Y., 1943.

Frank Lloyd Wright: Drawings for a Living Architecture, Horizon Press, 1959.

Frank Lloyd Wright: Writings and Buildings, The World Publishing Co., Meridian Books, 1961.

Horizon, American Heritage, Vol. 4, No. 2, November 1961.

Life Extension in Space Traveling Biospheres

Roy L. Walford

Requirements for simple duration of life are different for interplanetary versus star travel. Interplanetary travel is the modern equivalent of the Dutch successfully colonizing the Indies despite the fact that it took four years to get there and back by ship. Life extension was not necessary. By contrast, time requirements for biospheric star travel are demanding, increasing with distance from near to far stars. It has been variously estimated that a ship driven by a single-stage fusion engine could reach the nearest stars in forty years; with multi-stage fusion a round trip to Alpha Centauri (4.3 light years) might require thirty years; at 0.1 g acceleration for one year, then coasting, 120 years would be required each way to visit Tau Ceti (11.8 light years) (Forward, 1976). For near-star travel, we are dealing with these orders of magnitude for engineering and life endurance requirements. Quite different problems for survival, but perhaps not so different for engineering technology (since one could coast for an indefinite time) would arise for far-star flights.

Life span can be extended by controlled restriction of caloric intake; by slight lowering of internal body temperature; more severe lowering of internal body temperature, as by actual hibernation; or by freezing. These methods do not exhaust the possibilities for extending life span, but other approaches require a greater conceptual scientific leap, a deeper understanding of fundamental biogerontology such as how to regulate DNA repair rates, inhibit or neutralize free radical generation, or as yet unseen advances in the neurosciences. Much work is being done in all these areas (Finch and Schneider, 1985), but cannot be outlined in this brief report. Besides extending life span, the methodologies to be discussed may offer additional benefits for space travel.

Abundant animal studies since 1935 have shown that caloric restriction, to 90% to 50-60% of ad libitum intake, and provided that the food actually consumed is of high nutritional value (hence the catchphrase, "undernutrition without malnutrition"), will extend maximum life span of rodents and other species by 20 to 80% (Walford, 1983). There is reason to believe that with a high order of probability the method would work in humans; beginning with restriction in early childhood, this would mean at the outside a maximum life span of 180-190 years. Proportionate extension could be expected if restriction were started at a later time, for example 1/2 as much if at mid-life, and depending on the actual degree of restriction. Life extension by caloric restriction does not add old years onto old, but extends the period of youth and middle age, and, of additional importance for space colonization, the period of fertility. However, a life span of 180 years refers to the last survivor, the tail of the curve, not a working population. From a practical standpoint, the extension of useful working life possible by caloric restriction would be 20 to possibly 40 years. Additional advantages in relation to space travel would include lower food requirements (by 10% to 40-50%), lower disease susceptibility, and (possibly) some amelioration of the no-gravity induced condition of osteoporosis, since calorie-restricted animals do not lose bone so rapidly with age as normally fed animals (Kalu et al, 1984). The major advantage is that the methodology is available now and works.

Studies in poikilotherms demonstrate that great life extension can be achieved by long-term lowering of internal body temperature by a relatively few degrees (Liu and Walford, 1972). Calculations suggest that a readjustment of the thermostat in humans to maintain body temperature at say 33 degrees centigrade would yield maximum life spans of possibly 200 years (Rosenberg et al., 1973). Technology is not yet available to do this in homeotherms like mammals on a long term basis. Mammals can be rendered temporarily hypothermic. Most are tolerant of, i.e., under the right conditions can recover from, hypothermia down to 15 degrees C, but at least in acute experiments lack coordination at only 5 degrees below normal body temperature. It is not known whether very slow cooling would allow some adaptability, but it might do so as suggested by studies in Indian yogis (Walford, 1983). There are two types of acclimatization to cold environments (Hammel, 1964). That characteristic of most races is "metabolic acclimatization", in which shivering occurs and the metabolic rate is increased to maintain body temperature. Australian aborigines, by contrast, show "insulative-hypothermic acclimatization", in which shivering occurs less or not at all, and the body temperature drops slightly without an increased metabolic rate.

Substantial lowering of body temperature but still not to freezing would be equivalent to hibernation, and should yield an enormous extension of life span. Unfortunately the processes which control the onset of hibernation are unknown, although evidence exists for both sympathetic nervous system versus humoral factors (a hormone or circulating peptide) (Lyman et al., 1982). Control by a humoral factor would render the methodology more feasibly adaptable to ordinarily nonhibernating mammals like man.

Freezing is a real possibility and would have many advantages. Cells in suspension, including human lymphocytes and fibroblasts, can be frozen, maintained in liquid nitrogen, thawed many years later and be demonstrated to be fully viable. Thus, there is no built-in inability of the mammalian cell to survive freezing, and the fact that whole mammalian organs or organisms cannot yet be frozen and revived is a technological rather than basic science problem. The problem is that it has not been possible to lower temperature *at exactly the same rate* throughout the large volume of occupied space represented by a whole organ or person, resulting in marked hypersalinity in some cell compartments at the freezing point, with protein denaturation. A number of lower species (invertebrates) can survive freezing by inducing the production of cryoprotective agents. The highest order of animals able to do so are adult frogs (Schmid, 1982).

Additional advantages to freezing, and probably proportionately in other forms of temperature lowering, include the prevention of demineralization, lower food requirements, and resistance to damaging effects by radiation in space. X-rays (gamma-irradiation) produce tissue damage not so much directly as by the generation of free radicals, which then go on to damage DNA and other components of tissues. Fewer free radicals are generated in hypothermic tissues, and very likely none at all in tissues frozen to deep space temperatures. Frozen astronauts should keep well for thousands of years, hopefully not to serve as someone else's TV dinner at the end of their run.

Bibliography

Handbook of the Biology of Aging, by C. Finch and E. Schneider (Editors), 2nd edition, Van Nostrand Reinhold, New York, 1985.

Journal of British Interplanetary Society, A Programme for Interstellar Exploration, by R. L. Forward, 1976 (29:611-632).

Handbook of Physiology (Section 4: Adaptation to the Environment, ed. D.B. Dill, E.F. Adolph, C.W. Wilbur), American Physiology Society, Wms. and Wilkins, Washington D.C., 1964 (pp. 413-434).

Endocrinology, Aging and Dietary Modulation of Rat Skeleton and Parathyroid Hormone, by D.M. Kalu, R.H. Hardin, R. Cockerham, B.P. Yu, 1984 (115:1239-1247).

Gerontologia, The Effect of Lowered Body Temperature on Life Span and Immune and Non-immune Processes, by R.K. Liu and R.L. Walford, 1972 (18:363-388).

Hibernation and Torpor in Mammals and Birds, by C.P. Lyman, J.S. Willis, A. Malan, L.C. Wang, Academic Press, 1982.

Mechanisms of Aging and Development, The Kinetics and Thermodynamics of Death in

Multicellular Organisms, by B. Rosenberg, G. Kemeny, L.G. Smith, I.D. Skurnick, M.J. Bandurski, 1973 (2:275-281).

Science, Survival of Frogs at Low Temperature, by W.D. Schmid, 1982 (215:697-698).

Maximum Life Span, by R. L. Walford, W.W. Norton & Co., New York 1983.

The Biosphere prepares to send its mitoses into
space.

Cosmic Particles

Cosmic Particles and Earth's Radioactivity

Donald E. Paglia

Above the Biosphere the Cosmosphere pours in its electromagnetic radiations and its radioactive particles, some of which have already been impounded in the Geosphere while others shift about in the Biosphere itself. What happens with these energies that form, power, mutate and destroy life? THE EDITOR

A walled plain in the fourth quadrant of the moon bears the name of Heraclitus, the Greek philosopher who contended 2500 years ago that change was an inherent quality of the universe. Like the rivers that one "could not step twice in...for other and yet other waters are ever flowing on", so the cosmos continues in constant flux. Survival of any life form, therefore, ultimately depends upon the counterpoint quality, adaptability, a concept that Darwin extrapolated to include the evolution of species.

In similar manner, biospheres, as life systems existent in the universe, must of necessity be adaptable; for regardless of eventual location, change is their only certain encounter.

No other physical component of the universe is more illustrative of Heraclitean concepts than the radiations that light the heavens and power the stars. Radiation characteristics vary from one domain to another, and changes in one component invariably induce counterchanges in others: the polar aurora generated by particulate radiations from the sun represent a minor terrestrial example.

The universe is permeated by radiations. Those in electromagnetic form vary in wavelength from the long radio-frequencies of quasars to the shorter x- and gamma rays of stellar sources. These are accompanied by particulate radiation: among them electrons, protons, neutrons and the nuclei of various elements comprising heavy-particle cosmic primaries. In this expansive milieu, visible light is only a small segment of the broad spectrum.

TOTAL SOLAR ECLIPSE, March 7, 1970. Photograph by Jack Harvey. Copyright 1979 The Association of Universities for Research in Astronomy, Inc. The Kitt Peak National Observatory.

It is our purpose here to consider the radiation environment in terms of potential effects on biospheres; which, by definition, are entirely closed systems, except for the entry and exit of energy in the form of radiations. Light energy incident upon a biosphere is most dramatically converted to biochemical energy by photosynthetic processes and ultimately expelled as heat, i.e., radiation in the infrared region. Life forms, as we know them, require light energy for survival, but are paradoxically susceptible to injury by radiations of only slightly different wavelength or intensity or particulate forms.

This dependence/vulnerability dichotomy poses a primary challenge to biosphere viability and, therefore, requires detailed study, continued research and philosophic consideration. This section cursorily reviews some of the sources, forms and effects of the various radiations that may affect biosphere operations. The reader will immediately discern that uncertainty is the handmaiden of Heraclitean change, for many of the phenomena are incompletely defined, poorly understood and devoid of predictability.

Five principal sources of radiations will be considered: the Earth, other planetary bodies, the Sun, intergalactic space, and the biosphere itself. The interested observer will find that knowledge of each of these sources, as well as their effects, has accumulated exponentially over the past three decades with the advent of orbital and extraterrestrial instrument probes to complement earthbound instruments. In each instance, studies originating at a few specific research centers, generally under governmental aegis, have provided the bulk of the data.

The Earth's natural radioactivity has been extensively studied, for it provides the means for detecting uranium deposits that support the world's rapidly expanding nuclear industry. Low altitude aerial surveys with scintillation crystal detectors allow detailed mapping of natural background radiations and ore deposits and additionally define the fallout patterns of artificial radioactivity resulting from nuclear detonations. In the United States, these data have been provided primarily by the U.S. Geologic Survey working with the former Atomic Energy Commission, and by the Radioecology Division of the Atomic Energy Project, now the Laboratory of Nuclear Medicine and Radiation Biology, at the University of California in Los Angeles.

Planetary probes developed for NASA principally by the Jet Propulsion Laboratory of the California Institute of Technology have provided the first opportunities to measure some sources of radation directly, including the Van Allen belts that surround Earth and other geomagnetic bodies. Surface and near-space radiations of most of the planets and many of their moons have been sampled by Russian as well as American landers and fly-by vehicles.

Studies of solar radiation characteristics and flare activity require special telescopes with long focal lengths for high resolution, such as those operated by the University of Michigan, the Mount Wilson observatory near Los Angeles, and especially the Kitt Peak Observatory above Tucson, Arizona.

Many of these same organizations have been concerned with measurement of primary cosmic radiations, which include both electromagnetic and particulate forms. Because of their extremely high energies, experimental duplication of these radiations and exploration of their biological effects has been difficult and, in many cases, unobtainable with present technologies. Large-diameter accelerators, such as the alternating-gradient proton synchrotron at Brookhaven National Laboratory in New York, and similar, even larger instruments operated by the National Accelerator Laboratory and the European Atomic Energy Agency, are capable of producing high-energy particles comparable to those comprising a large portion of the cosmic-ray spectrum, but these facilities have been used almost exclusively for study of particle physics rather than radiobiology.

The advent of NASA's Space Transportation System (the Shuttle Program) has opened new opportunities for study of cosmic radiations relatively unaffected by atmospheric perturbations. Most STS missions carry instruments for cosmic radiation measurements, and many more are scheduled. The recent commitment to construct a permanent orbiting space station should provide the incentive to perform more experiments designed to assess potential biomedical hazards of these low-flux, but extremely energetic particles.

By contrast, information on the biological effects of non-cosmic radiations is abundant. Medical attention has focused on their potential benefits and harm ever since natural and artificial radioactivity and x-rays were first discovered. The National Medical Library in Bethesda is the most centralized repository of such data. Specialized areas of interest may be found at specific institutions: high-energy particle radiotherapy at Stanford University and at the University of California's Lawrence Radiation Laboratory, effects of internal emitters at Oak Ridge National Laboratory, and the biologic effects of nuclear fallout at U.C.L.A. and at the Brookhaven National

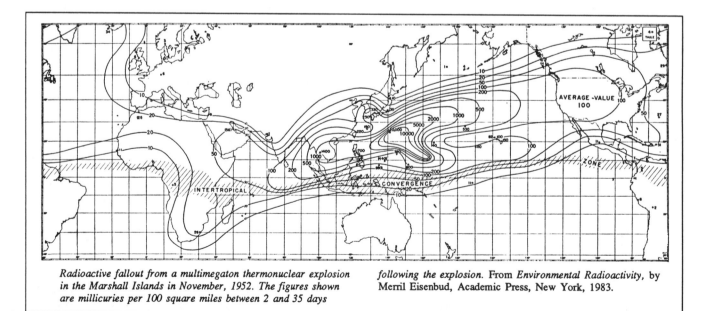

Radioactive fallout from a multimegaton thermonuclear explosion in the Marshall Islands in November, 1952. The figures shown are millicuries per 100 square miles between 2 and 35 days *following the explosion. From* Environmental Radioactivity, *by Merril Eisenbud, Academic Press, New York, 1983.*

Laboratory. The latter institution provides ongoing care for the Marshall Islanders accidentally exposed to mixed fission- product fallout from a thermonuclear detonation in 1954, the single largest resource for study of such effects on a human population.

For ease of study, these diverse forms, sources and effects of radiation have often been approached as isolated entities. Recently, however, this tendency has been supplanted by an integrated approach, recognizing the complex inter-relationships that exist among seemingly disparate phenomena in closed ecosystems. In a dramatic display of this concept, Congress recently commissioned NASA, the National Oceanic and Atmospheric Administration and the National Science Foundation to determine if technology was now sufficiently advanced to study Earth as a single closed ecosystem, i.e., a biosphere. Such a long-term international study of global habitability was justified by concern that certain conditions which are prerequisite to life are being jeopardized by increasing human modification and incursions. According to some authorities, for example, the outer boundaries of life-determinant conditions might be approached by the greenhouse effect on global temperature resulting from increased atmospheric carbon dioxide generated by fossil fuels, a phenomenon of radiation imbalance. These boundaries would certainly be exceeded by the deleterious effects of a nuclear holocaust, "nuclear winter" being

merely one component.

In terms of thermodynamic theory, the Earth (or any other biosphere) may be considered simply a small eddy in the Universe's constantly flowing river of entropy. Biospheric organization and complexity is not in violation of thermodynamic law, but occurs rather in harmony and balance with it. The precariousness of that balance requires continued study, understanding and accommodation within the Heraclitean milieu to preserve biosphere viability.

Radiobiological Considerations In Biosphere Operations

The following presentation is a cursory assessment of potential radiobiological hazards associated with the establishment and operation of a space biosphere.

Physical Aspects of the Radiation Environment

Personnel participating in an operation of this nature and the flora and fauna of the biosphere will be exposed to a radiation environment that is markedly variable in both character and intensity. Portions of this broad spectrum of radiations will be unlike any yet experienced

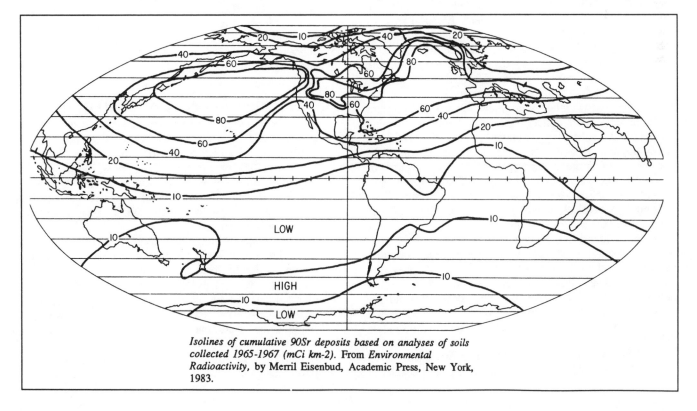

Isolines of cumulative 90Sr deposits based on analyses of soils collected 1965-1967 (mCi km-2). From Environmental Radioactivity, by Merril Eisenbud, Academic Press, New York, 1983.

on earth. Five primary radiation sources will contribute: Earth, the biosphere vehicle, sun, lunar or planetary surfaces, and intergalactic space.

Terrestrial Sources of Radiation

Terrestrial radiation per se is primarily confined to the infrared region and has been calculated to approach 0.06 watt/centimeters squared. The additional components of the earth's albedo consist of a wider energy range but are comparably negligible in amount. These are devoid of known deleterious effects on biological systems.

Radioactive isotopes may be present naturally in soil and earth crust materials or as a result of fallout from nuclear weapon detonations or reactor ventings. These are enormously variable in quantity, type and geographic distribution, but may be defined precisely for any given locale under consideration.

Intimately associated with Earth, although not of terrestrial origin, are the Van Allen radiation belts which may be of major importance to the present consideration. The radiations consist almost entirely of protons and electrons confined to two annular zones which are concentrated at the earth's magnetic equator. Traversal of these zones by a space vehicle may be neccesary if the advantage of equatorial acceleration is desired.

Van Allen radiations most probably result from decay of neutrons which are produced by cosmic ray interaction with the upper atmosphere. Electron streams from cataclysmic solar events may contribute additionally. Both zones contain numerous electrons ranging from 10 to the fourth power to 10 to the sixth power ev in energy. The inner zone is further characterized by numerous protons which are not detectable in the outer zone.

The narrow inner Van Allen belt has a minimum altitude of approximately 600 km above the Earth's surface and reaches its peak intensity at an altitude of 3000 to 3500 km. It is a mixed radiation source composed primarily of protons accompanied by two groups of electrons that vary in peak energies. The proton energy range is 40 to 700 Mev with an average of 120 Mev. Two populations of electons with energy peaks above 20 kev and above 600 kev are present in fluxes several times less than those found in the outer zone.

Radiation intensities in the inner zone are quite stable and apparently exhibit little temporal or spatial variation. The maximum dose rate from the proton component is on the order of magnitude of 100 rad per hour. The peak flux of electrons with energies up to 800 Kev will approach 2 x 10 to the tenth power/centimeters squared/second.

The broad outer Van Allen belt is first encountered at an altitude of 12,000 km. It reaches a peak intensity at approximately 18,000 km and extends to 55,000 km with progressively decreasing intensity. In some ways it resembles auroral radiation, since it consists primarily of low energy electrons. While these electrons populate a softer portion of the energy spectrum (up to a few hundred Kev), their fluxes are considerably higher than those found in the inner belt. For electrons of energy greater than 20 Kev, fluxes of 10 to the eleventh power/centimeters squared/second have been measured. A flux of 10 to the eighth/centimeters squared/second has been observed for that segment more energetic than 200 Kev. The latter, if unshielded, could produce surface dose rates of 10 to the fourth power rad/hr.

Marked variations in radiation intensity in the outer belt accompany variations in solar activity. At the onset of a magnetic storm, the intensities in the outer zone rapidly decrease. The recovery is equally rapid, and previous levels are exceeded before the fluxes gradually return to their baselines.

In summary, the radiations associated with the Earth consist of 1) low energy reflected photons, 2) naturally occurring and mixed fission-product radioisotopes, 3) a wide range of electrons in the two Van Allen zones, and 4) highly energetic protons in the inner zone. The first two are generally of negligible consequence because of their low intensity and energy, but specific areas may be sufficiently contaminated to pose biohazards. The third may deliver surface dose rates up to 10 to the fourth power rad/hr, dependent upon solar activity, and the last may irradiate an object at a rate of 100 rad/hr or greater, both thereby constituting potentially lethal biohazards for humans in slow traversal.

Vehicular Sources of Radiation

Radiation produced by space vehicle itself will be of greater concern when nuclear propulsive units become sufficiently sophisticated to allow their use in extraterrestrial excursions. Even now, however, low wattage auxiliary power units are available which utilize multi-curie alpha and beta emitters to activate thermocouples, but these self-contained units present a hazard only when disrupted.

Of greater immediate concern is the prospect of vehicular components acting as secondary radiation sources following primary irradiation. Secondary photon emission (bremsstrahlung) may result from deceleration of charged particles by the Coulomb fields of atomic nuclei or orbital electrons. The passage of fast electrons through matter is thus accompanied by a continuous x-ray emission ascribable to this phenomenon. The spectra of such radiations extend from zero up to the energy of the incident particle, but bremsstrahlung production is negligible for particles below 1 Mev energy. Due to mass differences, bremsstrahlung secondary to proton deceleration is smaller by a factor of 10 to the minus sixth power to 10 to the minus seventh power than that produced by electrons.

The efficiency of kinetic-energy conversion into bremsstrahlung increases proportionally to the electron energy and to the square of the atomic number of the stopping material. This becomes an important consideration in the construction of an appropriate radiation shield. For example, while 1 gram/cm aluminum would absorb a 2.3 Mev electron, the resultant bremsstrahlung would penetrate an additional 10-12 grams.

Within the inner Van Allen zone, electron fluxes of 2 x 10 to the tenth power/centimeters squared/second with energies up to 800 Kev would produce an incident surface flux of 10 to the sixteenth power electrons/second on a spherical vehicle of 2 m radius. This is equivalent to a current of 1.5 milliamps and effectively converts the vehicle into the target of an x-ray machine operating at a few hundred Kev and a 1.5ma current.

Irradiation with protons of greater than 0.5 Mev may also result in a secondary radiative process by interaction with nuclei of elements in the spaceship components. Energetic gamma rays (up to 17 Mev) are secondarily emitted in this process. These may present a hazard comparable to the x-rays of bremsstrahlung.

The probability of the proton-gamma nuclear reaction occurring increases with decreasing atomic number of the perturbing material. Appreciable numbers of protons in this energy range will be encountered only during traversal of the inner Van Allen belt and during solar flares.

Bremsstrahlung production then may be the primary problem in considering vehicular radiation emissions. Materials of low atomic number will absorb the incident electrons with minimal bremsstrahlung emission. The bremsstrahlung actually produced can then be absorbed secondarily by liners of high atomic number material.

Isolated periods of secondary gamma production from proton irradiation will considerably complicate the shielding problem.

Solar Sources of Radiation

Electromagnetic radiations in near space are primarily solar in origin. These cover a broad energy spectrum but are primarily concentrated in the visible wavelengths. Approximately 7% is ultraviolet (2000 to 4000 Angstroms). A much smaller component of hydrogen Lyman-alpha wavelength (1216 Angstroms) is present. At one astronomical unit from the sun, the latter intensity is only 6 x 10 to the minus seventh power watt/centimeters squared, compared to a total electromagnetic flux of 0.14 watt/centimeters squared (2 cal/centimeters squared/minute). The intensity of solar x-rays is lower by another order of magnitude. These x-rays have energies up to 90 Kev but most are below 10 Kev.

Hard x- and gamma rays are normally negligible but may increase to significant levels at the time of a solar flare. Indeed, it is the solar flare that presents the project with the greatest radiation hazard likely to be encountered in near space.

Flare activity is cyclic with an 11 year periodicity and a maximum activity of approximately 10 events per year. The actual occurrence of a flare is unpredictable, although observation of solar activity allows assignment of a high or low probability to a possible occurrence within the ensuing 5 days.

Magnitude and duration of flares are similarly unpredictable. Generally they last 10 to 100 hours, and during this period there is a massive ejection of protons, which comprise the primary hazard. Electrons and hard electromagnetic radiations accompany the primary proton emission.

Solar flare particles characteristically exhibit large local and temporal variations in flux and energy distribution. Proton energies vary from a few electron volts to 700 Mev, and some may reach the billion electron volt range. During the February 23, 1956 event, energies were noted to exceed 15 Bev.

Of 30 solar flares adequately documented, 6 were of sufficient intensity and duration to be lethal to humans. Fluxes of 5 x 10 to the sixth power protons/centimeters/second were measured. For the usual solar flares, dose rates of 35 to 50 rad/hour may exist for several days from protons of energies greater than 25 Mev. This dose rate doubles for some larger flares.

In the November 1960 event, protons in the 50 to 500 Mev range were calculated to approach 100 rad/hour in free space. The May 10, 1959 flare had a range of peak intensities of 10 to 100 rad/hour. Doses as high as 3 x 10 to the fourth power rad/hour are thought to be possible.

To summarize, primary solar radiations present little hazard except during unpredictable periods of flare activity during which lethal intensities of high energy protons are likely to exist.

Lunar and Planetary Sources of Radiation

Since a significant magnetic field is prerequisite to entrapment of charged particles, radiation belts of the Van Allen type may also be encountered around many planetary bodies. Surface radiations may result from decay of radionuclides in crust materials and from activation of crust elements by cosmic and solar particles.

Biological doses from surface sources on moons and planets have been calculated to be insignificant compared to the direct radiations of the sun and intergalactic space, and Van Allen regions.

Cosmic Sources of Radiation

Other galactic sources of ultraviolet radiations add a small component to the solar ultraviolet. Interstellar hydrogen produces further radiation in the Lyman-alpha region. Other portions of the electromagnetic spectrum, from radio wavelengths to gamma, also originate in galactic and intergalactic regions. All are considered to be of intensities insufficient to pose a biological hazard.

Particulate radiations of primary cosmic origin may present a hazard which is unique to outer space. Because of their extremely high energies, experimental duplication of these radiations and exploration of their biological effects has been difficult and in many cases unobtainable with present technologies.

Cosmic primaries consist predominately of protons (79-86%) and alpha particles (13-20%). Carbon, nitrogen and oxygen nuclei comprise approximately 0.78%. The remainder (0.22%) are nuclei of elements having atomic numbers greater than ten. Primaries as heavy as iron (atomic number = 26) have been identified.

Total particle energies as high as 10 to the nineteeth power ev may occur. The energy spectrum ranges from a few Mev to greater than 10 to the seventh power Bev per nucleon. Thus an iron nucleus with an atomic weight of 56 and an energy of 10 Bev per nucleon would present a total energy of 560 Bev. While some particles in this extremely high range will be encountered, the majority of the cosmic primaries possess energies of a few Bev per nucleon, and 90% are below 15 Bev.

Spatial and temporal variations in the fluxes are well established. During the 11-year solar cycle, exposure to heavy primaries may vary by a factor of two to ten, maximum intensities occuring at the time of minimum solar activity.

The greatest fluctuation occurs in those particles between 0.1 and 1.0 Bev per nucleon. This low energy range, however, is of considerable biological concern since there is a high associated probability that these particles will produce densely ionizing tracks in tissue. In free space, an omnidirectional flux of 2 particles/ centimeters squared/second exists. Near earth this is reduced by half. In addition, near any planetary body with an atmosphere, secondary radiations will be encountered, e.g., neutrons, mesons, and their decay products.

While the ratio of cosmic primary protons and alpha particles to nuclei of the heavy primaries is greater than 100:1, this ratio is reduced to 10:1 in regard to the total ionization produced in tissue equivalent material. This ionization may be sufficient to produce a dose rate of 15 to 35 millirad per day in free space.

To summarize, radiations of cosmic origin consist primarily of protons and alpha particles together with heavier nuclei and a negligible electromagnetic component. The particulate radiations cover an extremely broad spectrum, possibly reaching energies of 10 to the seventh power Bev per nucleon. Low dose rates (about 1 millirad/hour) are likely, but special consideration may be necessary for high-energy heavy particles regarding their biological effects. Ionization produced by some heavy particles may be of greater biological significance than indicated by their low dose-rate. Concentration of ionization occurs as some of these particles are absorbed in tissue-equivalent material. In a critical organ, this could produce a far more adverse effect than the same amount of ionization dispersed throughout a larger tissue volume.

Biological Aspects of the Radiation Environment

Interaction of Radiation with Biological Materials

Regarding the biological effects of radiation, two modes of action are pertinent to the high energy particles which may be encountered on extraterrestrial missions: star production and thin-downs.

Star production refers to the inelastic collision of an incident particle with an atomic nucleus in the tissue. The resultant disintegration produces an explosion of smaller high-energy particles and some electromagnetic radiations. The energy of the incident particle is dissipated over a large tissue volume with a decrease in biological effect.

Star formation is the predominant perturbation mechanism for particles exceeding 1 Bev/nucleon. In tissue, the probability of star formation exceeds the probability of a thin-down.

Thin-down production is generally an effect of highly-charged heavy particles which are densely ionizing. The specific ionization, or linear energy transfer, is proportional to the square of the charge and inversely proportional to the square of the velocity of the particle. In a thin-down, the incident particle is gradually slowed down by collisions with electrons, producing a track of ionization. The dislodged electrons (delta rays) produce secondary ionizations around the track approximately equivalent in biological effect to 20 Kev x-rays. The result is a small cone of ionization which increases in intensity toward the track terminus, thus the term, 'thin-down'.

A thin-down may encompass 15,000 cells in a cylinder of extremely intense ionization equivalent to 10,000 rads. This may occur several centimeters deep into the tissue, affecting a core 1mm long and 25 microns wide.

The low energy portion of the cosmic spectrum is preferentially absorbed by thin-down production. Particles with energies less than 100 Mev/nucleon have a 90% probability of terminating as thin-downs. This probability is negligible as the energies exceed 1 Bev.

Conventional dose terminology falters in this area. Knowledge of total energy absorption or ion production is insufficient to assess the biological significance of radiations when applied to these two modes of action.

The efficiency of damage production by radiation is related to linear energy transfer (LET). Thus, while cell death may occur at the center of a star, much of the energy of the incident particle is wasted peripherally. Concentration of the same amount of ionization in a thin-down, however, may become biologically significant in organs such as the hypothalamus or ocular lens where loss of a few cells is critical.

This problem has been approached experimentally using microbeams and heavy-ion linear accelerators. The

MAXIMUM AND MINIMUM MISSION DOSES FOR BEST AND WORST LAUNCH DATES DURING ACTIVE PERIOD OF CYCLE 19		
Mission duration	Maximum dose (rad)	Minimum dose (rad)
4 years	3492	2439
3 years	3229	974
2 years	2781	526
1.5 years	2415	176
1 year	2110	15
9 months	1963	2
6 months	1963	0
3 months	1962	0
1.5 months	1492	0
1 month	1452	0
2 weeks	1452	0
1 week	1452	0

The dose calculations from the solar-flare particles are very difficult owing to the wide range of energies and the complex shielding geometries presented by space capsules. A number of authors have examined the doses that would be received by space journeys of various durations during a recent solar maximum. These data are summarized in this table in which the doses are given for missions ranging from 1 week to 4 years. It is observed from these data that great risks may exist because of this source of radiation.

present consensus is that cosmic heavies have a relative biological effectiveness (RBE) of about 1 when compared to conventional radiations in producing injurious effects. Brain cell destruction by thin-downs is considered highly unlikely, since a 25 micron core dose equivalent to 400,000 rads was required to produce Betz-cell death. However, RBEs of 10 or more are considered possible by some, and present heavy-ion accelerators are not sufficiently energetic to study a very broad spectrum.

It has been calculated that a 70 kg man in free space can expect to sustain 100 cosmic primary hits/hour. This intensity is considered to be insufficient to constitute a biological hazard even for several weeks. Further experiments are necessary before this can be stated with assurance.

In the sequence of events that follows irradiation of biological materials, four stages appear definable. The physical stage is characterized by the actual absorption of radiant energy by the tissue. This occurs within 10 to the minus thirteenth power second, and during this period energy is transferred from the incident particle to the atoms of the tissue by ionization or excitation.

This primary radiochemical reaction occurs during the second stage and requires about 10 to the minus eleventh power to 10 to the minus ninth power second. The primary chemical substances resulting from the ionization are formed during this period. Excited molecules may undergo ionization by spontaneous dissociation or may revert to their original state by the emission of heat. New molecules and molecular fragments are also produced from ion-molecular collisions.

The highly reactive free radicals are of special import. In biological systems, these are primarily nonionized H + OH radicals derived from water. In the third state they interact with one another and with other molecules in the solution. A chain of chemical reactions probably occurs during which essential molecules may be injured and biologically harmful products may be formed. It is during this period of 10 to the minus sixth power second to a few seconds that the definitive biochemical injury probably occurs.

The final stage may require a few seconds or generations of time. It is the period required for formation of an observable biological lesion. This includes all of the reactions of the system to the chemical by-products of irradiation from a subcellular level to an effect on descendents.

It is thus apparent that prevention of the biochemical injury may be effected only during an extremely short period of time. Increased tolerances to radiation have been produced in some mammals by various drugs (e.g., sulhydryl compounds) and altered physiological states (e.g., hypoxia). Frequently, however, these have in themselves been injurious, and invariably the agent must be present at the time of irradiation. Subsequent therapy at present is of no value in radiation injury other than the usual value of supportive therapy in other clinically indicated circumstances, (e.g., antibiotics for infections, blood transfusions for bleeding, etc.).

Qualitative and quantitative variations in the four stages of radiation injury depend on the distribution of the absorbed energy within the organism, as well as its chemical composition. While some modification of the last three stages is possible in mammals, the ease of modification decreases as the radiations become more densely ionizing. For example, modification has not been demonstrable with the dense ionizations of alpha particles. A large portion of the radiation spectrum likely to be encountered on this mission will be characterized by high linear energy transfer and thus will fall into this category. The prospect of significantly altering the biological effects presently appears non- existent. Certainly for the foreseeable future, it is impractical to consider the use of protective chemicals or modified physiological states to reduce the radiation effects. Emphasis, therefore, must be placed on perturbation of the incident radiations by appropriate shield design.

Problems of Shield Design

It is clearly impractical to shield biosphere inhabitants completely from the ambient radiations throughout the excursion. A certain radiation dose must be accepted as a penalty for a successful mission. Simultaneously, the maximum permissible dose must never reach levels which might jeopardize the mission by adversely affecting performance.

Immediate whole body doses in the order of 100 rads may elicit acute clinical symptoms in humans. Biological damage is, of course, detectable at much lower dose levels, and there is a definite associated risk for development of late effects, (e.g., tumor formation, decreased life span, genetic mutations in the germ plasm). But clinically overt symptoms should not become manifest below 100 rad.

Beyond 125 rads of acute whole body radiation there is a reasonably high probability of developing nausea and vomiting. Mortality can probably result from as little as 200 rads. It would seem reasonable then to provide a shield which under any circumstances would permit no exposure greater than 100 rads to the occupants, and this amount only in emergency situations.

Traversal of the Van Allen belts at escape velocity will limit the whole body dose from this source to about 10 rads if a shield of at least lg/centimeters squared is available. Cosmic primaries will add another 2.5 to 6 rads over a 6-month period, though it must be recalled that this

component is of uncertain biological signature. Bremsstrahlung and other electromagnetic raditions will be negligible if the shield contains appropriate materials. The shielding problem, therefore, centers on protecting against the inner Van Allen belt and solar flare radiation, which is unpredictable in occurrence, intensity or duration. Until further information is available regarding solar flares it will be difficult to define shield thicknesses with precision.

Ideally, the shield might consist of a layer of low atomic number material to stop electrons with minimal bremsstrahlung production. A high atomic number liner, e.g., 0.25 cm lead or a carbon shield, could then absorb the residual bremsstrahlung. Unfortunately, the possibility of irradiation with protons greater than 0.5 Mev is high. Nuclear reactions therefore likely will occur between the protons and the shield materials if they are too low in atomic number. These reactions are exothermic: absorption of a proton may be accompanied by emission of a gamma ray where energy exceeds that of the incident proton. In some cases 17 Mev gamma rays may be produced. To reduce this secondary radiative process, an outside liner of high atomic number is optimal.

A multifactorial compromise is obviously necessary in designing an optimal radiation shield. The primary considerations are 1) minimum weight for maximum protection, 2) high atomic number material to reduce secondary radiative processes from nuclear reactions and Coulomb excitations and to absorb bremsstrahlung and 3) low atomic number material to reduce bremsstrahlung production and to fragment heavy primaries from cosmic sources.

One proposal is to provide a very thin outer layer of lead evaporated onto tin. This layer might be separated from the skin of the biosphere to serve secondarily as a meteor bumper. The skin could be constructed of a medium layer of aluminum, magnesium, or titanium, all of which provide structural strength and absorb protons and electrons by ionization loss. A final thick layer of hydrocarbons would attenuate a portion of the cosmic primaries.

Problem of Maximum Permissible Dose

On a theoretical basis it has been calculated that a human might receive five to ten acute exposures of 100 rads without significantly impairing his performance if these exposures were separated by sufficient recovery periods. An adequate period for a human to recover from the acute effects of 100 rads has been calculated to be about 120 days. This, however, seems optimistic and is not supported by sufficient experimental data. It must be emphasized that there is probably a 10 to 20% non-reparable injury that is additive, perhaps exponentially, and will therefore decrease the individual's tolerances to subsequent exposures as well as to increase significantly his probability of developing serious late effects.

An operating maximum of 50 rads might be required since this would insure against clinical symptoms of radiation injury jeopardizing the mission.

Therapy of Radiation Injury

As a clinical problem, radiation injury is little different from other disease entities. Since the prevention of disease is more efficacious than the cure, the best possible therapy for this potential problem is adequate shielding.

Basic clinical precepts apply equally to the diagnosis and treatment of radiation injury once it has occurred. Appropriate supportive therapy, instituted when clinically indicated, may save patients exposed to doses 2 to 3 times higher than those from which they might otherwise die. This is substantiated by extensive experimental work in animals and by a small amount of human experience secondary to critical accidents in reactors and fissionable-material processing plants.

TRIFID NEBULA IN SAGITTARIUS. Billowing clouds of hydrogen and helium glow from the radiation of stars with surface temperatures about 25,000 degrees centigrade. Radiation pressure and stellar winds from stars in the overexposed central area create a shock wave, pushing the gases outward. Dark lanes are opaque regions of dust and gas, and may be "nursery grounds" for new stars. Diameter: about 30 light years. Distance: about 3,000 light years. (Photograph courtesy of National Optical Astronomy Observatories, Tucson.)

Selected Reading List

Environmental Radioactivity, by Merril Eisenbud, Academic Press, New York, 1983.

Radiation Safety During Space Flights, by V.G. Bobkov, et al, translation by NASA of *Radiatsionnaya Bezopasnost' pre Kosmicheskikh Poletakh,* Atomizda, Moscow, 1964.

Ionizing Radiation: Levels and Effects, a report of the United Nations Scientific Committee on the Effects of Atomic Radiation to the General Assembly, U.N., New York, 1972.

Cosmic Radiation and Its Biological Effects, by V.F. Hess & J. Eugster, Fordham Univ. Press, New York, 1949.

Radiation Injury in Man, by E.P. Cronkite & V.P. Bond, Charles C. Thomas, Springfield, 1960.

Review of Medical Findings in a Marshallese Population Twenty-six Years After Accidental Exposure to Radioactive Fallout by R.A. Conard, D.E. Paglia, et al, Brookhaven National Laboratory Report BNL-51261, 1981.

The Cold & The Dark; The World After Nuclear War, by Paul Erlich, Carl Sagan, Donald Kennedy and Walter Orr Roberts, W.W. Norton & Co., 1985. A hard factual line of argument on the biological effects massive doses of man-made radioactivity will have on the biosphere. (See Information for review)

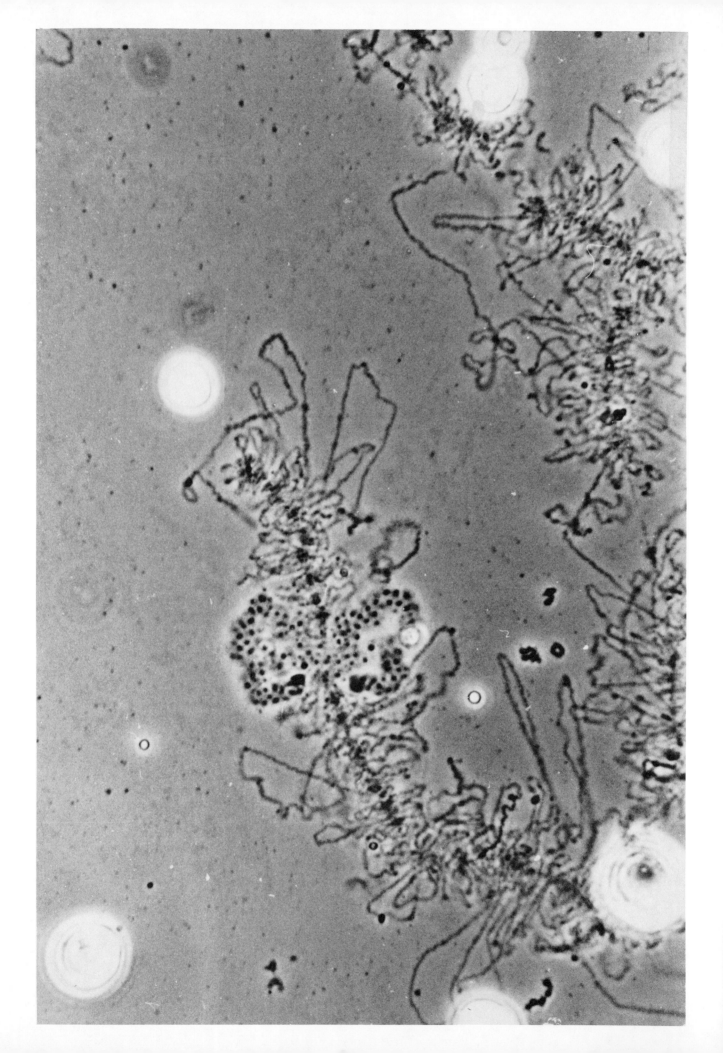

Genetics And Cloning

Genetics and Cloning

Donald A. Ritchie

Ah Love, could you and I conspire,
Would we not shatter this sorry scheme
of things entire
And rebuild it nearer to our heart's desire?
OMAR KHAYYAM

Dogma and Uncertainty

It is common knowledge that the foundation of genetics as a science began with the experimental breeding studies of the Austrian monk, Gregor Mendel. Born Johann Mendel, a farmer's son, he was given the name Gregor on becoming a monk -- a vocation chosen for its opportunity to provide an education. At the University of Vienna his aptitude for academic work was not well developed and he withdrew to the monastery at Brno in Moravia in what is now Czechoslovakia.

What is striking about Mendel's work is that it happened in a monastery with its atmosphere of dogma in that part of central Europe dominated by the autocracy of the Austro-Hungarian empire where science, and particularly biological science, was suspect. This was the situation in the 1850's in the Brno monastery that was to become the cradle of the science of genetics -- the most vital driving force in science in the latter part of the 20th century. That dogma and the uncertainty inherent in every scientific experiment and hypothesis should live so close together and yet enable science to flourish is a remarkable example of the quality to which human endeavor can aspire.

The truth of the matter is that Mendel's experiments crossing peas in the vegetable garden were conducted secretly between about 1858 and 1868. Although the results were published in 1866 in the Journal of the Brno Natural History Society, another 34 years were to pass before Mendel's work was rediscovered and its value recognized. The final note to this remarkable achievement

TRITURUS CRISTATUS CRISTATUS centrifuged preparation. End of left arm of chromosome XII including the pair of giant granular loops. Photograph courtesy of C.A. Thomas, Helicon Foundation.

is that after his death in 1884, having become the abbot, Mendel's papers were burned by his successor.

The essence of Mendel's conclusions, and the single most important discovery on which the entire basis of genetics rests, is that the characters of an organism are discrete units which are inherited in an all-or-none fashion. This put to rest the formerly held belief that the characters of a hybrid were a blend of those of the parents. We now call these characters genes.

Almost a century later came the second quantum leap in our understanding of genetics. This was the revelation by Watson and Crick in their 1953 paper in *Nature* of the structure of DNA and the mechanism, inherent in this structure, for the transmission of an exact copy of the DNA of the parent to the offspring. DNA is a major constituent of all chromosomes which are the vehicles of inheritance and it was known at this time that it was the DNA component of the chromosomes which carried the genetic information. The contribution of Watson & Crick was to define the structure of DNA as a double-helix in which the informational sequence along one strand of the polymeric molecule was represented in complementary form in the second strand. The base sequence along one strand therefore specifies the base sequence of the complementary strand. It was only a step from the elucidation of this structure to realize that when the two strands separate during DNA replication the two daughter molecules would be identical. The parent cell would, by this mechanism, have identical genetic information to its two daughter cells. This rule holds true for all organisms regardless of whether they are bacterial cells dividing by binary fusion or embryonic tissue in the developing human.

157

The Gene and the Genetic Code

The gene is the basic unit of genetic information. In spite of the existence of variations on a general theme the basic concept of a gene is of a linear sequence of DNA bases, the repeating unit of information, punctuated at either end by signals indicating where the reading of the sequence begins and ends. Chromosomes consist of tandem arrays of genes joined end to end, and held in complex structures by matrix proteins. The linear sequence of bases determines the linear sequence of amino acids of the protein molecule that is the product of that gene. DNA sequences in genes, therefore, transmit their information to amino acid sequences in proteins. Since chromosomes are compartmentalized in cell nuclei and proteins are made in the cell cytoplasm a means is required to transfer the genetic code from one cell location to another. This is achieved by messenger molecules composed of another form of nucleic acid, RNA, whose base sequence is a copy of the DNA base sequence. The DNA base sequence is read in groups of three such that each triplet of bases specifies a particular amino acid.

Within our own biosphere these constitute universal rules although, as with all laws, some exceptions do exist. There is no guarantee that other biospheres beyond our own planet will play their games with the same rules. Like the British legal system the genetic code has evolved and in another place at another time and with different conditions who can tell what might have happened? One of the objectives of space travel has for long been concerned with the search for other forms of life, and the nature of the genetic information of such organisms must be one of the first and fundamental questions.

The techniques of molecular biology are now available to determine the base sequences of entire genes or related groups of genes. This major breakthrough has opened the possibility of exploring evolution at the level of DNA. With this approach it will be possible to compare the changes in organisms at the primary level unencumbered by the complexities inherent in the study of whole organisms. Today's student of evolution is, therefore, as likely to be computer-bound looking at the intricacies of the use of coding triplets as he is to be found in the forests of a South Pacific atoll following the emergence of banding patterns on snail's shells.

Information Transfer in Cells

Genetic information is transferred at two levels. The first is from the gene to the gene product -- from DNA to protein. At this level the gene activity is confined to the cell or to the collection of cells that constitutes the organism. This form of information transfer is the basis of cellular metabolism and the regulation of that metabolism. By these gene functions the cell, and ultimately the organism, engages in those activities of energy conversion, growth, movement, hormone control, cell division and reproduction. The second level is the transfer of information from parent to offspring and the redistribution of that information to provide the pool of genetic variability on which evolution and adaptation depends. This transfer is the responsibility of the gametes or sex cells which upon fertilization produce the zygote whose development heralds the next generation. In microorganisms this process is usually achieved by the simple process of cell growth, chromosome duplication and cell division. The two processes of information transfer are quite separate and distinct but both are essential.

The Infinite Plasticity of Genes

Our discussion to date has concentrated on the high fidelity of the genetic information in terms of the formation of exact copies which are transmitted from generation to generation. This process perpetuates the identity of the organism and is the essence of the belief that 'like begats like'. This ensures the stability of the species. But we must be aware of two pertinent facts. First, stability is a valuable asset only so long as the ambient conditions remain stable -- change the ambience and stability loses its attraction. The second, and equally obvious point, is that genetic stability is only a relative term. We can be assured that two diamonds of different sizes will nevertheless be constructed of identical arrays of atoms. But take two people and it will be immediately obvious that their general resemblance is peppered with a variety of variations on the theme.

This variation, at least at the genetical level, is the product of mutations. Mutations are alterations of the DNA sequence -- we can think in terms of a consensus sequence with many minor modifications. These modifications, because they reflect changes to the coding sequence, will lead to modifications of the protein product in terms of its amino acid sequence. Now, the structure of proteins determines their properties and alterations to that structure will alter these properties. We can now appreciate that within the arena of the complex interactions between proteins and other biological molecules within a cell, these mutations will be expressed by differences in cellular activity. Translated to the level of the organism this produces the variation apparent among the members of a species.

Returning to the question of genetic stability we see mutation as the source of variation that provides the dynamic force to enable a species to meet a changing environment and succeed in its exploitation. While it is true that many mutations can alter the gene product to a point where its function is lost or badly affected, nevertheless the capacity to mutate is essential for a species to adapt. It is the biological force which allows evolution and speciation and in some instances, perhaps the majority, to extinction.

There is, therefore, a biological dilemma which centers around the infinite plasticity of genes. The concept of the species is based on the stability of the genetic material -- this is why the individuals within a species are similar and it is this similarity which identifies the species. Only members of the same species can breed and this is a force maintaining stability. On the other hand, variation is the basis of evolution and without this no progress can occur.

One last point should be made. The sexual process provides a means to exploit genetic variation since it serves to reassort the genes of the parents among the offspring. Sexual reproduction is the mode of generation of higher organisms. However for lower organisms, bacteria in particular, reproduction is asexual. Bacteria divide to produce daughter cells without the need for a partner. It is interesting to ask the question, ''Are higher organisms more successful than bacteria?'' Perhaps it is impertinent to question the importance of the sexual process but I am reminded of the words of Jacob Bronowski -- Ask an impertinent question and you are on the way to a pertinent answer.

The Exploitation of Genetic Variability

From the time man ceased to be a hunter and adopted the role of farmer he has exploited the genetic variability of his domestic animals and plant crops. In essence this is a simple process and goes on to this day. It entails the identification of desirable characters and restricting breeding to individuals bearing these characters. This can be likened to a process of purification in which a desirable product present in small amounts in a mixture is enriched. By a sequential process whereby at each stage the desirable product is fractionated from the contaminants a gradual increase in concentration of the product will occur. It is a process designed to reduce variability and to concentrate further breedings between individuals enriched for the selected trait.

This process has been highly successful as our cornfields and cattle meadows will testify. It has, however, two disadvantages. It is a very slow process requiring many generations of breeding experiments. Also it has its

limitations in the sense that, in spite of the possibility of further more desirable mutations occurring, the extent of the improvements that can be achieved depends on the pool of genetic variation in that species. This of course may be very large but it still has its limits.

The problem, of course, derives from an earlier discussion of the species concept which defines a species as a group of organisms between which breeding is possible. Conversely, different species cannot interbreed. The pool of variation would be considerably extended if the genetic variability of different species could be brought together. The advent of genetic engineering, or more properly, recombinant DNA technology, has brought this possibility much closer.

To highlight this issue we must focus our attention on DNA structure again. The process of genetic recombination as it naturally occurs in cells, brings together different DNA molecules within the same nucleus and permits them to exchange segments of molecules. This process occurs in the cells of the sex organs during the formation of eggs and sperm during the process of meiosis. This produces new gene combinations by rearrangements of the DNA of the homologous pairs of chromosomes in the diploid progenitor cells.

Genetic recombination requires a high degree of similarity between the chromosomes if viable gametes are to arise. This is one reason why genetic recombination between distantly-related organisms does not occur. Another reason is that a variety of imcompatibility barriers have been developed which preclude successful matings between disimilar organisms. The problems of crossing an animal with a plant are self-evident!

Recombinant DNA technology bypasses these barriers. This is partly because it uses DNA isolated from cells and is an *in vitro* technique and partly because it depends on DNA sequence homology of such a minor kind that makes all DNA molecules compatible.

The technology will be described in the catalogue. It is sufficient to make the point here that genetic engineering permits the unlimited formation of hybrid molecules regardless of origin. From this basis it will be clear that the potential for genetic exploitation in the forthcoming years will affect our own biosphere in ways that Mendel's wildest dreams in his monastery cell in Brno could not have improvised.

Codicil

In this essay I have attempted to set the scene in terms of my personal view of genetics. This has meant the subversion of detail and exceptions in the cause of clarity. My intention has been to stimulate interest rather than be a slave to pedantry.

The Catalogue
Genetics, Molecular Biology and the Nobel Prize -- The Gene Generals

The Nobel Prize is the ultimate accolade for the scientist. It is the prize above all prizes that identifies the scientist with the outstanding discoveries of his time. It is peer review in the most complete sense since the peer body in this case is on the global scale. In this respect, it is indicative of the seminal role of genetics and molecular biology in the ascent of man that this branch of human endeavor has been graced so often by the award of this prize.

A catalogue of the biosphere would be incomplete without summarizing this achievement. The catalogue is impressive and a glance at the increasing frequency of Nobel Laureates shows something of the rising impact of this branch of science.

1933 -- T.H. Morgan. For his contribution to the understanding of the fundamental nature of genes and chromosomes and the relationship of genes to physiology and medicine.

1946 -- H.J. Muller. Muller's work laid the foundation of our modern concept of mutations and the role of radiation in mutation.

1958 -- G.W. Beadle, E.L. Tatum & J. Lederberg. This work laid the foundations of modern genetics and molecular biology by showing the

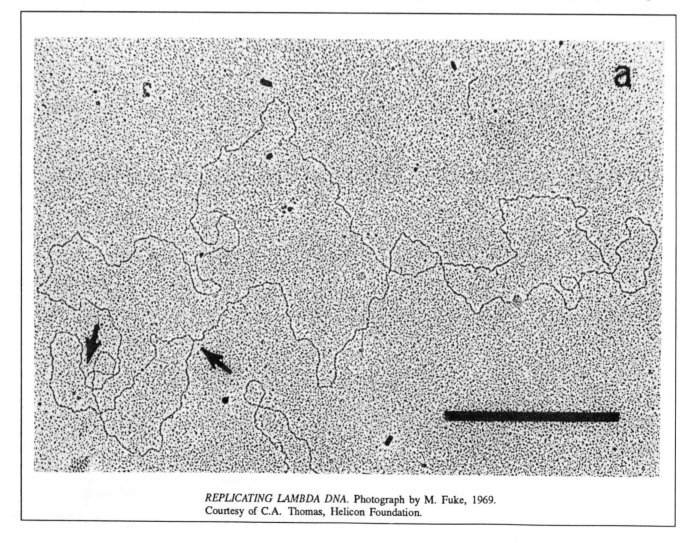

REPLICATING LAMBDA DNA. Photograph by M. Fuke, 1969.
Courtesy of C.A. Thomas, Helicon Foundation.

relationship between genes and the biochemical processes they control. Their work is embodied in the 'one gene -- one polypeptide' hypothesis indicating that polypeptides (or proteins) are the primary gene products. By working with simple microorganisms, molds and bacteria, they opened the field of microbial genetics which, complete with systems for genetic recombination, have provided much of our current understanding of gene structure and function.

1959 -- S. Ochoa & A. Kornberg.

The central role of nucleic acids as the genetic material (DNA) and the carrier of the information from the DNA in the cell nucleus to the cytoplasm for translation into proteins (RNA) was now established. The biochemical work of Ochoa with RNA and Kornberg with DNA showed that these biological molecules could be synthesized in the test tube -- technique which opened the way for much of the *in vitro* manipulation techniques of genetic engineering.

1962 -- M.H.F. Williams, J.D. Watson & F.H.C. Crick.

The elucidation of the structure of DNA and the mechanism by which the genetic message is copied and transmitted to the offspring is undoubtedly the single most important biological discovery of the twentieth century. It ranks with the elucidation of the structure of the atom, Newton's laws of motion or Galileo's revelation of the sun as the center of our planetary system.

1965 -- F. Jacob, A. Lwoff & J. Monod.

The DNA sequences of genes were known to be translated into the amino acid sequences of the proteins that play a central role in cellular metabolism. However, gene expression is not uniform and constant in all cells or at all times in the same cell -- gene expression is regulated. Using microbial systems, Jacob, Lwoff and Monod defined mechanisms for the regulation of gene expression in terms of the molecular switches which turn genes on and off. This discovery is the basis of modern views of control of gene action and cell development.

1968 -- R.W. Holley, J.G. Khorana & M. Nirenberg.

This work identified the genetic code: the relationship the sequence of bases on the DNA molecule and the sequence of amino acids of the protein product of the gene. The precise and spectacular biochemical analysis of this relationship provided the direct experimental proof of the universal triplet code.

1969 -- M. Delbruck, A.D. Hershey & S.E. Luria.

Three giants in the field of molecular biology. Their early entry into genetics during the second world war and their choice of the simple bacterial virus as a genetic system laid the foundations of molecular biology in all its diverse forms.

1975 -- R. Dulbecco, D. Baltimore & H. Temin.

Two lines of research culminated in advances in our understanding of cancer. Studies with bacterial viruses had set the pattern for analysis of the more complex animal viruses and animal viruses were identified as cancer-forming agents. Application of the molecular biology approach to cancer viruses provided the detailed background of molecular and gene interactions that directed research to the oncogene model that currently prevails.

1978 -- D. Nathans, W. Arber & H.O. Smith.

Studies of a general but otherwise unexceptional mechanism by which bacteria protect themselves from invasion by foreign DNA led to the identification of restriction enzymes. The development of genetic engineering as a major biological technology depends on these enzymes and their value has only just started to be exploited. Biotechnology and the current amazing advances in genetic analysis would not have been possible without this contribution.

GENE MACHINE. This is a commercial model, built by Cruachem of Scotland, which is partially automated. Simpler manual and more sophisticated fully automated machines are also available.   Figure 1

1980 -- F. Sanger, W. Gilbert & P. Berg.

For the development of techniques for determining the primary sequence of bases on DNA molecules and for the use of restriction enzymes to synthesize composite DNA molecules by slicing pieces of unrelated DNA together *in vitro*. Another major step in the establishment of gene cloning technology and the fine structure analysis of the cloned DNA sequences.

1982 -- A. Klug.

Klug's contribution was the refinement of methods for the visualization and analysis of complex biological macromolecules. Earlier work concentrated on the detailed structure of viruses. More recent studies have led to major developments in our understanding of chromosome structure in terms of an array of repeating sub-units -- the nucleasome.

1983 -- B. McClintock.

A classical geneticist whose work on unstable mutations in maize led her to the concept of transposable genetic elements ('jumping genes'). Such mobile gene sequences are now known to be widespread in nature and represent a major factor in mutation and variation. They have proved invaluable as tools for the analysis of gene structure and function.

1984 -- C. Milstein, G. Kohler & N.K. Jerne.

For their work in immunology and particularly for the formation of hybrid cells composed of antibody producing spleen cells and tumor cells produced the hybridoma cell which synthesizes specific antibodies from an immortal cell line. The use of monoclonal antibodies derived from such hybridoma cells has provided a major diagnostic tool for medical research and for identifying gene products from genetically-engineered DNA sequences.

Major Techniques

Genetics is a broad subject and uses a vast array of techniques. Molecular genetics is a high technology field which is rapidly developing and depends for much of its progress on techniques with a basis in chemistry and physics. The following catalogue is highly selected and concentrates on the advanced but widely used technology characteristic of modern genetics.

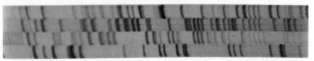

Figure 2

Gene Cloning

The essence of this technique is the *in vitro* splicing together of two or more DNA fragments derived usually from different sources and the subsequent propagation of this hybrid molecule. The aim is to isolate specific DNA fragments and derive large quantities of the purified sequence for analysis of gene structure or expression.

DNA is cut by restriction enzymes into small fragments of a few genes in length. Restriction enzymes are specific and cut the DNA at specific 4-6 base pair recognition sequences -- a given enzyme always cuts the same sequence. The type of cut enables two fragments cut with the same restriction enzyme to join together and the splice is sealed with a ligation enzyme. Providing the two fragments were cut with the same restriction enzyme they can be spliced together. This allows DNA fragments from any source to be joined with those from any other source.

The need to propagate the cloned DNA fragment is achieved by splicing the fragment to a vector molecule capable of replicating inside a cell. Vector molecules can be viruses or plasmids (supernumary circles of DNA

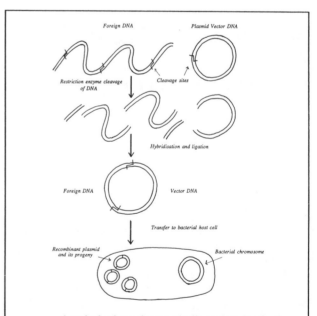

A typical scheme for genetically engineering foreign DNA by cloning into a bacterial plasmid vector. The circular plasmid DNA and the foreign DNA, both of which are double helixes, are cut at specific sites with the same restriction enzyme. This produces complementary ends whose base sequences can join. The joint is ligated to form fixed junctions between the ends of the insert and the vector. The plasmid with its hybrid insert is transformed into a bacterial cell to allow it to be maintained and replicated.

Figure 3.

present in bacterial cells and capable of self-replication). A scheme for gene cloning is illustrated in Figure 3. The most commonly used cloning systems employ plasmids as vectors and bacteria as the host for propagation of the vector DNA with its cloned insert. DNA molecules can be transferred from solution into bacterial and other cells where they will be stably maintained and reproduced.

Gene Banks

The entire genetic content of an organism can be cloned to form a gene bank or library of its DNA. This provides a source of material available to any geneticist in search of a specific gene sequence from that organism. Because higher organisms have a vast amount of DNA running to millions of genes the number of individual cloned fragments can be excessively large. This problem is to some extent circumvented by using high capacity vectors capable of accepting large DNA fragments. In this way it is possible to capture the complete DNA complement of a complex organism in a bank of about 10,000 separate clones. The researcher, having identified the clone of interest will then be able to subdivide the DNA insert into smaller fragments suitable for cloning into the low capacity plasmid vectors, thereby achieving further purification.

Gene Sequencing

The availability of DNA cloning techniques provides discrete, highly purified DNA segments suitable for further detailed analysis. A major breakthrough in DNA technology has been the development of methods to read the sequence of bases along a DNA strand. The cloned DNA provides a highly suitable source of DNA for sequence studies and this has led to remarkable advances in our knowledge of gene structure and the signal sequences which regulate gene expression. Figure 2 shows the end product of a typical DNA sequence experiment. The principle is simple and the technology is widely used. Radioactively-labeled fragments of DNA are synthesized enzymatically from the single strand of a cloned DNA segment from a known starting signal sequence.

Four enzyme reactions are made which correspond to the four DNA bases under conditions where copies of the strand to be sequenced are made as complementary strands. Each newly-synthesized fragment terminates at a different position but at a point corresponding to a known base. The collection of labeled fragments are separated by electrophoresis to give a ladder of fragments whose length can be determined. It is then a straightforward task to read up the four ladders, one for each base, and order the bases according to their distance from the fixed starting point. This amazingly powerful technique enables stretches of

200-300 bases to be read at a time and by using overlapping sequences the complete code of several viruses has now been determined as well as sequences from a whole range of organisms.

Gene Synthesis -- The Gene Machine

Man's ability to create entirely new genetic information has now been realized by chemical techniques which allow sequences of DNA to be synthesized *de novo*. At present this is a time-consuming task involving the addition of nucleotides (the DNA building blocks) in step-wise fashion. Currently technology is able to produce with reasonable ease and purity artificial DNA strands of up to 20 bases in length. This may not seem a lot when we realize that the simplest virus contains about 5000 bases but the technology will undoubtedly progress rapidly. In any case, it has already proved its vital role as a technique for producing artificial linkers for joining DNA molecules and for the site-directed mutagenesis of naturally-occurring DNA. Figure 1 shows a gene-machine. It may not look so impressive but the beauty of molecular biology is often seen by the highly-sophisticated nature of the work that can be done with relatively simple equipment.

Site-Directed Mutagenesis

Mutant forms of an organism or a gene are of vital importance to the geneticist -- these variant forms of the wild type provide the basic material for the comparative analysis of gene structure and function. Throughout its history genetics in all its branches of study has depended on the random mutational events that arise in nature or by the application of mutagenic treatments. Although these treatments can be controlled to some extent by the choice of mutagen it is not possible to produce mutations at specific sites. The value of site-specific mutagenesis is that a region of DNA, or even a base pair of potential significance can be altered and its effects analyzed. For example, an antibiotic may be improved by knowledge of its chemical structure, site-directed mutagensis of a region of functional importance will produce an altered antibiotic whose activity can be determined.

The Gene Machine, among other techniques, provides a means to achieve this major new approach to gene and protein modification. A short stretch of DNA is synthesized artificially such that one base pair differs from the normal DNA sequence. The normal sequence can be removed and replaced by the modified artificial sequence. Reintroduction of this modified DNA into the cellular background will enable effects of the altered sequence to be monitored at the gene product level. This technique is becoming increasingly widely used for specific DNA modification and we can expect major breakthroughs from this approach.

Blotting and *In Situ* Hybridization

A major difficulty in the isolation of a specific gene sequence is its identification. We have discussed the techniques of gene cloning and the construction of gene banks. They provide a large number of cloned DNA sequences from an organism but they don't identify that particular sequence of interest. At the level of cloned DNA all DNA sequences are much the same. The solution to this technical problem comes from the fact that at the level of base sequence different cloned DNA molecules can be distinguished. If, therefore, a probe is available whose sequence corresponds to that of a particular DNA molecule, or a part of it, this probe can be used to pick out the sequence of interest from all the others.

Probes are specific because their base sequence will match only that of the specific complementary sequence. Probes are usually radioactively-labeled to allow detection and can be used in a variety of ways using methods which form hybrids between the probe and the sequence it is designed to detect.

The identification of a particular cloned sequence from a bank of clones can be done at the point where the vectors carrying their cloned inserts are established in bacterial cells. Each bacterial cell and its progeny will carry a different clone. Bacterial colonies on the surface of a Petri plate are transferred, or blotted, to sheets of nitrocellulose paper to which their DNA will be bound at the exact locations of the colonies. The blot is exposed to the labeled probe which will hybridize only to the DNA of that colony containing the specific complementary sequence. By detecting the site to which the radiolabel has hybridized will identify the specific colony bearing that cloned DNA sequence.

The same approach can be applied to the entire chromosome content of a cell to localize the position of a particular gene sequence. In this case, the well-established technique of spreading out mitotic chromosomes on a microscope slide is used to allow each chromosome to be unambiguously identified. The spread chromosomes can then be immersed in a solution of the specific probe and the site of the complementary chromosome sequence identified by its highly-localized radioactivity.

Cell Fusion

Genetic interactions between organisms occur when their genetic information is brought together within the same cell. This is true for fertilization when cell fusion occurs between gametes. However, it is also possible to fuse together a whole range of cells to form hybrids. This includes somatic or non-sexual cells from plants and animals and also bacterial cells and is not necessarily restricted by species barriers. The value of such a technique is manifold -- it has permitted the construction of hybridoma cells for the production of monoclonal antibodies, and the analysis of hybrid mouse/man cells has led to the localization of a variety of genes on human chromosomes. In bacterial systems it has permitted the construction of genetic hybrids from cells that do not normally interact and thereby has led to the formation of inter-strain recombinants.

As far as we can tell all cells are capable of fusion under appropriate conditions. The basic requirement is that the cells should be in the form of protoplasts -- that is cells with a cytoplasmic membrane but no cell wall. Animal cells are normally in this form but for plant and bacterial cells the cell wall must be enzymatically removed prior to fusion.

In the case of bacterial protoplasts they can be regenerated back into normal, walled cells. Even more striking are plant protoplasts which with the right blend of treatments, can be regenerated to form whole, seed-bearing plants.

This catalogue of techniques is, for reasons of space, a limited selection based on some of the more advanced and therefore potentially more exciting developments in genetic technology.

Literature Sources for Genetics, Molecular Biology and Biotechnology

As with any scientific discipline the information base for the subject is distributed among a wide variety of publications. These run from the scientific journals as the source of primary experimental data, through to textbooks, which provide a current digest, to popular articles more appropriate for the general reader. The number of journals and abstracts would fill the page. Only a few are listed here. For general reading of a technically competent nature on genetics consult one or all of the following publications: *Cell; Nature; Science; Proceedings of the National Academy of Sciences, U.S.A.; Biotechnology; Scientific American.*

Textbooks

Genetics, by J.R.S. Fincham, Wright PSG, London, 1983.
Genetics, by C. Avers, Willard Grant Press, Boston, 1984.
A History of Genetics, by A.H. Sturtevant, Harper &

Row, New York, 1965.

Modern Genetics, by F.J. Ayala & J.A. Kiger, Benjamin/Cummings, California, 1980.

Genetics, by U. Goodenough, Saunders College Publishing, Philadelphia, 1984.

Molecular Biology, by D. Friefelder, Van Nostrand Reinhold Co., New York, 1983.

Gene Expression (Volumes I-III), by B. Lewin, John Wiley & Sons, New York, 1980.

Molecular Genetics, by G.S. Stent & R. Calendar, W.H. Freeman & Co., San Francisco, 1978.

Gene Function, by R.E. Glass, Croom Helm, London, 1982.

Genes, by B. Lewin, John Wiley & Sons, New York, 1983.

Recombinant DNA, by J.D. Watson, J. Tooze & D.T. Kurtz, W.H. Freeman & Co., New York, 1983.

Principles of Gene Manipulation, by R.W. Old & S.B. Primrose, Blackwell, Oxford, 1984.

Gene Cloning, by D.M. Glover, Chapman & Hall, London, 1984.

Biotechnology, by J.E. Smith, Edward Arnold Ltd., London, 1981.

Biotechnology Corporations

The last 10 years has seen a remarkable growth of the biotechnology industry largely based on developments in gene cloning and recombinant DNA technology. This development is largely confined to North America, Europe and Japan and has taken three forms. The large established industrial corporations with established interests in bio-medical and agricultural products have committed themselves to expanding their biotechnology interests. A variety of new and often small private organizations largely funded by venture capital have emerged to exploit recombinant DNA technology for commercial purposes. Universities, often with industrial and venture capital funding, have established biotechnology centers to monopolize on their academic expertise.

The list of these organizations is long and is continually expanding as the potential benefits are more widely appreciated. The following list gives the financially most successful of those companies in the second category.

Biogen (Switzerland)
Bio-Logicals (Canada)
Bio-Response (U.S.A.)
Cetus (U.S.A.)
Collaborative Research (U.S.A.)
Damon (U.S.A.)
Enzo-Biochem (U.S.A.)
Flow General (U.S.A.)

Genentech (U.S.A.)
Genetic Systems (U.S.A.)
Genex (U.S.A.)
Hybridtech (U.S.A.)
Molecular Genetics (U.S.A.)
Monoclonal Antibodies (U.S.A.)
Novo Industri A/S (Denmark)
Pharmacia (Sweden)

Major Conferences

Because of the rapid theoretical and technical development in genetics, molecular biology and biotechnology and the need for the fast spread of information there has been a marked growth in conferences. The interested reader wishing further details is recommended to consult journals such as *Science; Nature* and *Biotechnology.*

Laboratory Courses

To meet the growing demand for training in the techniques of genetics, molecular biology and biotechnology a number of laboratory technical courses are now offered. These courses are usually of about 2 weeks duration and generally are organized for about 20 research workers. Often these courses require some background in the relevant field and are particularly geared to the younger scientist wishing to gain entry to a new area of technology. Some large organizations such as EMBO (European Molecular Biology Organisation) and FEMS (Federation of European Microbiological Societies) and ICRO (International Cell Research Organization) support an extensive program of such courses. In other cases they are organized by individual laboratories. These courses are usually very intensive and while largely laboratory-bound, will also cover theoretical aspects of the subject.

As with the conferences, the menu is constantly changing and the classified sections of journals such as *Nature* and *Science* and also the *Biotechnology* journals provide an excellent source of information that the interested reader is recommended to consult.

Centers for Research in Genetics & Molecular Biology

In selecting this list of laboratories for research in genetics and molecular biology, I have taken notice of several factors. The problem is in the definition of centers of excellence. By the criterion of Nobel Prizes we would have to say that the U.S.A. and Europe constitute the 20th century source of the most profound scientific discoveries. A recent Japanese report, the MITI Report, identified the national sources of innovation in science and technology since the end of World War II and the report showed the top three to be the U.K. (55%), U.S.A. (15%) and Japan (5%). But we must bear in mind several facts in defining good places to do research. The wealth of a nation is clearly of extreme importance. The national priorities of a country often lean towards the application of science rather than fundamental discovery. The organization of science plays a major role as does the political attitudes of a country. Educational opportunity is yet another, and we must not forget that many scientists have migrated from all over the world to North America and Europe and their talents have therefore been lost by their mother country.

It is with these thoughts that I have selected a list, albeit incomplete, of research laboratories. I have tried to be representative and have made no attempt to assess their position in the list. This would not be the right approach in my view and they are listed randomly to fortify this point.

Research Laboratories

Dept. of Biology, Massachusetts Institute of Technology, Cambridge, Massachusetts, U.S.A.

Max-Planck Institut fur Zuchtungforschung, Koln, F.R.G.

Institute for Biophysics, Polish Academy of Sciences, Warszawa, Poland.

Institute Radiobiologie Cellulaire, CNRS, Gif sur Yvette, France.

Lab. of Molecular Biology, State University of Ghent, Netherlands.

Zentralinstitut fur Genetik und Kulturpflanzenforschung, Academy of Science, Gatersleben, GDR.

National Institute for Medical Research, London, U.K.

National Institute of Genetics, Mishima, Japan.

European Molecular Biology Laboratory, Heidelberg, F.R.G.

Dept. of Biochemistry & Molecular Biology, Harvard University, Cambridge, Massachusetts, U.S.A.

MRC Laboratory of Molecular Biology, Cambridge, U.K.

Institute of Virology, Glasgow, U.K.

Salk Institute, San Diego, California, U.S.A.

Beatson Institute for Cancer Research, Glasgow, U.K.

Laboratorium voor Genetica, Ghent, Belgium.

Dept. of Biochemistry, University of California, Berkeley, California, U.S.A.

Cold Spring Harbor Laboratory, Long Island, New York, U.S.A.

Dept. of Biological Sciences, University of Warwick, U.K.

Dept. of Molecular Biology, University of Edinburgh, U.K.

Institute of Molecular Biology, University of Oregon, Eugene, Oregon, U.S.A.

Centro de Biologia Molecular, Universidad Autonoma, Madrid, Spain.

Instituto di Genetica, Biochimica ed Evoluzionistica del CNR, Universita di Pavia, Italy.

Institute of Cellular & Molecular Pathology, Brussels, Belgium.

Imperial Cancer Research Fund Institute, London, U.K.

Cancer Research Laboratory, University of Western Ontario, Canada.

Dept. of Microbiology & Immunology, University of California Medical Center, San Francisco, California, U.S.A.

Molecular Biology Laboratory, Napoli, Italy.

The John Innes Institute, Norwich, U.K.

Dept. of Biochemistry, University of Strasbourg, France.

Division of Molecular Biology, Netherlands Cancer Institute, Amsterdam, Netherlands.

Laboratory of Molecular Biology, NIH, Bethesda, Maryland, U.S.A.

Dept. of Biochemistry, Stanford University Medical School, California, U.S.A.

Institut fur Molekularbiologie, Universitat Zurich, Switzerland.

Whitehead Institute, Cambridge, Massachusetts, U.S.A.

Biogen Research Corporation, Cambridge, Massachusetts, U.S.A.

Institut fur Genetik, Universitat zur Koln, Koln, F.R.G.

Division of Biology, California Institute of Technology, Pasadena, California, U.S.A.

Institute of Molecular Genetics, USSR Academy of Sciences, Moscow, U.S.S.R.

Max-Planck Institut fur Moleclare Genetik, Berlin, F.R.G.

Dept. of Microbiology, Biozentrum, University of

Basel, Switzerland.

Laboratory of Genetics, Faculty of Agriculture, Kyoto University, Japan.

Lehrstuhl Moleculare Genetik der Universitat Heidelberg, F.R.G.

Dept. of General Genetics, Warszawa, Poland.

Institute de Biologie Moleculaire, Universite de Geneve, Switzerland.

Tata Institute for Fundamental Research, Bombay, India.

Dept. of Genetics, Biology Centre, Kerklaan, Netherlands.

Dept. de Biochemie et Genetique Moleculaire, Paris, France.

McArdle Laboratory for Cancer Research, University of Wisconsin, Madison, Wisconsin, U.S.A.

Dept. of Embryology, Carnegie Institute of Washington, Baltimore, Maryland, U.S.A.

Dept. of Molecular & Population Genetics, University of Georgia, Athens, Georgia, U.S.A.

Dept. of Medicine, Stanford University School of Medicine, Stanford, California, U.S.A.

Dept. of Microbiology & Molecular Genetics, Harvard Medical School, Boston, Massachusetts, U.S.A.

Institute for Chemical Research, Kyoto University, Japan.

Lehrstuhl fur Genetik, Universitat Regensberg, F.R.G.

Institute of Molecular Biology, Slovak Academy of Sciences, Bratislava, Czechoslovakia.

Plant Breeding Institute, Cambridge, U.K.

Dept. of Genetics, Monash University, Australia.

Institute of Molecular Biology, Bulgarian Academy of Sciences, Sofia, Bulgaria.

Dept. of Genetics, University of Glasgow, U.K.

Institute of Molecular Genetics, Czechoslovak Academy of Sciences, Praha, Czechoslovakia.

Recombinant DNA Laboratory, University of Helsinki, Finland.

Dept. of Biology, Kyushu University, Fukuoka, Japan.

Dept. of Genetics, University of Canberra, Australia.

Dept. of Genetics, University of Liverpool, U.K.

Dept. of Botany, Magadh University, Bakhtiyarpur, India.

Centre de Biochimie et de Biologie Moleculaire du CNRS, Marseille, France.

ARC Unit of Nitrogen Fixation, University of Sussex, Brighton, U.K.

Central Institute of Microbiology & Experimental Theraphy, GDR Academy of Sciences, Jena, G.D.R.

Dept. of Genetics, University of Leeds, U.K.

Institute of Biochemistry & Biophysics, Warszawa, Poland.

Institute of Plant Physiology, Szeged, Hungary.

Centro de Investigacion Sobre Ingeneria Genetica y Biotechnologia, Mexico City, Mexico.

Institute of Biophysics, Czechoslovak Academy of Sciences, Brno, Czechoslovakia.

Institut fur Physiologische Chemie, Universitat Munchen, F.R.G.

Dept. of Microbiology, Gdansk, Poland.

Laborataire de Biologie et Genetique Moleculaire, Universite Paris Sud, Orsay, France.

Dept. of Population & Evolutionary Biology, Rijkuniversiteit Utrecht, Netherlands.

Departamento de Bioquimica, Universidad de Santander, Spain.

Dept. of Fermentation Technology, Osaka University, Japan.

Dept. of Microbiology, University of Liege, Belgium.

Dept. of Biochemistry & Molecular Biology, Technical University of Berlin, F.R.G.

A Last Word

In this brief entry to The Biosphere Catalogue I have attempted a global view in keeping with the spirit of the publication. This has meant that much of value and interest has been sacrificed at the altar of selectivity. My aim has been to provide the grape and not the wine and my hope is that I have passed on some of the intense excitement of my chosen field of study. If a few sparks begin to smoulder then it will not be difficult for that fortunate reader to search for further fuel.

Plant Tissue Culture: General Characteristics & Agricultural Applications

Toshio Murashige

Starting with Haberlandt's first experiments that were published in 1902 and, perhaps, until twenty years ago, plant tissue cultures were intended mainly as tools of botanical experiments and were practiced in only a handful of academic laboratories. By virtue of their isolation from the plant, developmental studies of specific organs and tissues were possible without the interference by correlative influences. Among the significant contributions of tissue culture investigations were the discoveries by Skoog and his associates in the mid-1950's of the cytokinin class of plant hormones and the regulation of organ formation by balances between the cyokinins and auxins. Auxin tends to enhance root formation and inhibit shoot initiation, whereas cytokinin stimulates shoot initiation and represses root formation.

The practical agricultural applications that are evident today were initiated in the early 1960's by Morel's observation that shoot apex culture served as a superior alternative in clonal multiplication of orchids. The major research in agriculture currently involves the development of *in vitro* techniques, particularly those of protoplast and microspore cultures, to aid plant hybridization and variety development. However, the practical applications of such techniques remain unrealized. In contrast, significant advances have been made in the employment of tissue cultures to enhance clonal propagation. Diverse cultivars, including orchids, foliage plants, and some trees, are already being produced *en masse* in several commercial tissue culture facilities.

Hundreds of cultivars and species are being reproduced asexually in commercial laboratories of all sizes. But commercial laboratories perform few experiments to adapt nutrient formulations and refine procedures for specific crops. The major experimental effort aimed at developing specific propagation methods still resides in academic institutions, perhaps unwisely. The extensively propagated crops include nearly all indoor foliage plants; some flower crops and landscape ornamentals; a few vegetables and field corps; some fruit varieties; and a number of forest genera.

Tissue culture is an important method of establishing pathogen-free stocks. And because plants are recoverable from single cells and protoplasts of many species, plant tissue culture has rapidly gained prominence in the latest heralded field of genetic engineering. Plant tissue culture is, more than ever, a significant tool of biological experimentation. More astonishing, however, is the major role it now pursues in agricultural research and applications:

(1) Rapid clonal propagation
(2) Elimination of pathogens
(3) Development of superior cultivars
(4) Production of biochemicals

General Characteristics

Plant tissue culture identifies collectively plant cell, protoplast, tissue, and organ cultures. The common features are asepsis (elimination of pathogens) and development in artificial nutrient medium and controlled environment. The origin in each instance is an organ or organ section; but only organ cultures are intended to retain and enhance the organ's characteristics. The others range in development from dissociated cells in liquid suspension to complete plants in an intermediary callus.

Aespsis is achieved by surface sterilization of the plant part used as the explant, steam sterilization of the nutrient media, and carrying out operations in a workstation provided with filtered air. Specially designed culture vessels are often used to maintain asepsis.

Nutrient media of plant tissue cultures are diverse in composition and are furnished as liquids and gels. Minimal constituents are inorganic salts, including all mineral elements that are essential to plant development; sugar, usually sucrose; one or more B-vitamins, especially thiamine, nicotinic acid and pyridoxine; inositol; and water of relatively high purity. Growth and differentiation of cultured tissues are determined by the proportions of hormonal supplements, particularly auxin and cytokinin. Amino acids, adenine, phenolic derivatives, and other morphogenic substances are frequently added to enhance some species and developmental processes.

With the exception of orchid cultures, the incubation of which is sometimes carried out in greenhouses, plant tissue cultures are normally maintained in rooms or chambers with relatively controlled light and temperature. Prescribed photoperiods, fluorescent lamps (with significant emission in the blue and red regions), and specified light intensities play critical roles in plant tissue culture development. Plants are regenerated mainly through a sequence of adventitious shoot formation, using a variety of tissues as explants, and rooting of individual shoots; or by enhancing auxiliary branching in shoot tips, followed by rooting of shoots. Both processes are relatively slow; nevertheless, *they are often several million times faster than traditional cloning counterparts.* The most rapid plant multiplication can be achieved through somatic cell embryogenesis. It is still under development, although already being applied to a few crops, e.g., date and oil palms. All three methods are laborious and can benefit substantially from mechanization. To that end, encapsulation or fluid drilling of somatic embryos appears most promising.

The main objective of clonal propagation is to reproduce uniform plants; tissue culture enables its attainment at a faster rate. Tissue culture can be especially advantageous in increasing propagules of plants that have been newly freed from pathogens, or new varietal selections and introductions. It can hasten domestication of uncultivated plants and their development into new crops. Parental plants can be cloned in large numbers by tissue culture to increase the availability of hybrid seeds.

Plant propagation by tissue culture is not without risks. The method does not guarantee exclusion of pathogens, even though this is frequently claimed. More important, the cultivar traits may not be reproduced, even though the derived plants are clonal. Frequency of aberrants depends on the cultivar; it is also progressively elevated in successive subcultures.

The production of pathogen-free plants enables the achievement of yield and quality commensurate with a variety's inherent potential. Disease-related extinction of germplasm can be prevented. And international exchange of propagules can be conducted without risking disease spread. Each of these benefits are attainable by tissue culture. Moreover, that of propagule exchange by tissue culture can also ensure exclusion of insects, mites, nematodes, and other pests.

Macroscopic parasites are easily excluded by tissue culture. However, microscopic and systemically infecting agents, such as viruses, viroids, and mycoplasmas, can only be eliminated through special procedures.

Pathogen testing of regenerated plants is critical. No plant should be assumed to be pathogen-free, even though special precautions were observed in obtaining it. Moreover, the pathogen tested plants should not be propagated in large numbers and placed in production, unless reproduction of cultivar traits has been ascertained.

Several *in vitro* techniques are at hand for immediate application in varietal improvement. Desirable genetic variants can be isolated from cultured cells and protoplasts, or by screening plants regenerated from cultured cells and pollen. A sugar cane cultivar with resistance to Fiji virus was the product of screening plants regenerated by tissue culture. Plants with tolerance to cold, salinity, herbicides, and a variety of pathogens have been isolated by screening somatic cells or regenerated plants of carrot, rice, wheat, corn, tobacco, potato, and sugar can. Higher sugar yields have been encountered among variant plants from sugar cane callus. Rice and corn plants that produced lysine-rich grains have also been attained.

Prospects

In the last twenty years, plant tissue culture has progressed from experimentation in a few botanical laboratories to major applications in numerous agricultural concerns. Utilization of plant tissue culture has also extended into molecular biology. Extensive successes in genetic engineering may be anticipated in the years ahead, largely through a combination of cell culture, protoplast manipulation and recombinant DNA methodology. Insertion of selected genes into plant cells will be aided by additional vectors, such as organelles and transposons. The successes will be evident in the form of major crops with new genes with resistance to diseases, tolerance to soil and climatic stresses, resistance to herbicides, higher photosynthetic efficiency, capacity to fix atmospheric nitrogen, higher yields, and improved nutritional and other product qualities.

Pathogen exclusion by tissue culture will be the accepted, if not demanded, practice for the major clonally propagated crops.

There will also be further exploitation of tissue culture in clonal propagation. The successes will eventually extend to all fruit and forest trees, as well as vegetables, cereals, legumes, and other currently seed-propagated crops.

Plant Tissue Culture: Future Applications

Stephen Storm

Tissue culture as a method of clonal propagation is the most important invention affecting managed ecosystems since horticulturists learned to propagate plants by placing cuttings in the soil. In the 50 years that have passed since the first continuous culture of tomato roots, tissue culture has become the preferred method for commercial propagation of many plants.

Another important potential for tissue culture is in plant collecting, inventorying and germ-plasm preservation. At the cellular level many plants can be cryo-preserved in very small spaces. It may be possible to place in stable orbit deep frozen plant cells, the biosphere's ultimate safe deposit vault. Plant collectors may someday venture into the field with a miniature tissue culture lab in their backpack and return with many more plants than is now possible.

For the future, cloning of plants and related technology holds great promise. Perhaps the most interesting is the creation of entirely new genera of plants through protoplast fusion. Also somaclonal variants with hitherto unknown but desirable characteristics may provide plants for hostile environments. And again the mutation of plants grown *in vitro* is often seen and may give rise to plants important to the biosphere. The farthest out speculations, using a combination of tissue culture techniques, suggest the ability to design and create plants for the hostile environment of space. By establishing a continuum between Earth conditions and, for example, Martian conditions, and proceeding by small steps it might be possible to develop plants capable of living on some more favorable parts of the present Martian environment.

Whatever the future holds, tissue culture can serve as a tool with which man can dramatically alter the rate and direction of evolution.

The following is a catalogue of plant tissue culture associations and laboratories engaged in the development of this field.

Associations

The International Association for Plant Tissue Culture operates through national correspondents and publishes a monthly newsletter which is included in the cost of membership. Following is a list of some national correspondents which should give most everyone access to the Association.

USA

Roberta H. Smith
Texas A & M University
Box 2132
College Station, Tx. 77843

USSR

Raisa G. Butenko
K.A. Timiriazev Institute of Plant Physiology
USSR Academy of Sciences
Botanicheshajd 35, 127273
Moscow, USSR

Japan

Hiroshi Harada
Institute of Biological Sciences
University of Tsukuba
Sakura-mura, Niihari-gun
Ibaraki-ken, 305

France
Abdellatif Benbadis
Laboratoire d'Histophysiologie Vegetale
12 Rue Cuvier
75005 Paris

United Kingdom
Keith C. Short
Trent Polytechnic
Clifton Lane
Nottingham NG11 8B.NS

Israel
Jonathan Gressel
Plant Genetics
The Weizmann Institute of Science
76100 Rehovot

India
P.S.Rao
Bio-Organic Division
B.A.R.C.
Bombay 400085

Indonesia
E. Noerhadi
Jurusan Biologi
Institut Teknologi Bandung
Jalan Ganesha 10
Bandung

Mexico
Manuel Robert
Departamento de Genetica y Fisiologia
Centro de Investigacion Cientifica de Yucatan
Apdo. Postal 87
Cordemex 97310, Yucatan

Australia
Martin Barlass
CSIRO Division of Horticulture Research
Private Mail Bag
Merbein VIC 3505

Brazil
Otto J. Crocomo
CENA /USP, CEBTEC FEALQ
ESALQ /USP 13.400 Piracicaba SP

Taiwan
Chi-Chang Chen
Institute of Botany
Academia Sinica
Taipei

Plant Tissue Culture Laboratories

For a comprehensive listing consult the Handbook and Directory of Commercial Laboratories, *Plant Propagation by Tissue Culture*, published by Exegetics Ltd., 1984.

France
Etablissements Georges Delbard,
Pepinieres Roseraires,
Malicorne,
03600 Commentry
A major French nursery recently expanding into the American market. Produces a range of horticultural plants.

Belgium
Station des Culture Fruitieres et Maraicheres
Chaussee de Charleroi 234
B-5800 Gembloux

Australia
Burbank Tissue Culture Laboratory & Research Center
Pacific Highway
Tuggerah, P.O. Box 403
Wyong, NSW 2259
One of the largest Australian tissue culture enterprises. Special emphasis on woody plants for agricultural and plantation use. Offers contract tissue culture production, consultancy and research services.

New Zealand
Bio-Tissue Products
44 Challinor St.
Hamilton
Tissue culture technques for plant propagation, plant breeding, virus-eliminations and high health indexing, and production of mycorrhiza for blueberries. Services include micro-propagation, consultancy, *in vitro* export/import, and chemical analysis.

Germany
Robert Mayer Gartenbau -- Specizlkulturen
Postfach 110204
Hornthalstrasse 47a
8600 Bamberg
Specializes in raspberry plants with other

species such as Gerbara daisies, apple and plums.

England

Twyford Laboratories, Ltd.
Boltonsborough, Glastonbury
Somerset
10 years experience in orchard propagation, now uses *in vitro* techniques on herbaceous ornamentals, woody plants, and vegetables. Established reputation in meticulous virus testing and disease -- indexing of all propagated material.

South Africa

Malanseuns Nurseries
Brits Road
Pk./PO. Rosslyn
Pretoria 0200
Experimental work on a wide range of woody plants, primarily for ornamental horticulture. Species include Magnolia, Olive, and Holly.

United States

S.B.V. Plant Laboratory P.O. Box 771
Oracle, Arizona 85623
A recently established laboratory involved in research and production of a wide variety of plants with emphasis on tropical and sub-tropical fruits and ornamentals.

Native Plants Inc.
University Research Park
360 Wakara Way
Salt Lake, Utah 84103
A large micropropagation lab capable of producing 3-4 million tissue cultured plants per year. Wide variety of species available from vegetable crops, to forest trees and various plants of pharmaceutical interest.

Journals

HortScience
In Vitro
Journal of Plant Cell, Tissue and Organ Culture

Reference

Plant Propagation by Tissue Culture, Handbook and Directory of Commercial Laboratories, by E.F. George and P.D. Sherington, Exegetics Limited (Eversley, Basingstoke; Hants, RG27 0GY, England), 1984. A compilation of information appearing in journals and research reports. A useful book if one does not have access to a major university library or other bibliographic source. The directory of laboratories will be of interest to those who wish to participate in this emerging industry.

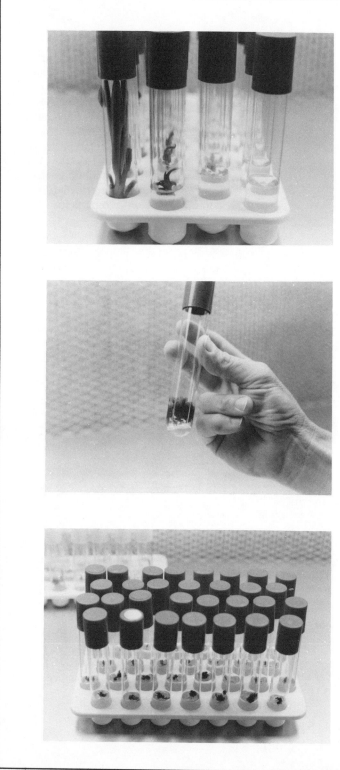

From right to left:
Meristem explant – Day 1
Proliferating callus – Day 21
Emerging plantlet – Day 45
Full size plantlet ready for greenhouse – Day 90

One tube of Boston Fern tissue is enough to inoculate 40 more tubes.

In one month each of those 40 tubes will inoculate 40 more, and so on.

Analytics

Joe Hanson

In order to observe
One must learn how to compare. In order to compare
One must have observed. By means of observation
Knowledge is generated; on the other hand, knowledge is
    needed for observation. And
He observes badly who does not know
How to use what he has observed.
            BERTOLT BRECHT

Complexity and Organization

Ever since I became vaguely aware of what's going on in the universe, I've been fascinated by the fact that one of the prime tendencies of the elements is to form themselves into ever more complex structures; ever more complex systems; ever higher levels of organization.

A few billion years ago on a small planet we call Earth, some organic molecules formed themselves into viruses; viruses evolved into bacteria, fungi, and the like; these, in turn, somehow seem to have given rise to single-celled plants and animals. Once the cell, with its information packed nucleus and its protective outer membrane was formed, life began to reach beyond the microscopic: jellyfish, worms, starfish, insects, spiders, lobsters, sharks and rays, boney fishes, frogs and toads, lizards, snakes, turtles, dinosaurs, mammoths, rats, horses, camels, apes, pigs, humans, and cockroaches.

Some, maybe nearly all, of these life forms apparently weren't content with just being wonderfully complex all by themselves; they formed complex societies of complex individuals. Ant colonies, bee hives, porpoise and whale schools, and human civilizations are just a few of the more familiar examples. But almost all animals live in some sort of a social organization and so, by the way, do plants.

So, I'm intrigued with the idea that everything in the universe seems to have some innate compulsion to strive for higher orders of organization and complexity.

Where Biospherics Fits

Perhaps the most complex of the complexities that evolved here on earth is the whole uneven spherical shell of stuff and activity which covers the entire planet from hundreds of meters below its crust to thousands of meters into its sky: the dynamic planetary shell we call the biosphere. Reduced to its irreducible minimum simplicity, the biosphere is an incredibly complex system of solar energy-driven oxidation/reduction (redox) reactions. Differential heating and cooling and gravity changes as Earth's moon orbits and Earth and Moon both spin and orbit the Sun, result in tides, ocean currents, wind and weather; these are the primary mixers in the biospherical mixing bowl. Photosynthetic life (plants, algae and photosynthetic bacteria) capture some of the photons sent our way by the sun's thermonuclear furnace and use this energy to drive reductive chemical reactions which assemble carbohydrate molecules from carbon dioxide and a menu of other inorganics including hydrogen, nitrogen, phosphorous, and sulfur, among other things. Photosynthesis, then, is the light-driven biochemical reduction reaction which uses solar energy to create living organic material from non-living inorganic matter. It gives off oxygen as a by-product, by the way, and the 20% or so of oxygen in Earth's atmosphere was probably mostly contributed by photosynthesis.

Now, remember that carbon dioxide, needed by the photosynthesizers, is a by-product of the oxidation of carbon compounds. Of course, oxidation can come under a variety of brand names like explosion of dynamite, rocket propulsion, a fire in the fireplace, and biological metabolism. Shooting guns, animal metabolism, forest fires, and bacterial decomposition of organic detritus into inorganics are all oxidative reactions that put carbon dioxide into Earth's atmosphere and waters. Compared to the carbon dioxide contributed by bacteria, the carbon dioxide of wars, all animals, and forest fires to Earth's carbon dioxide reservoirs are less than trivial. It is not that any one microorganism contributes very much, it is that there are near infinite numbers of the little fellows metabolizing away almost everywhere on Earth where it is warmer than a deep freeze and cooler than an oven. The

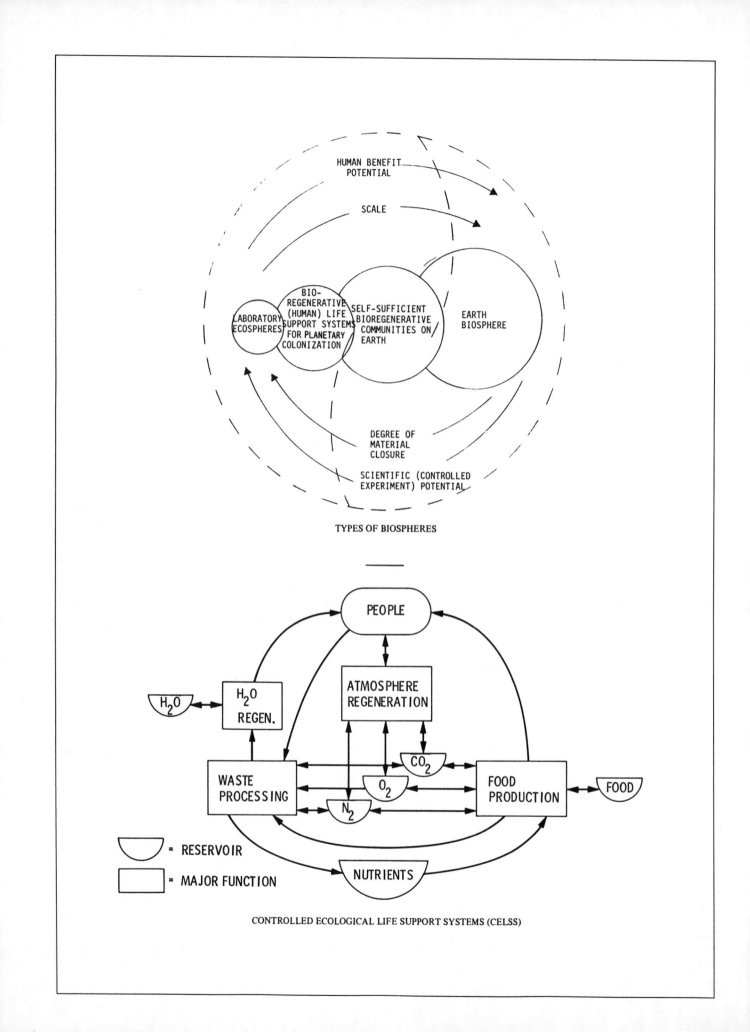

TYPES OF BIOSPHERES

CONTROLLED ECOLOGICAL LIFE SUPPORT SYSTEMS (CELSS)

meek may not inherit the Earth, but without its microscopic detritus processors, the biospheric machinery would quickly grind to a halt as its carbon dioxide tank became dry and its inorganic building blocks became locked up in organic wastes.

The bottom line is that the biosphere is spherical, functionally as well as structurally.

I used to call this cycle "bioregeneration". That's a pretty good name because, in fact, everything is regenerated. But, since I ran into the Ecotechnics people and was introduced to their term, "biospherics", I think I like their's a little better. To me, "biospherics" connotates both the spherical structure and the spherical dynamics of self-sustaining, bioregenerative systems.

Now, with that understood, how many basic types of biospherical systems is it useful to think about? In my view there are four: (1) tiny research "ecospheres", (2) biospherical (human) life support systems needed for extended space travel and for colonizing other planets, (3) resource-conserving approaches to living, and (4) the biosphere of Earth.

The Game for Humans -- Maybe

One of the things going on at the Jet Propulsion Laboratory, where I work, has the nickname (acronym) SETI -- Search for Extraterrestrial Intelligence. This work monitors the various subspectra of the electromagnetic spectrum (mainly from low frequency to ultra high frequency radio wavelengths) which reach Earth from outer space. Using the latest in information theory techniques, they analyze these radiations to determine if any of them are sufficiently non-random that they may have been generated by intelligent beings. So far, the results are negative.

Considering the number of galaxies in the known universe, the number of dying stars (like our sun) in each galaxy, and the number of planets that could be orbiting around each star, is it possible that none of them other than Earth has experienced the magic intertwined sequences of energy and matter which, on Earth, evolved a biosphere with forms of life capable of grasping, understanding, and communicating ideas? I suggest that within a couple of million light years from here, we may be it. There may not be any other civilizations out there, at least not in our neighborhood of a million light years or so.

If we are it, then one of the games we might play is to learn to manage our own planet well enough to preserve it as a productive and pleasant base of operations and then to gradually expand our civilization on out into the nearby galaxies -- those within a few thousand or few hundred thousand light years. It could be fun, but we will have to understand biospherics if we are to do it.

Since the second two rings in Figure A are covered elsewhere in this catalogue, I would like to offer a brief summary of current work relating to the first two -- laboratory ecosystems and biospheric human life support systems.

Laboratory Ecospheres

Dr. Clair Folsome, in his laboratory at the University of Hawaii, has some hermetically-sealed 25 cc. vials containing sand, sea water and varieties of procaryotic organisms that have been sustaining themselves for a decade; they will probably continue indefinitely. Dr. Folsome is now beginning work with materially-closed systems containing higher aquatic animals which will be as large as five gallons. He and I have some future dreams of hermetically enclosing systems as large as a house. Meanwhile, the smallest self-sustaining ecospheres which contain multicelled plants and animals so far are my 1000 cc. creations upon which Folsome and I perform research and which Engineering and Research Associates of Tucson, Arizona markets under the tradename "SEBRA Ecospheres".

"An ecosphere or laboratory ecosphere is a photon-fueled ecological oxidation-reduction system which perpetuates itself for a year or more and has internal dynamics (bioelemental cycles). Ecospheres do not contain humans. Humans may employ ecospheres as subjects of research. Such research may lead to eventual understanding of the physical, chemical, biological, and thermodynamical networks which must function within certain tolerances in order for given types of plants and animals to survive within materially-closed, energetically-open ecosystems. Such understandings may be very useful in understanding how to design, build and operate biospherical human life support systems for space travel and for colonizing other planets and they may be useful in understanding how to manage Earth's biosphere and its subsystems." With the definition as a launch pad, let us now look at who is doing what in "ecosphere biospherics".

Clair E. Folsome, Ph.D., Department of Microbiology-SNY201 -- University of Hawaii -- Honolulu, Hawaii 96822. Telephone: 808-948-8386.

Dr. Folsome has been working with materially closed, energetically open microbiological ecosystems since 1967. This, to the best of my knowledge, certainly makes him *the* pioneer in this new field. Since he and I became associated in 1982, he and his graduate students have also been working with macrobiological systems. They began by performing experiments which Dr. Folsome and I designed on the shrimp-algae experiments which Dr. Folsome and I came up with in the late 1970's and, after some exploratory work, are now beginning some investigations on materially closed systems containing boney fish. If these latter systems persist (they are three months old at this writing), they will mark the first known success with vertebrates in materially closed environments.

Thus far Folsome and his students have performed a variety of experiments using hundreds of ecosystems; one Ph.D. has been earned, as has an M.S., and another Ph.D. is nearing completion. Seven open literature publications have been produced by this work.

Among the experiments performed in this laboratory are: monitoring of oxygen and carbon dioxide cycles as indicators of system stability and instability, determinations of apparent quantum efficiency, ATP-GTP determinations of biomass, and monitoring of procaryote/eucaryote ratios as indexes of system state. As it is with any emerging field, the University of Hawaii laboratory has received precious little funding for pursuit of closed ecosystem research. This fact, I think, makes Dr. Folsome's accomplishments very impressive indeed.

Laboratory facilities include a high resolution mass spectrometer, recording infrared, visible and ultraviolet spectrophotometers, radioisotope scintillation counters, and a bewildering array of micro-computers. These, of course, are in addition to the standard biology wet lab facilities. The laboratory and its associated offices are located on the second floor of Snyder Hall on the University's Manoa campus overlooking Honolulu and overlooked by the Koolau mountain range. It is a nice place to work.

Joe A. Hanson, Jet Propulsion Laboratory -- California Institute of Technology -- 4800 Oak Grove Drive -- Pasadena, California 91109. Telephone: 818-354-8148.

The shrimp-algae materially closed, energetically open ecosystems which I began demonstrating in 1979 grew out of some earlier work I had done at the Oceanic Institute in Hawaii before I joined the Jet Propulsion Laboratory (JPL). Being an ecologist by academic background and a systems theorist/engineer by trade, I suppose it was natural that I should become somewhat obsessed with the possibilities for self sufficient bioregenerative systems. I am not certain how long ago all this started, but I do remember bringing my obsession with me to JPL.

Sometime in 1977 NASA initiated its Controlled Ecology Life Support System (CELSS) program and it seemed to me that I could demonstrate how the shrimp-algae closed ecosystems might be of some real value in understanding how to go about developing CELSS that would support humans in extended space travel and on other planets. NASA did not leap at the opportunity I

offered, however, and I found myself in the business of convincing others that I was, in fact, reasonably sane. This, of course, could only be done by proving that the little closed ecosystems I was talking about really could be demonstrated. Fortunately, the JPL environment is not by any means well designed to supress scientific creativity. However, it does take a little time to prove that something can persist for years. Neither NASA nor I had yet heard of Folsome's work.

By mid-1981, the CELSS program manager at NASA, the CELSS lead center (NASA Ames Research Center) and principals at various universities associated with the CELSS program had become interested in my results and in Folsome's work (Folsome and I were now in contact by telephone at least), and the work being done by Dr. Basset Maguire at the University of Texas, Austin. This interest was sufficient for the CELSS program manager to be in a position to fund me to organize and chair a small, invitation-only workshop concerned with the viability and potential research value of materially closed, energetically open ecosystems. The workshop was held in January 1982 and, I think, was a successful beginning toward the initiation and recognition of a new branch of ecological science.

Since the workshop, NASA has been in a position to provide a small amount of funding to permit Clair Folsome and I to collaborate in our research. JPL is not by charter a NASA center for biological research. JPL's mission is the unmanned exploration of space. Therefore, even though there are some advanced instruments here at JPL which offer real promise for the study of closed ecosystems, it has not been possible for me to establish a laboratory even remotely comparable to Clair's at the University of Hawaii. Thus it makes sense at this time for the work to be carried out in Clair's laboratory with me collaborating by telephone, mail and occasional visits.

I still maintain some of my original systems in a corner of a laboratory at JPL -- now five years old and still going strong -- but the real work is being done by Clair and his students. Clair and I are now working on a new proposal to NASA under the aegis of NASA's "Biospherics" program. Perhaps in 1986 things will begin moving a little faster thanks to this new program.

Loren C. Acker, President, Engineering Research Associates -- 500 North Tucson Boulevard -- Tucson, Arizona 85716. Telephone: 602-881-6555.

Late in 1983 Loren saw one of my shrimp-algae systems on the desk of one of my associates. Engineering Research Associates manufactures advanced specialty medical instruments. Loren expressed interest in my systems as commercial specialty items and it was not long after that he and I began talking seriously.

During the past two years, Engineering Research Associates (ERA) has added *Ecospheres* to its product line, ERA has developed some impressive laboratory and production facilities for Ecospheres. Ecospheres have been sold nationally, have received a good deal of attention in the media, and a fair amount of interest has been shown in foreign countries.

When it comes to materially closed, energetically open ecosystems, ERA is interested in marketing attractive products that will remain so, which includes, of course, remaining very much alive throughout storage, display, shipping and whatever their owners do to them. With its orientation on objectives such as these, ERA has developed an advanced algology laboratory where isolation and culture of the most attractive and shrimp-compatible algae possible are pursued. In addition, ERA has to be extremely sure of the health of the shrimp before they enter the Ecospheres so, not only are the animals kept in true clean room conditions, but there is also a continuing activity directed toward isolating and identifying any pathologies and pathogens which might enter the facility with a new batch of shrimp or algae. Finally, ERA has developed lighted bases for its Ecospheres which allow them to be maintained in places in offices and homes where the ambient light conditions are insufficient.

Whatever the future for ERA, it has already contributed significantly to our knowledge of closed system ecology and to the very difficult task of convincing the world out there that materially closed, energetically open ecosystems smaller than Earth's biosphere are not,

after all, impossible.

Frieda B. Taub, Ph.D., College of Fisheries-WH10 -- University of Washington -- Seattle, Washington 98103. Telephone: 206-545-2115.

Frieda Taub, although she does not work with completely closed ecosystems herself, does work with ecosystems which are nearly materially isolated. Moreover, her interest in materially closed ecosystems and her contributions to past and present closed system ecological dialogues certainly warrant her inclusion here.

Frieda Taub's work is currently funded by the Environmental Protection Agency (EPA) and is directed toward the development of essentially self sufficient microcosms to be used in a large number of laboratories throughout the country as mechanisms for establishing indexes of the ecological effects of environmental contaminants at various concentration levels. She has been pursuing this work for several years and it has now reached the point that the systems and laboratory protocols that she and her staff have developed are being tested at several other laboratories. In a recent telephone conversation, Dr. Taub mentioned that the results of the tests thus far are encouraging.

In the same conversation, she mentioned some new laboratory instruments and techniques she and her students are beginning to explore and some ideas she has for applying the laboratory systems and protocols she has developed during the past several years to assessments of the potential effects of genetically engineered microorganisms on certain ecosystems in which they may be loosed, intentionally or accidentally, and thereby come into competition with the naturally occurring organisms in that ecosystem. Although Dr. Taub and I have not been in close contact since shortly after the January 1982 workshop, I will be surprised if she does not become a major participant in the new field of closed system ecology as it gains recognition and momentum during the next decade or two.

Basset Maguire, Ph.D., Department of Zoology -- University of Texas -- Austin, Texas 78712. Telephone: 512-471-7473

Dr. Maguire began his work with materially closed, energetically open ecosystems around the middle of the 1970's. He experimented originally with three types of fresh water ecology aliquots containing algae, microscopic metazoans and microorganisms.

SEBRA ECOSPHERE -- Closed system ecology

I am extending my earlier analysis of required material flows in minimal human-support agricultural systems. Although requirements per person vary depending on the individual and the conditions (amount of work done, temperature, etc.), average daily required per person major material flows between the people and the supporting system are approximately: food, 615 grams; oxygen, 1712 grams; carbon dioxide, 2354 grams, "waste", 912 grams; and water, 190 kilograms. Through the use of a variety of crops which have appropriate high yield and/ or nutritional quality, about 68 square meters per person will be necessary for the food-producing plants if currently most efficient culture techniques are used. (For more detail see "Ecological Problems in Extra-Terrestrial Life Support Systems", by B, Maguire, Jr., pages 373-390 in Space and Society: Challenges and Choices, *P. Anaejionu, N.C. Goldman and P.J. Meeks (Editors), Vol. 59, Science and Technology Series, American Astronautical Soc., 1984.)*

Other work in my lab includes experimental and/or theoretical research on the nature of the interacting mechanisms which together determine the structure and operation of biological communities (with or without humans). For example, there are important problems having to do with possible deleterious effects of human-carried microorganisms on the plants upon which people on extra-terrestrial missions may depend for food, oxygen and carbon dioxide uptake. In addition, there are various other kinds of possible problems having to do with long term patterns of change of or stability of ecosystems. This is true both for human supporting agro-ecosystems and natural ecosystems (and parts of natural ecosystems). We currently are studying a number of the important ecological dynamics and patterns by experimentally enclosing, manipulating, and observing (parts of) various aquatic and terrestrial ecological systems. We enclose them so that they cannot exchange material with the outside world (except that for some systems we provide some exchanges, but only including those over which we have exact

control). We have been able to maintain various of these systems for different periods of time, and have charted the enclosure-caused changes in others. From these experiments and observations we have learned much of the ecological mechanisms involved and now know how to exert considerable control over them.

BASSETT MAGUIRE

Dr. Maguire heads a large and well-equipped laboratory at the University of Texas and has a number of students working in biospherics. He has several publications related to closed system ecology in the open literature and has collected a wealth of data.

NASA Biospheric Research Program,
Dr. Maurice M. Averner, Contact -- NASA Code EBR -- Washington, D.C. 20546. Telephone: 202-453-1525.

NASA's Biospheric Research Program is new as of fiscal year 1985. It has been structured into four categories intended to focus a variety of individual research projects on broader areas of biospheric interest. The four categories are: (1) wetlands research which is presently directed to regions along the eastern United States, (2) coniferous forest research which is presently concentrated in Sequoia National Park, (3) tropical forest research which is presently concentrated in the Amazon, and (4) global biogeochemical modeling.

All four categories are intended to encourage investigations of the interactions of biological processes with regional biogeochemical cycling. Investigations include ground gas flux measurements, nutrient transport flux measurements, associated above-ground vegetation or biomass measurements, and mathematical modeling. It is the intent of the program that all ground data eventually be correlated with remote measurements taken from spaceborne instruments. The future intent, of course, is to develop a capability to monitor the dynamics, health and well-being of Earth's biosphere from orbiting spacecraft in a comprehensive and routine fashion.

Biospherical Human Life Support Systems

When humans venture into any environment for which they are not naturally equipped, they need some sort of life support in order to survive for very long. Commercial airlines routinely fly us at altitudes so high that we couldn't survive for even a few hours without pressurized cabins and heating systems. They even serve us food and drink and provide restrooms so that we are not uncomfortable and grumpy. The airline example is an example of an ''open'' life support system. Supplies are carried on board, used up, and wastes are disposed.

Scuba diving gear is another example of an open life support system; the air is carried in a pressurized tank and used up during a dive. Submarines, both conventional and nuclear, have open life support systems. The same is true of the life support systems which NASA employed in Mercury, Gemini and Apollo to the Moon. The present Space Shuttle life support system is also an open one. Even the more advanced life support system that will sustain humans in the forthcoming NASA Space Station, although it will recycle some wastes, will not recycle human metabolic wastes back into food; so it will not be a complete bioregenerative life support system. *However,* there are tentative plans at NASA to test bioregenerative human life support systems aboard the Space Station, probably in the late 1990's or early 2000's.

In the Space Station, orbiting Earth at an altitude of only a hundred-plus miles, bioregenerative life support is not really required. Carrying food and other supplies up to the Space Station and bringing waste products back to Earth will be a routine for Space Shuttles.

But what if we want to send more people further out into space and for longer periods of time? NASA has tentatively determined that a manned space mission which cannot conveniently be resupplied from Earth and which involves somewhere around 100 person-years or more is the point at which self-sustaining, bioregenerative life support systems will be required. Without such systems, the mass of the supplies that would have to be carried plus the size and mass of the structures needed to carry the supplies would become economically prohibitive. Space biospherics must evolve if we're to migrate very far into space; it is a simple matter of economics.

To the best of my knowledge there are only two activities aimed at achieving bioregenerative life support systems for space travel. One is NASA's Controlled Ecology Life Support Systems (CELSS) program which has been under way since 1978; the other is a new project, Space Biospheres Ventures, now being managed by the Institute of Ecotechnics.

NASA's Controlled Ecology Life Support System (CELSS) Program

Dr. James H. Bredt, Contact -- NASA Code EBR -- Washington, D.C. 20546. Telephone: 202-453-1540.

The long-range goal of the CELSS program, of course, is to develop bioregenerative human life support systems which will permit human space travel and human colonies on other planets to continue for decades and longer without the need for resupply from Earth. The nearer-term objectives have to do with building a base of scientific knowledge concerning the growth of plant and animal foods in space, the recycling of organic wastes and developing a testable theoretical base for coupling human metabolism, food production, waste processing, and on-board energy sources to form a self-sustaining, self-sufficient, bioregenerative life support system. Progress toward the near-term objectives has been underway since 1979 at a variety of universities, private research facilities and NASA centers. The long-term goal probably will not be reached until well into the 2000's unless national policy dictates an accelerated program with a commensurate budget. At present the CELSS budget is quite modest by federal agency standards -- a few million dollars annually.

Space Biospheres Ventures

See Space Biospheres section.

Research Papers for Further Investigations on Closed Ecological Systems

Selected by the Editor from a computer search conducted by Dr. Peter Warshall on the National Technical Information Service database consisting of government-sponsored research, development, and engineering plus analyses prepared by federal agencies, their contractors or grantees.

Birth of Space Plant Growing, by A. Mashinskiy and G. Nechitaylo, NASA, Nov. 1983. The attempts, and successes, to grow plants in space, and get them to fully develop, bloom and produce seeds using orchids are presented. The psychological advantages of the presence of plants onboard space vehicles and space stations is indicated.

Utilization of Urea, Ammonia, Nitrite, and Nitrate by Crop Plants in a Controlled Ecological Life Support System (CELSS), by R.C. Huffaker, D.W. Rains and C.O. Qualset, California Univ. -- Davis Plant Growth Lab., NASA sponsored, Oct. 1982. The utilization of nitrogen compounds by crop plants is studied. The selection of crop varieties for efficient production using urea, ammonia, nitrite and nitrate, and the assimilation of mixed nitrogen sources by cereal leaves and roots are discussed.

Air Pollutant Production by Algal Cell Cultures, by F. Fong and E.A. Funkhouser, Texas A&M Univ. -- College Station Dept. of Plant Sciences, NASA sponsored, Aug. 1982. The production of phytotoxic air pollutants by cultures of Chlorella vulgaris and Euglena gracilis is considered. Algal and plant culture systems, a fumigation system, and ethylene, ethane, cyanide and nitrogen oxides assays are discussed. Bean, tobacco, mustard green, cantaloupe and wheat plants all showed injury when fumigated with algal gases for 4 hours. Only coleus plants showed any resistance to the gases. It is found that a closed or recycled air effluent system does not produce plant injury from algal air pollutants.

Mineral Separation and Recycle in a Controlled Ecological Life Support System (CELSS), by E.V. Ballou, San Jose State Univ. -- California Dept. of Chemistry, NASA sponsored, March 1982. Steps that may be taken in a program to analytically define and experimentally test key mineral control concepts in the nutritional and waste processing loops of a CELSS are delineated.

Nutrition and Food Technology for a Controlled Ecological Life Support System (CELSS), by P.E. Glaser and J.A. Mabel, Arthur D. Little Inc. (Cambridge, Massachusetts), NASA sponsored, May 1981. Food technology requirements and a nutritional strategy for a CELSS to provide adequate food in an acceptable form in future space missions are discussed.

Plant Diversity to Support Humans in a CELSS Ground-Based Demonstrator, by J.M. Howe and J.E. Hoff, Purdue Univ. (Lafayette, Indiana), NASA sponsored, June 1982. Factors that influence the human nutritional requirements envisioned in a controlled ecological life support system ground-based demonstrator and on bioavailability experiments of Ca, Fe and Zn. Interrelationship of protein and magnesium on Ca retention is also described.

Nutritional and Cultural Aspects of Plant Species Selection for a Controlled Ecological Life Support System (CELSS), by J.E. Hoff, J.M. Howe and C.A. Mitchell, Purdue Univ. (Lafayette, Indiana) -- Dept. of Horticulture, NASA sponsored, March 1982. The feasibility of using higher plants in a controlled ecological life support system is discussed. Aspects of this system considered important in the use of higher plants include: limited energy, space, and mass, and problems relating to cultivation and management of plants, food processing, the psychological impact of vegetarian diets, and plant propagation. A total of 115 higher plant species are compared based on 21 selection criteria.

Controlled Ecological Life Support System: Research and Development Guidelines, by R.M. Mason and J.L. Carden, Metrics Inc. (Atlanta, Georgia), NASA sponsored, May 1982. Results of a workshop designed to provide a base for initiating a program of research and development of CELSS are summarized. Research recommendations are presented concerning the following topics: nutrition and food processing, food production, waste processing, systems engineering and modelling, and ecology-systems safety.

Plant Diversity to Support Humans in a CELSS Ground-Based Demonstrator, (Final Report: Jul. 1, 1979-Oct.1, 1981), by J.M. Howe and J.E. Hoff, Purdue Univ. -- Dept. of Foods and Nutrition, NASA sponsored, Oct. 1981. Human nutritional requirements information based on current knowledge are developed for inhabitants envisioned in the CELSS ground-based demonstrator. Groups of plant products that can provide the nutrients are identified.

Space Flight Feeding and Space Food Systems. January, 1972-August, 1981 (Citations from the International Aerospace Abstracts Data Base), (Rept. for Jan. 1972-Aug. 1981), National Technical Information Service (Springfield, Virginia), Aug. 1981. Citations in this bibliography cover the principles, systems, and diets for closed-ecology life support in space habitats.

Thermodynamic Considerations in the Support of Life for Long Space Voyages, (Final Report), by A.S. Iberall and S.Z. Cardon, General Technical Services Inc. (Upper Darby, Pennsylvania), NASA sponsored, Nov. 1979. The essential requirements for the maintenance of life, particularly human life, on isolated space missions of long duration were investigated through the study of extended irreversible thermodynamics. The characterization of a four trophic level system was developed. Questions of stability are discussed.

Biological Systems for Human Life Support: Review of the Research in the USSR, by Y.Y. Shepelev, NASA, Dec. 1979. Various models of biological human life support systems are surveyed. Biological structures, dimensions, and functional parameters of man-chlorella-microorganism models are described. Significant observations and the results obtained from these models are reported.

Trophic Models: Was Elton Right, by S. Cousins, Open Univ. (Milton, England) -- Energy Research Group, Oct. 1978. The Eltonian pyramid, relating populations of animals to their size distribution, is reconsidered as a mathematical model in ecosystem energetics.

An Induced Environment Contamination Monitor for the Space Shuttle, by E.R. Miller and R. Decher, NASA -- Marshall Space Flight Center (Huntsville, Alabama), Aug. 1978. The Induced Environment Contamination Monitor (IECM), a set of ten instruments integrated into a self-contained unit and scheduled to fly on shuttle Orbital Flight Tests 1 through 6 and on Spacelabs 1 and 2, is described.

The MIT/Marine Industry Collegium Opportunity Brief No. 7, Closed-Cycle Aquaculture, by Massachusetts Inst. of Tech. Cambridge Sea Grant Program, National Oceanic and Atmospheric Administration sponsored, May 1977. Opportunities for near-term entry into a small but potentially profitable market for oysters and clams, raised in closed-cycle environments. A specific operation is now underway at the University of Delaware of a partially recycled environmentally controlled algae/oyster husbandry system.

Problems of Creating Biotechnical Systems of Human Life Support, by I.I. Gitelzon, Leo Kanner Associates (Redwood City, California), NASA sponsored, April 1977. Various aspects of the cultivation of higher plants as a possible link of a biological life support system.

Biological Evaluation of Various Space Cabin Atmospheres, (Final rept. Jan. 1-June 30, 1966), by R.W. Hamilton, G.F. Doebbler, C.H. Nuermberger and H.R. Schreiner, Linde Div. Union Carbide Corp. (Tonawanda, New York), Aug. 1966. Evaluation of the physiological consequences of exposure to several possible spacecraft atmospheres by means of a specially designed closed system. Atmospheres contained oxygen and nitrogen, helium, argon or neon.

The Biological Problems of Space Travel (As Urhajozas Elettani Problemai), (Edited translation) by Sandor Lukacs, Foreign Technology Div. Wright-Patterson AFB Ohio, Aug. 1967. A general review is given of some biological aspects involved in space travel.

A Month Alone with Chlorella, by S. Starikovich, Leo Kanner Associates (Redwood City, California), NASA sponsored, July 1975. Results of an experiment wherein a subject lived in a hermetically-sealed, 4.5 cu.m. room for 30 days.

Immunological Problems of Closed Environments and Gnotobiology, by K.A. Lebedev, Joint Publications Research Service (Washington D.C.), Oct. 1971. Analysis of published data makes it possible to draw the conclusion that the prolonged stay of animals and man in closed environments leads to simplification of indigenous microflora, which in turn leads to a reduction of the immunocompetent system. Ways of preventing reduction of the organism's immune system under conditions of prolonged space flight are discussed.

Bios

A group of Russian scientists and engineers are working on the Bios Project, a 315 cubic foot, partially closed, life-support system made of stainless steel for use in long-range space travel. Bios researchers have been engaged in experiments over the past twenty years at the research center located in Siberia to establish atmospheric and biological reproduction processes in a materially closed system. The latest experiment involved two men, a scientist and an engineer, inhabiting the 315 cu.ft. enclosure for a five-month period -- the time necessary to travel to Mars. Their work centered around producing their food, analyzing, monitoring and controlling the biological and atmospheric equilibrium. THE EDITOR

Pittsburg, 1955, before the Environmental Act.

Global Pollution: Analysis, Monitoring and Control

Walter E. Westman

Truth comes as conqueror only to those who have lost
the art of receiving her as friend. TAGORE

General Principles of Global Pollutant Circulation

During the blush of environmental concern in the 1960's and 1970's, legislators drafting pollution control legislation were guided by the axiom that "Everything must go somewhere". It was assumed that "somewhere", however, was not too far from the source. Hence the 1970 Clean Air Act in the United States defined regional "airsheds" within which pollutant concentrations were to be held to an acceptable level. Water quality legislation in the U.S. before 1972, and in the United Kingdom, Australia, and elsewhere today, was designed to maintain certain zones of a water body at a level of cleanliness suitable for a particular human use of the water (e.g., fishing, drinking). Toxic wastes were buried in landfills, often without sealing the landfill at the bottom. In each case an important assumption was made: that natural forces would eventually "assimilate" or degrade the pollutant to harmless form.

In the 1970's and 1980's, environmental scientists gathered increasing evidence that this assumption was no longer tenable. Some pollutants, being elemental in form, can be degraded no further, and build up in available pools, especially with the aid of microorganisms. Hence such toxic elements as mercury, selenium, lead and arsenic can be converted from inorganic to organic form by microbes. In organic form, the substances are readily taken up by higher organisms, and concentrate in the tissues of organisms as one is eaten by another in the food web. Hence concentrations of mercury may be found at levels 100,000-fold higher in the tissues of freshwater invertebrates than in the surrounding water, due to the

Photograph by W. Eugene Smith, untitled, 1955. Courtesy of the Center for Creative Photography, University of Arizona. Copyright the heirs of W. Eugene Smith.

process of bioaccumulation. Far from being degraded, wastes containing toxic elements are partitioned among sediments, water, air and living tissues, and continue to recycle between these components indefinitely. Synthetic organic substances, such as many pesticides, plastics and other industrial materials, also are subject to this process of bioaccumulation and recirculation for many years, since microbes have not evolved metabolic pathways to break down these new substances rapidly. Hence we have seen the buildup of DDT, PCBs and other synthetic organic substances in various media and in wildlife to hazardous concentrations. Residues of DDT and PCBs are found in mothers' milk and in wildlife of remote polar regions.

One of the mechanisms for rapid global circulation of pollutants released at a point on the earth is the injection or slow upward movement of pollutants into the stratosphere, some 16,000 meters above the earth. At this height, very strong winds carry the pollutants across oceans and continents within days and weeks. Recognition of this phenomenon came when ecologists were able to detect radiation in the lichens, caribou, and the thyroid glands of Laplanders of the Arctic derived from radioactive particles released by atmospheric nuclear weapons testing in the South Pacific in the 1950's. Radionuclides injected into the stratosphere over the South Pacific would rain out over North America within a few days to a few weeks. Gradually it came to be recognized that this global circulation of pollutants applied not only to radionuclides, but to stable gases and other particles as well.

If a gas is not broken down by atmospheric reactions (mainly with oxygen and sunlight) in the lower atmosphere (trophosphere), it will soon rise to the stratosphere and be circulated globally. Thus chlorofluorocarbons and nitrous oxide are examples of synthetic and naturally-produced gases, respectively, which rise to the stratosphere and are gases, respectively, which rise to the stratosphere and are distributed globally. These gases do react with ozone, however, and since ozone occurs in relatively high concentrations in the stratosphere, they are slowly reducing the concentrations of stratospheric ozone, permitting a rise in penetration of damaging ultraviolet rays to the earth. The latter is both a source of skin cancer, and an increased source of energy which can alter global temperature and other features of climate. In March 1985, a draft Convention for the Protection of the Ozone Layer was signed in Vienna by representatives of many governments.

Even gases which do not reach the stratosphere can be lofted by wind currents in the troposphere and carried long distances. Hence in the 1960's, Scandinavian countries observed rising levels of acidity in their precipitation, arising from sulfur and nitrogen oxides emitted by coal burning in the United Kingdom, hundreds of kilometers to the southwest. By the 1980's, acid deposition, not only in rain, but in dust, dew, fog and snow, was recognized as a growing regional problem. Sophisticated tracking of air masses by their chemical "signatures" of dust and other trace contaminants by Kenneth Rahn and others at the University of Rhode Island permitted verification that acidifying gases released in the midwestern U.S. were migrating to the northeast, causing "acid rain" to fall over New England. Similarly polluted air from the U.S. caused increasingly acid rain to fall over Canada.

Once acid rain falls upon vegetation and soil, it mobilizes trace elements such as iron, zinc and aluminum, which proceed to run off into water supplies. Acid water in household pipes of copper or lead can also solubilize these toxic elements, so that the effects of acid gases initially emitted into the air may soon appear as severe problems of toxic accumulations of metals in water. Thus the problem of "acid rain" illustrates both the large scale at which pollutants can be transported rapidly, and the fundamental interconnectedness between air, water and land as routes for cycling of pollutants. Recently an international Convention on Long Range Transboundary Air Pollution was adopted by some governments. The International Union for the Conservation of Nature passed a resolution in 1984 asking all contracting parties to this convention to reduce their total sulphur dioxide emissions by at least 30-50% by the end of the decade as compared to 1980 levels.

By the mid-1980's environmental scientists have come to view the circulation of pollutants as global in scale, affecting every compartment of the biosphere. Hence new techniques for analyzing and monitoring pollutants at these large scales are being developed.

Research and Monitoring

Global monitoring of pollution is currently being approached by accumulating large data bases from monitoring on the ground, but satellites are starting to play increasingly important roles. The Global Environmental Monitoring System (GEMS) exists to coordinate the collection of standard measures of a variety of environmental parameters from different countries, for entry into a single computerized data base. GEMS is coordinated by the United Nations Environmental Programme. To obtain regular monitoring data from remote locations, however, requires new methods of data collection and transmission. Fiber optic cables, small fibers that transmit light along them, are now being used to monitor chemicals in remote locations such as deep wells and groundwater tables. Techniques are being developed to beam information from such monitoring devices directly to satellites for transmission back to a computer data base on earth. The National Aeronautic and Space Administration (NASA) and the National Oceanic and Atmospheric Agency (NOAA) in the U.S., as well as Canadian, Australian, European and Soviet space agencies are working on the use of satellite images to detect pollutant concentrations, and pollutant damage on earth.

As one example, NASA is sponsoring, through its research initiatives in Global Biology and Global Habitability, work to monitor the release of nitrous oxide gas from a variety of biome types. Using satellite imagery, NASA scientists are working to detect levels of chemicals in foliage that will help predict, with the use of ecosystem stimulation models on computer, the rate of emission of nitrous oxide due to decomposition of litter and soil organic matter. This information will then be integrated between biome types using satellite imagery to classify the earth's vegetation and other earth cover types, yielding global estimates of nitrous oxide release that can be monitored over time.

Globally-oriented research on environmental processes is rapidly becoming an international goal among biospheric scientists. The International Council of Scientific Unions (ICSU) is currently developing proposals for an International Geophysical and Biological Decade in which the world's scientists would address, in a cooperative and concerted way, questions regarding global climate, terrestrial life, oceans, and the transfers of material and energy between media. This research is fundamental to the understanding of biospheric pollutant circulation, and can be expected to yield new insights into the manner and extent of biogeochemical cycling of global contaminants.

Organizations Concerned with Global Pollution at the Level of Policy and Management:

United Nations Environmental Programme, P.O. Box 30552, Nairobi, Kenya; Telephone: 333930, Cable address: UNITERRA, Nairobi; Executive Director: Dr. Mostafa K. Tolba.

International Union for Conservation of Nature and Natural Resources, Avenue du Mont-Blanc, 1196 Gland, Switzerland; Telephone: 022-643254, Cable address: IUCNATURE GLAND; Executive Officer for the Commission on Ecology of the I.U.C.N.: Maarten Bijleveld.

World Wildlife Fund, 100 Park Avenue, New York, New York 10017, U.S.A.; Telephone: 212-889-8006.

World Resources Institute, 1735 New York Avenue, Washington D.C. 20006, U.S.A.; Telephone: 202-638-6300; President: Gus Speth.

Worldwatch Institute, 1776 Massachusetts Avenue NW, Washington D.C. 20036, U.S.A.

National Organizations Concerned with Global Pollution

In the United States:

Environmental Defense Fund, 444 Park Avenue South, New York, New York 10016; Telephone: 212-686-4191.

Natural Resources Defense Council, 122 E. 42nd Street, New York, New York 10168; Telephone: 212-949-0049.

Conservation Foundation, 1717 Massachusetts Avenue NW, Washington D.C. 20036; Telephone: 202-797-4300.

U.S. Environmental Protection Agency, 401 M Street, Washington D.C. 20036; Telephone: 202-655-4000.

U.S. Council on Environmental Quality, Executive Office of the President, 722 Jackson Place NW, Washington D.C. 20006.

In Canada: Environment Canada, Ottawa, Canada K1A 1CB Telephone: 819-997-1731

Research Organizations Concerned with Global Pollution

Resources for the Future, 1616 P Street NW, Washington D.C. 20036, U.S.A.; Telephone: 202-328-5000.

National Aeronautics and Space Administration, Washington D.C. 20546, U.S.A.

National Oceanic and Atmospheric Agency, c/o Dept. of Commerce, Washington D.C. 20235, U.S.A.

U.S. Environmental Protection Agency, 401 M Street, Washington D.C. 20036, U.S.A.

Institute for Terrestrial Ecology, 68 Hills Road, Cambridge, England; Director: J.N.R. Jeffers, Ph.D.

Center for Intermedia Transport of Pollutants, University of California, Los Angeles, 405 Hilgard Avenue, Los Angeles, California 90024, U.S.A.; Director: Dr. Sheldon Friedlander.

Center for Ecosystems Research, Cornell University, Ithaca, New York 14853, U.S.A.; Director: Dr. Simon Levin.

Journals Publishing Articles on Global Pollution

Acid Rain Digest
Ambio
Atmospheric Environment
BioScience
Environmental Conservation
Environmental Pollution Series B.
IUCN Bulletin (1196 Gland, Switzerland)
Journal of Environmental Quality
Nature
Science
Tellus
UNEP News (P.O. Box 30552, Nairobi, Kenya)
Water, Air, and Soil Pollution
Water Resources Research

Recent Books Discussing Global Pollution

Living in the Environment (4th Edition), by G.T. Miller, Jr., Wadsworth, Belmont, California, 1985. A broad-ranging textbook on environmental science, providing an excellent introduction to a variety of global pollution issues, including both qualitative and quantitative descriptions of the nature and extent of the problems.

SCOPE Report 21. The Major Biogeochemical Cycles and Their Interactions, Wiley, New York, 1983. A compilation of review articles by ecological experts on the cycling of major elements (carbon, nitrogen, sulfur) globally, providing a basis for understanding the effect of human perturbations on the global cycling of these elements, and the compounds in which they are found. Assumes some background in chemistry and ecology.

SCOPE Report 22. Effects of Pollutants at the Ecosystem Level, P.J. Sheehan, D.R. Miller, G.C. Butler & P. Bordeau (Editors), Wiley, New York, 1984. A compendium of articles dealing with ways of studying the effects of pollutants as they interact with all ecosystem components -- air, water, soil, biota -- at a site or in a region. Case studies of pollutant effects on ecosystems are also discussed. Intended for the professional ecologist.

Ecology, Impact Assessment, and Environmental Planning, by W.E. Westman, Wiley-Interscience, New York, 1985. A textbook discussing the social and natural science fundamentals needed to predict and evaluate the effects of human disturbances on natural ecosystems. Includes legal, economic, and planning approaches, as well as detailed discussion of ecological methods of impact prediction. Intended for the student and professional.

State of the World, by L. Brown, W. Chandler, C. Flavin, C. Pollock, S. Postel, L. Starke & E.C. Wolf, Worldwatch Institute, Washington D.C., 1985. A series of articles dealing with the current state of knowledge regarding a variety of global environmental problems. Useful for policy makers as well as students and professionals.

The Global 2000 Report to the President, by the Council on Environmental Quality and U.S. Department of State, reprinted by Penguin Books, 1982. A study, based on governmental data bases and computer modeling, characterizing trends in the global supply of materials, energy, food, and extent of pollution. Intended for use by policy makers, but also a useful source of data. Data bases and details of models are found in Volumes 2 and 3 of the Report.

Annual Report of the U.S. Council on Environmental Quality, Washington D.C., 1985. (Published annually since 1971.) The report provides detailed tabulations of the current state of pollution of air and water, as well as coverage of land use issues and species conservation. In some years, detailed discussions of global environmental problems are included, and some mention of these is found in each volume.

Plant Analysis

Robert Raffauf

The Plant Kingdom stands between the sun and our eventual extinction; without it, life as we know it on this planet could not exist. Aside from the obvious uses of this green barrier as sources of food and shelter, our earliest written records include references to Man's use of plants for a host of purposes which, if not adding to his enjoyment of his environment, have at least increased his tolerance of his place in it. In spite of current preoccupations with worlds and environments other than his own, it is likely that studies of the Plant Kingdom will continue, if not increase, as he tends to saturate the planet with himself and his works.

The beginnings of plant chemistry lie in a distant past, in primitive processes of extraction, distillation and fermentation. Its status as a discipline of its own began with the isolation of morphine from the ancient drug opium early in the 19th century. Rapid and parallel development of the disciplines of chemistry and pharmacology have since permitted the isolation and identification of many of the specific compounds responsible for the effects observed through the empirical uses of plants in ages past. Much of the emphasis was placed on those plants which had been used as drugs and hence on their direct usefulness to Man himself. The enthusiasm for such studies continues; several thousand plant constituents of many chemical types are now known, and some of them have been associated with plants used in other cultures for such things as psychedelics, contraceptives, insecticides and antibiotics. We have not, certainly, discovered them all nor, unfortunately, do we yet know or surmise the purposes which the majority of them may be presumed to serve in preserving the delicate balances operating in the biosphere as a whole.

In recent times there has been a noticeable trend toward the study of the role of plants in these balances rather than from the viewpoint of their immediate economic importance. A few examples come to mind: inter-relationships between plants themselves ("plant communication"); their resistance, or lack of it, to disease (plant antifungal agents); the relationship between plants and the animals which feed on them or are discouraged from doing so (insect antifeedants). Such problems are beginning to attract the attention of the plant chemist whose basic interests lie in the chemical nature of the compounds involved in these interactions. He may be satisfied with the accomplishment of isolating and identifying them; he may seek their origins in the biosynthetic pathways leading to their formation in plants; he may attempt to relate his findings to the work of the botanist in the sense that his studies may be of value in the solution of problems of plant classification and evolution. At the same time he may supply other researchers with clues to the nature of the interactions of plants with other species. In any case, he does not function in isolation and it is this multidisciplinary nature of his work which offers the challenges of the future.

Literature

The literature of plant chemistry is vast; a comprehensive listing of appropriate titles is beyond the scope of this catalogue. The following titles offer an introduction to its many facets. References therein will lead the reader to areas of special interest, e.g., alkaloids, steroids, flavonoids, etc.

Books

Pharmacognosy (12th Edition), by G.E. Trease, & W.C. Evans, Balliere-Tindall, London, 1983.

Chemotaxonomie der Pflanzen (6 Volumes), by R. Hegnauer, Birkhauser Verlag, Basel, Stuttgart, 1962-

1973.

The Organic Constitutents of Higher Plants (4th Edition), by T. Robinson, Cordus Press, N. Amherst, MA, U.S.A., 1980.

Secondary Plant Metabolism, by M.L. Vickery & B. Vickery, Macmillan Press, Ltd., London/University Park Press, Baltimore, MD, U.S.A.,
1981.

Journals

Phytochemistry, Pergamon Press, Oxford, New York, Frankfurt, Sydney.

Journal of Natural Products, official organ of the American Society of Pharmacognosy and the Lloyd Library and Museum, Cincinnati, OH, U.S.A.

Chemical Abstracts, published by the American Chemical Society, Chemical Abstracts Service, Ohio State University, Columbus, OH, U.S.A.

Equipment

Extraction of dried, milled plant material with appropriate solvents can be accomplished in several ways varying from simple percolation to the use of industrial equipment designed for the purpose. The choice of apparatus depends largely on the size of the sample and the preferences of the operator. Other than the standard laboratory apparatus available from supply houses throughout the world, modern chemistry uses a variety of sophisticated instruments for the identification and characterization of chemical compounds whether natural or synthetic. In current practice, the use of *gas and high performance liquid chromatography, polarimetry, ultraviolet, infrared, nuclear magnetic resonance and mass spectrometry* are routine. There are many manufacturers and many models of these instruments. See, for example, *Guide to Scientific Instruments,* published annually by the American Association for the Advancement of Science, Washington DC, U.S.A.

In our own laboratory, under the auspices of the Institute of Ecotechnics, Inc., we are attempting to develop a field kit for the screening of plants for major types of chemical constituents under all but the most primitive conditions. This should assist plant-collecting expeditions to make on-the-spot assessments of the desirability of bulk collection for eventual chemical evaluation as well as permit monitoring various plant organs for the presence of a desired constituent.

Botany

No chemical investigation should be undertaken without botanical identification and documentation of the plant to be studied or the eventual probability of obtaining such information. University botany departments, botanical gardens, national herbaria can be of assistance in this regard. Reference may be made to *Index Herbariorum* (7th Edition), by Bohn, Schetema and Holkema, Utrecht/Antwerp; Dr. W. Junk B.V. Publishers, The Hague/Boston.

Plague Analysis

Paul Rotmil

An epidemic. The word means a disease spreading through a community for some period of time, affecting people and/or animals (or even plants). However, most laymen associate the word with an outbreak of a highly contagious disease, for example plague, and as this book is not meant exclusively for medics, we will use the latter definition. It would be beyond the scope of an entire encyclopedia, let alone a short paper, to give an account of the tremendous impact various epidemics have had on the biological, social and economic evolution of mankind, and the epidemics limited to the animal or plant world are not to be forgotten, or taken lightly.

In the beginning of genus homo there were probably no big epidemics -- the size of a community being too small to harbor a serious contagious disease for a long period, and travels were infrequent and slow. The only way to introduce a new germ would have been with wild animals, but even those do not usually travel very far -- except when forced to by an earthquake, fire, drought or simply lack of food. The disease agents in each community must have been of a relatively low virulence. A germ which rapidly kills all the victims (host organisms), or incapacitates them severly so they cannot hunt or gather the food -- such a germ does not survive for a long time itself. In that way, nature has selected out of all the microorganisms and parasites those somehow less virulent (less dangerous). In much the same way people around gained immunity at least in some degree. A recent example would be the story of a cholera germ -- vibrio cholerae. The old, 'classical' vibrio did not travel well -- except with water. It gave almost invariably a severe disease or nothing. But recently there appeared a new strain, called el toro. Patients infected with it can show a whole spectrum of symptoms, from subclinical (without any noticeable symptoms), through mild to the most severe cases. Patients with mild symptoms, or no

symptoms at all can travel and the vibrio can disseminate. As the size of the community increases, it becomes possible even for the more virulent germs to propagate within it and still have a suitable number of susceptible hosts left. Finally it becomes possible for some of the diseases to be present in a community at any period of time -- it becomes endemic. Then people start to travel farther, faster and in greater numbers enabling the disease agent to stay alive during the passage, and introducing it into new environments, new hosts unprotected by evolution -- sometimes with disastrous results. Our examples are by necessity taken from recent history and quite well known; we can assume that similar mechanisms were valid even for prehistorical times. In such a way a dreaded killer, the plague, has been brought to Italy by sailors in the beginning of the XIV century and spread throughout the European continent, killing an estimated one-third to one-half of the population, and changing the economic and socal structure of Europe. On the other hand, the well-known and, for European stock, quite benign measles depopulated vast areas in the new world unaccustomed to it. In much the same way syphilis became a deadly disease when introduced to Europe, and salvarsan and penicillin alone cannot account for its now reduced virulence.

People were always trying to combat the epidemics and other diseases. Various religious and magic practices were mixed with many more or less reasonable treatments. Then people noticed that at least some of the diseases were contracted by close contact with other patients. It took somewhat longer to find out about transmission through animals (except obvious things like rabies) and arthropods. Among many names worth mentioning will be Edward Jenner who gave us the first vaccination; Louis Pasteur and Robert Koch who proved microorganisms to be cause of the diseases; John Snow who gave us the epidemiological approach, Ehrlich and Domagk who were the fathers of chemotherapy, and many, many others. Their work has inspired many biographies and an interested reader will not find it difficult to get hold of the literature.

The methodological tools inherited from these pioneers allowed people to control many of the epidemics. some of them were fought by changing some parts of our ecological system, like draining the marshes to get rid of the mosquito-born epidemics. On the other hand, some of the ecological changes were unintentional and not advantageous, like the changing biology of the mosquito.

Changing of an ecologic system for other purposes such as building huge water reservoirs, can affect adversely the pattern of many diseases in the vicinity (bilharzia, mosquito-transmitted diseases, etc.).

A complete eradication of disease would be indeed a very radical change in the biosphere, but until now we can boast of only one such achievement -- smallpox. Most of the other classical killers are now quite well contained, even in the third world (except perhaps malaria), and we do not have to fear them, provided a decent standard of health services can be mentioned. But new terrors are coming up. Some of those are soon rendered innocuous by hard work of many people as, for example, Legionnaires Disease, but others like AIDS still menace the world.

This paper does not pretend to give a reader a summary of current knowledge of epidemics in general or any particular one -- it is written to whet the appetite. Those still hungry should search in textbooks not only of medicine, but history, biology and other subjects in order to get a broad view of the whole problem. Serious students should be able to get help and information from the nearest medical faculty, from the local or national health authorities, or from the regional offices or headquarters in Geneva.

Buckminster Fuller's schematic of the relationships possible within a system of seven vectors, illustrating the non-additive mathematics which makes synergy possible. Courtesy of Buckminster Fuller Institute.

Organizations

Norman Myers

Now we come to the boundary which separates
actual scientific research from the decision-
making process. GREGORI KHOZIN

We all share a single Earth-Home. So who shall fix the housekeeping?

An immediate answer: governments. For sure, governments do a lot to safeguard our planetary habitat. Only a government can establish national parks and other protected areas. Only a government can oversee a nation's forests, look out for grasslands, check soil erosion, protect coastlines, impose anti-pollution measures, and keep an eye open for other aspects of the community's nature endowment. But governments tend to be preoccupied with "real concerns" such as health, defense and the like, which means that nature often ranks low in the pecking order of priorities. Moreover, governments are inclined to do no more on the nature front than they believe their citizenry wants, and often enough the citizenry is little aware of the need to safeguard soil cover, threatened species and the like. Ask John and Jane Citizen what they think about the natural-resource base that underpins their very livelihood, and they may have only a hazy idea of what is involved.

So the people who make most of the running are, to use their official if ungainly title, non-governmental organizations, or NGOs. These citizen activists raise the alarm when things go wrong and they agitate to make things go better. They raise funds, they devise projects, and they do a hundred and one things on behalf of us all. They initiate, they stimulate, they catalyze, they prod and push, and they wave a flag generally for the biosphere -- not only for their particular patch of the biosphere, but for the entire earth ecosystem. Above all, they spread the message, and try to get others to become committed to the cause as well. Without the World Wildlife Fund, Friends of the Earth and a host of others, we would all be the poorer.

Most of these NGOs operate off shoe-string budgets. Indeed they have next to no resources with which to "busy body" governments into action, or to confront corporations that despoil the environment. Yet they are surprisingly effective, and they generate a remarkable return on each scarce conservation dollar. Some observers might suppose that a bunch of private persons, operating out of small offices, cannot stand up to Big Government and Mega-Corp. But they might reflect on the track record of NGOs in the United States during the past two decades. In response to their activities, there has been a series of annual Earth Days, the government has set up the Environmental Protection Agency and the Council on Environmental Quality, the statute books bulge with major new laws, the populace enjoys far cleaner air and water, and "environment" is now a force to be reckoned with.

In other fields, too, the United States has been transformed thanks to NGOs -- and these further efforts demonstrate the surprising amount of political muscle that can be mobilized by NGOs. American society has experienced one revolution after another, in the form of women's lib, civil rights, the anti-Vietnam movement, and consumerism. In all of these fields, the initial impulse has come from grass-rooters, with the government following on when it finally had no alternative. Yeah!, then, for NGOs.

At the international level, too, NGOs can be remarkably effective. It was largely due to NGOs in a dozen different countries that the United Nations finally got its environmental act together. After years of pressing, the NGOs finally persuaded governments to call an international meeting to face up to the situation of a deteriorating biosphere. So governments of the world met at the Stockholm Conference on the Human Environment in 1972. In turn this led to the establishment of the United Nations Environment Programme, or UNEP.

UNEP is an example of how, at international level,

some of the action is undertaken by official bodies -- but only some. International agencies such as UNEP are in a position to do much. But they in fact accomplish all too little, due to back-sliding on the part of their member governments. UNEP's budget is a mere $30 million a year (contrast the U.S. EPA: $3 billion), yet it endures one annual struggle after another to get even this sum approved. The problem is that UNEP, like several other agencies of the UN system, can scarcely be characterized as international. Rather it is dominated by *inter-governmental* committees, which means that it reflects the nation-state system writ large, with all the competitive rivalries that entails -- a far cry from the collaborative spirit and the One-Earth vision that we require to safeguard our biosphere.

In any case, we find that all too often the basic problem lies with lack of political commitment. Our leaders have not yet gained the planetary vision that is needed: they do not understand the nature of One-Earth living. The most crucial ecological concepts remain beyond the grasp of many politicians, as witness those who seem to think that a food chain is a line of supermarkets. Many might even be hard pressed to define the term "biosphere." So at international level, as well as at national level, there is a major role for NGOs and their ginger-group activities. Fortunately a number of NGOs are decidely international in scope. The World Wildlife Fund is an obvious instance, with its national organizations in 25 countries. The sister agency of WWF, the International Union for Conservation of Nature and Natural Resources, serves as a focus for conservation concerns via its 750 members spread around the world. Friends of the Earth has affiliates in 17 countries. A good number of similar "networking" bodies bear the banner for environmental issues that are international in scope. Without these NGOs and their campaigns on behalf of our common heritage, the biosphere would be in worse shape than it is.

While not possessing a fraction of the economic or political clout that is enjoyed by governments or major corporations, the NGO community can, when it acts together, prove far more effective than some observers may suppose. They build a "citizenry consensus" of transnational scope, thereby enabling environmental matters to be tackled at a level above the purview of individual nations. An effort of this sort enables NGOs to make an "end run" around governments that are overly preoccupied with individual interests. To the extent that NGOs engender a spirit of "global constituency", they can assert what political leaders cannot always afford to proclaim. Partly in response to the energetic lobbying of NGOs, more than 120 governments have now established environmental agencies of one kind or another, by contrast with a mere dozen or so at the time of the Stockholm Conference.

How do NGOs actually set about their tasks? In terms of strategy overall, they perform three central functions. They alert the public to the global environmental predicament. They mobilize opinion in support of environmentally sound policies. They intervene directly in the political arena. These are the three principal thrusts of NGO planning.

But how does all this work out in practice? Well, translated into action terms, NGOs blow the whistle on undiscovered problems, such as the fuelwood crisis. They monitor the environmental performance of governments, agencies, corporations and other major institutions. They educate the media and opinion leaders. They work at grass-roots levels with local authorities, in order to exemplify their goal of "thinking globally, acting locally". They establish dialogue with private enterprise, persuading industry and commerce that it is in their economic self-interest to maintain the natural-resource base that sustains us all -- through, for instance, "environmental audits" of corporations' activities. They seek to do work with labor organizations, on the grounds that trade unions express a growing interest in all aspects of lifestyles, including the environmental dimension: they help unions to formulate policies on environmentally acceptable technologies and products. They build close relationships with the media, persuading television, newspapers, and the like, to highlight environmental issues: they supply much material, in the form of information and analyses of environmental issues, that the media can readily use. They work with inter-governmental organizations such as EEC and OECD, in order to integrate environmental concerns into every field of activity: they help, for instance, to shape "blueprint responses" to problems such as transfrontier pollution. Perhaps most important of all, NGOs play a watchdog role vis-a-vis governments, pressing them to undertake environmental legislation, and to enforce regulations already on the statute books, to re-examine concepts of development, and to support international bodies in the environmental field (were it not for the efforts of NGOs, the U.S. government's funding for UNEP might have been cut more severely still).

As a measure of what NGOs can achieve, let us look at their track record in a few countries. In the United States, a consortium of NGOs made common cause during the 1970's, and pressured the government to extend the provisions of its excellent National Environment Protection Act to those federal agencies that operate beyond the territorial domain of the United States, notably the Agency for International Development. Without the NGOs' sustained effort, finally pressing the government as far as the court room, it is unlikely that the U.S. Administration would have adopted such a splendid leadership role in environmental affairs among the community of nations throughout the 1970's. In Indonesia, where NGO bodies have proliferated to an extraordinary total of over 400, the Minister for Environment and Development Control makes no secret of the support he receives from citizen activists, who help to pressure the government into a more sensitive stance on environmental issues. In Malaysia, the Consumers Association of Penang, working in conjunction with the Friends of the Earth Malaysia, has persuaded the government to be more stringent in its regulation of mining impacts, pollution of rivers and other water bodies, and over-use of tropical hardwood forests. In Costa Rica, a bevy of NGOs has supported the conservation efforts of two successive presidents during the 1970's, with the result that Costa Rica now has a larger percentage of land under protected status (parks, reserves and the like) than any other country in Latin America. In Kenya, a coalition of NGOs interested in energy has accomplished far more tree planting during its first couple of years existence than the government achieved during the previous five years.

Not only are NGOs becoming more effective. They are becoming more numerous. At the Stockholm Conference there were only a few dozen NGOs present, almost all of them from North America and Western Europe; while Third World NGOs would have fitted round one small table. Today there are thousands of such bodies, large and small -- and by far the most rapid growth has been in Third World countries. At the time of UNEP's 10th birthday celebrations, Third World NGOs turned up in entire throngs.

At a time when the general public is becoming disenchanted with the capacity of governments and international agencies to resolve the world's problems, there is a fast-growing niche for NGOs. Fortunately NGOs are recognizing their opportunity, and there has been a veritable outburst in their numbers. In the opinion of this writer, who has operated on the environmental scene in all major regions of the earth during the past 25 years, there is no more hopeful portent for the future than this recent proliferation of NGOs.

So much for some general thoughts about organizations that do the housework for our common living space on the one Earth-Home. Let us now look at a selection of them in individual detail.

Government and Inter-Government Bodies

Whatever the limitations of government and inter-government bodies, a number do a generally good job.

The U.S. Environmental Protection Agency

As an example of a national agency with a good track record, the U.S. EPA undertakes a coordinated attack on environmental problems, notably pollution (waste materials, pesticides, toxic substances, radiation and so forth). It brings under one roof some 15 programs which had earlier been scattered throughout several agencies of the U.S. government; and it beefs them up into a single cohesive program. Its functions include the setting and enforcing of environmental standards, research on environmental problems, and help for states and local authorities. Established in 1969, the agency had a rough ride in the early 1980's, but is now recovering some of its fine reputation.

United Nations Environment Programme

P.O. Box 30552, Nairobi, Kenya

Despite its many disappointments, both in terms of poor government support and internal deficiencies, the main achievement of UNEP is the continuing fact of its existence. The agency reflects the desire of governments to tackle collective problems through collective endeavor -- and that gesture in itself is worth a good deal. Being the first U.N. agency to be located in a developing country, UNEP *could* still amount to a solid effort to safeguard our common biosphere, were its member governments to wish it so (and were it to get a new leader).

As a measure of what UNEP can achieve, the Mediterranean clean-up plan stands as a breakthrough in "environmental politics." The sea, bordered by 18 nations, has been dying through pollution from land and shipping alike -- thus threatening the 100-million-a-year tourist trade, plus several major fisheries. By dint of some fancy diplomatic footwork, UNEP persuaded all nations involved (except Albania) to get together around a table -- including such traditional enemies as Israel and Syria, Egypt and Libya, Greece and Turkey, and France and Algeria. Eventually the participant states acknowledged their joint problem, and agreed on a common Action Plan. Result, the Mediterranean is now well on the way to recovery. Further result, the blueprint for a cleanup is being applied in 12 other regional seas of the world.

Man and the Biosphere Program

UNESCO, 7 Place de Fontenoy, Paris

Set up in 1968, the Man and the Biosphere Program, or MAB as it is known, specifically aims to look at man-disturbed environments rather than pristine-nature environments. It tries to account for both positive and negative types of human impact, in order to assist developers, exploiters, land-use planners and conservationists with regard to future encroachment on natural environments. This is a first-rate approach, insofar as much of the biosphere will shortly bear the distinct imprint of man's hand. In other words, it is a pragmatic and down-to-earth (so to speak) attempt to map out the most productive ways for us to intervene in the biosphere.

Regrettably, MAB has not been nearly so successful as was once hoped. True, some of the national affiliates, notably U.S. MAB, do a good job. But the head office in Paris, under its parent organization UNESCO, has suffered from bureaucratic inertia and lack of creative insight. Moreover, the spirit of the Paris-based endeavor has tended to be esoterically scientific, without enough "real world" integration. In short, a somewhat stultified outcome. More's the pity, since we urgently need innovative strategies for management of our living space. Worse, MAB has recently run into further problems as a result of the U.S. withdrawal from UNESCO (which does not, fortunately, affect the U.S. sub-program). Nor has UNESCO felt inclined to cooperate as much as it might with UNEP, which it sometimes sees as a rival organization. Overall result, the problem of "turf rivalries" within the UN system seems to have won out.

The World Bank

1818 H Street NW, Washington D.C.

The Bank's environmental record has been distinctly spotty, to put it at its best. But the Bank leads development banks in general, by establishing an Office of Environmental Affairs in its headquarters in Washington DC. While the Office does not enjoy so much influence as it would wish, it supplies environmental impact assessments for major projects, and it has been instrumental in modifying certain projects to make them environmentally acceptable. In other words, the Office helps ensure that development is *sustainable* development. The marginal extra costs of environmental safeguards range between one percent and four percent; and the long-term return on the investment is often as high as any of the Bank's other investments.

Equally to the point, the Bank's approach to tropical forests now represents some of the most enlightened forestry found anywhere. After promoting production forestry (logging and other forms of exploitation -- or rather over-exploitation) until the early 1980's, the Bank has now shifted its emphasis to protection forestry (watershed management, conservation units and the like). Still more important, the Bank has undertaken the daring initiative of asking what -- just what -- is needed to tackle the key problem of tropical deforestation. After all, tropical forests represent, potentially at least, the richest

stock of natural resources on earth, by virtue of their huge numbers of species and their vast genetic reservoirs. They are also the least developed of all major ecological zones, "developed" being understood here in the proper broad sense of the word, definable as "subject to sustainable use of whatever outputs, whether material goods or environmental services, that will best serve the long- term interest of human communities around the world, now and for ever." At the same time, tropical forests are being depleted more rapidly than any other biome, at a rate which will leave little within another 50 years at most.

The Bank's visionary initiative is to look at problems, *and* the opportunities they imply, on five fronts: commercial timber, fuelwood, watersheds, protected areas, and research/training. Cutting across all these five sectors is a single dominant theme, that of forestry's relationship to its ancient foe and potential ally, agriculture. The price tab for the Action Plan runs to $5 billion a year until the end of the century. Large as this sum sounds, it would generate handsome payoffs. Moreover, were the developed-world nations to pick up half the tab, in light of the many benefits they receive from tropical forests (material goods, genetic resources, climate regulations, etc.), the cost would still represent only the equivalent of one can/pint of beer per taxpayer per month. If the Plan is widely adopted, it will surely save more species, at least one million by the end of this century alone, than the next one dozen conservation initiatives put together; and it will help protect the most exuberant expression of life ever to appear on the face of the planet.

Non-Governmental Organizations

International Union for Conservation of Nature and Natural Resources

1196 Gland, Switzerland

IUCN, as it is known, was founded in 1948 to serve as a reservoir of scientific expertise on conservation matters, and to act as a clearing- house for information. It works through a secretariat plus five Commissions, dealing with Species, Protected Areas, Ecology, Law and Education. Its 521 members are, curiously enough, made up of a mixture of governments, government agencies, international bodies, scientific institutions, research bodies, private interests and citizen-activist groups -- an exceptionally polyglot bunch of organizations that nevertheless operate together fairly well in support of the Union's aims (58 states, 121 government agencies, 313 national NGOs, 24 international NGOs, and 5 affiliates). During the 1950's, IUCN found it needed to get into field projects; lacking funds, it engineered the establishment of the World Wildlife Fund to raise money (see below). Now that its projects are starting to be managed as well as financed by WWF, IUCN is increasingly taking on the role for which many observers believe it is best suited, that of a "think tank" body that looks at long-term problems and opportunities of environmental affairs.

World Wildlife Fund
1196 Gland, Switzerland

The biggest save-species body anywhere, WWF comprises 24 national organizations and an international headquarter. Since its startup in 1961, it has raised over $95 million for threatened wildlife ($10 million in 1984), and has supported 3000 projects in 131 countries.

Friends of the Earth
1045 Sansome Street, San Francisco, California

With its international headquarters in the United States, FOE has affiliate organizations in 30 countries. Founded in 1969, it is active in many environmental fields, including wildlife, pollution, and rational use (not just preservation) of natural resources. One of the most activist of NGOs, FOE is in the forefront of political lobbyists. With only a small membership and very limited funds, it achieves much through little.

Greenpeace
2007 R Street NW, Washington D.C.

Primarily dedicated to preservation of marine ecosystems, Greenpeace campaigns vigorously against the slaughter of whales, seals and other marine mammals. It also campaigns against the dumping of toxic and radioactive wastes in oceans, the testing of nuclear weapons, and the growing blight of acid rain. With headquarters in Washington D.C., Greenpeace favors "direct" action, for instance the obstruction of whaling ships on the high seas; while these activities may sometimes be illegal in a strict sense, they are invariably non-violent.

Sierra Club
530 Bush Street, San Francisco, California

Originally dedicated to the enjoyment and protection of wilderness areas in the United States, the Sierra Club now promotes the responsible use of the entire biosphere; while its headquarters are in San Francisco, it runs an International Office in New York. Forthright in its aims and activities, it does not hesitate to go to law in order to further its goals. With 54 chapters right across the United States, it operates a broad program of outdoor activities, such as backpacking, white-water trips and mountaineering.

National Audubon Society
950 Third Avenue, New York, NY

One of the oldest and largest conservation organizations in the United States, Audubon carries out education, research and action programs to preserve wildlife and natural areas, and to safeguard the biosphere on which all life depends. With around 500 chapters across the United States, the Society provides information and encourages action to tackle many environmental problems.

Environment Liaison Centre
P.O. Box 72461, Nairobi, Kenya

Set up in Nairobi in 1974 as an NGO counterpart to UNEP, the ELC serves as a "network nerve center" for environmental NGOs around the world, and especially for Third World NGOs. It now has around 250 members in 70 countries, mostly Third World, and thus serves two valuable functions: it helps environmental NGOs in all parts of the world to keep in touch with what is going on in other parts of the world; and it acts as a two-way conduit between the environmental NGO coummunity and UNEP.

The ELC discharges the first of these functions admirably. Unfortunately the second has not proven so productive, through no fault of the ELC. Despite fine commitments made at the Stockholm Conference, UNEP allocates less than 10 percent of its Environment Fund budget to NGO activities, and the $3 million in question goes mainly to a mere five organizations, out of the hundreds that deserve support. Moreover, UNEP's overall liaison with NGOs has steadily declined, ostensibly through lack of interest in pursuing a relationship that could be mutually supportive.

Natural Resources Defense Council
1725 I Street NW, Washington D.C.

Mainly staffed by several dozen attorneys in its offices in Washington, New York and San Francisco, NRDC principally seeks to support environmental values by mobilizing the full force of the law. It concerns itself with pollution, nuclear safety, toxic materials, wildlife protected areas, coastal zones, energy and forestry; and it pursues these issues not only within the United States, but in the international arena. NRDC frequently heads up a consortium of environmental interests in the United States, in order to challenge, for example, government agencies in court. By virtue of the "political muscle" that NRDC represents through its leadership role, it has been instrumental in several major institutional advances, for example requiring that AID take account of environmental concerns in its development projects throughout the Third World.

Consumers Association of Penang

No. 87, Jalan Cantonment, Pulau Penang, Malaysia

One of the most effective NGOs in the Third World. Founded in 1970, this pressure group tackles pollution, inappropriate technology, deforestation, over-fishing and the like. It has repeatedly stood up to the government, invoking the law when need be, even though the government has been inclined to "lean on" the organization. Well-informed and vociferous, CAP represents grass-roots activism at its best.

Asociacion Costarricense para la Conservacion de la Naturaleza

(Costa Rican Association for the Conservation of Nature)

Apdo. 8-3870, San Jose, Costa Rica

Known as ASCCONA, this private organization is made up of a diversity of local conservationists and environmentalists. Despite its unprepossessing title and makeup, the Association has been one of the main reasons why Costa Rica has established an exemplary record in the management of much of its natural-resource base. Under two enlightened presidents during the 1970's, the government brought as much as 30 percent of the country's forests under protected status, as parks, reserves, conservation units, etc. No other country in Latin America has achieved anywhere near this amount. The areas include the Corcovado Park in the Osa Peninsula, which, only a little over 100 square miles in size, encompasses virtually the last sizeable patch of undisturbed lowland rainforest on the Pacific coast of all Central America.

European Environment Bureau

29 Rue Vautier, Brussels, Belgium

Located in the city that houses the secretariat for the European Economic Community, the EEB serves to coordinate the activities of some environmental NGOs in Europe. Despite its very limited resources, the EEB has been remarkably successful, especially with regard to agriculture within the Community and deforestation in the tropics. It exerts much skillful leverage with the EEC secretariat.

League of Conservation Voters

317 Pennsylvania Avenue SE, Washington D.C.

This American organization amounts to a non-partisan, political campaign committee that promotes the election of public officials who are committed to the environmental cause. It also evaluates the environmental records of Senators and Congressmen, and of candidates for the Presidency.

New York Botanical Garden

Bronx, New York

Though it hardly sounds like an activist organization, the NYBG supplies $1 million a year for conservation-oriented research in the tropics. This is no small amount, out of the mere $30 million that is generated worldwide for research in tropical biology of whatever sort.

Missouri Botanical Garden

P.O. Box 299, St. Louis, Missouri

Another leader in conservation-oriented research in the tropics, MBG generates rather more than $1 million a year for overseas research, with emphasis on tropical forests. Its findings help conservationists to plan parks and other protected areas, and to foster rational and self-renewing use of tropical forests.

Institute of Ecotechnics

24 Old Gloucester St., London WC1 3AL England

The Institute convenes two annual conferences for leading scientists, and thinkers interested in evolution; one on Man in Aix-En-Provence, France, and the other on Biospheres in Tucson, Arizona.

In addition, the Institute consults ten projects, two on the oceans and eight on four continents for their contributions to biospheric and cultural evolution.

Finally, the Institute has set up programs at several of these projects so that qualified applicants can gain "hands-on" as well as theoretical experience.

Worldwatch Institute

1776 Massachusetts Avenue NW, Washington D.C. 20036

A leading center for information and analysis, the Worldwatch Institute looks at whatever major trends and new activities impinge upon our biosphere. The Institute publishes an annual survey, *State of the World*, which is a first-rate way for the citizen to keep abreast of what is happening -- and what should be happening, and what should not be happening. The Institute also publishes about half a dozen booklets each year, which are compact compendiums of state-of-the-art knowledge on e.g. pollution, recycling, forests, fisheries, soil erosion, international debt, spread of deserts, the ozone layer, etc. -- masterpieces of condensed review, emphasizing simplification while avoiding over-simplification.

World Resources Institute

1735 New York Avenue NW, Washington D.C.

Probably the leading think tank in the environmental field, WRI engages in policy studies and resource analysis with respect to e.g. carbon dioxide, toxic wastes, tropical forests, genetic diversity, multinational corporations, and the U.S. stake in the global environment. Publishes an annual assessment of current trends, *World Resources Review*, being a strongly data-based evaluation of where we are headed, and what the outcome (whether positive and negative) will be. Also publishes occasional booklets on, e.g., pesticides, which are excellent rundowns on the state of play with particular respect to policy appraisals.

Centre for Science and Environment (India)

807 Vishal Bhavan, 95 Nehru Place, New Delhi 110019

A leading NGO in India, the Centre serves as a source of information on every aspect of India's environment: the ecological zones, modes of exploitation, population, development, the natural-resource base, exploitation patterns, conservation strategies, etc. Publishes periodic versions of *The State of India's Environment*, a "must" book for anyone who wants to know about environmental matters in the country with the second largest populace, the sixth greatest industrial output, and the most diversified agricultural system on the planet.

Chipko Movement

Parvatiya Navjeevan Mandal, Silyara, Tehri-Garhwal, U.P., India

The Chipko Movement originated in the mid-1970's, as deforestation in the Himalayan foothills brought all manner of ecological backlash for human communities living downstream. In the monsoon season of June 1978, crop damage and livestock loss amounted to $2 billion. So local people decided to save "their" trees from the axe, through their tree-hugging movement. So successful has this initiative proved, that extensive areas of forest have been reprieved. There could hardly be a more graphic demonstration of the capacity of grass-roots people to take measures for their own support.

Club of Rome

Via Giorgione 163, 00147, Rome

Founded in the 1960's by Aurelio Peccei, now unfortunately deceased, the Club comprises just 100 persons from academia, industry, the research community, politics, etc. Despite the small number of members, the Club has had extensive influence, starting with its *Limits to Growth* in 1972. Of course, the Club is not nearly so exclusive as its membership may imply: it calls on a broad range of professional expertise while making its global-scale appraisals of the human predicament in the midst of an over-loaded biosphere.

Fundacion Natura

Ecuador

Has recently published an environmental profile of the country, as a first step to initiate sound environmental management. Provides school teachers with educational materials. Provides expert advice to government agencies and other institutions.

Indonesian Environmental Forum (Wahana Lingkungan Hidup Indonesia)

Jl. Suryopranoto No. 8 Jakarta Pusa, Indonesia

Founded in 1980, it aims to increase community participation in environmental activities throughout the country. Its fields of activities include communication and information amongst the NGOs themselves, between NGOs and the society, NGOs and the government; training and education to improve the effectiveness and efficiency of the organization's programs; and program development to provide technical assistance needed by the NGOs.

References

Conservation Directory 1985, National Wildlife Federation, Washington D.C.
World Directory of Environmental Organizations, Second Edition, The Sierra Club, San Francisco, California, 1976.

The trail begins.

Photo courtesy of Lute Jerstad Adventures International.

Tours, Travels and Adventures

Sandra Parker

It is necessary to travel.
It is not necessary to live.
ANCIENT PROVERB

Four Vectors: Space, Time, Biome and Culture

What is the biosphere? Scientists specialize in producing elucidations of this question; engineers enlighten us with insights of its marvelous design; artists reflect its essential beauty; philosophers its cosmic significance; managers its needs; and mystics its transcendental influence. But only by joining those who traverse this planet as adventurers will we ever understand in our being what the biosphere is.

The experiential method is and since man first stirred on this planet, has been, the only method by which we can achieve a direct perception of where we live. Where we or you or I live is not on, say Dillon Drive in Omaha, or Downing Street in London, or Red Square in Moscow, but *in* the biosphere.

Tours, travels and adventures offer the means for exploration of the biosphere, whereby we may experience within our own being the far-reaching and varied effects produced by this unified multiplicity.

The ancients understood this necessity to travel without which one could not live, that is, live in the sense of being a 'Citizen of the Biosphere'. Animals, though they move, are bound to their own biome; plants to their econiche in the biome; but man has the potential for, at minimum, four-vectored travel: space, time, biome and culture.

Modern day tourism according to Oriol Pi-Sunjer, Department of Anthropology, University of Massachusetts, "fundamentally involves the merchandising of fantasy." But, the marketing of fantasy is *not* the object of Tours, Travels and Adventures. In our terms, a tourist is one whose experience remains in his own time and culture -- although he may move through space and change biomes. A traveler/adventurer by contrast, experiences each vectorial change afforded by travel, making contact with the culture he or she is visiting, sensing the effect on the organism of a different biome, experiencing human life in a different moment in historical time from whence he came. That experience, in some magical way, produces a transforming effect on the individual such that we cannot help but hope to also experience when the adventurer fascinates us with tales and anecdotes of other worlds.

The desire to travel, to venture to other worlds, appears to be as old as man himself. "Long before the dawn of recorded history, people had been marking out the world's great natural highways, the most accessible routes through formidable mountain ranges, across barren deserts, over treacherous waters." Today, man has an unparalleled opportunity for travel and adventure -- some think the 'age of exploration' really begins now that we have the means to travel to the far reaches of the earth's surface, to delve deep into its vast oceans and finally, to soar up through the atmosphere which forms the boundary of the biosphere and enter the limitless adventure of Space.

Robert Hahn, F.R.G.S., World Explorer

Tour Companies
Society Expeditions

723 Broadway East -- Seattle, Washington 98102, U.S.A. 206-324-9400. T.C. Schwartz, Director.

Society Expeditions' brochures read like a lesson in natural history of our globe -- not only are remote villages, islands and even countries listed, but brief descriptions of their history, culture, wildlife are also given. As their 'Expedition Cruising' brochure states, "We believe travel should enrich the mind as well as excite the senses." Each voyage of this series therefore has onboard scholars and scientists who present lectures and who are available to informally instruct the passengers on each area visited. Private dinners, folk festivals, cultural presentation performances are all part of the journey whether on the Trans Siberia Special, India's Palace on Wheels, or the nostalgic Paris-to-Istanbul Orient Express. Society Expeditions' tours range from the North Pole to Antarctica, from Yemen to the Amazon, from Tibet to the Galapagos. Whether a person wishes to brave the barren Northwest Passage on an exclusive voyage, or luxuriate on a gourmet adventure in the wine country of France, or experience the special cultures of Greenland or Papua New Guinea, Society Expeditions offers the choice and the opportunity. And many of the tours can be combined to expand the experience.

Special Expeditions

720 Fifth Avenue -- New York, New York 10019, U.S.A. 212-765-7740. Sven-Olaf Lindblad.

Venturing to India, sailing the waters of Baja California and Alaska, and safariing in Kenya and Tanzania, Special Expeditions conducts first class expeditions to some of the more exotic and remote areas of our globe. Accommodations, whether on shipboard, in palaces or in tented camp, are comfortable and suited to the country being visited; transportation is also selected according to the area being studied, whether by air, four-wheel drive vehicles, rafts or private railway; itineraries are mapped out and scheduled at a leisurely pace for optimum appreciation of the cultures and environments visited: guides knowledgeable with each destination assist tour participants with a more informed understanding of it and groups are kept small for maximum attention and ease of travel.

The Potala

The Potala must be acknowledged as one of the most awe-inspiring edifices built by man. It is set in the world's highest country, and by all odds the hither-to most remote and inaccessible on this planet. Doubtless the aura of mystery and inaccessibility add to the wonder of Tibet and The Potala -- but those factors alone are only a part. The sheer magnificence of The Potala's design, its staggering dimension and its eye-filling richness of content make it stand unique. We have all seen photographs of the regal way in which it looms above the Tibetan capital of Lhasa.

However, lest the impression be gained that it is simply a mammouth deserted edifice it must be added that it is also an active living 'people' place even today. The private quarters of the Dalai Lama in exile are of course uninhabited. They are as he left them in 1959 when he fled to Sikkim and on to India -- but they are far from deserted since they became the holiest and most sought-to-be-visited part of the palace by the countless devout pilgrims who wend their patient way, with burning yak butter lamps in hand, up countless steps through a galaxy of chapels, past chanting monks intoning prayers from the sonorous beat of yak-skin drums.

It is without doubt therefore that the 'livingness' of the Potala gives much to its wonder. It is not 'tourist peopled' -- it is not a monolithic 'dead monument' to some bygone era -- but a living, venerated place of pilgrimage by other-worldly people, on a part of our globe where few of us, for reasons not entirely of our own choosing, have ever been. *Donald L. Ferguson, Member, Circumnavigators Club*

Orient Express. Courtesy of Society Expeditions.

As you set out for Ithaca, then pray that your road is long. May the summer mornings be many when you enter harbors seen for the first time... C.P. Cavafy

Adventure Travel Specialists

And there are adventure travel companies specializing in programs to unique destinations created by the biosphere.

Mountain Travel India

1/1 Rani Jhansi Road -- New Delhi, India. 523-057. Telex: 315061 TREK IN. Vira Mehta.

Adventure Travel Nepal

P.O. Box 243 -- Durbar Marg -- Kathmandu, Nepal. 12706. Telex: 2216 TIG TOP. Basant Mishra.

Founded in 1964, Mountain Travel was the first trekking company in the world and is the only company to have had ten Sherpas stand on the summit of Mt. Everest. Besides servicing major expeditions in the Himalayas, both Mountain Travel India and Mountain Travel Nepal guide climbing on peaks open to nonexpeditionary ascents. Experts in special interest areas such as natural history, anthropology or religion can be provided for groups which wish to explore a particular aspect of Himalayan life.

Under the name Tiger Mountain, the two companies operate special lodging facilities and associated adventure trips in Nepal, Kashmir, Ladakh and south India. For example, travelers can journey three days on a river/camp trip with the final destination of Tiger Tops Jungle Lodge. Or the monastaries and bazaars of Leh can be experienced from Ladakh Sarai, a yurt tent camp in the Indus Valley. Or the jungle of Nagarhole National Park can be explored from the Kubini River Lodge, the renovated hunting lodge of the Maharaja of Mysore in south India.

Lute Jerstad Adventures International

P.O. Box 19537 -- Portland, Oregon 97219, U.S.A. 503-244-6075. Lute Jerstad.

"Take one step beyond!" Lute Jerstad adventure travel focuses on Asia and northwest United States -- whether it be a trans-Himalayan trek in India including relaxing days in the luxurious houseboats of the Vale of Kashmir, a trek through the Sherpa valley near Khumba at the base of Mt. Everest, a leisurely trek-tour combination or sightseeing odyssey throughout Asia, or whiteriver rafting and horsepacking in wilderness areas of North America. Asian treks and programs are handled by Mountain Travel India and Nepal and Lute Jersted serves as North American agent for the two companies. "Our unblemished safety record and enviable lists of 'firsts' throughout the world set us apart."

POTALA. Photograph by Donald L. Ferguson.

Peruvian Andean Treks E.I.R. LTD.

P.O. Box 454 -- Cuzco, Peru. 84/225-701. Telex: 52003 PE PB CUZCO. Peter Robinson.

Andean Treks Unlimited

707 6223-31 Avenue N.W. -- Calgary, Alberta T3B 3X2 Canada. 403-228-7177.

Southern Peru is a favored location for observing Halley's Comet as it passes near the Earth. Peruvian Andean Treks will be conducting an Observation trip of this phenomenon in April 1986. But on a regular basis, this adventure travel company conducts trekking programs in the Andes, led by tour guides who have all lived and studied in Peru. Except for their Andean Classic nontrekking tour, all programs are camping expeditions into the near and far reaches of these Peruvian mountains with all gear carried by llamas. Professional logistics support for expeditions into the Andes is offered from their Cuzco office. Besides trekking programs, birding trips are conducted in one of the largest areas of tropical rainforests in the world, the Many National Park of Peru's Amazon jungle.

Encounter Overland

267 Old Brompton Road -- London, England. 01-370-6951.

"The originators of long-range journeys by expedition truck across Africa, Asia and South America", Encounter Overland offers 'Brief Encounters (4-56 day treks and safaris) and 'Transcontinental Expeditions' (7-31 week long-range expeditions) to young adventurers committed to being fully involved in travel and to searching "the remote, the interesting, the beautiful, the mysterious and the challenging" in 70 countries on the

Tours, Travels and Adventures

three continents. "The continents themselves supply the challenge -- each one of us involved and backed by meticulous preparation, the best equipment, powerful vehicles and leadership by people of presence and experience. There is an easy flexibility linked to the expeditions' self sufficiency. This can maintain us off the worn paths and enables us to seek alternatives and to vary itineraries." Encounter Overland has agents appointed throughout the world and each expedition is thus made up of a pool of cross-cultural participants. This, plus the ability to journey over little-traveled routes via expedition trucks, results in a rich variety of cultural and environmental experiences.

Adventure Center

5540 College Avenue -- Oakland, California 94618, U.S.A. 415-654-1879. Telex: 910-366-7092. Merle Friedenberg, Director of Marketing

Westcan Treks

1414 KensingtonRoad N.W. -- Calgary, Alberta T2N 3P9 Canada. 403-283-6115. Telex: 038-27912.

'The Adventure Travel Specialists' -- adequately describes the wide range of activities offered to most parts of the world -- trekking the outer Hawaiian Islands; overlanding Asia, Africa and South America; exploratory holidays in Europe and Asia; and adventure holidays in Australia and New Zealand -- everything from one-week Himalayan treks to a nine-month trans- Africa overland expedition in a four-wheel-drive truck. Or London to Kathmandu in thirty-one weeks. "The main idea behind all our trips is to encounter the different peoples and cultures and to experience them as fully, and authentically, as possible. Although not academically oriented, each trip is a whole series of individual learning experiences. We tend to really 'get out there' -- camping with the Pygmies of the Ituri Forest of Zaire, trekking with Tibetan traders in Nepal, staying in villages with the Shipibo Indians in the Amazon region of Peru, getting the local hairstyle by women of Timbuctoo, etc." Worldwide adventure travel.

Adventure Center and Westcan Treks are agents in North America for Encounter Overland.

Himalaya

1802 Cedar Street -- Berkeley, California 94703, U.S.A. 415-540-8031. John Gage, President.

"In a hundred ages of the gods, I could not tell you of all the glories of the Himalaya". Himalaya Trekking and Wilderness Expeditions invites you to journey into a World of High Adventure, not only to Nepal, Kashmir/ Bhutan, China/Tibet, and Pakistan, but to the Pacific Region of New Zealand, Thailand, Papua New Guinea and the Japan Alps. Trips range from easy walks to mountaineering expeditions and all trip leaders are widely traveled and knowledgeable of the regions explored. Participants are encouraged to travel at their own pace and family treks are included in Himalaya's program.

"Our trips focus on contact with local people as they follow the season of rhythms of mountain life as well as the quiet beauty of the lands they inhabit".

Sobek Expeditions, Inc.

Angels Camp, California 95222, U.S.A. 209-736-4524.

The most complete compilation of adventure travel trips and tours must be Sobek's *Adventure Book II*, listing "1,000 journeys to the rivers, lands and seas of seven continents". Sixty tour companies' programs are included -- only those companies which have a proven high level record of competence and those which offer one-of-a-kind destination itineraries. From cycling in India to rafting the Colorado River, from birding the Okefenokee Swamp to trekking the great Himalayas -- it's all there, all corners of the globe covered and all adventure possibilities listed. It is just a matter of choosing.

Sobek International Explorers Society, a membership organization, offers updates on member-only expeditions and special travel activities as well as discounts on trips listed in the *Adventure Book II*. The Society "is dedicated to the preservation and protection of the world's wildernesses, and has as its principal goal the intelligent use and continual discovery of the undeveloped lands they inhabit."

Southwest Safaris

P.O. Box 945 -- Santa Fe, New Mexico 87501, U.S.A. 505-988-4246. Bruce Adams.

The Four Corners Region of the southwest United States is a vast and natural setting for rich cultural, archaeological, geological and geographical discoveries and studies and Southwest Safaris attempts to integrate the many and varied aspects of this grand panorama. "Bush flying is the safest, most time-economical form of transport over the unfathomably complex terrains of the southwest, offering grand views of complicated landscapes impossible to interrelate solely from the ground. On the other hand, there is no substitute for strolling barefoot in the sunset across golden-hued sand dunes, for jeeping through mazes of rainbow-colored buttes, or for rafting down deep, twisting canyons and exploring hidden cliff dwellings".

Flamingo Travel Limited

Nairobi Hilton Hotel -- City Hall Way -- P.O. Box 45070 -- Nairobi, Kenya. 331360-27927. Telex: 22314

FLAMINGO.

No previous camel-riding experience is required for this five-day walking and camel safari in Kenya -- needless to say. Up to twelve guests can be accommodated on each caravan consisting of riding and baggage camels led by young Samburu warriors. Daytime is spent riding, and walking, through the rugged and remote African countryside, and nighttime is spent in traditional-style hunting camps with dinner around the campfire. All camels of this safari come from a private camel farm and are "well mannered and gentle creatures, each individually named with its own rather superior personality".

Malamute Power of Vermont

Box 442-A -- RD1 -- Williston, Vermont O5495, U.S.A. 8O2-482-2548. Ed Blechner.

"Some night travel may be attempted if conditions are favorable. With wolves howling in the background and the dogs answering, this trip will be the highlight of the winter." (exerpt from the North Woods Canadian tour). During all of Malamute Power's excursions, participants experience dogsledding or dogpacking with teams of purebred Alaskan Malamutes. They also learn harnessing techniques, dogsled driving, cold weather cooking, snowshoeing, cross-country skiing, emergency snowsheltering, and how to stay comfortable and warm. But the emphasis is on enjoyment and appreciation of the environment and "the wonderful and individual personalities of the beautiful and friendly animals".

China Passage

302 Fifth Avenue -- New York, New York 10001, U.S.A. 212-565-4099.

China Passage offers bicycling tours throughout the People's Republic of China. Because the bicycle is the major transportation for the people of China, these tours offer opportunities for traveling along with, and thus meeting, the people of this special country. Two wilderness walking tours and a coastline fishing adventure are also offered to those who wish to experience the Chinese countryside and culture close-up at a relaxed and leisurely pace. Cycling and walking are interspersed with boat, train and small-van transport.

Ocean Voyages

1709 Bridgeway -- Sausalito, California 94965, U.S.A. 415-332-4681. Telex: 470561 SAIL UI. Mary Crowley, Director.

"Ocean VOYAGES is adventure -- traveling the horizons of the earth's last frontier". On a world-wide fleet of both luxury sailing and motor vessels ranging from 2-participant boats to 3- and 4-masted Barques, Ocean VOYAGES offers relaxing sailing vacations, long ocean passages, racing yacht charters for seasoned sailors, scientific research expeditions, and specialty boats for filming projects. Voyages are scheduled in South, Central and North America; the Pacific, Mediterranean and Indian Oceans; and the Caribbean. In addition to these regularly scheduled trips, special charters for individuals as well as groups can be arranged. Flexibility in sailing locations around the world, degree of sailing participation, duration of voyage, and type of vessel is paramount with Ocean VOYAGES. "Whether you are landlocked with a yen for adventure, or an experienced sailor wishing the thrill of a different rig and new exciting locations -- or anyone simply wanting the most refreshing and exciting holiday of a lifetime, Ocean VOYAGES has the boat for you."

Educational Adventure Tours

Organizations exist which specifically offer educational adventure journeys to special destinations of our globe. In approach and underlying all the differences is a goal of inner peace through better understanding and acceptance of oneself, and world peace through better understanding and acceptance of other peoples and cultures.

Experience is the best teacher. The following are a few experiential programs.

Natural History Tours

Nature Expeditions International

P.O. Box 11496 -- Eugene, Oregon 97440, U.S.A. 503-484-6529. David Roderick, President.

Nature Expeditions International -- "Wildlife and Cultural Expeditions to unique Environments of the World". Nature Expeditions originated in the college classroom in the form of short courses in natural history. Since then these courses have taken to the road (or ocean, river or mountain) and have become a combination of vacation adventure travel and discovery through "education in its widest and best sense -- seeing, touching, understanding and appreciating what the world has to offer". Successful educational touring requires strong leadership and every NEI leader has traveled extensively or lived in his tour-destination country and speaks its native language.

Biological Journeys

1876 Ocean Drive -- McKinleyville, California 95521, U.S.A. 707-839-0178. Ron LeValley.

Whales, Whales Whales! -- the title of one of Biological Journey's natural history trips and the focus of many other expeditions they conduct from Baja Mexico, along the west coast of North America, through to the many straits and passages of Alaska. But whales share the natural history tour spotlight with birds and wildlife of such diverse destinations as the Galapagos, Machu Picchu, the Amazon and East Africa. "We emphasize direct involvement with the earth's great wilderness areas and combine a joy and celebration of the earth's wonders with sound natural history education. Our trips reflect our own personal interest in the biology of whales and birds, but all include exposure to the broad range of life around us."

Walking along the Great Rift Valley in Kenya, East Africa.
Photograph by David Roderick, courtesy of Nature Expeditions International.

Geo Expeditions

P.O. Box 27136 -- Oakland, California 94602, U.S.A. 415-530-4146.

Limiting tour group size in order to minimize impact on the peoples and ecologies of destinations visited, Geo Expeditions conducts travel programs throughout Latin America, Asia and Africa. Special highlighted tours include archaeology studies of Mexico and Belize, Birds of Thailand, Orang Utangs of Indonesia, and wildlife safaris into Rwanda and Zaire, homes to the mountain gorilla. All tours emphasize regional culture and natural geography and are conducted by a tour leader who has academic or professional expertise on the region visited.

In addition to regularly scheduled tour programs, Geo Expeditions can organize special expeditions for museums, associations, schools and private groups interested in ornithology, culturology and trekking.

Kingbird Tours

P.O. Box 196 -- Planetarium Station -- New York, New York 10024, U.S.A. 212-866-7923. Ben King, President.

"If there is a choice between good birds and comfort, KingBird will always choose the birds". Ben King is one of the most experienced bird-tour leaders to Asia and uses his expeditions for data collecting and ornithology field work. He conducts both birding tours and scientific expeditions to China, Indonesia, Thailand, Burma and Hong Kong. He stresses that his tours are rugged and that long predawn-to-dusk days are spent solely on walking and birding in remote and beautiful locations. "Camping is roughing it. However, the opportunity to live outdoors and awaken to the dawn chorus far transcends inconveniences".

Victor Emanuel Nature Tours and Photo Safaris, Inc.

P.O. Box 33008 -- Austin, Texas 78764, U.S.A. 512-477-5091. Victor Emanuel, Director.

"One of nature's most captivating evolutionary achievements -- the living bird". The living bird serves as model for VENT's beautifully illustrated brochure which recaps their natural history tours to some of the richest birding areas of the world in North, Central and South America, the West Indies, Africa and Australasia. All tours are conducted at a relaxed pace, thoroughly covering a few select areas rather than crowding in as many locales as time would permit. "The Victor Emanuel philosophy is that birding should encompass both the asthetic enjoyment of remarkable creatures and the acquisition of broader knowledge of our natural world".

As a recent extension of their nature tours, Victor Emanuel has chosen various destinations rich in scenic beauty and natural history subjects to conduct photographic tours and workshops led by well-known and published naturalist photographers.

Oceanic Society Expeditions

Fort Mason Center -- Building 'E' -- San Francisco, California 94123, U.S.A. 415-441-1106. Birgit Winning, Expedition Director

As the travel/expedition branch of the Oceanic Society (an organization "for people who love the sea") many of the educational adventure programs take place on ships -- luxury sailing yachts, sailboats, dive boats, motor vessels and even rubber rafts. But Oceanic Society Expeditions also offers land based trips near the water -- natural history tours to Sri Lanka, the southern tip of South America and Kenya. The spotlight of each expedition is the vast array of plant, animal, fish and bird life which abounds at each destination. To enrich the experience of wildlife sightings, a professional naturalist/guide accompanies each tour giving informal instruction. Whale watching in Canada, Alaska and Mexico is a speciality of a number of trips, but swimming with dolphins is also an unusual and attractive feature of the Grand Bahama expedition.

"This is a water planet and we are all members of an Oceanic Society".

Museums, Zoos and Organization Tours

British Museum Society

British Museum -- London WC1B 3DG England. 01-637-9983.

The British Museum selects a number of countries with important architectural and cultural tradition as destinations for membership tours. The chosen destinations vary each year and museums, churches, castles, palaces, monasteries and gardens are highlighted during European and Asian trips.

Smithsonian Associates Travel Program

A&I 1278 Smithsonian Institute -- Washington D.C. 20560, U.S.A. 202-357-2477.

Smithsonian Associates Travel Program covers the globe visiting unique cultural and ecological regions from Turkey to Mexico, from Scotland to the Galapagos, from Kyoto to "Los Angeles in Style". And all trips are accompanied by an expert-lecturer on the area and subject being covered -- whether it is the opera in New York or wildlife sanctuaries of India. The emphasis of the program is relaxed learning in fascinating environments with stimulating fellow travelers, Associates of the Smithsonian Institution in Washington DC.

Royal Geographic Society

1 Kensington Gore -- London SW7 2AR England. 01-589-5466.

As the focal point for British geographical and exploration activity, the Royal Geographic Society conducts scientific expeditions throughout the world. For the lay person, it conducts tours to select destinations, viewing and studying the wildlife, geography and peoples of the area visited. All tours are accompanied by a Society expert who has traveled extensively in the particular destination. Previous investigative tours have included a West Himalayan walking tour, a camping tour of Iceland, a wildlife and archaeological study of Swaziland, and a retracing of Darwin's voyage on the *Beagle*. As the Society is dedicated to discovery and exploration throughout the world, its tours offer epic journeys to all member participants.

Betchart Expeditions Inc.

10485 Phar Lap Drive -- Cupertino, California 95014, U.S.A. 408-245-9517. Telex: 171596 AAACOM SUVL. Margaret Betchart, President.

A person wanting to join an in-depth natural history tour with a museum or zoo would do well to contact Betchart Expeditions as they work exclusively with such organizations. Led by well qualified naturalists, expeditions include exploration of the national parks of Brazil, viewing of millions of monarch butterflies in Mexico, and studying the unique isolated wildlife of Hawaii with such groups as the World Wildlife Fund and the San Diego Zoo.

The Nature Conservancy

1800 North Kent Street -- Arlington, Virginia 22209, U.S.A. 703-841-5300.

The Nature Conservancy is a conservation organization which selects and acquires or protects jeopardized areas of highest ecological value and species diversity. Originally founded in the United States, it now works with conservation colleagues in Canada, the Caribbean and Central and South America to form an international network of institutes to assure the perpetual preservation of natural plant and animal diversity. Priority emphasis is being placed on Costa Rica, Colombia, Peru, Bolivia and Mexico due to the rapid extinction of highly diversified species existing in these regions. The eventual goal of this international program is to expand the network worldwide.

Surveying in the Santa Valley of Peru. Dr. David Wilson is aided by Earthwatch volunteer. Photograph by Steve Benjamin, courtesy of Earthwatch.

In the United States, most Conservancy preserves are open to the public and some preserves offer special tours and visitor programs. As most of the Central and South American Conservancy programs are conducted in national parks, the public is again welcome to explore the specially selected wildlife environments.

Schools

National Audubon Society Expedition Institute

Northeast Audubon Center -- Sharon, Connecticut 06069, U.S.A. 203-364-0522.

"Wild America is Our Campus". Concerned for the quality and environmental significance of the traditional classroom, Audubon Expedition Institute offers experiential education through small investigative camping groups which use the global environment as its unbiased classroom and teacher. Each 'class' travels by bus to a variety of traditional communities, ecoregions and educational centers, and interacts with political groups, conservation organizations and specialist experts in fields such as geology, anthropology, ecology and astronomy. Many graduates from the Institute have gone on to conservation, outdoor and environmental careers.

Boulder Outdoor Survival School, Inc.

University Station -- P.O. Box 7215 -- Provo, Utah 84602, U.S.A. 801-224- 5183.

Survival techniques such as trap and snare construction, primitive direction finding and fire building, shelter construction and plant identification are taught during rigorous courses in the wilderness environment of Utah's badlands. Though not living off the land, participants with a minimum of equipment learn how to live and cooperate with nature and how personally to live intensely and simply. Students are required to be physically fit and committed mentally to complete this extremely challenging course.

High Country Guides and Packers School

Box 6326 -- Wetaskiwin, Alberta T9A 1G1 Canada. 403-352-9965. Bob Silverthorne, Director.

"High Country's average school day is twelve hours. You will be learning from the time you roll out of bed in the morning until bedtime each night. Yet, there is time to share tales of the trail around the campfire and leisure time for reading and riding". To prepare students for a career in guiding and outdoor recreation or the serious backcountry traveler for adventure into the wilderness, High Country offers a Recreational Horse Packer course (horse and mule handling and use) and a Mountain Hunting Guide and Packer course (includes a wilderness journey into the Canadian Rockies). To successfully complete these courses, a student must display practical expertise as a field farrier and in veterinary skills, low impact wilderness use, camp craft and hunting skills.

Wilderness Outfitter and Guide Service

Box 97 -- Cortaro, Arizona 85230, U.S.A. 602-721-6906.

Frank Roubieu, director of Wilderness Outfitter and Guide Service, has an answering service as he is "out on the range" a great deal. He has conducted numerous endurance rides throughout the southwestern United States, but during winter seasons he conducts mountain survival training courses and regular mountain trail rides for adults with all levels of horseback riding experience and expertise. The rides incorporate informal exercises in environmental awareness and observation training on horseback along with specific horse care and handling techniques. Longer endurance rides or custom trips can be arranged.

Cowboy Stories

Staring into the campfire on a clear, cold February night in the Sonoran desert, we listened to Frank Roubieu recalling life out on the range -- of the characters he has encountered and with whom he has traveled, of wild nights in town and peaceful days in the mountains -- all tales punctuated with laughter of rememberance. Cowboy stories.

With a faraway look in his eye and a calmness in his voice, he speaks of the freedom of the range -- of venturing wherever his path leads with no responsibilities except to himself and his horse. He is one of the last of his kind -- the open range rider in the style by which the Wild West was tamed. "Once I traveled for two months all alone and loved every minute of it. I come and go as I please and this gives me a feeling of independence and absolute freedom, of peace of mind and happiness few people will ever experience, of a closeness to God and a love of nature".

In the introduction to Frank's book, Horseman Survival in the Wilderness, *he encourages readers to learn how to better understand and work with horses, then "one day you may climb into the saddle, chirp to your pack horse, wave to your envious friends -- and follow my trail into the wilderness. You and your horse, one together. When you get out there, look for my sign. Ask around. You'll find me, Frank Roubieu, saddle tramp. Sit by my fire and we'll swap stories".*

Work / Study Programs

Expedition R/V Heraclitus

24 Old Gloucester Street -- London WC1 3AL England. 01-242-7367. Telex: 885960 ECOHUB G. Robert Hahn, Director.

Those questing for new worlds to master may well find them aboard the R/V Heraclitus. The Institute of Ecotechnics' "Round the Tropic World" Expedition, ending in March 1986, aboard this research vessel is a multi-disciplinary program to explore jungles, coral reefs, and cetacean movements while operating its Sea and Space Training Program consisting of seamanship, navigation (celestial and satellite), communication, group dynamics, gestalt theater, diving, ethnoecology and working with the classic wind/wave systems of the planet. A new expedition commences in 1987.

Apprenticeship programs of varying time periods are available to individuals interested in intensive seagoing instruction and adventure.

Some crew aboard make halophyte collections and others, studies of the dugong and of whale locations and sounds as part of the Institute of Ecotechnics' cooperative programs with the Environmental Research Laboratory of

211

the University of Arizona and Cetacean Seas Research.

Oceanic Research Foundation Ltd.

Dangar Island, N.S.W. Australia. 02-455-1275.
David Lewis.

Oceanic Research Foundation undertakes independent marine-based research in the waters surrounding Australia as well as those of the Antarctic and Indonesia.

Headed by Dr. David Lewis, an initiated Polynesia navigator and first man to sail single-handed to the South Pole, Oceanic Research Foundation offers intense exploratory expeditions of high degree -- "in the tradition of Australia's pioneering adventurers."

Expedition Advisory Center

1 Kensington Gore -- London SW7 2AR England. 01-581-2057.

The Expedition Advisory Center provides advice and services to explorers and expedition organizers. Center publications include reports on past expeditions, a register of those planned for the future and members available for them, expedition consultants and suppliers, and information on expedition organization in all climates. Training seminars conducted by the Center include such topics as Underwater Expeditions, Expeditionary Medicine, Conservation Matters for Expeditions and their annual Planning a Small Expedition.

Earthwatch

10 Juniper Road -- Belmont, Massachusetts 02178, U.S.A. 617-489-3030. Mary Blue Magruder, Director of Public Affairs.

Earthwatch England

Brook Green Studios -- Dunsany Road -- London W14 England. 01-602-5203.

Earthwatch Australia

43 Victoria Street -- McMahon's Point N.S.W. Australia 2060. 02-929-5677.

Archaeology, anthropology, paleontology, primatology, and ethno- musicology -- just some of the work/study programs Earthwatch conducts throughout the world. Professionals and lay persons alike are invited to join expeditions to numerous research sites to assist university investigators with their field work data collection. No special skills are required -- only an interest to participate in studying the Mayan civilizations of Belize and Guatemala, videotaping the folkdances of Japan's Ryukyu islands, counting trees in a Panamanian tropical rain forest, or excavating ancient ritual sites on the Cook Islands of Polynesia -- to name just a few Earthwatch

projects.

"Earthwatch supports the efforts of scholars to preserve the world's endangered habitats and species, explore the vast heritage of its people, and promote world health and international cooperation. By making these efforts accessible to citizens, Earthwatch strives to increase public understanding of science and improve the quality of life on earth".

Wildlands Research

3 Mosswood Circle -- Cazadero, California 95421, U.S.A. 707-632-5665.

Participants join backcountry research teams as working field associates helping qualified researchers look for answers to important environmental problems. As field associates, participants choose among wildlife, wildland and wildriver projects in the Mountain West, Canada or Alaska. Previous fieldwork experience is not necessary as all skills are taught on-site by resource specialists. Areas of study range from recovery of Roosevelt Elk population since the 1980 eruption of Mount St. Helen, to environmental analysis of options for future wilderness area usage. Projects occur entirely in the field and, while there is time for solitude and relaxation, they are not simply vacations. "Field work sometimes means long days and uphill trails in not always ideal weather. At times, research can be frustrating, repetitive, or just plain hard work; but it is also a rare and fascinating opportunity to explore our wildlands firsthand, while striving toward shared goals with experienced researchers and new friends".

The Cousteau Society

930 West 21st Street -- Norfolk, Virginia 23517, U.S.A. 804-627-1144.

'Project Ocean Search' is a series of short, intensive field-study programs conducted by a Cousteau Society team and Jean-Michel Cousteau. Open to anyone over sixteen years of age and in good health, and diving ability or scientific experience not prerequisites, each expedition is limited to 35 participants and travels to a remote area to study its biology and ecology and man's relation to its environment. Expedition members participate in an ongoing reef ecosystem dynamics study as well as other special projects of special interest. Lectures accompany project study and organized field trips.

Crow Canyon Center for Southwestern Archaeology

23390 County Road 'K' -- Cortez, Colorado 81321, U.S.A. 303-565-8975. Ed Berger, Director.

Crow Canyon conducts an archaeology program open to professional archaeologists and lay persons interested in participating in discoveries of prehistoric man in North America -- precisely, the Anasazi of southwestern Colorado, the ancestors of modern-day Pueblo Indians.

Archaeological field schools stress disciplined and educated research in all phases of archaeological work including field excavation, mapping and data recording, laboratory analysis, and washing and sorting of artifacts. The comprehensive educational programs are the exchange given for an individual's contribution to the Crow Canyon site excavation. "By becoming directly involved in the daily work of archaeology, you will develop a deeper understanding of the methods which apply to all sciences -- attention to detail, the process of interpretation and deduction, and interrelationships of different disciplines. This is an opportunity to see science being practiced in the real world".

Kunstakademie Atelier Beuys

Postfach 200271 -- 4000 Dusseldorf -- West Germany 0211/326720. Joseph Beuys.

In 1982, the German artist, Joseph Beuys, undertook a project to plant 7,000 oak trees in the town of Kassel, "an achievement of urgent necessity to the biosphere and to the pure matter of ecological coherence...the action should yield to a complete modification of the way of life as well as to the reorganization of human society and to the whole ecological environment". The process of tree planting will subsequently continue in other towns of Germany and then throughout Europe.

Volunteers are invited to participate in this experience of social sculpture wherein life and art are blended together. Beuys rates as one of the key avant-garde figures in today's art.

Dolphinlab

P.O. Box Dolphin -- Marathon Shores, Florida 33052, U.S.A. 305-289-1121.

Dolphinlab studies dolphins through the disciplines of patterns of animal behavior, goals and methods of communication, behavior modification as practiced by dolphin trainers, and care of captive dolphins. Associated fields of study are whale biology, ecology and conservation as well as Florida Keys reef ecology, marine ornithology and shark studies. Field study work includes identification of animal species, monitoring of endangered species, and assistance with Florida Keys animal and bird sanctuaries.

Environmental Opportunities

Box 684 -- Fitzwilliam, New Hampshire 03447, U.S.A. 603-357-3122.

"Serving environmental job interests throughout the United States", Environmental Opportunities is a monthly publication of environmentally related jobs and internships presently available including administrative, teaching, research, planning and seasonal positions. Job-wanted listings as well as a recap of upcoming courses and environmental activities are also included in the bulletin. This publication is sponsored by the Environmental Studies Department of Antioch/New England Graduate School.

Celestial Navigation

Since the beginning of his existence, man has turned his eyes and imagination skyward. We, too, can gaze up at those same stars and dream of the ultimate travel adventure -- to sail among them. Modern space science has brought us to the point wherein a select number among us have made that journey and now the biosphere itself prepares to make the mitosis that will enable permanent travel.

Like all educated travelers venturing to destinations never traversed before, we will study about the region to be explored -- for background information will enrich our experience and, since we most likely have a few years before this ultimate spacial journey is possible, we can make an earthly tour of an area rich in facilities dedicated to the study of the planets and stars of our cosmos -- *Tucson, Astronomy Capital of the World*. This tour will give an idea of the complex support developing that will back up the movement of biospheres into space.

Concentrated in northern and southern Arizona in the southwestern United States, and centered around the University of Arizona in Tucson, are astronomical sites open to the interested general public as well as educational institutions reserved for those who wish to delve deeper into the questions of the origin and evolution of our universe. A self-guided tour to these sites would find us peering into telescopes, touching meteorites fallen from the skies, reviewing the manned and unmanned space programs conducted by various countries of the world, and gazing at fantastic photographs of planets, asteroids, moons, galaxies and comets -- pictures taken from land-based observatories and those returned to us from space-borne vehicles. Even photographs of our own planet Earth taken from beyond our Moon.

Our study tour begins with a visit to the Grace Flandrau Planetarium at the corner of Cherry Avenue and Hawthorn Street in Tucson, Arizona, U.S.A.

Grace Flandrau Planetarium

Cherry Avenue and University Street -- Tucson, Arizona 85721, U.S.A. 602- 621-4515.

For an overall introduction to a study of space and the space sciences, Flandrau Planetarium presents special astronomy and space sciences programs nightly to the public in its Star Theater, as well as a permanent exhibition on the features of our cosmos. Specially designed programs for school children are conducted along with the "Eyes of the Universe" lecture series presented in conjunction with the Steward Observatory.

Steward Observatory

Cherry Avenue and Second Street -- Tucson, Arizona 85721, U.S.A. 602-621- 2288.

Steward Observatory, established in 1916, continues to be the research and educational institution of the University's Department of Astronomy. Since the construction of the "All American Telescope" in 1922 -- at the time the largest telescope wholly constructed (both optics and structure) in the U.S. -- the Observatory has continued to increase its facilities so that today the University has telescope sites on the campus itself, Kitt Peak, in the Santa Catalina Mountains, on Mt. Hopkins and on Tumamoc Hill near downtown Tucson. In addition to ground-based facilities, Steward Observatory staff are engaged in research with air-borne equipment and space probe astronomy.

The Observatory has been involved with public education and, since its inception in 1922, has conducted a Public Evening Series -- "The Eyes of the Universe", an astronomy research lecture series.

Individual and/or group tours can be arranged to the various Observatory facilities.

Kitt Peak National Headquarters

950 Cherry Avenue -- Tucson, Arizona 85719, U.S.A. 602-327-5511.

Kitt Peak National Headquarters houses the laboratories and instrument shops for the National Observatory located south of the city. The Observatory is funded by the National Science Foundation and is under the management of the Association of Universities for Research in Astronomy (A.U.R.A.) which is an association of 17 universities with well-developed research and graduate training programs in astronomy and which manages Kitt Peak and her sister facility, Cerro Tololo Inter-American Observatory in Chile. Also housed here are the headquarters for the National Optical Astronomy Observatories including the National Solar Observatory and the Advanced Development Program, the latter program working on the National New Technology Telescope.

Lunar and Planetary Laboratory

Cherry Avenue and University Street -- Tucson, Arizona 85721, U.S.A. 602-621-6963.

As part of the Department of Planetary Sciences of the University, the Lunar and Planetary Laboratory is an interdisciplinary research center which uses astronomical observations, spacecraft-based instruments, laboratory analyses and theoretical investigations to study the origin and evolution of the planets of our solar system. A space station is scheduled by NASA to be in orbit in 1992 and implanted on the station will be a telescope developed by the Laboratory in conjunction with NASA's Ames Research Center to view the Universe with a clarity never before possible. Celestial bodies and possibly entirely new planetary systems will be observed for the first time ever.

Housed within the Laboratory is the Space Imagery Center which contains more than 500,000 images of the planets of our Solar System. The Center encourages the study of its maps, photo-and cartographic-products by planetary researchers and the interested public.

Individual and group tours of both the Lunar and Planetary Laboratory and the Space Imagery Center can be arranged.

A new division of the Laboratory, the Arizona Center for Space Resources, is being established in 1985 to serve as a global information and communication center coordinating the various aspects of the subject of space resource utilization. Educational seminar and workshop programs will be conducted and the Center will be a multi-disciplinary forum for all scientists, governmental agencies and industrialists involved in work and research into space-based resource exploitation.

Optical Sciences Center

Cherry Avenue and University Street -- Tucson, Arizona 85721, U.S.A. 602-626-2836.

The Optical Sciences Center which is the University's facility for graduate education and research in the field of optics, covering such diverse disciplines as atmospheric studies, remote sensing computer-aided image enhancement, laser physics telescope design, and optical design and fabrication. Included in the Center are classrooms, an optical polishing facility, and electronics and instrument shops.

Individuals interested in graduate-level optics study can arrange a visit of the Center, as can groups.

McMATH SOLAR TELESCOPE at the National Solar Observatory, Kitt Peak, Arizona, courtesy of National Optical Astronomy Observatories.

Astronomical League

P.O. Box 12821 -- Tucson, Arizona 85732, U.S.A.

Tucson Amateur Astronomy Association

Information through Flandrau Planetarium or the Astronomical League.

Associated information on amateur space study activities can be obtained from the Astronomical League Headquarters. The League promotes the science of astronomy by coordinating the activities of local amateur astronomy societies by expanding contacts of those societies and of individual members.

As a League member, the Tucson Amateur Astronomy Association conducts meetings and programs such as astrophotography, fabrication of mirrors and telescopes, planet and galaxy observation, field trips and, of course, stargazing.

L-5 Society

16 East Elm Street -- Tucson, Arizona 85719, U.S.A. 602-622-6351.

Located near the University, the L-5 Society dedicates its efforts towards public education regarding worldwide space activities and space industrialization and habitation. Educational techniques include space career conferences for adults and children, a speakers bureau for schools and organization, a legislative activity telephone information line and political action committee, a press information service for professional writers and a public library at the Tucson headquarters.

Kitt Peak National Observatory

P.O. Box 26732 -- Tucson, Arizona 85726, U.S.A. 602-623-5796.

Southwest of Tucson on the Papago Indian Reservation, is Kitt Peak National Observatory which contains the world's largest collection of telescopes and

facilities for stellar, solar and planetary observation and research by residential and visiting astronomers and scientists from all parts of the globe. Among the telescopes on Kitt Peak are two solar telescopes including the 1.5 meter McMath, the stellar 4-meter Mayall, and six others utilized for the study of galaxies and stars. Kitt Peak is also the site of the National Optical Astronomy Observatories' National Solar Observatory.

Self-guided walking tours with supporting films are available daily and guided tours are offered on weekends.

Fred Lawrence Whipple Observatory

P.O. Box 97 -- Amado, Arizona 85640, U.S.A. 602-398-2432.

Farther south is the Fred Lawrence Whipple Observatory on Mt. Hopkins in the Santa Rita Range, an astronomical research facility of the Smithsonian Astrophysical Observatory. In conjunction with the University of Arizona, the multi-mirror telescope was built and is operated here -- a revolutionary design utilizing six individual reflecting telescopes in array to produce one large focused image. It is the third largest telescope in existence and serves as a prototype for still larger ones. The multi-mirror telescope is used in the study of infrared and optical astronomy. Other astronomical instruments on Mt. Hopkins investigate cosmic radiation and spectroscopy of galaxies, stars and planets.

Scheduled guided tours on reservation basis depart three days a week during March through November from Amado for the Mt. Hopkins site.

Catalina Mountain Observatories

Information can be obtained through the Steward Observatory.

Northeast of Tucson are two University of Arizona observatories on Mt. Bigelow and Mt. Lemmon. Photography, photometry and spectroscopy are techniques used in research conducted at both observatories.

Visits to these sites are by special arrangement only.

Casa Grande Ruins

Highway 77 -- Coolidge, Arizona 85228, U.S.A. 602-723-3172.

'The home of the cruel and bitter man who looked through holes in his house to salute the sun' -- the present Pima Indian language translation for the Casa Grande ruin located half way between Tucson and Phoenix. Continuing studies suggest that openings in the thick adobe walls of this ancient building were specifically placed for observing the Sun, Moon and possibly other planets, and for marking the equinoxes and summer solstice. The possibility that eclipses could be predicted by mooncycle observations through certain west wall openings, suggest that the prehistoric Hohokam Indian residents of Casa Grande were extremely advanced in astronomy and mathematics.

Casa Grande Ruins site and visitors center are open to the public daily. Self-guided tours accompanied by periodic informational talks are available throughout visiting hours.

Center for Meteorite Studies

Arizona State University -- Tempe, Arizona 85287, U.S.A. 602-965-6511.

On the Arizona State University campus just south of Phoenix, is the Center for Meteorite Studies, a research facility for the study of the phenomenon of meteorites, their origin, falls and types.

A permanent public exhibition in the Center displays examples from its large and very important collection of meteorites along with an educational presentation on the subject.

Meteor Crater Enterprises Inc.

121 East Birch -- Suite 210 -- Flagstaff, Arizona 86000, U.S.A.. 602-774-8350.

In Flagstaff, northern Arizona's center for space science studies, lies the best preserved evidence of meteorite impact on the Earth -- the Meteor Crater. Created around 20,000 BC by a meteorite calculated at 63,000 tons and traveling at 12 miles per second, the Crater is the first proven meteoritic impact crater site in the world.

Its terrain has proven to be a natural laboratory for crater studies of the Moon and, as such, as been used as a training site for Apollo astronauts in preparation for a lunar landing. Their study of crater mechanics and geology enabled them to better comprehend what they later encountered on the Moon.

To acquaint the public with the Crater and with other planetary surfaces and interiors, an educational exhibition of meteorites, the dynamics of meteors, and crater formation is on display at the Crater's Museum of Astrogeology. Adjacent to the Museum is the Astronaut Hall of Fame which traces the progress of manned space programs. The exhibitions and crater viewing area are open to the public every day.

U.S. Naval Observatory

Astronomical Observing Station -- Flagstaff, Arizona 86002. 602-779-5132.

The Astronomical Observing Station, one of three sites which make up the U.S. Naval Observatory. The purpose of the Observatory is to provide accurate time and other astronomical data essential for safe navigation at sea, in air and in space. To accomplish this, the Flagstaff Station conducts continual observations to determine the position and motion of the Sun, Moon, planets and principal stars using a transit circle telescope. The Station also conducts research with conventional reflector and refractor telescopes.

The Station does not conduct regularly-scheduled tours, but limited special viewing of the facility can be arranged by advanced appointment.

Lowell Observatory

P.O. Box 1269 -- Flagstaff, Arizona 86002, U.S.A. 602-774-2096.

Famous for the discovery of Pluto and the theory of the expanding universe, is Lowell Observatory which continues its astronomical research into planets, satellites, asteroids, comets, galaxies, quasi-stellar objects and the Earth's atmosphere. The Observatory also maps the surfaces of the planets in support of the space missions. Its Planetary Research Center coordinates the International Planetary Patrol which is a worldwide network of telescopes photographing the planets on a regular basis, and the Center's collection of planetary images is the largest in the world. The Observatory contains complete facilities for astronomical research.

Guided tours are conducted weekdays with Friday night visits during the summer months.

United States Geological Survey

2255 North Gemini Drive -- Flagstaff, Arizona 86001, U.S.A. 602-527-7022.

Closely affiliated with NASA, Geological Survey scientists have participated in every one of the lunar and planetary missions conducted by the Space Agency. Due to the similarity of the terrain surrounding Flagstaff and that of the surface of the Moon, Apollo astronauts trained at this planetary data facility for the geological experiments they would conduct during the lunar landings. As well, the excellent telescopic observation conditions of the area facilitate lunar and planetary mapping.

In addition to research into the origins and the geological evolution of the planets and solar system, the Flagstaff Branch of Astrogeology Studies is conducting terrestrial studies of the geological resources of the southwestern United States and the environmental effects of utilizing these resources. Research conducted at the Survey not only involves data analysis and synthesis, but also development of techniques for collecting and processing this data.

Facilities at the Survey include a comprehensive lunar and planetary data library, the Planetary Data Facility which houses data on missions and planets, the Computer Center Division, the Photogrammetry Unit -- an advanced image processing facility wherein computer enhancement photography techniques are developed and applied, and the Cartographic section which produces geological, shaded relief and topographic maps of the planets from computer data and from manned and unmanned exploratory spacecraft.

No scheduled tours are conducted but can be arranged with prior notice.

'Very Large Array' National Radio Astronomy Observatory

P.O. Box 'O' -- Socorro, New Mexico 87801, U.S.A. 505-835-5011.

Nearby in northern New Mexico is the Very Large Array, one of several radio telescopes operated by the National Radio Astronomy Observatory for the study of cosmic objects such as our sun and other planets of our galaxy, other distant galaxies and even quasars at the edge of the universe. Comprised of 27 moveable, disk-shaped antennas, the Very Large Array collects radio signals from each antenna and collects them in a central location where they are studied by resident as well as visiting astronomers from around the world. The Array site also houses a complete data analysis and image display computer center for experimental research.

The grounds of the Array are open to the public every day for self-guided walking tours. Group tours can be arranged.

Space Travel

Space -- the ultimate in adventure travel -- to be gliding among the planets, stars and other heavenly bodies of our solar system -- to be gazing back through space to our own planet Earth. Science fiction launched our imaginations beyond Earth's atmosphere and now science reality can launch our physical beings there too. Our dreams begin to come true.

The past quarter century witnessed the journeys of the first space travelers -- Soviets, Americans, Canadians, a German, Vietnamese, Mongolian, Frenchman, Saudi Arabian, and Indian. Presently the Chinese train astronauts for manned flight before the end of the centery and Japan works on its own preliminary manned space shuttle designs. The thrust for the majority of future manned space programs is towards development of space colonies or space stations which, once established, will allow for the exploitation of resources and the industrialization of space, heralding the new era of human habitation of space.

Certain forecasters envision that within the next quarter century men and women will orbit the Earth, living and working in these permanent space stations; a lunar base will generate; colonies will conduct research on Mars; and the pioneers into space will develop new systems for habitation of the further reaches of our universe.

As yet there is little in the literature per se, but various authors feel that citizen participation in space flights could realistically become an integral and economically viable part of any manned space programs already in existence. For example, in the United States, various proposals have been tendered for modification of the Shuttle to accommodate from 20-80 passengers for flights of hours to weeks in duration. These proposals emphasize that the equipment and potential exists now for making space available to a greater number and broader range of people. The experience of these space travelers would enrich the world-wide storehouse of data regarding future space station design requirements and additional number of voyages into orbit would hasten the progress of all space programs around the world.

The reality of space travel today has as much captured the spirit and imagination of Earthlings as those science fiction stories of our youth. People speak in fantastic and excited voices of going 'out there'. Moon landings and manned space journeys have not demystified the heavens but have only increased the enthusiasm through eloquent expression of astronaut experiences in space.

Europe: European Space Agency

Headquarters -- 8/10 rue Mario Nikis -- 75738 Paris Cedex 15 France. 273.72.91. Telex: ESA 202746 The cooperative organization of European states in space technology and research for peaceful scientific purposes.

United States: National Aeronautic and Space Administration

Public Affairs Office -- Washington D.C. 20546, U.S.A. 202-453-1000.

Canada: Canada Center for Space Science

100 Sussex Drive -- Ottawa, Ontario K1A 0R6 Canada. 922-02-11. Telex: CNP 534433 NRC SPC OTT.

India: Indian Space Research Organization

Department of Space -- F-Block Cauvery Bhavan -- District Office Road -- Bangalore 560 009. 7-73-22. Telex: 845499 DOS IN.

If I Were To Be Welcomed Aboard...

Boarding the Space Shuttle would be for me the Kingdom of Fantasy. I have fantasized riding in Space beginning in grade school when I saw a weekly newsreel on John Glenn. At the time I am sure I never imagined my fastasy might come true. Later I realized space exploration was a growing sector of our society and in my lifetime it might be possible to pay for a ride to the moon. I started saving!

Little did I know that the events in my life were preparing me for such an incredible adventure. I have learned to navigate and survive in the wilderness which builds self reliance. Next I developed the skill to become airborne, acquiring my pilot license with a furor of passion. Now I had another tool in which to experience my environment.

Now the opportunity to apply to become the Teacher in Space has presented itself. As I labored over the application it became clear to me that I was a likely candidate and that I could adapt to a 'Shuttle life-style'. I just need the right person to say 'Welcome Aboard'. And if it doesn't happen this year...I'll continue to save my money.

Cyn-d Turner, Applicant, United States Teacher in Space Program

Soviet Union: USSR Academy of Sciences

Intercosmos Council -- Leninsky Prospect 14 -- 117901 Moscow V-71.

Japan: National Space Development Agency of Japan

2-4-1, Hamamatsu-cho -- Minatu-ku -- Tokyo. Telex: KDD 28424 NASADA J 28424.

Peoples Republic of China: Chinese Academy of Space Technology

P.O. Box 2417 -- Beijing. 89-22-50. Telex: 22473 CCSC CN.

complete launch vehicle services to anyone promoting the beneficial development of space. Works in close alliance with the European Space Agency.

Space Biospheres Venture

P.O. Box 689 -- Oracle, Arizona 85623, U.S.A.

Research and development project for study, creation and production of materially closed, energetically and informationally open biospheres, as a potential means of establishing permanent manned stations in space or on other planets.

Argo Venture

18 Victory Park Square -- London E2 9PF England. Lord Young of Dartington, Chairman.

Research into reproducing the atmosphere of Mars in a closed system and potential of vegetation growth therein. Also, sociological study of group dynamics.

Space Studies Institute

P.O. Box 82 -- Princeton, New Jersey 08540, U.S.A. 609-921-0377.

Founded in 1977 by Gerard O'Neill, the Space Studies Institute supports and conducts research towards the utilization of space resources.

Space Settlement Studies Project

Sociology Department -- Niagra University -- Niagra, New York 14109, U.S.A. 716-285-1212. Stewart Whitney and William MacDaniel, Co-Directors.

The Project objective is to organize and coordinate persons involved with the requisite social planning that must precede establishment of human communities in extraterrestrial space.

Space Age Publishing Company

3210 Scott Boulevard -- Santa Clara, California 95054, U.S.A. 408-988-0952.

Publishes weekly *Space Calendar*, noting space-related events around the world for upcoming week, and bimonthly *Space Age Review* with space articles of timely concern. Space Age Review Foundation has produced an in-depth Space Shuttle Passenger Project to demonstrate possibilities of transporting large numbers of people in space.

L-5 Society

1060 East Elm -- Tucson, Arizona 85719, U.S.A. 602-622-6351.

Actively promotes development of space activities and human habitization of space through public education.

Space Camp -- Alabama Space and Rocket Center

Tranquility Base -- Huntsville, Alabama 35807, U.S.A. 205-837-3400.

Experiential learning program for children, and now adults, in astronautics, the science of travel beyond the education.

Space Camp -- Alabama Space and Rocket Center

Tranquility Base -- Huntsville, Alabama 35807, U.S.A. 205-837-3400.

Experiential learning program for children, and now adults, in astronautics, the science of travel beyond the earth's atmosphere. Participants world-wide.

Kansas Cosmosphere and Discovery Center

1100 North Plum -- Hutchinson, Kansas 67501, U.S.A. 316-662-2305. Max Ary, Executive Director.

As an outgrowth of the city's planetarium, the Kansas Cosmosphere and Discovery Center houses the Hall of Space museum exhibiting one of the most significant collections of space artifacts in existence, both of traditional and hands-on items. The Center is highly respected for its expertise in restoration of space gear both for themselves and for other museums.

On Your Own

Probably the best way for the prepared individual. For inspiration, read about Kropotkin's life, Walt Whitman's *Open Road*, Thoreau's *Walden*, Doughtey's *Arabia Deserta*, Melville's *Typee*, Aldo Leopold's *Sand County Almanac*, and Celine's *Journey to the End of the Night*.

Information

The object of knowledge and the instrument of knowledge cannot legitimately be separated but must be taken together as one whole. P.W. BRIDGMAN

This last section to the catalogue lists key books, journals, and other sources concerned with the integrity of the biosphere. Of the books reviewed, some are classics and perhaps out-of-print. Check with libraries and second-hand bookshops. They are worth every effort it might take to find them.

The Biosphere

By V.I. Vernadsky, an abridged version based on the French edition (forthcoming from Synergetic Press).

Vernadsky's great work of 1929, *The Biosphere*, remains unpublished in English although *Vladimir Vernadsky* (English translation) published by MIR in Moscow is a welcome sourcebook, as is this abridged publication.

E. Suess of Vienna University first used the word *biosphere*, but it fell to Vernadsky to give the first great presentation of its scale, its laws, its past, its probable future, and reveal man's proper place in the universe, namely as part of the biosphere of planet Earth.

Vernadsky sees the direction of evolution as indicated by the biogenic transfer of matter; first by organisms alone, and then by constructions of animals such as termites, now most spectacularly by man's cultures.

Like Darwin, he seizes upon the multiplication of life as its chief feature, but where Darwin emphasizes the evolution of species from the competition thus imposed in a limited environment and so creates Biological Evolutionary Theory, Vernadsky emphasizes the pressure of life upon the material surroundings, and how the sun powers this relentless process of ever-increasing alteration of the Earth's crust. "The movement of living matter resulting from the multiplication of organisms operates with an astonishing regularity. It takes place on the surface of the dry land, in the ocean, in lakes and ponds and in the air. In the form of parasites it even penetrates the interior of living bodies. Without ceasing, for myriads of years this movement has been performing gigantic geochemical work, spreading the energy of the sun and the matter of the biosphere about the earth's surface...at each moment there are hundreds of millions of tons of living matter in the biosphere, always in a state of movement. Such colossal masses of living matter are created and decomposed through death, birth, metabolism and growth within 24 hours that no one could possibly count the number of beings which are born and which perish unceasingly." It is dubious that anyone can understand biospherics who does not master Vernadsky.

Gaia: A New Look at Life on Earth

by James Lovelock, FRS, Oxford University Press, 1979.

Gaia -- "the hypothesis, the model in which the Earth's living matter, air, oceans, and land surface form a complex system which can be seen as a single organism and which has the capacity to keep our planet a fit place for life." Lovelock extended the range of the analytical technique of gas chromatography by developing, among other devices, the electron capture detector. He used this device "to barter" his way through the various scientific disciplines and around the planet in quest of Gaia, which name he uses as shorthand for the above hypothesis.

The book contains a subtle and closely reasoned argument based on exploring the planet physically, measuring its atmosphere, applying the laws of equilibria and information that contain next only to Vernadsky, the most thorough statement of the proposition that man is not the measure of all things, but rather that he is a part of the self-regulating biosphere, a being that has lived over three and a half billion years.

"From a Gaian viewpoint, all attempts to rationalize a subjugated biosphere with man in charge are as doomed to failure as the similar concept of benevolent colonialism.'' Anyone interested in biospherics must read this book as well as Vernadsky's *The Biosphere*, since not only do they produce the key concepts but introduce the requisite vision on the right scale and intensity.

Five Kingdoms: An Illustrated Guide to the Phyla of Life on Earth,

by Lynn Margulis and Karlene U. Schwartz, W. H. Freeman and Company, 1982.

Biospherics deals not only with life but the incoming cosmic energies and the biogenic transfers of matter and the consequent alterations of the crustal and atmospheric earth, but nonetheless life is the force that mediates between radiation and matter. In this wonderfully illustrated and intelligently written volume, Margulis and Schwartz take the reader wisely and brilliantly through the *Five Kingdoms of Life* (as first proposed by Whittaker) and then through the 89 phyla that they recognize: 16 moneran (the non-nucleated cells that created the biosphere and maintained it for its first 2.5 billion years), 27 protoctist, 5 fungal, 32 animal, and 9 plant.

The five kingdoms are shown as three levels: the *monera*, the *protoctista* (nucleated cells), and the three nucleated larger forms *plantae, animalia, and fungi* pursuing three different eco-strategies; production, consumption, and absorption.

The book claims to be, and is, ''a catalogue of the world's living diversity.'' The innovation of Margulis and Schwartz has been to ''make the taxonomic level of phyla conceptually comparable throughout the Five Kingdoms".

If you have time for only three books on the biosphere, and you must deal with these issues as manager, scientist, artist, adventurer, citizen, or student, following Vernadsky and Lovelock, you must obtain Margulis and Schwartz. These three books are on the highest level of conceptual reordering of our dealing with ourselves in the world.

Five Kingdoms has text, illustrations, and definitions. A realized work of love and knowledge.

The Evolution of the Biosphere

By Mikhail M. Kamshilov, Mir Publishers, Moscow, 1976.

''We are witnessing a revolutionary transition from evolution governed by spontaneous biological factors (the period of biogenesis) to evolution governed by human mind, to the period of noogenesis.'' In this brilliant exposition, Prof. Kamshilov, a student of Vernadsky, who headed the microbiology laboratory of the Institute of Biology of Inland Waters, reviews the cosmic and planetary preconditions for the evolution of life, the biospheric circulation and deposits of matter, and charts the emerging course of evolution itself.

Kamshilov distinguishes four major stages in the evolution of the earth's biosphere, and assesses the present situation as the movement to harmonize the technosphere not by a regression to a Rousseauian fantasy but by intelligent cooperation with the laws governing the biosphere.

''Human technology is not anything alien to the biosphere but a qualitatively new stage in the latter's development.'' Biospheric evolution proceeds towards higher degrees of organization and information. Life acts as a huge negentropic factor. This natural metaphysically organizing ability of the biogenetic phases of the biosphere will be accelerated in the noogenic phase.

Kamshilov calls for the creation of new types of multi-disciplinary research institutes to ''constitute the conscious human equivalent of the selecting function of the biosphere, which will admit for growth only such innovations that do not undermine its basis.'' A major work that illuminates the mechanism of the biosphere, it greatly rewards the reader.

Global Change

Edited by T. F. Malone & J. G. Rocderer, ICSU Press/Cambridge Univ. Press.

''Is the time ripe to launch a cooperative interdisciplinary, international program to illuminate the complex and synergistic physical, chemical and biological processes in the Sun-Earth system that determine its changes?'' This volume, the edited proceedings of the 1984 symposium convened by the International Council of Scientific Unions at its 2Oth general assembly in Ottawa, heralds a major integration of man's sciences. The ICSU, a federation of twenty scientific unions and seventy-one national academies effectively acts as the world non-governmental organization of scientists. In the midst of a two-year study of their proposed ''International Geosphere- Biosphere Program -- Global Change'' the papers presented here offer an excellent overview of the knowledge gained to date on systems studies in atmosphere-hydrosphere, life systems, lithosphere, sun and space, monitoring technology and the impact of man.

The timeliness of such an international project, as Dr. Malone notes in his preface, stems from four factors: increasing recognition that biotic and non-biotic components of the biosphere are ''inextricably intertwined"; man now impacts the biosphere on a scale unprecedented for a single life species; the accelerating needs for sustainable biological productivity of the developing nations; and finally, state-of-the-art technics can accomplish the daunting task.

''An incredible array of observational tools is now

provide global surveillance, to chemical techniques that measure substances in parts per trillion. The sophistication of communication technologies, the capacity of computers, and the methodology of systems analysis have literally exploded in recent years. Such advances have brought within real time the analytical, data-handling and data-management techniques required...''

The Earth Spirit

By John Michell, Thames and Hudson.

Definitive formulation of three cosmologies: the nomadic, where ''perambulating each year the wide range of their native territory, they traced the steps of the gods who first created it, thus living out a cosmogony in which every spot, every feature of the landscape had its mythical significance, reflected in the activities that took place there. Time was cyclical, not linear; creation was a continuous process, and the spirits (of trees, animals, springs) that promoted it were eternal.'' After this Heraclitean ''all is flux'' mode of the wanderers comes the geomancer who makes a sacred architecture with two aims: ''to preserve the landscape of the golden age and to make it support a large settled population.'' The Chinese landscape of temple, farm, and city, and the ancient megalithic temple structures and bylines of Britain are examples of this agricultural paradigm.

North America, Michell states, exemplifies the third kind, sites chosen only for economic value by commercial-industrial interests and to whom neither the Earth-nature (biosphere) nor the settled agricultural 'sacredness' (culture) need be taken into consideration except as free dumping sites for waste, and supplies of material to be processed into commodities, where wants take the place of needs and dreams.

The illustrations are chosen from Michell's long immersion in the remotest corridors of great art and architecture and by Michell's uncompromising eye for the beautiful and the essential.

Our Green and Living World: The Wisdom to Save It

By Ayensu, Heywood, Lucas & Defellips, Smithsonian Distribution.

The plant life of the planet is examined from cultural, artistic, religious, ecological, economic, and scientific points of views with aim of generating the wisdom needed to live within it as stewards and not plunderers.

Indira Gandhi's epilogue sums up:

''There is not and has never been any contradiction between conservation and development. The two must go together. Development is distorted without conservation.''

Do not be deceived by the lavish illustrations. The book is written by knowledgeable and practical men and contains within its lovely presentation a practical program, a well-worked-out conceptual approach, and a number of pearls from the realm that its subtitle rather boldly proclaims for itself.

Green Inheritance: The World Wildlife Book of Plants

By Anthony Huxley, Gaia Books, London, 1984.

Anthony Huxley in this beautiful book documents the wealth plants contribute to the biosphere. They protect and enrich soil and watersheds; they fuel, fibre, timber, shade, spice, feed, perfume, intoxicate and medicate; and offer hidden gardens to delight, exotic landscapes to explore.

Crafted with evident love, the book dazzles with stunning photographs and illustrations, and presents fascinating histories of plant development and use. A WWF book written in the context of a frightening loss of plant genetic diversity and habitat -- the biosphere loses one species per day in 1980, expected to rise to one species per hour by 1990; and 20 hectares of plant habitat per minute at present -- the book demonstrates ''we must save the plants that save us.'' A must book and a treasure.

Behind the Mirror

By Konrad Lorenz, Methuen, 1977.

An extraordinary work in which Lorenz makes ''the human mind an object of scientific investigation demonstrating that the specifically human functions and characteristics of man reveal themselves in their uniqueness precisely when one regards them through the eyes of a scientist as the products of a natural creative process.'' ''This attitude,'' Lorenz continues, ''rests on the realization that our cognitive apparatus is itself an objective reality which has acquired its present form through contact with and adaptation to equally real things in the outer world.'' In this classic work, Lorenz succeeds in unifying his work in metaphysics (he had been elected to Immanuel Kant's chair in Konigsberg), in evolution (where he was foremost in creating ethology, the science of animal behavior), and in medicine (where his interests in pathology led to many fruitful insights) to a point of great interest to biospherics: he sees civilizations as the flower and fruit of nature linking man to cosmic realities and shows how their pathologies related to the disjunction of the objective organs of cognition in man and the objective reality beyond man due to human cultures which do not realize, allow for the fact ''that all knowledge derives from an interaction between the perceiving subject and the object of perception, both of which are equally real'' and therefore must be equally studied.

A profound, brilliant and satisfying book that points the way toward achieving a true lasting culture, wherein man can integrate himself into the biospheric process without losing, rather enhancing, all his considerable uniqueness, by studying the backside of his mirror, the physiology of his reflections.

FILM

Genesis of a Genius

Film produced and directed by Dr. Bernhardt Lotsch, Austrian Academy of Science, Institute of Environmental Sciences, Vienna. 0043-222-937-302.

This film portrays the roots of *comparative ethology* in the childhood and life of Dr. Konrad Lorenz. Basic experiments, observations of the imprinting phenomena, nature versus nurture -- key principles in the study of animal behavior -- are presented in this one hour film designed for a popular science audience. In German and English and available directly from Dr. Bernhardt Lotsch or the ORS, Austrian Broadcasting Corporation.

Four film interviews with Dr. Konrad Lorenz, by Dr. Lotsch, are also available from the Institute for Scientific Films (I.W.F.), Nonnenstieg 72, D-3400 Gottingen, F.R.G.

Technics and Civilization

By Lewis Mumford, Harcourt, Brace & World, Inc., New York & Burlingame, 1934.

"...While anthropologists and archaeologists paid due attention to the technical equipment of primitive peoples...the broader influence of technics upon human cultures was hardly touched on: the useful and the practical still stood outside the realm of the good, the true, and the beautiful.'' Lewis Mumford in this penetrating study analyzes the social conditions that laid the basis for the advent of the machine culture in the West (prototypically the monastery, mine and military) and elaborates three periods in its development: eotechnics, characterized by the use of water and wood; paleotechnics,

with coal and iron (the period simplistically known as the "Industrial Revolution"); and neotechnics, with its use of electricity and alloys.

From its origins in a new world view which devalued the living for the mechanical, the spontaneous for the regimented, which moved increasingly from utensils, apparatus, tools and utilities to the automatic "power" machine, Mumford traces the impact and assimilation of the machine and points to what he terms the emergence of a biotechnic technics -- a man/machine/environment symbiosis where technics are employed in the service of life.

An invaluable book for the study of the interplay of technosphere, human society and the biosphere.

Caste and Kin in Kathmandu Valley

By Christoph von Furer Haimendorf.

Haimendorf's magisterial study of the intricate social system of the subcontinent as exemplified at one of its most highly evolved centers shows how mankind organized itself during the 10,000 year agricultural interregnum between biosphere-controlled nomad and biosphere-damaging technoman. The system of priests, warrior-rulers, trader-guildsmen, and farmers nowhere reached higher perfection than here and Haimendorf got it all.

Triumph of the Nomads: A History of Ancient Australia

By Geoffrey Blainey, Revised Edition, 1982.

A Professor of Economic History at the University of Melbourne, Blainey applies the exacting methods of studying German or American economic history to the nomads of Australia, and concludes that theirs was an economic triumph. They kept a balanced population (all the women had specialist knowledge in abortion and population, a ceremonial but effective warfare was practiced), they understood climate and seasons, enjoyed a varied diet, and probably worked less than a forty hour week. So as students know from many nomadic studies, nomads had the leisure to develop pilgrimages, art, fashion, cosmology, funerals, complex social relations of courtesy and, in the case of Australia, at the conservative count, over 300 languages.

What was man like as a being that integrated with the biosphere, limiting himself to non-plague proportions? This book perhaps gives the most complete, authentic account of the at least million-and-a-half years' Golden Age before the Neolithic Revolution which spawned the accelerating series of Revolutions to today's Scientific-Technical Revolution.

Blainey is by no means a romanticist; the triumph he

speaks of is a bottom line sustainable profit of a cooperation with a continental segment of the biosphere that gave around 300,000 people (1 per 10 square miles) a way of life for ten to fifty thousand years, parts of which survive today after two centuries of European conquest as a significant strand of Australian culture. The symbiosis between culture, technics, and biosphere may be capable of a higher level than the nomadic culture and biosphere, but it is our only comparative model for a non-exponential growth way for man, and its lessons can be ignored only at great peril.

Feng-Shui

By Ernest Eitel, Synergetic Press, London, 1984. Commentary by John Michell.

Originally published in 1873, the Rev. E. J. Eitel's *Feng-Shui* was the first treatise written on the subject and is now amongst the most important texts to our understanding of Chinese thought and cultural tradition. This new edition contains a commentary by John Michell and a bibliography and provides a valuable introduction to the Chinese art of feng-shui -- the science of landscape -- giving an often surprising insight into the town planning and factory development of the West. "Feng-shui offers a principled but highly flexible code which can be referred to overall matters of architectural design, city planning and the use of the countryside." A fascinating book beautifully presented and illustrated.

To the Ends of the Earth: The Great Travel and Trade Routes of Human History

By Irene Franck and David Brownstone, A Hudson Group Book, 1984.

A unique work in which we are taken on a journey through time and space exploring almost fifty of the world's great historical travel and trade routes. Irene Franck and David Brownstone have compiled "the first and only historical guide to all of the world's main travel and trade routes," illustrated with maps, linecuts, photographs and travelers' accounts of the biosphere which have carried the life-giving sustenance of human civilization.

"Much of the romance and adventure of human history flows from the world's great travel and trade routes, and much of the stuff of human history stems from the development of these routes. The Silk Road, the Santa Fe Trail, the Appian Way, the Spice Route, the Wilderness Road, the Amber Routes -- these and two-score other highways and seaways have for tens of thousands of years shaped the course of history."

Franck and Brownstone "have long thought that the earth is, in essence, only a single place, and that political boundaries only temporarily fracture the interconnections between all the people and areas of the world." Their work brings new insights to the student of the biosphere interested in history of man's activities. They found that "long before the dawn of recorded history -- people had been marking out the world's great natural highways, the most accessible routes through formidable mountain ranges, across barren deserts, over treacherous waters. Tens of thousands of years ago, when humans were producing the great cave paintings of Western Europe, some of their kin had already traversed the more than 8,000 miles of the Eurasian Steppe Route. European traders on the Santa Fe and Chihuahua trails were following pathways taken by Native Americans thousands of years before, as they coursed down through the Americas. While humans were still working with stone alone, people were routinely traveling across the Sahara Desert. When China sent its first emissaries along the Silk Road, at the beginning of the Christian era in the West, they heard there ancient legends of Chinese travelers from long before. And when the Egyptians were building their great pyramids, shipments of precious cinnamon were reaching them by sea from East Asia." A thoroughly satisfying work whose value is as enduring as its subject, *To the Ends of the Earth* is a must for any biospheric explorer. Writing from their love for history and travel, Franck and Brownstone have created a door through which we may enter and partake of the experiences of those who have marked out the pathways of the biosphere opening up for us the 'open road' of adventure and historical exploration.

The Limits to Growth: A Report for the Club of Rome's Project on the Predicament of Mankind

By D.H. Meadows, D.L. Meadows, J. Randers & W. Behrens, Signet, New American Library, 1972.

The Limits to Growth initiated a decade of debate by making available the results of sophisticated computer modeling and forecasting of five key vectors of global economy: population, agricultural production, natural resources, industrial production and pollution. Their conclusions were a bombshell: the limits to growth will be reached sometime within the next 100 years and will be accompanied by a catastrophic decline in population and industrial capacity.

At the 1973 United Nations Conference on Population at Bucharest, the study encountered violent opposition from the Catholic Church because of birth control implications, the Soviet Union and China because they maintained they were not part of the problem, and some Third World countries who feared a freeze on their industrializing activities. Unfortunately this political reaction temporarily obscured the intention of the book to present a new way of approaching these problems (systems dynamics) and to open a wider forum on the implications of open-ended exponential growth.

The tide has recently turned -- the polemics have abated -- with researchers' revisions of the original studies. Soviet scientists (N. Moiseyev and others) have expanded the modeling from purely economic ones to include parameters of economics, politics and biosphere. The Catholic hierarchy and most Mullahs, though not an increasing number of their thinkers and followers, remain in total opposition to any practical means of birth control.

Though some objections can be raised to certain assumptions and omissions of the original study -- e.g. the impact of the ephemeralization of modern technics, possible expansion into space, their failure to consider different national modes of development presupposing a political homogeneity, treating the biosphere as a passive spectator -- the book remains the seminal and still highly relevant study of long-term prospects of human activity in our biosphere. Moiseyev's model can be seen as an extremely useful attempt to deepen and develop this model, coming closer to the biospheric constraints. But the fundamental reality that there *are* limits to growth remains true.

The Universe and Civilization

By Sevastyonov, Ursul & Shkolenko, Progress Publishers, Moscow, 1981.

"The creation of space settlements with a closed ecological circuit means essentially the creation of artificial planets where development of independent civilizations is, in principle, possible. The possibilities for man's existence in the infinite Universe becomes unlimited." "The Universe is a vast screen...on which earthly problems are projects; in turn it serves as a means of formulating and solving earthly problems." The book contains a very provocative Systems-Structural Analysis of the cosmicisation of human activity giving a theoretically complete map to locate any cognition in a 16-level system culminating with a *cosmic individual* using *cosmic instruments* to study *cosmic objects* under *cosmic conditions*. Anyone interested in knowledge theory will instantly perceive a goldmine.

"The movement from earth's biosphere towards biospheres in man-made space constructions may in time be replaced by a movement in the opposite direction, from these biospheres to the Earth. It may very well be that space will produce more promising models for the organization of the biosphere on our planet." For a feel of

the imaginative creative synthesis of philosophy, biospherics, noospherics, and space being made by the Soviets, this book is a must. A powerful and inspiring conceptual effort.

From Vinland to Mars: A Thousand Years of Exploration

By Richard S. Lewis, Quadrangle, 1978.

The book takes up its theme in three parts: (1) completing the first reconnaissance of the earth, the discovery of the Americas, Antarctica, Gondwanaland, Pangaia, the shifting and alternating magnetic poles, the great ocean ridges and mantles; (2) the moon; (3) the planets;and leaves with the implication that exploration of the stars will soon follow.

For any who wish to gain a historical-factual basis for understanding the location in time-space of Biosphere 1, and the possible location of many others.

Lewis views intra-species competition as the driving force that impels homo sapiens sapiens to ever further exploration, in other words, that it is operated by biospheric rules. The Soviet-American, the Soviet-Soviet, the American-American, the German-German, German-American, and German-Soviet intraspecific competitions are very well described, as well as the struggles between Vikings, Scott and Amundson, Filchner and Shackleton, etc.

The Greening of Mars

by Michael Alleby and James Lovelock, Andre Deutsch, London, 1984.

"The provision of oxygen was much simpler than that. The Martian soil was rich in pernitrates, highly oxidized substances that liberated oxygen when they were warmed...in fact it was necessary only to collect soil and store it at ordinary room temperature for oxygen to be liberated." A highly provocative and engaging book for students of biospheres -- knowing how the "terran" biosphere operates, how would one seed and nurture the potential Martian biosphere?

Lovelock and Alleby intelligently choose to utilize the given conditions on Mars rather than attempt to recreate the Earth biosphere -- indeed Mars offers many advantages: it requires less that half the escape velocity, 38% the weight -- taking the load off both bodies and architectural structures, etc.

Their scenario is simple and daring -- it presupposes no miracle technology nor people.

"People who migrate to pioneer new lives in new lands are usually of an independent turn of mind. Terran history shows that many of them quarreled with the authorities in the countries they left..." Indicative of the intellectual present moment, scientists have refused to leave the book in the ''sci-fi'' section and serious evaluations and conferences develop its thrust.

From eco-logist (the knowledge of the house or world) and eco-nomist (the rules of the house) man transforms to eco-poeist: house or world- *maker*. ''We think, and we dream...an era in human history has ended, and an era has begun, and the split human race henceforth must pursue more or less parallel paths. More? or less?...the list is long of those who have believed the future to be impossible.''

A Case for Mars

Edited by Penelope J. Boston, Vol. 57, Science and Technology Series. An American Astonautical Society Publication, 1984.

''The establishment of manned bases on Mars is a practical, unifying goal for the entire United States space program for the next century.'' ''In the broadest terms, the ultimate goal of space exploration appears at this time, to be the creation of, or associating in, an interstellar culture. In order for this goal to be realized, we must first become a solar system culture.'' This book, capably edited by Penelope Boston, brings together the results of the wonderful Case for Mars Conference held in Boulder, Colorado in 1981, the first overall formal studies of the problem since 1971. And the results show how Mars contains the best possibilities for the first Biospheres to leave our planet to make their home. How do-able it all is.

The Cold and the Dark: The World After Nuclear War

By P.Ehrlich, C. Sagan, D. Kennedy & W.O. Roberts, W.W. Norton, 1984.

''I no longer feel that a single biologist can remain exempt from involvement in the issue of nuclear war...The enemy is not the Soviet Union or the United States, but the nuclear weapons themselves.'' An unusual book in form, a record of a conference, *The Cold and the Dark* is unique in content: a scientific study of the future if one political option is carried out -- nuclear war.

Hundreds of American and many Soviet scientists participated in this study, climatologists, biologists, physicists, mathematicians. With no dissension they arrived at the same conclusion: nuclear war must be stopped, and by that they mean the possibility of one, or the biosphere itself faces the loss of most of the higher species, and mankind the loss of itself.

An impeccable inspiring record of science in action on perhaps its most meaningful field of inquiry. No one interested in the biosphere can afford not to master the data, line of argument, and conclusions of this ongoing study.

For further data contact: The Center on the Consequences of Nuclear War, 3244 Prospect Street NW, Washington D.C. 20007.

Weapons and Hope

By Freeman Dyson, Cocophon Books/Harper & Row, 1984.

''I would submit that the first thing we have to do...is to wean ourselves from this fatal and pernicious doctrine of first strike.'' George Kennan quoted by Dyson.

Dyson does not in this deeply meditated book mention directly the effects of large-scale nuclear exchange on the biosphere, preferring to emphasize its destruction of humanity aspects, particularly Americans and Russians, however it is clear that he regards the prevention of Nuclear Holocaust as political objective number one.

Dyson's own military career began as Operations Research Officer for a British Strategic Bombing Command in World War II, then as a physicist at Princeton Institute of Advanced Studies he had opportunities for exchanging feelings and views with Oppenheimer, a high level specialist in Atomic Strategy (the Baruch Plan), and went on to become consultant to the Defense Department and the Arms Control and Disarmament Agency. In addition, he has been active inside the Coalition for Nuclear Disarmament and so has participated in popular as well as arcane political realities.

The very basis of the nuclear arms race, the interplay of the American first use doctrine opposed by the Soviet premptive first strike counterforce doctrine opposed by the Americans Mutual Assured Destruction doctrine, is here thoroughly set forth with a full historical accounting of its origins, development, and prospects. Six other possible concepts of American-Soviet strategy are then set forth taking into consideration the differing history and strategies of the two antagonists. The seven concepts cover the range of possible approaches, and Dyson does not shrink from evaluations of practicality even when those considerations go against his personal preference.

Besides the practical aspects, Dyson emphasizes the virtue of Hope, ''the will to struggle against obstacles even though they appear insuperable'' as the major spiritual force needed to rouse a sufficient number of both Warriors and Victims to action.

He argues and shows in convincing detail that the great step forward is to understand that the American military doctrine of first use of atomic tactical weapons is the driving force of the arms race, and that with the driving force removed, a ''Live and Let Live'' policy between Counterforce and MAD can give a stable situation for time to negotiate major reductions in, if not eliminate, nuclear weaponry.

From a biospheric point-of-view *The Cold and the Dark* presents scientists' best informed view of the consequences of Atomic War; *Weapons and Hope* a remarkable man's dispassionate intellectual, compassionate emotional and spiritually hopeful program to begin to reverse the terror, a program designed to be acceptable to the people (Victims), to American and Russian soldiers (Warriors), and to the American and Russian rulers.

Obtain these two books, master them, and you will become a center of understanding on how to help deal with the major threat to the biosphere on whatever level you are operating.

The Population Bomb

By Paul R. Ehrlich, Sierra Club, 1968.

"Man can undo himself with no other force than his own brutality -- The roots of the new brutality...are in the lack of population control." "Basically...two kinds of solutions to the population problem (if one doesn't understand exponential growth, one may deny the problem, of course, though it does not go away). One is a birth rate solution...ways to lower the birth rate. The other a death rate solution in which ways to raise the death rate...find us." Before the death rate solution sets in full force, however, the biosphere (called in this book 'the planet') begins to deteriorate so that man is bringing down the entire level of life before meeting his own fate.

This book unfortunately has, as several others reviewed here have, out-of-date predictive scenarios intended at the time for illustrating possibilities. Ignore or skip through these, but the spine of the book makes an extremely cogent argument hardly to be found so unequivocally stated elsewhere, and solidly based on the author's scientific and conservationist work.

In addition the book has its place in history as one of the awakeners in understanding homo sapiens sapiens' biological menace to the biosphere and thus eventually to itself as it fouls its own habitat.

Doubling any number means that the last term of the series exceeds the cumulative total of all the preceeding terms. Take the series 1,2,4,8,16,32. 32 is greater than 1+2+4+8+16.

The Restoration of the Earth

By Theodore B. Taylor and Charles C. Humpstone, Harper & Row, 1973.

"This book is less concerned about pollution problems than how to go about solving them." The authors show conceptually how the strategy of dealing with all potentially significant pollutants could be implemented by the application of a guiding principle they call "containment".

FILM

Koyaanisqatsi: Life Out of Balance

Film produced and directed by Godfrey Reggio, music by Phillip Glass.

The first movie that shows the biosphere and its dealings with homo sapiens and homo sapiens' activities viewed from a biospheric scale.

There is no dialogue or narrative line. Eerily pullulating images, imploding and exploding to a slick-as-glass hypnotic musical score produces an organic effect of awe and wonder. The collective funeral pyres of industrial civilization parade before us, as if embodying a force of nature, like a volcanic eruption or cyclonic storm.

Hauntingly beautiful time-lapse photography of urban life around the planet and of great natural phenomena, puts the viewer into a higher state of perception, as if one were a Martian observing the eccentric activities of a terrestrial form of life.

The life that is 'out of balance' is our way of life. *Koyaanisqatsi* invites our active thought about the role of man in the biosphere.

"We began by questioning two assumptions: that man is wise enough to determine how much man-made change the biosphere can support and that the way to environmental salvation lies through changing spiritual or ethical values. Discarding both, we have asserted that man has and should exercise the ability to insulate the biosphere from human activity at a cost that is not unthinkable or beyond measure, but within the range of prices that we pay for other services." An invaluable conceptual scheme for handling biospheric policy that takes into consideration law, institutions, economics, technics, and thought by two men whose credentials are brilliantly grounded in preparatory studies (Harvard law, Cornell theoretical physics), accomplishments (Nuclear Space Propulsion Project and 60's Civil Rights), understanding the establishment (AEC and IRS policy) and, most importantly, developing the ability to clearly present a complex subject while answering the standard objections of the status quo.

Skip any of costs or technics that are dated, but grasp the approach if you are, or wish to be, one of the policy makers of a biosphere-oriented humanity.

Operating Manual for Spaceship Earth

By R. Buckminster Fuller, Simon & Schuster, 1969.

Critical Path

By R. Buckminster Fuller, St. Martin's Press, New York, 1981.

"Cosmic evolution irrevocably intent upon completely transforming omnidisintegrated humanity from a complex of around-the-world, remotely-deployed-from-one-another, differently colored, differently credoed, differently cultured, differently communicating and differently competing entities into a completely integrated, comprehensively interconsiderate, harmonious whole." R. Buckminster Fuller makes a paradigm jump from traditional analytic thought to a total systems approach; from ideology and credo to direct perception ('no more second-hand god'). Trained in world ocean naval strategy, Fuller re-examines all previous thought and makes explosive conceptual breakthroughs: the mathematics of synergetics, comprehensive anticipatory design science, the advent of ephemeralization, among others.

A man of unflinching intellectual and moral courage, Fuller's views of existing power structures and belief systems may infuriate -- but he provokes thinking in his reader. His history traces the line of the Great Pirates who control the planet because of advantages inherent in their whole planet reality thinking -- deflecting potential opposition by encouraging provincial nations and cultures and specializing the brighter individuals. Fuller challenges us to achieve our destiny -- to succeed on Spaceship Earth.

Operating Manual introduces the sweep of Fuller's ideas, while *Critical Path* urgently assesses the human present moment, and includes extraordinary sections on evolution, the acceleration of technical revolutions, and the self-disciplines which forged this towering thinker.

"Whether it is to be Utopia or Oblivion will be a touch-and-go relay race right up to the final moment. Humanity is in 'final exam' as to whether or not it qualifies for continuance in universe as *mind,* with the latter's access to the design laws -- called by science 'the generalized principles' -- governing eternally regenerative Universe."

Buckminster Fuller Institute

1743 S. La Cienega Blvd., Los Angeles, Ca. 90035, (213) 837-7710.

In 1927 Buckminster Fuller began an experiment: to see what the "little individual" could do on behalf of all humanity -- to discover the effectiveness inherent in individual initiative; to document the results that would come out of shifting the focus of one's life from earning a living to making the world work. During the course of the experiment Bucky has touched many aspects of life, from being the first person to scientifically confirm humanity's capability to make the Earth a complete physical success, to uncovering nature's own geometrical coordinate system, to designing specific "livingry" artifacts such as the geodesic dome, to creating the World Game for practically demonstrating the most effective use of Earth's resources. Through lectures and workshops around the world and over twenty books and thousands of published articles, he directly shared his perspective and experience with millions of people, illuminating certain key principles and ideas which are vital to the 'critical path' ahead.

Fuller Archives include letters, world resource research files, manuscripts, blueprints, project reports and documentation, film, video and audio tape, photos, slides, models, new clippings and mailing list of people who have been associated with Fuller's work.

If there is any one conclusion to be reached from Buckminster Fuller's life experiment, it is that an individual can have an important impact on the quality of human life.

Information

Man and Biosphere

USSR Academy of Sciences, Nauka Publishers, 1984.

An important selection of papers relating to Soviet efforts in the framework of Man and the Biosphere.

Part I takes up Ecology and the Science of Biosphere and should not be neglected by anyone wishing to deal with biospherics. Particularly to be noted is the paper by Babayev et al on Ecological Problems of Nuclear Energy which takes a quite different angle than common in the USA and UK.

Part III on Reserves and Species Protection will also be invaluable to anyone in these fields.

Part II on Integrated Problems of Nature Conservation contains a mix of papers: the one on the Tula Abatis forests is a vivid example of a regional study.

The Gaia Atlas of Planet Management

By Norman Myers (General Editor), Pan Books, 1985.

"Maps and analyzes a living planet at a critical point in its history -- as one species, our own, threatens to disrupt and exhaust its life support systems. It charts the growing divisions in the human family." Divided into seven sections: Land, Ocean, Elements, Evolution, Humankind, Civilization and Management, each considered from the standpoints of Potential Resources, Crises, and Management Alternatives.

The Atlas uses the word Gaia following James Lovelock for what many others, including this catalogue, call Biosphere, the union of the life forms, atmosphere, stratosphere, ozone layer, hydrosphere, and much of the lithosphere into a dynamic unity that has its own self-regulating and evolutionary properties.

The Atlas represents a remarkable effort on the part of Norman Myers and staff, to successfully bring together in a form useful to the public, inspiring to specialists, and invaluable to educators, a Biospheric Atlas. This Atlas should companion your Atlas of World History (political-social-economic-demographic).

The Living Planet

By David Attenborough, Colins, London, 1984.

Based on the BBC television series, *The Living Planet* introduces the basics of the biosphere in a beautifully illustrated and readable form. A good introduction to the subject of our planet as a living unit and its individual elements.

Life Itself

By Francis Crick, Simon and Schuster, New York, 1981.

The theory that life on Earth has come from another planet is not a new one, but Francis Crick has presented scientific backup for this idea in *Life Itself*. This support is based on the fact that the genetic code for all living matter, with minor differences in mitocondria, is identical; concluding that all life on Earth evolved from the same source. Crick's Directed Panspermia theory postulates that the source is bacteria transported from a higher-technology civilization of a far distant planetary body and deposited on our oceans about 4.5 billion years ago, about the time life was forming on Earth. He presents compelling arguments in support of his theory in this thought-provoking book on the origin of life on the planet Earth.

Atmospheres

By J. P. Barbato and E. A. Ayer, Pergamon Press, Oxford, 1981.

The atmospheres, the gases surrounding planets, of Earth, Mercury, Venus, Mars, Jupiter, Saturn, Uranus, Neptune and Pluto are discussed in terms of origin, composition, thermal structure and meteorological phenomena.

World Ocean Atlas

Edited by S.G. Gorshkov, Commander-in-Chief of the Soviet Navy, Pergamon. Vol. 1, *Pacific Ocean;* Vol. 2, *Atlantic and Indian Oceans;* Vol. 3, *The Artic Ocean.* All one needs to say about this global work, which includes a synthesis of data including the IGY, IGCY, and IYQS year programs, and of course all Soviet and foreign data accummulated in the USSR, is that if you or your institution has serious interests in the Biosphere and/or Ocean, you cannot afford to be without it even at Pergamon's price.

The charts combine superb technics with beauty.

The Atlas plan contains seven sections: History of Ocean Exploration, Ocean Bed, Climate, Hydrology, Hydrochemistry, Biogeography, Reference and Navigation-Geographical Charts.

This reviewer has not seen the Arctic Ocean volume which has not yet been released by Pergamon, but it is probably a safe assumption that it will be at least as fine as the others since this is the ocean on which the Soviets have their frontage.

The Times Atlas of the Oceans

Edited by Prof. Alastair Couper, Times Books Ltd., 1983.

What ocean species eats giant squid nine metres in length? How deep in the ocean is life found? What is the 'contiguous zone'? What is a pterpod? The answers to these questions and almost any other concerning the oceans can be found in the latest atlas from Time Books Ltd. Recognizing the importance of the oceans "regarded as the last major frontier on earth for the exploration and development of resources to sustain mankind in the future," Prof. Alastair Couper has compiled an authoritative and beautifully illustrated atlas with over 400 maps, illustrations and color photographs. Organized into four major divisions -- The Ocean Environment, Resources of the Oceans, Ocean Trade and The World Ocean -- each major section is accompanied by an appendix and bibliography and the entire work is indexed and contains a glossary of ocean-related terms.

For the student of the biosphere, such a comprehensive work has obvious value, but the approach taken by Couper and *The Times* makes this an invaluable resource for anyone with an interest in the oceans. Their approach in this atlas "goes a long way towards explaining physical and biological interactions, the trans-national character of living resources, the reasons behind the flow of merchant ships and deployment of naval vessels, management concepts, and the legal regime of the oceans. It provides an informed starting point for a sound understanding of the ocean- resource system involving man and the marine environment." A pleasure to use, *The Times Atlas of the Oceans* combines the beautiful with the beneficial, a masterwork by Prof. Couper and the 27 contributors.

Geophysics in the Affairs of Man

By C.C. Bates and T.F. Gaskell, Pergamon Press, Oxford, 1982.

Exploration geophysics and its influence on world civilization is traced from World War I to present. The interaction of government, academic and industrial geophysics is presented along with discussions of plate tectonics and a basis for ban of further nuclear weapons testing. A valuable reference work for geophysicists and related professionals.

The Language of the Earth

Edited by F. Rhodes, Pergamon Press, Oxford, 1981.

Not just another geology text, *The Language of the Earth* paints a broad stroke about the earth science as it relates to philosophy, poetry and prose, the arts, and humor, as well as about the scientists involved in it.

The Year of the Whale

By Victor Scheffer, Charles Scribner's Sons, New York, 1969.

A fictional story based on fact and observation, *The Year of the Whale* follows the early growth of a sperm whale from its birth in September in the northeast Pacific, weaving into the story as it flows along information on and accounts of experiences with whales throughout the world. As a specialist and researcher on the study of marine mammals, Schaffer relates the reciprocal interaction between whales and the man who studies them and, through his story, emphasizes the beauty of this mammal and its importance to our world.

The Year of the Gorilla

By George Schaller, University of Chicago Press, 1964.

The Year of the Gorilla is a personal account of the two years Schaller and his wife spent in Central and East Africa studying the mountain gorilla, *Gorilla gorilla beringei*. At the time the expedition was proposed, 1957, most of the literature on this large ape consisted of exaggerated fantasy and rumor. Little factual information was known as to its life undisturbed in the wild. Schaller's book, as well as his scientific monograph, *The Mountain Gorilla: Ecology and Behavior* (University of Chicago Press, 1963), reveals the gorilla to be a shy and and content ape wishing only to be left alone but, as all of us must do, facing the limits of specialist adaptation in a changing biosphere.

African Genesis

By Robert Ardrey, Delta Books, New York, 1963.

"A Personal Investigation into the Animal Origins and Nature of Man." Ardrey, a playwright and "generalist" who traveled throughout Africa, theorized that man is descended from *Australopithecus africanus*, the last animal before man. These killer apes became extinct in Africa about the same time as the emergence of man on that continent. Human aggression and affinity for weapons he sees as a direct inheritance from these apes. Our nationalism derives its strength from their social territoriality. Ardrey traces social characteristics from insects and birds through the higher animals to the apes and then to man to demonstrate the fallacy that man is unique among the animals; that his aggressiveness is just a result of modern-day society. Based on evidence emerging over thirty years of scientific work, Ardrey presented a "contemporary revolution" in evolutionary thought -- revealing a theory that had been in existence for some time but not widely known. The book gives an exciting flavor of the days when it was first realized homo sapiens sapiens had definitely evolved along with the biosphere.

The Growth and Development of Birds

By Raymond J. O'Connor, Wiley & Sons.

Treats the species decisions as to energy use and adaptations to ecological demands from almost every aspect, from differential physical development to star navigation. Birds make a wonderful way to study energetics transformations in the biosphere because the demands of flight preclude any excess capital formations. The book has the advantage of being tightly written so as to provide a definite thinking effort from the reader instead of being facts laid out as forgettable problems.

The Body

By Anthony Smith, Allen & Unwin, London, 1985.

"...mankind is no isolated being...another bit of biology, and therefore much of the animal kingdom is entirely relevant to his body, his mechanism of sperm transfer, his sex ration, his brain, his sense of smell...not an isolated bit of creation, like a meteor...flown in from somewhere else." "...this book regards a pumping heart as more interesting than a heart failing to pump." Specific and interesting examples illustrate and add resonance to general topics: hemophilia is accompanied by Queen Victoria's reactions to it and the presence throughout her vast family network.

The closest anyone has come yet to seeing the human species as a part of the biosphere on a sustained scientific, medical, and historical basis, that its being and functions have been developed by part of the world of life, and in turn act within the world of life.

Topics range from Suicide to Old Age to Speech to Skin to The Senses to Lactation to Contraception to the Growth of Babies. Erudite, witty, useful, and a guide.

Indian Practical Civil Engineers Handbook: The Standard Every-Day Reference Book for All Engineers

By P.N. Khanna, Engineers' Publishers, P.O. Box 725, New Delhi 110001.

An extraordinary accomplishment, this Handbook does not presuppose working in a technical world divorced from the biosphere but goes into fascinating and always practical detail about soils, materials, estimating labor time needed, water supply and sewage, arboriculture, irrigation, bridges, with a just regard for India's biomic features, differentiating between ghats, plains, and other regions.

"The book (has been) bought right from Chief Engineers down to subordinates and not only from all corners of India, but also from abroad." "Very little originality, no finality or perfection is claimed." However, it is comprehensive, useful, educational, economical, and highly recommended to any individual or organization doing field work, and as a model of style to those engaged in technical transcriptions.

Journals

Key Environments, series, Pergamon Press.

Key Environments is a series of books, each spotlighting an important locale threatened by pollution and exploitation, e.g. Antarctica, Amazonia, the Sahara Desert. This series is an attempt to bring together in one set of books, important scientific and accurate information on the environmental changes occurring in these key regions and their possible future consequences.

The Conservation Review, series, Webb and Bower, Exeter, England.

The *Review* is a series of yearly summaries of the Conservation Foundation on ecological and conservation activities and subjects published in an attempt to encourage readers to join the conservation movement. Emphasis is placed on industry to participate in this movement and recognition is given to those companies which display support to the Foundation's efforts which are world-wide.

Environmental Conservation, published quarterly, Elsevier Sequoia S.A., Lausanne, Switzerland.

"The international journal devoted to maintaining global variability through exposing and countering environmental deterioration resulting from human population-pressure and unwise technology." Concern for the present and future of "Earth's fragile Biosphere," *Environmental Conservation* focuses on articles concerning "rational uses f resources, foreseeing ecological consequences, enlightened environmental policy, anti-pollution measures, low-impact development, environmental education and law, and ecologically sound management of all land and fresh water, sea and air." An intense concentration of information on world-wide conservation efforts and activities. A year-end summary of articles and contributors from the year's quarterly issues is given.

The Environmentalist, published quarterly,

Science and Technology Letters, Kew, England.

"The International Journal for All Professionals Concerned with Environmental Awareness." *The Environmentalist* serves as an international meeting-ground for diverse environmental interest groups, whether they be governmental bodies, industry or ecologists. The journal's focus is education on issues and problems as well as guidelines for solution to global and local problems. It also provides information on environmental conferences and work groups throughout the world.

Ecological Abstracts, bimonthly publication,

Geo Abstracts Ltd., London.

Published six times yearly, *Ecological Abstracts* includes marine, tidal and estuarine, freshwater, terrestrial, applied, and historical ecological abstracts as well as a section on general theory, methods and techniques. Contributions are international.

World Conservation Strategy, International

Union for Conservation of Nature and Natural Resources, Gland, Switzerland.

Commissioned by the United Nations Environmental Programme and funded jointly with the World Wildlife Fund, the *World Conservation Strategy* aims "to help advance the achievement of sustainable development through the conservation of living resources." The *Strategy* defines its objectives (and obstacles to their achievement) to human survival and wellbeing, outlines the framework for action on national and subnational level, and describes actions for stimulation of support of these conservation objectives. Specific priorities, e.g. desertification, extinction of species, organizational and personnel problems, are set.

Appendix

Institute of Ecotechnics Conceptual Model For Managing Projects As Integrated Parts of Biomes Which Are Integrated Parts of the Biosphere

The Institute of Ecotechnics developed, tests, and uses the following conceptual model for project managers to deal comprehensively and incisively at the biomic (regional) level in a way that shows how to integrate their activity with long-term steady state, interrupted by cosmic shocks and "jumps" in biospheric evolution.

Firstly, the particular ecosystem of a biome is identified, and, for the purpose of including human emotions and associations, called a region: for example the Kimberly Savannah region of Western Australia.

Then I.E. makes a survey of existing conditions on 12 levels of ever more complex organization from two parallel and interacting forces, nature and culture.

Natural Science Levels	Cultural Science Levels
Teleosphere (Directions of Evolution)	Ecumene (Noosphere)
Biosphere	Civilization
Biome	Culture
Ecosystem	Creative Ideas
Communities	Communities
Groups (Species)	Task Groups
Organisms	Organisms
Soil (Cells)	Health/Medicine
Macromolecules	Food/Objects
Atoms	Materials
Fields	Power
Heat	Information/Concepts

Each level requires its methodology: for example, heat, information, and concepts are fundamentally studied by thermodynamic laws; each quickly loses the ability to do work without special insulation, wind up in "frozen disorder" and require continuing inputs (redundancy) to keep up the free energy (available to do work). Each region must be carefully appraised for its heat, information and conceptual inputs, treatments, and disposal of "waste" of each, and the project manager endeavors to raise the free energy component, lower the entropic component, and keep to a minimum the new inputs required by using more efficiently the existing sources, or if he/she must introduce new sources, that they harmonize with the eco-region.

At this stage one can evaluate the project's first level contributions to the eco-region: to what extent does it contribute entropic or negentropic forces to other eco-regions? To what extent does it import these forces into its own eco-region and from which other eco-regions? Within the eco-region the same analysis can be applied.

With this conceptual model the biospherically-oriented manager can assess his/her actions by whether they contribute to overall growth of ability to do work (potentiality) or by increasing disorder constitute a destructive act. Furthermore the model allows direct qualitative assignments of value (by making sure all important variables are considered) as well as facilitating detailed quantitative calculations where necessary. The manager can see where feedback loops are indicated and proceed to ever finer approximations to reality in stable situations or make quick adjustments in crisis situations with the confidence that he/she is a biospheric citizen. With time, experience, and ripening judgement he/she can make quite accurate synergetic total project moves from a thorough "soaking" in the twelve levels.

This catalogue, for example, addresses itself to the ecumene concerning the teleosphere, and studies the directions of evolution, what possibilities these afford the noosphere.

Index

Index

Index

Index

Index